ART EDUCATION
Its Philosophy and Psychology
Selected Essays

The Essay and Monograph Series
of The Liberal Arts Press

OSKAR PIEST, FOUNDER

Art Education

Its Philosophy and Psychology

Selected Essays

By

THOMAS MUNRO

THE BOBBS-MERRILL COMPANY, INC.
A Subsidiary of Howard W. Sams & Co., Inc.
Publishers   Indianapolis, New York, Kansas City

PREFACE

The field of art education is commonly understood as limited to the visual arts, both "fine" and "applied" or "useful." It thus includes painting, sculpture, the graphic arts, architecture, furniture, ceramics, textiles, and other arts addressed primarily to the sense of sight; sometimes, in addition, the visual phases of dance and ballet, theater, and motion pictures. In principle, education in these arts includes their theory and practice; their history, appreciation, and criticism as well as their techniques of production and performance. It includes not only the imparting of such techniques but the fostering of original, creative work by students in the various media concerned. It includes the preparation of teachers and administrators in the field, as well as research and theory on the psychology, aims, and methods of instruction in the visual arts. Actually, few if any institutions cover so large and diversified a field in detail; most of them specialize on one or a few arts and approaches to them, for students of a certain age and interest. Some specialize on teaching art as a phase of general education; some on the training of professional artists.

The term "art" has had many meanings, and is still used in various senses. For the Greeks and Romans, *techné* and *ars* included not only aesthetic skills but also purely utilitarian ones such as agriculture, mining, medicine, and war. Now the latter are usually called, instead, applied sciences or branches of engineering or technology. This restricts the modern concept of art to skills and products which are used or intended to stimulate satisfactory aesthetic experience. They may have other functions as well, as architecture has in serving utilitarian, religious, and political ends; but they are classed as "arts" in so far as they aim at beauty, visual interest, or some other aesthetic value. The tendency now in scientific discussion is to class them so whether or not they actually succeed in achieving beauty or in satisfying people aesthetically. Thus a work of art can be either beautiful or ugly, and a man can be a good artist or a bad one.

Although the concept of art is usually restricted in college catalogues to the visual arts, elsewhere it is often extended to cover music and literature also; even to such "lower-sense arts" as perfume and cooking, in so far as they seek to give aesthetic satisfaction. Aesthetics and cultural history now favor this broad interpretation of "art." Theoretically, music and poetry can claim to be "fine arts," quite as well as painting and sculpture can. There is much to be gained by considering them all together as partly similar, partly different modes of artistic expression and sources of aesthetic experience. In education, there is now a tendency to emphasize the interrelation of the arts in cultural history and in school projects involving two or more media. In the lower grades especially, and in surveys and orientation courses on the higher levels, the visual arts are now frequently presented in close relation to music and literature.

The essays in this book, while focused mainly on the visual arts, try to see them in the larger context of art and art education in the broad, inclusive sense. Instruction in a particular skill or subject, such as drawing or picture appreciation, is not considered in isolation, but as an integral part of the whole curriculum, and of the student's whole mental and emotional development within a social, cultural environment.

It is in this way that the following essays can be said to deal with the philosophy and psychology of art education. Only occasionally do they discuss the specific, technical problems of contemporary philosophy or the detailed, laboratory and statistical researches of present psychology. But they do attempt to see the field of art education steadily and whole, in relation to the aims and requirements of a good life for the educated, well-balanced human being in modern Western civilization. Little is said about particular classroom procedures or studio devices and equipment. These change from day to day, often with no clearly defined objective. Much is said here, on the other hand, about the main types of activity and subject matter which art education should involve on successive levels in order to secure the greatest individual and social benefits. Many of these are now frequently neglected. Such questions as these are kept in mind throughout the book: What kinds of educated human beings are we trying to produce with our curricula and costly, elaborate equipment for the study of the arts? How well are we succeeding in this? What is the ultimate value of the skills and information we convey, in making students not only professionally qualified but creative, constructive citizens, able to enjoy life in a civilized way and to contribute something to the cultural level of the communities in which they live?

In a field where recent psychology is still too often ignored, where obsolete assumptions about art and its place in human experience still hamper progress, a basic reorientation has long been needed. Old issues such as that between academic discipline and free expression, tradition and originality, reason and emotion, art for art's sake and art for moral, social or practical ends have had to be restated with due respect for all these competing values. The place of art education in a modern, industrial democracy, in an age of vast economic and political change and ideological conflict, has had to be newly assessed with due respect for the artist's freedom and for his social responsibility. Certainly, the essays cannot claim to have solved these problems; but they try to direct the reader's attention to some fundamental ones, with which he may have to cope as artist or as teacher in the generation ahead. They point to a number of areas in great need of further research, experiment, and discussion.

Much is said in these essays about the relation of art education to art itself, and to contemporary trends in art and criticism. Art education in recent years has been revolutionized and sometimes partly paralyzed by recent trends in art and criticism. On seeing the old, academic rules and standards flouted by leading artists and critics of the day, with nothing definite to take their place, the art teacher has often resigned himself to a merely passive, noncommittal role, content with imparting facts and techniques, and telling the student to do whatever he likes with them. The result has been an overemphasis on information and technique, along with much vagueness, confusion, and evasion in regard to aims and values. Too little has been said about the nature and worth of the product and the uses to which the techniques can be put. Much is said in these essays about aims and standards. In this, it overlaps the field of its companion volume of essays, *Toward Science in Aesthetics,* which deals more thoroughly with basic questions of function, form and value in the arts.

In addition to emphasizing the visual arts, I have emphasized certain approaches to them, such as aesthetics and museum education, in which I have had most intensive experience. This has been mainly in university departments of art and philosophy, in art museums, or in a combination of both. It has allowed me to see art education

in a larger perspective than most art teachers do, in that persons of
every age and many interests, many types of cultural background
come to the art museum for appreciation, history, and practice in the
arts. On the other hand, I do not pretend to discuss the arts from
the standpoint of a professional, practicing artist. Through international contacts, I have been fortunate enough to see a little of the
problems and tendencies of art education in other countries, and of
attempts such as that of UNESCO to deal with it on a world scale. The
museums with which I have been associated (the Barnes Foundation and the Cleveland Museum of Art) have been especially interested in modern art and educational activities. Through this interest,
and with the aid of foundation grants, I have been able to participate in several projects of research and experiment in art education.
In this regard, I remember with gratitude the wise friendship and
timely assistance of the late Frederick P. Keppel, of the Carnegie
Corporation.

In the Cleveland Museum of Art during the past twenty-five years,
I have had the privilege of leading an alert, highly qualified educational staff in a continuous program of experimental teaching. It has
comprised not only appreciation but studio work for children and
adults in various media. It has included instruction in music, dance,
and theater arts as well as in drawing, painting, modeling, and crafts.
Many of the ideas in these pages have evolved through years of
weekly staff discussions, and it is a pleasure to express warm thanks
to my colleagues there for this happy association. My university
work—at Columbia, Pennsylvania, New York University, Rutgers,
and Western Reserve—has been largely in the historical and theoretical approaches to the arts. Here again, I have been fortunate in the
close co-operation of colleagues in the studio approach at neighboring
institutions, many of them practicing artists of distinction. From the
college and graduate level, and as chairman of a university division
of art, one has to survey the whole educational ladder in the field.
One often has to ask oneself why this ladder in the arts has so many
missing rungs and weak supports, why college students and prospective teachers are often so poorly prepared, and what can be done
about it. These questions are discussed in the opening essays, several
of which first appeared in the yearbook *Art in American Life and
Education*. It was most instructive and pleasant to work as chairman
of the committee of able, experienced artists and teachers who pre-

pared this book for the National Society for the Study of Education with the aid of over seventy contributors.

The present book brings together those of my essays on art education, written during the past thirty years, which have seemed worth making more accessible in book form to students and teachers. The earliest, about a visit to Franz Cizek in Vienna, dates from 1925, when I was associate educational director of the Barnes Foundation, under A. C. Barnes and John Dewey as president and educational director. I was then enjoying an invaluable opportunity to learn something about art, aesthetics, and the philosophy of life from these two great, though very different teachers, as well as from George Santayana during my European visits.

I have tried to eliminate unnecessary repetitions and comments of merely local or transitory interest in assembling the essays. But certain key ideas recur in different contexts: notably, the importance of art education for the development of a broadly balanced, harmonious personality and for the selective transmission of the world's cultural heritage. I have often stressed the role of the art museum as a new educational agency, with yet unrealized possibilities for active public service. Throughout, I have emphasized the need for intelligent thinking and planning in the field, with all the aid that science and philosophy can give, as opposed to excessive reliance on blind tradition, dogmatic rules, mystic inspiration, or irrational impulse.

ACKNOWLEDGMENTS

Having saluted, in the Preface, the memory of some old friends and teachers, I would like to offer thanks as well to some younger ones, including present colleagues and students. From them I hope always to continue learning. Much cherished is the long and friendly association with the staff and trustees of the Cleveland Museum of Art, especially its president, Harold T. Clark, and its director, William M. Milliken. Their constructive interest in educational work along new, experimental lines has made possible, not only this book, but the experience on which it is based. I am indebted to Mrs. Louise M. Dunn, now emeritus, who did much to develop the museum's educational work before I came on the scene; and not least of all to those who now ably help to manage it—Edward B. Henning, Dorothy Van Loozen, and Ronald Day. In writing and editing the present book of essays, my wife, Lucile Munro, has been of constant help and encouragement. Mrs. Dorothy S. Kroko, Miss Dolores Filak, and Miss Adeline Schirripa have given expert aid in editing and preparing the text.

Cordial thanks are extended to those who have given permission to republish previously copyrighted material: Mrs. A. C. Barnes, President of the Barnes Foundation; the National Society for the Study of Education; the Public School Publishing Co.; the *Educational Encyclopedia;* the *Magazine of Art;* the American Federation of Arts; the Eastern Arts Association *Bulletin;* the Western Arts Association *Bulletin;* the *Journal of Aesthetics and Art Criticism;* Henry Hope and the *College Art Journal* and *Parnassus* of the College Art Association; Francis H. Taylor and the Worcester Art Museum *Bulletin;* the *Journal of Experimental Education; Progressive Education;* the *Bulletin* of the Cleveland Museum of Art; Trevor Thomas and the Unesco Documents and Publications Service, publishers of *Education and Art;* Edwin Ziegfeld, and *Art Education Today,* published by Teachers College of Columbia University.

T. M.

CONTENTS

ART EDUCATION
Its Philosophy and Psychology

AESTHETIC EDUCATION AS A PART OF GENERAL EDUCATION

1. The psychological approach

Aesthetic education deals primarily with the arts. It includes their production and performance, and also their appreciation, criticism, history, and theory. But aesthetic experience and aesthetic education are not limited to works of art. They can be directed also toward nature, toward human beings, and toward other products of man besides the arts. Aesthetic education, as broadly conceived, tries to develop aesthetic abilities in relation to all kinds of object. It deals with experiences of beauty, ugliness, and other aesthetic qualities, wherever they are found. It deals with aesthetic and artistic processes wherever they occur, in the fine arts and in the daily work of ordinary people. It is concerned with the nature of these abilities and processes, including individual differences and talents; with their hereditary basis in man's physical and mental endowment, and the development of educational methods which will best favor their healthy, beneficial growth.

"The aesthetic" in a stricter sense is concerned with the perception and appreciation of art and other beautiful objects rather than with their creation or performance. *Aesthetic* experience in this narrow sense is distinguished from *artistic* experience, which occurs in the creation, designing, manufacture, execution, and performance of art. Aesthetic education in this narrow sense is instruction in the perception, use, enjoyment, and criticism of works of art rather than in techniques of production and performance.

Aesthetic experience is not necessarily derived from art, but art is one of the best sources for it. In such experience, the attention is focused upon some outer sensory stimulus such as a work of art or a scene in nature. This object tends to arouse in the observer not only perceptual responses, but those of understanding and perhaps of guided fantasy, as in reading a story or watching a film play. In aesthetic experience, one may consider problems and general ideas,

3

as in a mystery story or a meditative lyric. But one's attitude is compliant: one follows the train of thought of the author or his characters. The aesthetic attitude is said to be "disinterested," in not
involving strong personal desires or efforts to possess or accomplish
something. But it is not completely devoid of a conative element.
In watching a play, one may hope and fear for the hero's success. But
the emphasis is on observation and understanding. Toward painting
or music, the aesthetic response stresses an attempt at clear, full,
complex perception of sensory qualities and details as organized in
space or time. It involves some attention to suggested meanings as
in understanding the words in a poem. It involves conative and emotional responses of welcome, admiration, enjoyment, or the opposite.
The artistic attitude is not purely aesthetic. It is necessarily practical
in part, as when a painter tries to represent a flower in paint on
canvas, or write a poem about it. He may contemplate the flower
aesthetically, but he must also solve practical problems in the control
of a medium to produce an external form, express his own ideas, and
communicate them to others.

In the case of young children, the appreciation of art can best be
taught along with creative production and performance. Aesthetic
experience and the appreciation of art are not restricted to a passive
attitude of quiet looking or listening, as in a museum or concert hall.
Both can occur in the midst of activity or practical use, as in enjoying the beauty of a house or garden while actively using it or making
a picture of it. Through experimentation with different materials
and instruments of the arts, through attempting to express his
thoughts and feelings in an outward medium, to control his hands
or limbs, to build and communicate, the student learns to think out
and control his own ideas and feelings. In so doing he tends to become more conscious and highly developed mentally, and more able
to appreciate the artistic products and expressions of others.

Aesthetic experience is not necessarily an attempt to repeat the
experience of the artist, although the two have some elements in
common. The thoughts and feelings of the tribal artist who carved
an African fetish are too different from those of a civilized modern
to be recaptured fully. It would usually not be worth while for the
observer to repeat all the artist's efforts to solve his technical problems and produce the finished form. Appreciation may begin where
the artist left off. It may include some understanding and admiration

of the artist's skill in overcoming difficulties, but it can also go on to a full, free, and thorough perception, understanding, evaluation, and enjoyment of the work of art itself as a finished product. Appreciation of a work of art may involve far more mental development, maturity, and skill than the production itself, as when an expert critic or psychologist analyzes the drawings of a young child or a neurotic patient. In the case of a great work of art, the observer may perceive only a few superficial and fragmentary aspects of it and may miss its deeper meanings, its more subtle, perceptual relationships. A student can come back again and again to the study of a single great work such as the cathedral of Chartres or the *Divine Comedy* of Dante, and may learn to appreciate them more fully and deeply as his own mind develops. Indeed, a modern observer can in some respects understand such a work of past art more fully than its contemporaries did, through seeing it in historical and scientific perspective. In other respects, the modern may perceive the work less fully and adequately, being out of sympathy with the religious or other attitudes which inspired it. On the whole, our appreciation of past art grows with our powers of sensitive perception and intellectual understanding.

There are narrow limits to the amount of technical skill in the practice of art which any individual can acquire during a lifetime. He must specialize intensively to practice any art well, especially in the present age of competition. No one can learn to play all the instruments of the orchestra well, or dance well in all the great national styles, or paint with mastery in the Chinese, Persian, Impressionist, Renaissance, and other styles of painting. The artistic phase of education must be somewhat specialized, especially for those who look forward to a professional career. On the other hand, there are no limits to the range of art appreciation which is possible to the educated modern adult. He can learn to perceive and understand the essentials of form and style in all the great arts and periods of art.

The term "fine arts" is ambiguous, being sometimes restricted to the visual arts and sometimes including music and literature, both of which claim to be as "fine" as painting or sculpture. The more precise term "visual arts" is coming into use to designate those arts addressed primarily to the sense of vision. "Art" does not imply a lack of utilitarian or functional aim. Architecture combines utilitarian and aesthetic aims and values in the same art and the same product. The same can be said for many of the so-called minor, decorative arts, such as furniture, textiles, and pottery. The old antithesis between the aesthetic and the practical, the fine and the useful, expressed not only the social cleavage between the leisure class and the working class in the aristocratic social order, but also the dichotomy between mind and matter, the spiritual and the physical, in a dualistic psychology and metaphysics. The present tendency is to bridge over these gulfs in theory and practice, and to emphasize the continuity between aesthetic and practical activities, treating them as differences in degree only. Nevertheless, it is recognized that an artist has a right to specialize at times on his own distinctive problems: upon form, expression, and technique, without being constantly distracted or called upon to serve too many political, moral, practical, or other interests. The same is true of aesthetic experience and aesthetic education. They have their own distinctive values, which should not be ignored or unduly subordinated to others.

Aesthetic education is now based on increasing knowledge about the development of personality from infancy to maturity. The value of children's aesthetic and artistic activities is appraised in relation to the interests and abilities of the child at each successive age level. One must realize the much shorter span of attention which is possible for the young child, and his inability to follow sustained lectures or planful activities over a long period of time. His stage of development calls for greater spontaneity and playfulness in all activities. His thought and behavior are simpler and more undifferentiated than those of adults. His approach to art and aesthetic experience must be less specialized and systematic than that of the older student. Although young children are alike in certain respects, they differ greatly in intelligence and in perceptual and imaginative ability. There is a difference also among children's artistic expressions, even at a very early age; in their power to externalize a vivid, active psychic life of perception, feeling and fantasy into some objective form of symbolic shapes, colors, words, or sounds. Aesthetic education tries to adapt its methods and techniques of instruction to such individual differences, including a tendency toward introversion or extroversion.

Art and civilized aesthetic experience differ widely according to the culture in which they operate. One can understand them only by studying the various culture patterns into which adult life and thought are organized in various times and places. Aesthetic psychology is learning much from ethnology and cultural history. It is distinguishing between the human mind as it operated in medieval Europe and as it operated in China in the Sung Dynasty or in a Polynesian island before the coming of the white man. Aesthetic psychology is also learning from recent advances of individual psychology and psychoanalysis. It is profiting from greater knowledge about normal and neurotic types of personality and their origins: about the inner, subjective fantasy life of these various types, and its relation to art. Education itself is one of the greatest potential laboratories for psychological research on the effects and values of different kinds of art on students of various types and ages.

Studies have been made of the development of drawing ability in individual children over a period of years. Typical stages and sequences occur, as in the advance from "schematic" or conceptual drawing toward greater and greater realism. Ordinarily, older children reach a stage of fairly realistic representation. At present, nonrealistic, post-impressionistic, and nonobjective styles are fashionable in advanced art circles. Some older students complete the circuit and return from realism to renewed interest, on a mature level, in the schematic and nonrepresentative types of drawing and painting.

Young children enjoy spontaneous play with art materials and media of different kinds; they like the simple activity of handling clay, paints, brushes, either alone or in small groups. Very young children do not co-operate well, but joint projects become easier in later childhood. As the child grows older, he tends to become more critical of his own artistic efforts, and more aware of excellence in adult art and in the work of his more skillful associates. He is also more distracted in later childhood by scholastic and other interests such as the requirements of promotion to advanced vocational training or college entrance. He is increasingly influenced by contemporary adult art and attitudes toward art, by the tastes of others, including children a little older than himself. He is sensitive to ridicule and to praise or condemnation, and is quick to change his own attitudes toward art in response to social pressures. He becomes more aware of the social, political, and religious currents about him, and of commercial and professional attitudes toward art. The child grows up into a culture and constantly tries to adjust his own individual desires and aptitudes to the value system of the group in which he lives. He tends to imitate the tastes of persons he admires, and to reject those of persons whom he dislikes or scorns. The status of art in the community and the kinds of art which are praised or disparaged tend to direct the growth of his own aesthetic nature along certain lines.

Aesthetic development implies a steady increase in powers of discrimination among perceptual qualities and images, and increasing power of complex, organized perception and composition. It implies a progress from the naïve to the critical, analytical attitude toward works of art. It implies increasing knowledge about art and acquaintance with varieties of art, so that the mind becomes stocked with a richer supply of memory-images of different types and styles. Such a developed mind has greater power of perception and discrimination in encountering any new work of art. Even though the object is unfamiliar, the individual can compare it with memories of other works of art.

One cannot say, from the modern standpoint, that there is such a thing as "good taste" in the sense of an absolutely correct judgment of artistic value. Artistic value changes in relation to social conditions. The taste of the adult is not necessarily right for the child, or the taste of the connoisseur for the beginner in art. Different types of art are good for different persons. Nevertheless there is good taste in the sense of highly developed, trained, sensitive powers of perception and aesthetic response. Its conclusions are not necessarily binding upon others, but it allows experience on a high mental level. However, all too often progress in knowledge and in special training is accompanied by a loss of enthusiasm and emotional vitality, which militates against aesthetic enjoyment and creative vigor. The humanistic ideal in aesthetic education is to maintain the fresh spontaneity, enthusiasm, sensitivity, and power of learning which are common in youth, along with the greater knowledge and skill of educated maturity.

Many children lose interest in the arts during adolescence. Many of them remain on an arrested level of development of knowledge and taste. Those who continue in the arts tire of play and free expression, and demand more definite instruction in techniques and information. Teachers of art on this level must try to keep alive an interest in art and in continued growth and learning in the field.

The transition must be made in later childhood and adolescence from spontaneous play with art materials to a more serious, disciplined handling of adult techniques and styles. Here art museums, libraries, phonograph records, and color prints are of great assistance. They help the child learn how to enjoy adult art discriminatingly while continuing to express himself in a chosen field. The problem is to encourage the child to absorb the cultural heritage of adult art without becoming slavishly imitative, or without mere copying of what has already been done. He must be shown how to perceive and stock his mind with images from art and nature, and to use these creatively, reconstructing them, selecting and emphasizing what appeals to him most, and thus producing a form which embodies something of his own individual personality. Sex differences become increasingly important at this stage. The girl normally develops greater interest in such arts as clothing, textiles, flower arrangement, and interior design, while the boy develops more in architecture, community planning, photography, and carpentry—in general, in arts and media requiring more muscular strength or involving a practical or vocational turn of mind.

Psychology shows us how different kinds of art can serve the psychic and emotional needs of youth at different stages of development. No one kind of art is necessarily best for all ages and types of youth. Some art which adults consider inferior and trivial may be exactly what the adolescent needs at his particular stage of development. Popular art which appeals to him may seem too erotic and sentimental to the adult. Within limits, as dictated by the moral standards of the community, such art may be of value. It is a mistake to pick out certain kinds of art as great, or as the latest trend in sophisticated adult circles, and force these on children of all ages and types.

2. The philosophical approach

The present age is one of deep and widespread conflict among ideologies, new and old. One such conflict is between the naturalistic philosophy, based on empiricism and scientific rationalism, and the various forms of supernaturalism. Some of the latter are dualistic, maintaining the reality of both mind and matter, body and soul; some are idealistic or panpsychist, maintaining that only mind or spirit is real. Another basic issue is between the authoritarian, dogmatic, or totalitarian attitude in conduct and evaluation, and the liberal, humanistic attitude which stresses the right of individuals and minorities to work out their own destinies, with due regard for the interests of others—to think for themselves, to experiment in art and in moral and social policies. A third issue is that in moral and aesthetic value theory, between absolutism and objectivism, on the one hand, and subjectivism and relativism, on the other.

Naturalism, in the philosophic sense, had its origins in Greek atomistic materialism as set forth by Democritus, Epicurus, and Lucretius. At first confined to the physical sciences, naturalism has spread to the biological and social sciences, to the study of thought and human behavior in psychology, and now to the subjects concerned with value: ethics and aesthetics. Naturalism doubts the existence of disembodied spirits; it holds that life and mind occur only as activities of physical organisms. It disbelieves in magic and miracles, insisting on the regular order of nature, wherein no effect occurs without a natural cause. It involves an interest in nature and human life on earth rather than in heaven and a future life.

In Renaissance art, the growing interest in nature was at first expressed in representations of the human body and of animals and plants; later, in scenic landscapes. In science, it was expressed in curiosity about the hidden causes and processes of things. A related trend was humanism: the respect for human life on earth; the interest in man and his affairs, including individual personalities. These trends were shown in realistic portraiture (painted and sculptured) and in realistic stories and characters in literature. Humanism in the Renaissance involved extreme admiration for Greek and Roman art; it often disparaged useful labor by contrast with fine art and philosophy. In later centuries, naturalistic humanism took on a more practical cast, through the influence of such philosophers as Francis Bacon in seventeenth-century England. He called for the improvement of life on earth through the observation and understanding of nature and through the invention of devices for curing man's ills and satisfying his wants. Still later, the rise of democracy led to further changes in the spirit of humanism; to less admiration for the classical ideal and greater admiration for the common man and his problems.

In the Renaissance and later, naturalistic humanism involved an enthusiasm for "naturalistic representation"; that is, for visual and factual realism. These were shown in the representation of human anatomy and of spatial perspective. Fantastic visions and distortions of anatomy gave place to the attempt to render faithfully scenes on earth as they would actually appear to a single spectator who regarded them from a single viewpoint at a single moment in time. The modern philosophic naturalist does not necessarily prefer the naturalistic style in art. For he now sees that even mysticism and idealized or romantic fantasy in art are expressions of human nature. Such art can produce valuable aesthetic experience here and now on earth. It is consistent with naturalistic philosophy to work out designs or expressive forms in art which serve as interesting objects of visual perception for their own sake or for their symbolic meanings. A modern naturalist can enjoy and approve modern abstract, distorted, or nonobjective painting more than conservative, realistic art.

Naturalism in metaphysics does not necessarily imply a "materialistic" attitude toward life and values. A philosophic materialist can fully agree that "spiritual" values, including moral, artistic, and intellectual ones, are superior to those of crude physical satisfaction and of money and mechanical power. The liberal naturalist holds that achievement of the highest spiritual values requires a healthy, free bodily life and a just social order in this world.

Absolutists in aesthetics have never been able to agree on the specific nature of beauty and value in art and their so-called laws; on how they are to be recognized in genuinely good art or conveyed in education. The supposedly self-evident, provable "laws" of beauty and good art, proclaimed by dogmatic idealists, are extremely broad, vague, and inconsistent. From the Renaissance through the eighteenth century, it was generally accepted in Europe that the principles of Greek and Roman art were universal and permanent standards of perfection. Now they are regarded only as one of many great traditions, each with its own aims, styles, and values for us today. There is room in art for endless progress in the future.

The opposites of absolutism and objectivism are relativism and subjectivism. These trends were carried to extremes by some of the early Greek Sophists and Epicureans. They proposed a negative skepticism; an individual anarchy of tastes, according to which there is no such thing as beauty or value in general. They rejected general standards in art, holding that beauty is merely the pleasure and preference of the individual, and that whatever any individual likes at the moment is beautiful for him. The bearing of such extreme relativism on aesthetic education is obvious. On this basis, the teacher can never criticize a student as right or wrong or grade one work of art as better than another, except as an expression of his own personal taste. A teacher cannot hold up to the student any works of art as great in themselves or worthy of emulation. He cannot logically give any one student in art a higher grade than another or recommend him for special opportunities on the basis of superior talent. In its extreme form, relativism prevents any attempt at discriminating the better from the worse in art or in other realms of value. Some art teachers become timid and inert, fearing to criticize or influence the student.

Such extreme negativism is not a necessary implication of modern naturalism, which is less individualistic than ancient Epicureanism, and more scientific. Modern naturalism places more emphasis on the cultural, intersubjective nature of value standards. It is more positive and constructive in attitude, and does not hesitate to formulate standards in art and ethics, of a tentative and experimental character.

Such standards, like any other hypotheses, are man-made products and are developed out of human experience in art and other fields. They express the tested, cumulative wisdom and discernment of humanity of a particular culture up to the present time, and are subject to further revision through experience. Human beings are not all completely different; no individual is completely unique. They all resemble each other in many ways, primarily in that normal humans are equipped with the same basic physiological endowment of sensory, nervous, intellectual, and emotional functions. They also differ individually and according to cultural background, but not completely. To the extent that humans resemble each other or fall into certain recurrent types and groups such as those of sex, age level, or intelligence, tentative standards are possible. They can be developed as in the fields of nutrition and medicine. Different kinds of individual need different foods and medicines. What is good for one may be poisonous for another; hence one cannot prescribe any one kind as best for all. There are certain psychic, mental, emotional needs which differ to some extent from person to person and age to age, but not completely. Many types of art have come down to us through thousands of years and still satisfy and benefit persons of a certain age or type. Experimental aesthetics, aided by educational experiment, seeks to discover the effect of certain types of art on certain types of person under certain circumstances. It seeks to develop generalizations regarding such tendencies or potencies in art. These operate as standards of value, in so far as a certain kind of aesthetic effect is desired. Some effects of art are aesthetic and hedonistic; they consist in giving pleasure, entertainment, or the highly developed aesthetic enjoyment of the connoisseur. Other effects of art are utilitarian, moral, political, social, or otherwise nonaesthetic. In this category are the long-range, indirect effects of art on the development of personality. Generalizations about the effect of art must now be very tentative and flexible, for we know too little about the psychic needs of different kinds of person, or about the effects of art upon them. We know little, for example, about the actual effects of stories and films of crime upon different kinds of children and adolescents.

The individual preference and aptitude of students must be given considerable scope. At the same time, educational authorities have the right and duty to require a study of what they consider to be best in world art, and what they consider most valuable in the general education of students in a certain cultural group. Such judgments of value are subject to change. Teachers of art are entitled to grade and criticize the work of students, but they should do so in a tentative and not a dogmatic way. They are under the obligation to make their standards as clear and conscious as possible—to point out the specific qualities in art which they deem desirable, and why.

The naturalistic worldview is sometimes distorted along illiberal, coercive lines. One such extreme at the present time is that of Marxist Communism. Based in theory on a dogmatic materialism, and persistently attacking religious traditions, it is often regarded in Europe and Asia as the only alternative to a traditional Christian or other religious ideology. The possibility of a moderate, liberal naturalism or deism is not widely realized there. Marxian Communism has developed a new form of absolutism and oppression. It appeals not to the will of God or to eternal truth or principles of value but to party discipline. The official party line in Moscow as to good or bad art, and as to what the artist or art teacher must or must not do, is subject to frequent, radical, and often unexplained reversals. Achievements for which the artist or teacher is praised at one time may lead to his imprisonment or death a little later. Art becomes largely an instrument of political regimentation, rather than a means to free cultural development.

To Rousseau and other Romanticists of the eighteenth and early nineteenth centuries, we owe the modern democratic emphasis on freedom in art and education. We owe to them the belief, further developed by John Dewey and others, that the child should be encouraged to feel, think, observe, discuss, and experience for himself throughout the educational process. The Romantic emphasis on freedom, impulse, and emotion has also been carried to extremes, as in opposing all discipline in school, all leadership by teachers, all general rules and prescribed subject matter. Within limits, and balanced by the opposite emphasis upon order and reason, it remains a valuable element in our present cultural heritage.

Modern liberal humanism preserves a moderate, restrained optimism as to the future of mankind and of art. It rejects the medieval assumption that man is weak, helpless, and corrupt by original nature. It is no prey to the anguish, pessimism and defeatism of the existentialists. It is still confident, in spite of the modern tragedy, in the eventual power of man to progress through his own unaided efforts, and through a wise use of scientific knowledge and control. Such progress is by no means certain or automatic, however. Modern humanism assumes that art can progress along with other branches of civilization. This does not imply that contemporary art is better in all respects than ancient. Art progresses in developing new types of form, technique and expression, new insights into nature and human nature, and new sources of valuable experience, and in contributing these to the common fund of man's inheritance. The cultural heritage in art progresses in becoming steadily more rich, varied, informed, skillful, infused with realistic understanding of man and his place in the world. World art is now being poured together from every tradition into one vast, diversified cultural heritage, which is being placed at the disposal of all students everywhere through education. In this task, liberal humanism proposes a reasonable balance between order and freedom, emotion and reason, tradition and radical innovation, self-expression and careful craftsmanship.

An important factor in the scientific approach to aesthetic education is the development of aesthetics itself as an empirical science, rather than as a branch of abstract philosophy. Based on psychology and sociology as well as on the intensive study of works of art themselves, it is becoming an enlightening influence in aesthetic education.

There is room in modern humanism for many liberal varieties of religious and philosophic creed. It does insist, however, that a paramount aim of man must be improvement of the quality of experience or conscious living in this life; not merely for the privileged few, but for everyone. Art is and always has been one of the most powerful instruments for producing good experience of many different kinds. These change from age to age, and differ according to the individual. Art is constantly discovering new ways to make life worth living as we go along, by adding to its immediate delightfulness and significance. In addition, art can contribute to mental development and social adjustment. It is the task of aesthetic education to see that all these values, together with those of science and other studies, are achieved in a balanced, harmonious way on every level of schooling.

3. Aims of aesthetic education

So conceived, aesthetic education has the following principal aims:

(1) It should *foster the aesthetic and artistic strains* in individual personality through active exercise and application in the observation, production, performance, and discussion of works of art. The aesthetic and artistic strains in personality do not constitute a distinct, separate faculty, but consist in certain distinctive applications of the common psychophysical functions and processes. Their development must proceed hand in hand with the development of other functions and abilities. The general aim of education, from this point of view, is to achieve a balanced, developed, well rounded, highly conscious, normal, healthy, and happy personality, not only at maturity, but at every stage of growth. Aesthetic education can exercise and train many of the functions which are neglected when education becomes too bookish, verbal, and intellectual, or too narrowly practical and vocational. It should seek to develop perceptual skill in looking at, listening to, and reading complex artistic forms. It should seek to develop a sense of values in art and in the experience of art, and above all a love of art and of the life of which it is a part.

Development of the artistic and aesthetic strains in personality is not a purely subjective, mental process. It should involve increasing control of hands, arms, limbs, voice, and other parts of the body in executing artistic techniques, under the direction of a controlling mind, imagination, and purpose.

(2) Another aim of aesthetic education is to convey to every student as much of the *cultural heritage of the world's great art* as he can effectively absorb and utilize. Aesthetic and artistic abilities require this heritage for their nourishment. Past and present works of art are among the materials out of which the modern individual builds his own personality and contribution to society. Through conveying the most valuable elements in the artistic heritage to every student, we can help him to become deeply and broadly educated— a citizen of the world as well as of his own local community and national, racial, or religious tradition. The cultural heritage should be presented to him gradually, in such quantity and selection as he can best absorb, understand, and enjoy at each stage of development. There should be a general transition from the easy to the difficult, from the local and familiar to the more remote and difficult elements in the heritage. On the whole, each nation and community should emphasize its own traditional arts. At the same time, it should lead the student to appreciate other traditions and world art as a whole. The student should come to compare the works of people of his own locality with those of others, so that he may become aware of their distinctive values and limitations, and of how the arts of his own community can be developed and enriched without losing their characteristic flavor.

(3) Aesthetic education should help to prepare the student for *vocational and professional success,* for a career which will gain him a livelihood and at the same time perform a constructive service to society. It should help the student to choose his or her life work intelligently and to prepare for it in a realistic, effective way. Such a career may be in the arts or elsewhere. The student can best choose among various types of vocation by observing and working in different ones, so as to find out the one for which he is best fitted. Today, careers in the arts have multiplied; they include not only the traditional occupations of painting, sculpture, and architecture, but also industrial designing, commercial art, art education, museum work, journalistic criticism, scholarly research, publishing, and the management of artistic activities, such as theaters, orchestras, and com-

munity recreational centers. Art education in the school should familiarize the student with the opportunities in art which are open at home and abroad. Art can also help inform the student about other careers, including those in science, business, medicine, and politics. By means of accurate films, photographic displays, stories, radio and television, the student can be vividly shown the nature of work in various fields; what it means to be an active participant in each; what the rewards, advantages, and disadvantages are, and what types of person can best succeed in them. The arts are too often taught without reference to the financial difficulties of such a career, and the problems involved in making a living by it. Painting should be presented not merely as an art or technique, but as a possible vocation or avocation, with advantages and limitations. As the student grows older, he should have more and more opportunity to learn those techniques and skills which may help him make a living, along with those which are of more purely aesthetic or cultural rather than practical or monetary value. They are not mutually exclusive, but each deserves separate attention at times.

(4) The fourth main aim is the use of the arts for *developing constructive, co-operative citizenship*. The arts are a powerful means of developing a sense of respect and understanding toward persons of other groups. Not all art is peaceful and tolerant in attitude; on the contrary, some is expressly designed to inflame emotions of hatred and prejudice. A selection must be made by educators of types of art which best contribute to intergroup understanding. Even the arts of destructive and vicious propaganda can be studied with profit. They can be analyzed as to their actual operation and dangers, so as to immunize the student against lies and misrepresentations. Art can be used to develop a friendly attitude among students toward each other; in children of one group (racial, religious, or otherwise) toward others. The arts offer many opportunities for co-operative projects in and out of school, in which children can learn, early in life, the joy and the value of subordinating their selfish desires in a collective enterprise. Students of all interests can learn the importance of art as a social function, and of artistic products in the civilized community. They can learn to take pride in their community buildings, parks, playgrounds, museums, municipal theaters, and common possessions, so as to discourage vandalism and to encourage civic improvement.

4. Methods of aesthetic education

Specific *methods* will and should vary considerably from place to place. They will be determined in part by the dominant interests and character of the community: for example, by its degree of industrialization, mechanization, and urbanization—whether a community is a rural or a metropolitan one; the nature of its resources and equipment; the nature of the careers and opportunities available. The whole culture pattern of the community helps determine methods of instruction: the religious and ethnic character of the population; climate and physical resources. Local influences combine with national and international trends in art and science to determine details of the program.

Two general principles follow from a genetic, developmental approach to art education; that is, from regarding it as a phase in the individual's growth from infancy to maturity within a particular cultural environment. One is the principle of *progressive differentiation and specialization* as the student grows older. The other is the principle of *increasing purpose and systematic control*.

In the lower grades, education in the arts and other subjects should be most undifferentiated in the sense of not being divided into separate subjects. Art activities here are continuous with other activities. The children pass easily and without noticeable break from an artistic to a factual, scientific, or historical approach. Art activities are bound up with others. Subjects and activities change frequently from day to day, though preserving a basic continuity. Art activities in the lower grades are varied, extensive, and comparatively unsystematic. The children observe a great variety of objects in art, in nature, and in the life around them, learning gradually to distinguish them. The sequence is genetic and psychological, related to their changing interests and abilities, rather than logical or theoretical. They can try their hands informally at a great variety of media and tools in the arts, such as finger paints, modeling clay, rhythm and percussion instruments, simple wind instruments, singing, building with blocks, and telling stories. Activity is playful in the sense of being directly enjoyable and not too severely regimented; but this does not exclude an atmosphere of serious work or the desire to learn and perform each task with care. Adult standards of perfect craftsmanship and organization are not required; interest and vitality are more important. Nevertheless, an effort is made to develop gradually a respect for accurate craftsmanship and for finishing at least some definite part of the task one has begun. The teacher can easily go too far in allowing habits of laziness, carelessness, or impatience. Free individual experiment is encouraged within the arts, but the teacher does not stand by in a completely passive way. She is constantly present to exert a gentle influence in the direction of growth, system, and understanding, without undue haste or pressure.

As the student climbs the educational ladder, his work necessarily becomes more specialized; he comes to realize the difference between the scientific and aesthetic attitudes; between various styles in each art; between fact and fancy; between truth, fantasy, propaganda, and personal opinion. At certain points along the way, he is given more opportunity to concentrate upon the field of his choice: upon manual or intellectual work; art, science, administration, housework, or business. He can specialize more and more intensively, but is never permitted to lose all contact with the broader approach. Complete specialization on a single skill or subject is to be discouraged from the standpoint of liberal education until the last phase of schooling. Along with his field of concentration, he should if possible continue some studies which develop understanding and interest toward all constructive, civilized human thought and action. He should continue to develop as an alert-minded citizen of the world while becoming a capable specialist in some chosen vocation. Even in adult education, after formal schooling has ceased, the alert and growing individual will constantly try to see his own personal and local problems in a wider context of world problems and developments. During the last few years of schooling, there will necessarily be specialized courses, and studies and particular projects within these courses, which focus the attention on a narrow range of problems for the sake of utmost precision and perfection. But at other times during the day or year, the student can be drawn once more to contemplate these intensive studies in their larger framework of his own life's program and of events in his community and the world.

Never should a technique be taught in complete isolation, as a pure, unrelated skill or method. It should always be taught as a means to an end, whether that aim is practical or aesthetic. It is subject to change in the light of new aims, new styles of art, and improved methods for achieving them. The intelligent student should never be forced to concentrate long upon the purely mechanical, external, manual phases of technique apart from the mental ones. The development of planning and imagination should go hand in hand with the acquirement of skills. He should be led to ask why, to what end he is learning this or doing that; why this particular technique is the best way so far to achieve certain goals, although it may be improved in the future. In that case, he will have to learn a new technique or change the old one. Techniques are never finished or permanent. The student who learns only a set of mechanical skills will soon find himself out of date in a changing world; the one who has learned basic principles and methods of creative thought can grow with the times.

There are many ways of narrowing down the field of effort as the student grows older. Too often we think that specialization in art must be made in terms of a single art or technique. In teaching the history of art, we wrongly assume that specialization must be in terms of time and place; that the scholar must limit himself to a certain period and nationality in the history of art. In modern education, many other kinds of specialization are important. One can specialize on the general, theoretical approach to art. In art history, one can specialize upon the relations between art and some other factor in civilization, such as religion or economics. An artist can specialize on the relations between pictures and music in the film. Education is trying to develop new syntheses, new borderline or interdepartmental studies, new ways of selecting and interrelating activities and subject matter in art.

On the higher levels education in art, as in other subjects, should be increasingly planful and systematic. From the casual, impulsive play of early childhood, the student can be led into a more consciously directed, continuous program. Free impulse must gradually come under the flexible guidance of intelligent purpose, individual and social. In a democracy, every citizen is encouraged to learn how to plan and evaluate his own activities rather than merely taking orders from a boss or dictator. Young children are encouraged to think out what they are doing and why. In art, they plan constructive programs for the group: joint projects such as staging a play, painting a mural, or visiting a museum. Some of these may last for several days or weeks as their attention-span lengthens. Older children can orient themselves in larger chronological frameworks of history, looking backward to the dawn of civilization and ahead to ideal goals. They can plan their individual lives in a tentative and flexible way, subject to change.

Whereas, in the lower grades, art appreciation has little of the intellectual element, this element develops gradually in the higher grades. First experiences in art are largely sensory, manipulative, and affective. One handles things, jumps about, sings, laughs, runs, builds, looks and listens, all in rapid and irregular succession. Occasionally, one asks an intelligent question or gives an intelligent answer, especially under the guidance of the teacher. But there is no attempt at systematic logical theory. In the higher grades, one tries to connect ideas in more complex patterns of fact and implication. Some of these are historical, some geographical or social; some are logical and theoretical. In later childhood and adolescence, one learns the principles of abstract mathematics and of other sciences. In art, one may likewise advance to a discussion of aesthetic principles: of the psychology, morphology, and sociology of the arts.

The older student's work in art can become more systematic, whether or not it is vocational in aim. Every civilized individual has many different plans and connected activities which he carries along together or in alternation. Some are limited to holidays or vacations, but are dropped, and renewed again. The civilized adult, though practicing a vocation far removed from art, may maintain an intelligent amateur interest in music or in the collection of some type of art, such as porcelain or etchings.

To emphasize the increasingly intellectual and purposeful character of higher education is not to say that it should be entirely devoid of the play spirit or of casual, unplanned experiences. There is an important place for careless relaxation in the life of the busiest, most responsible executive. In these tense, disturbed times, everyone needs occasional hours, days, and, if possible, weeks of relaxing diversion. It may be secured by a change of work, as from the cares of government to the new difficulty of learning to paint or to play tennis. It may be attained through casual, aimless wandering through the woods or playing with children. The realm of art is one we can enter to advantage, either with a purpose and a serious problem or for the sheer delight of manipulating a medium or letting our eyes and ears feast upon the beauties of form. All are good, and all can be educational in the fullest sense. The best policy is to change now and then from a purposeful to a planless, from an intellectual to a sensory or emotional approach. For one who practices or teaches an art professionally, it provides challenging work rather than play. For a painter or a government official, music may provide restful recreation. Serious studies in the arts, if rightly conducted, will help one to enjoy the arts more keenly through deeper understanding and clearer perception. Enjoyment is not necessarily diminished by knowledge. This may happen if the knowledge is undigested or irrelevant, unrelated to active appreciation or creation. A dead weight of facts is obstructive to both enjoyment and creation. But facts and skills can be learned in such a way as to increase enjoyment and effectiveness.

Another common error in aesthetic education is to suppose that technical skill is needed only in the production and performance of art. Appreciation also has its skills and techniques. The training of the eye to perceive complex and subtle relationships in painting or in architecture; the training of the ear to perceive complex form in a symphony—these are techniques which require careful study. Many artists and erudite art historians never acquire them. In time they can become automatic and effortless, contributing to fuller enjoyment on a high mental level.

5. Materials and equipment

The *subject matter* of aesthetic education will vary greatly according to the nature and resources of the community and of each particular school. Wealthy, metropolitan institutions may have rich resources for the study of art. But these are not necessarily decisive and can be counteracted by bad methods of education. On the other hand, a great teacher in a rural school, with only the simplest equipment, may produce a high level of appreciation and creative power in students.

In general, the desirable materials for aesthetic education may be classified under two headings. One group consists of *works of art* for observation, together with *supplementary material* for understanding them. Here the range of desirable materials is limitless. It includes all the great styles and products of world art from primitive times. It includes original works of art in museums, augmented by international circulating exhibitions. It includes the still greater range of reproductions of art now available, which have revolutionized the teaching of art history and appreciation. We now have faithful color prints of paintings, together with films and lantern slides in color. We can show the student great architecture through the eye of the motion picture camera, as if he were traveling through, around, and upon it. There is a tremendous range of phonograph records of European, oriental, and tribal music from all parts of the earth. Radio and television help diffuse both popular and classical art to the masses. We now have libraries of great world literature in translation as well as in the original. Well-selected anthologies concentrate the best of this into textbook compass for the student. Urban centers have their theaters for drama, dance, and film. Such materials for the study of world art should be supplemented by travel. Many cannot be transported or well shown in reproduction. Funds are needed to help students travel to distant art centers, where they can see the great museums and masterpieces of architecture directly.

The second type of necessary material consists in the *raw materials and tools for the performance and production of art*. Studios are needed, including small ones where an individual can at times work in privacy, away from distractions. The range of materials and instruments varies according to the arts concerned. Some are extremely simple, ranging from pencil and paper for the poet or draftsman to complex apparatus for making color films with sound accompaniment, and to the precision tools of architecture and industrial design. Aesthetic education as a whole requires so vast and expensive an array of such materials and tools that no school or city school system can expect to have them all; an attempt to do so would entail unnecessary duplication. A well-planned national educational system should see to it that a few specialized centers are established, each with adequate equipment for learning and practicing some complex, difficult art such as architecture, community planning, or motion picture production. The simpler, less expensive materials, required for many arts, can be more widely diffused. For children, they include crayons, paints, clay, and building blocks. Simple materials are needed for young children to create and express themselves more directly. In music, there has been too much emphasis on learning adult musical instruments such as the piano by young children; a beginning can be made with much simpler instruments. There is no reason why children should not compose music or literature before they can write down a musical score or a verbal manuscript. If the school possesses a machine for recording music and speech, children and adults who are untrained in notation can record original compositions which can afterwards be corrected and written down by others. Motion picture films and tape recorders are useful in teaching orchestral composition, dancing, and similar arts.

It should be emphasized that such complex mechanisms are not necessary for the production of great art, and that excessive devotion to them may actually militate against high quality. Mechanisms are and should be the servant of the artist, and he should not be overwhelmed by them, especially at an early age. But the present age is one of increasing mechanization and industrialization. The artist who is confined to simple hand tools and methods is likely to be out of touch with his age. For those who can master and direct them, mechanical methods can provide increase in power. The mental ability to direct them well is an important goal of aesthetic education. It requires attention to the intellectual, imaginative, and emotional phases of artistic experience, as well as to external tools and technique.

✒ II ✒

SOME BASIC PROBLEMS IN ART EDUCATION*

1. Current issues and conflicting answers

All the chief issues as to the nature and values of the arts in contemporary society carry over into art education. In addition, new problems arise there as to the best selection of activities, equipment, and subject matter; as to the best methods of instruction in dealing with different types of student and curriculum in different environments. According to the way we answer the questions, "What are the best kinds of art?" and "How can art best serve society?" certain implications will follow as to the best ways of teaching art. Methods of art education have on the whole followed successive trends and styles in art itself: once setting the student to emulate Greek, Florentine, or Dutch masters; then gradually opening the doors to Impressionist and Post-impressionist aims and techniques. As leading architects and industrial designers come to stress functionalism, simplicity, and new materials, the teachers of these arts follow suit; not all at once, but after the new trend has become respectable.

Issues in regard to the psychological, sociological, and evaluative aspects of art are also educational issues, or have an immediate educational bearing. What we believe as to the nature of art abilities and the mental processes involved in creation and appreciation will influence our ways of trying to develop these abilities in students. If we believe that art ability is restricted to the talented few, we shall be inclined to restrict art instruction to these gifted students; but if we believe it to be more universal, we may favor making such opportunities available for all. If we believe that art is an effeminate luxury of the idle rich, we shall not be inclined to spend much money on it in the public schools. What we believe as to the social functions of art will influence our ways of relating art to the rest of the curriculum, will make us present it as detached and trivial, or as

* Published in its original form in *Art in American Life and Education,* 40th Yearbook of the National Society for the Study of Education (Bloomington, Ill.: Public School Publishing Co., (1941)), pp. 16–45.

25

an integral, vital factor in society. If we adhere to strict academic standards of value in art, we shall probably insist that students be drilled in accordance with them, made if possible to like such art and to produce it. If, on the other hand, we like to see an artist express his personal outlook in unusual ways, even when these are not beautiful by accepted standards, we shall be more tolerant of children's experiments in self-expression. If we believe that painting and sculpture are the only arts worthy of the name, we shall restrict the scope of art courses accordingly; or we may react to the opposite extreme of looking down on the "fine arts" as trivial, and restricting educational recognition to the "practical arts" alone.

Any policy can be carried to an unwise or absurd extreme. This includes the policy of according more recognition to the useful, everyday manifestations of art, and of avoiding the narrow, genteel snobbishness of the "fine art" tradition in the past. No doubt the latter has been heavily overemphasized in many college art departments and museums. But it should not be inferred that the value of art is to be appraised entirely in terms of everyday utility or of the greatest enjoyment of the greatest number of people. Painting and sculpture should not be too hastily brushed aside as unimportant in the new enthusiasm for practical arts. There may still be a place for the production and enjoyment of visual, as well as musical, forms that have no utility other than to provide objects for aesthetic contemplation. There may still be a place for the types of art that stress pure decoration, fantasy, amusing entertainment, and the expression of abstract ideas remote from immediate needs. In our eagerness to make art function in the lives of common men, and in our insistence that art ability is not confined to the aristocratic few, we need not rush to an indiscriminate leveling of values. There may still be certain kinds of art that are too difficult for untrained or insensitive minds to enjoy, yet quite as valuable socially as the popular forms of art, or more so. There may be talented individuals, and a few geniuses, who deserve special treatment. They may come from any social or economic class.

Just how to balance these sets of values is a perennial issue in art and art education. At present, there is perhaps greater danger of a too narrowly practical attitude toward the claims of art on the part of school educators than of the opposite extreme. It would be unfortunate if art education were to be justified only on the basis of tangible returns in cash, comfort, or that vague catchword "social adjustment." It would be unfortunate if potential leaders in art were lost to sight through exaggerated emphasis on mass education.

Not all the issues in art education arise from issues in the outside world of art production and consumption. Some are more indigenous to the educational realm itself. Education in youth is not now regarded merely as preparation for later life, but as a period of life that has its own intrinsic values. Deciding on the right sort of art education is not, therefore, merely a matter of deciding what sort of mature artists or art appreciators we wish to produce. Even if we knew that no students were to become artists, and that none would have access to art in later life, there would still be reason—so much the more reason—for letting them practice and enjoy the arts in school. Art is coming to be recognized as a necessary part of general education for all persons, on all age levels—necessary to the full exercise and development of personality, especially in its sensory, emotional, and imaginative aspects, and in muscular co-ordination.

But how shall art as an element in general education for all be related to art as vocational training for the few? What relative emphasis shall be placed on the two modes of approach? To what extent shall a broad, cultural view of art be required of all? To what extent shall intensive technical skill be sacrificed to it? To what extent shall free, individual experimentation be encouraged in all? To what extent shall the money available for art education be spent on students for whom it is to be a vocation? And to what extent shall these students be taught specific, salable techniques and styles? To what extent and how early shall they be given the practical viewpoint of factories and commercial studios? Shall students be encouraged to be original and experimental, to express their own interests and outlooks, or to please the public? Or can both be done at once? Some kinds of originality are salable, of course. And it is not without value in character development to learn how to do a technical job in a professional way. In overemphasizing personality, students' preferences, emotional adjustment, and so on as aims of art, there is danger of sentimental vagueness, of losing the real educational values of self-discipline, habits of work, respect for sound craftsmanship, and definite knowledge. Yet few educators today, in democratic countries, propose returning to the set rules and repressive disciplines of the old academic education.

In so far as art is regarded as a phase of general education rather than as training in a marketable skill, certain definite problems are raised. How can the stages in art education be adapted to those in personality development and general education, so as to become a phase in normal growth? How can they be made continuous from age level to age level, from lower to higher grades, avoiding the gaps and dislocations that now exist? How can studies in the appreciation, history, and criticism of art best be co-ordinated with those in technique and creative production? How should the emphasis be placed as between the two groups? Should there be much or little study of past art? How can museum or other studies of past art be made to contribute to creative originality, instead of making students imitative or merely scholarly? How can studies of art best aid in conveying the cultural heritage of past civilization and also give the student an ability to understand and cope with present civilization? What manual skills and technical knowledge are of value in general education for the student who will not become a professional artist? Should every child acquire some facility in using his hands to control a visual art medium, as he learns to use words for expression and communication? Which media should he work with; how many; and at what ages?

Each art and each medium raises its own additional problems. For example, in drawing, should students draw directly from observation of nature and from past works of art, or only from memory and imagination? If from all, in what proportions? Is copying other works of art necessarily bad? If not, how and to what extent can it be done beneficially? To what extent should historical and other factual knowledge of the subject matter of art be required of students; and to what extent should students be allowed to "use their imaginations" in representing a subject?

How can art activity be used to develop mental and emotional health and stability in the student? What does psychoanalysis imply as to the possible psychotherapeutic uses of art, and how reliable are these implications?

From the standpoint of directors and supervisors, administrative problems may appear as most important. What teaching personnel and what physical equipment are necessary for art work on various levels, and in various types of school? What portion of the total budget does art deserve? How important is supervision, and what should the supervisor do? Should art be taught mostly by regular classroom teachers or by special teachers? If the latter, how should art be related to other subjects? At what school level should art and other subjects be departmentalized? How should elementary school art differ from junior and senior high school art, and these from college, graduate, and professional school art? How can continuous progress in art from one school level to the next be facilitated? How can students' achievements on each level be evaluated and recorded? What standards of achievement can fairly be demanded on each level, for promotion to the next higher? How can attention to individual needs, especially of gifted students, be reconciled with the needs of ordinary students? How can large-scale education in art be standardized in desirable ways (e.g., equipment and schedule) without becoming inflexible? How large should art classes be, and what maximal teaching load is desirable?

Still heatedly argued back and forth is the question of "integration" versus "isolation"—shall art be taught as a separate subject and department, or be merged with others, as in the project method, core curriculum, and similar procedures? If the former, how can it be kept from excessive specialization, aloofness, and artificiality? If the latter, how can it avoid being overwhelmed by other approaches and made a mere handmaid to other departments, as in the making of posters for English and social studies? Shall it be taught with emphasis on distinctively artistic aspects, such as color, design, and perspective, or with emphasis on "social significance"—on art as a means of social reform, realistic description, and propaganda?

To all these questions more than one answer is possible. On most of them, art teachers tend to divide into two main camps: first, the so-called "progressive" wing, favoring comparative freedom for the student, a psychological and sociological approach, and integration rather than the subject curriculum; secondly, the more conservative wing, sometimes called "academic," favoring more discipline, required knowledge and technique, and more intensive, directed, systematic study of a limited realm of art. The former camp inclines to be more sympathetic to modern Post-impressionist art and to liberal politics; the latter to conservative politics, realism, and traditional standards in art. But such views do not always go together, and most art teachers object to being definitely labeled. They are conscious of the unwise extremes to which both attitudes have been carried: the one to absurd freakishness and pampering of children's whims; the other to stodgy, repressive conventionality. Most art teachers regard themselves as being at a happy medium between the two extremes, and as combining in their approach both sets of values. Nevertheless, vigorous disputes still arise over details of method and content.

Another administrative problem that is coming to the fore is that of providing opportunities for students to see good art, past and present, originals and reproductions. To try to teach art without showing good examples reduces art instruction to students' groping experiments or to rules and teachers' demonstrations. It is like trying to teach musical composition to students who never hear good music; yet all too often that sort of teaching is attempted. Sooner or later the school budget must face the task of supplying necessary materials for art as it does for chemistry. These will include, of course, artists' materials also—the traditional types, such as paints and clay, and the more complex apparatus of twentieth-century art, especially in the industrial fields and in theater arts.

2. The preparation of the art teacher

One's attitude toward the preparation of art teachers tends, if consistently thought out, to be largely determined by one's attitude on the problems mentioned above. If one believes that a certain kind of art is best, and that students should be trained to produce and like it, then one will believe that teachers in turn should be trained so as to make them capable of achieving these results. Methods of educating art teachers, accordingly, tend to proceed from beliefs or assumptions regarding the best kinds of art, the most valuable kinds of skill in producing or appreciating art, and the principal values to be derived from a study of art. In defining ultimate objectives, the emphasis may be laid on the student's own benefit through vocational skill, culture, and development of personality, or both; or on the student's potential contributions to society. The latter may be interpreted in terms of a liberal ideal of free creative enterprise, or in terms of economic production, or in terms of solidarity, obedience, readiness to fight and die for the state, as in dictatorial regimes today. In any case, the rightness of any teacher-training program is decided largely on instrumental grounds—in terms of what kind of instruction we wish the prospective teacher to be able to give.

Naturally, various lines of thought part company on this question, as on the prior aesthetic and educational issues themselves. There are teachers of prospective teachers who believe their charges should be fitted primarily to convey certain techniques of art as effectively as possible, including the requisite manual skills and technological information, and also a certain set of artistic ideals and standards. There are those who believe their task is to develop highly trained research scholars in art history, who can in turn make their own students into highly trained scholars. There are those who believe the art teacher's primary task is to develop in students a broad culture, independent habits of imagination and expression, emotional adjustment, and similar personality traits. They will believe, accordingly, that the art teacher's own training should be organized primarily to make him capable of developing these traits in students.

Of course, it is not necessary to choose one or another of these policies exclusively. Most teacher-training institutions would probably recognize all (except some of the dictatorial ones) as desirable and would claim to be working more or less for all of them, directly or indirectly. But real and considerable differences of emphasis arise in practice. They are manifested in the relative amounts of work in various fields required of prospective art teachers.

Time was when no very complicated requirements were imposed upon a prospective teacher of art. The guild system was often fairly strict in recognizing a man as a master craftsman whose qualifications would fit him to rule the lives of apprentices and to convey to them the ideals and skills of his craft. Under the freer individual methods of instruction that followed, anyone who could persuade others that he knew his craft could set up as a teacher or employ apprentices. Later on, vocational schools, some of them managed by craft unions, have again raised standards and organized systematic courses of instruction; but they have been almost entirely concerned with technique. Hence the principal requirement for teaching in them was technical. If a man was a good craftsman himself, it was assumed that he could teach his craft without bothering to study methods of teaching.

Meanwhile colleges and universities were teaching art from another aspect, mainly from that of history and literature, especially of the classical, medieval, and Renaissance periods. They were interested very little, if at all, in producing artists, but rather in conveying knowledge about the history of art. Positions were opened for men and women to teach art history and appreciation in the increasing number of colleges throughout the country. Graduate instruction was arranged—primarily for prospective teachers of art history —and degrees were established requiring advanced knowledge and ability in historical research. But ability to practice art was not (and still is not) considered a necessary qualification for college art professors. Nor is there much disposition to require courses in education of a prospective college art teacher. Ordinarily he is exempt from state certification requirements. But he does, in a liberal college, have to study many other academic subjects besides art, and hence presumably he does acquire a fairly broad cultural background.

The tremendous rise of "education" or pedagogy as a profession and a subject of study in this country has altered the situation considerably, especially with respect to the preparation of teachers for public and private schools of the elementary and secondary levels. Along with this has gone the increasing belief that studies in art are of value in the general education of all children, even for those who will not become artists; also that art instruction should aim at a variety of goals in addition to technical skill. It should help produce personality traits, integrate the curriculum, and so on. For these reasons it is urged that a prospective art teacher should devote a considerable amount of time to studying educational courses, such as the philosophy and psychology of education, teaching methods, and so forth, in addition to practice teaching. State teachers' certificates have enforced this tendency by demanding a certain amount of prescribed work in education. Professional art schools, universities, and teachers colleges have all been drawn into service to supply art teachers. They have been required to provide (at least by co-operation with some other institution) for the pedagogical, as well as the technical, training of their charges.

The course of study for the prospective teacher of school art is continually being widened to include more and different studies, each of which can be reasonably defended as desirable. Teachers of the practice of art, however, usually oppose giving up much time from the technical work that they believe necessary. Not a few leaders in the subject of education are coming to agree with them and to point out that required courses in education are often of little value as actually taught, and that, in any case, too many are required. At the same time, too little work in art history and theory is required in many teacher-training institutions.

It is difficult to generalize, because of the diverse conditions prevailing in different institutions and localities, but it seems fairly evident that various types of institution for preparing art teachers have developed on very different lines, and that much dislocation has resulted in the field as a whole. Teachers of art in the colleges are being prepared with heavy or exclusive emphasis on the historical approach to art, with fairly good cultural background, but with little or no technique in the practice of art, and little or no study of educational methods. Teachers of art in the schools below college level are being prepared with some technique and some educational methods, but often with little art history or theory, and little general cultural background, as evidenced by the small number of courses required in literature, history, and science. Teachers of professional art or craft instruction tend in their preparation to specialize on technique and to sacrifice all the other alternatives to some extent, except as they are forced to a broader preparation by certification requirements.

One result of these divergent lines of training has been to differentiate excessively between various types and levels in art instruction. College art has been decidedly different from, and unrelated to, the type of art done in secondary schools. Secondary school art is often very different from elementary art, because of greater departmentalization and concentration on technique. Art work in vocational high schools again is very different from art work in general, academic high schools. This dislocation appears as lack of continuity in progression from grade to grade, lack of definite requirements for each grade, and lack of co-operative understanding between art teachers at various points in the educational process.

Progress is being made in improving the training of art teachers, mainly through the gradual recognition by each institution and school level of what it has been neglecting. College art faculties are coming to include practicing artists as well as historians in their faculties, and to recognize practical art experience as desirable, if not strictly necessary, for the college art teacher. Prospective teachers of school art are being required to study more art history and theory, which they have lacked. But the exact distribution of time and the organization of curricula still present many issues.

Ideally, it would seem that all courses for the training of art teachers should be made longer, with more possibility of including all the desirable types of subject matter. But it is hard for any one institution alone to raise the requirements. Moreover, the profession of teaching art must compete with practical opportunities afforded by the industrial and commercial arts, in which financial rewards are sometimes high and educational requirements low. No doubt, further progress can be made through having administrators place a premium on adequate preparation in appointing teachers, and through concerted action by teacher-training institutions and teachers' associations. The problem is not solved by putting down on paper a fine array of required courses, topics of study, and so on. Everything will depend on how well these are taught and learned; and this in turn will depend on the quality of the persons engaged in them. It is to be hoped that the profession of art teaching, as well as the practice of art, will attract more broadly qualified persons to enter it, by its financial as well as its intangible rewards. This will necessitate better conditions of work, an easier teaching load, more secure tenure of position, and salary and retirement provisions commensurate with ever-rising standards of proficiency.

✬ III ✬

A PSYCHOLOGICAL APPROACH TO ART AND ART EDUCATION*

1. Aims of art education from a psychological standpoint

Modern psychology has deeply affected education in all fields. It has led us to realize that, in all branches of education, we are trying to direct the development of human beings. These are the basic materials with which we work; and the more we understand them, the more effectively we can control them for their own benefit and that of society. Teachers, too, are human beings, each with a peculiar set of strong and weak qualities, desires, and emotions. They affect the educational process in ways not always foreseen or intended. The content of education itself consists of products and records of human thinking and striving. The ideas and skills, the books, machines, and works of art that we ask children to study are expressions of human nature, and all are to be understood more clearly in the light of psychology.

Art especially is a warmly personal subject, though not always so presented in schools and colleges. It is concerned directly and constantly with human individuals and groups rather than with impersonal facts or logical abstractions. It deals with concrete experiences and their objects: with emotive sense-images, aspirations, loves, and hates. The forms and activities of art can be fully understood only in the light of the motives that inspired them and the experiences they arouse. Psychology should and will illuminate these for us, although so far it has made only a slight beginning in the study of behavior and experience in the realm of art.

Success in art depends to an unusually high degree upon obscure personal factors in the student, the teacher, and the mature artist. It depends on configurations of desire, imagination, and feeling that we now understand very dimly. No amount of technical skill or information alone will produce creative artists or discriminating appreci-

---

* Published in its original form in *Art in American Life and Education* (1941), pp. 249–286.

35

ators. Routine methods, and even the most apparently logical courses of study, are often unavailing. Many teachers are eager to make their students "creative," and often fondly believe they have done so, only to see the capable student become a mediocrity, while some neglected "ugly duckling" of the class may go on to produce surprisingly original things. Educational idealists hold up the goal of producing a new culture, including new advances in art. But there is little evidence that we know how to educate for artistic creativeness.

The psychological approach to education regards teaching in all subjects, on all age levels, as an attempt to *develop abilities* rather than to convey an inert mass of knowledge; as an attempt to foster inborn aptitudes, to harmonize and direct them into channels desirable from the social as well as the individual standpoint. There are many sorts of mental ability, all involving a co-operation of basic functions, but differing to some extent as to what functions they emphasize. We recognize some abilities concerned especially with manual or with other forms of nerve and muscle co-ordination, some with powers of visual or other sense perception, some with various sorts of memory, some with understanding of abstract concepts. There are powers of creative imagination, powers of enjoyment, and powers of critical judgment. All are exercised in art and may be developed through it.

The teaching of any subject may be appraised in terms of how well it succeeds in developing valuable mental and bodily abilities. Too often we teach science without asking how we can best develop powers of scientific thinking rather than mere understanding and memory of past scientific discoveries or mere ability to apply them in a mechanical way. Too often we teach art without asking how we can best develop the power to think and imagine artistically—to create and appreciate art. We teach it, in other words, as a set of mechanical skills or historical facts, apart from the mental ability to use these skills and facts constructively. We sometimes profess a desire to develop creative originality and powers of appreciation in students, and then proceed to teach as if the creation of art were merely a matter of manual technique and the following of set rules of composition, or as if appreciation were merely a matter of knowing historical facts about art.

Some theorists would reply that neither appreciation nor creative ability can be taught, and that all we can hope to do in art education is to train the hands and memories. That is a psychological assumption for which there is no other evidence than the frequent failure of past educational methods. The fact remains that we know little about what constitutes the process of artistic creation or that of appreciation, or what factors enable some individuals to achieve greater ability in these processes than others do. Both are essentially problems of psychology. If we ignore them or rest content with dogmatic assumptions about them, our educational principles remain to that extent unscientific and unintelligent. The situation points to one outstanding need, and that is for more careful systematic study and experiment in the psychology of art—not in isolation, but in relation to general psychology.

That art is a powerful means of influencing children, and thus of educational control, is evident if we consider the hold of motion pictures, comic strips, and illustrated stories upon the imagination of youth. True, these are not always good art, but they do attract and stimulate to an extent that school art and other school studies often fail to achieve. Vivid, dramatic techniques of presentation, visual and otherwise, can vitalize all sorts of school work and make learning easy. Well-meaning efforts of educators and moralists, on the other hand, are often hampered by dullness and abstractness. These facts are bound up with the larger fact that art is a powerful means of social control in general. It operates effectively in the dictatorial state, and we should not forget the long history of religious art in the service of various creeds and cults or the present influence of advertising, political cartoons, and posters. Whether we consider the educational process in a narrow sense or consider the whole process of social control, the same fact is evident: that art is an instrument of incalculable power, too often left to selfish interests and neglected by the public-spirited. To use it better, we must understand better how it affects and can affect human nature; how it moves the springs of human action, belief, and emotion. This is fundamentally a problem for psychology, to be approached through a study, not of art alone, but of art in relation to the basic factors of personality as well.

A consistent analysis of educational aims from the standpoint of psychology leads again to the old Greek conception of a well-balanced, harmoniously developed *personality*. Each individual is born with a number of rudimentary functions, to which others are added during maturation. They develop into complex types of perception, imagination, reasoning, desire, preference, purpose, and evaluation, as well as into powers of manual and other bodily co-ordination. All these can be actively exercised, controlled, and refined through the activities of art—in some respects, more directly and effectively there than in any other branch of human culture. A consistent effort at balanced development of personality would include attention to these and to their manifestations in aesthetic experience. In other words, the perceptive, imaginative, and effective components of personality should be fostered and developed through the educational process, along with the bodily and intellectual components. All are active and spontaneous in young children. But too often they become neglected, repressed, and atrophied in older students and adults, with the result that the adult personality is mutilated and disbalanced, with many of its potential functions arrested and immature.

This situation cannot be blamed entirely on formal education. In large part, it is a result of maladjustments inherent in our civilization. Life closes in upon the older child; repressive customs and competitive responsibilities force him to give up, one after another, the development of abilities he might ideally have pursued to fruition. But education could counteract these repressive forces much more than it does, through achieving a better balance in its own activities. From the psychological standpoint, an excessive share of the educational process—more and more as the child grows older—is devoted to intensive, and sometimes fatiguing, training of a few selected nerves and muscles, especially of those concerned with reading the printed page, understanding abstract ideas, and memorizing facts. The functions thus neglected by formal education do not become entirely inactive, however. They are stimulated outside of school, often by irresponsible agencies, in sensational and undisciplined ways, thus producing dissociation between the school and outside interests, and sometimes antagonism to the school as dull and prosaic. A considerable advance toward correcting this fault has been made in recent years, especially in the lower grades of school. Where made, it has always involved a greater emphasis on activities in the visual and other arts, including those of the theater.

In addition, art activities are being increasingly employed as a corrective for mental and nervous maladjustments in both children and adults. Their therapeutic value results in part from bringing into active play muscular, sensory, and other functions that may have been too little exercised in a sedentary life, thus restoring balance and helping to rest the overfatigued nerve centers. In part, it results from helping the individual to externalize his interests and divert some attention from himself and his anxieties. Meanwhile, the growing popularity of art activities for leisure recreation on the part of normal people, especially professional and office workers, gives a clear indication of their value in helping to correct the tiring overspecialization of urban life.

It is not implied that the development of individual personality should be the sole aim of education. That would be to overwork a single psychological conception. We also aim, for example, at transferring to all children, so far as they are able to receive it, those elements in our *cultural heritage* that seem most important for intrinsic enjoyment and practical use. That choice can never be made with complete objectivity or finality, but must be made by each generation of educational leaders in the light of its best powers of judgment. It involves a compromise (different in different types of school) between the requirements of vocational training and those of a broad cultural background. The latter, as far-sighted vocational advisers realize, is not to be advocated merely for the sake of leisure enjoyment, but also for its direct contribution to powers of advancement in any skilled occupation.

The selection and emphasis must be adapted to the mental age level of the student. Certain things can be understood, enjoyed, and used by older students and not by younger. Certain types of art can be appreciated and profitably studied by the twelve-year-old and not by the six-year-old. Certain technical activities, such as enameling, are too difficult for the very young. How shall these be graded, presented in order of sequence, so as to be adapted to the student's present stage of development? How can they be organized into a continuous program of advancement toward the more difficult and mature, without gaps or confusing dislocations? These questions can be answered, in regard to art or any other subject, only in the light of genetic psychology; after a study of the normal development of interests and abilities through maturation and the principal types of deviation in such growth. We shall consider them more fully in a later section of this chapter.

Formal education in all countries has been remiss in developing the artistic and aesthetic, the perceptual, imaginative, and emotional strains in personality. Several causes have impelled many educational administrators in recent years to adopt a consciously "hard-boiled" attitude, to disparage and disfavor expressions of imagination and feeling. Some (by no means all) administrators and school boards are opposed to art that is not "realistic" and practical. For the young child, they are intolerant toward fairy tales, myths, and fanciful pictures. They insist that children spend their time instead on factual studies of modern industry, transportation, and the like. Even the "progressive" wing of recent educators, consciously revolting from the classical, aristocratic education of yesterday, has tended toward a heavy emphasis on social and economic realism, often at the expense of imaginative art. The latter it sometimes condemns as "escape from reality," and many of its leaders would restrict the study of art to realistic portrayals of the contemporary social scene. Thus, whereas the old classical education at least paid some attention to the Bible and to Greek and Latin literature, with their rich content of myth, fantasy, and folklore, the modern education gives the child comparatively little of these cultural traditions, indispensable for appreciation of past art.

Even from the standpoint of realism, these attitudes are narrow and incomplete. They assume, and lead students to assume, a false psychology which ignores the tremendous force of sensuous, willful, emotional, and often irrational factors in life; the proneness of all mankind to fantasy-building of one sort or another. They lose the great power of art to deal directly with such factors, and to refine and organize them into some degree of rational adjustment with the rest of life. Through ignoring the actual importance of art in present society, they conceal from the student important vocational opportunities and resources, even in commerce and industry themselves.

Inadequate attention to art in education is due in part to confusion between the broad and the narrow meanings of the term "art"; in part, it has been due to a narrow conception of art in the minds of professional teachers of art. In a very broad sense, "art" includes not only the visual arts but also literature and music, so that educators sometimes feel that they are doing enough for art when they include some study of literature and music. Thus the development of visual ability is neglected. In a very narrow sense, "art" is often restricted to the "fine arts" of drawing, painting, sculpture, and decorative design. Overemphasis on these fine arts by art teachers tends to exclude the industrial and commercial arts, furniture, clothing, the handcrafts, city planning, and even architecture (aside from temples and cathedrals). As a result, the administrator gets an exaggerated impression of the impracticality and triviality of all visual art. He comes to think of art education merely in terms of flower painting, clay modeling, abstract decoration, and what seem to him crude efforts by children at pictorial self-expression. "Art appreciation" becomes identified in his mind with sentimental effusions about pictures, and ineffective attempts to make children like them. Those responsible for art in education have too often failed to put it forward so as to show its true power and substance, its true utility, practicality, and realism.

Psychologically, the goal of developing the aesthetic and artistic strains in personality is not necessarily achieved by merely including one or more "art courses" in the curriculum. Such a perfunctory solution often serves merely to conceal the basic neglect. For art can be taught merely as trivial play—pleasant for little children, tedious to older ones—or as unimaginative technique or dry scholarship on higher levels. If we are to understand the psychological importance of art, we must first regard it broadly—not as a special accomplishment or luxury for the few or as a mere avocation for leisure amusement, but as covering a group of activities almost universal in scope and concerned with basic human interests.

The wide range of phenomena concerned becomes more evident as soon as we think, not only of the artist or producer of visual art, but also of the appreciator, the consumer, the enjoyer, and the user of art. For everybody falls in some way under this latter category. It includes, not only those addicted to art galleries and museums, but also every reader of illustrated books, magazines, and newspapers, whether the illustrations are drawings or photographs. It includes every patron of theaters and motion picture shows; every wearer of clothes, jewelry, and other accessories of costume. It includes every inhabitant of a house and garden or an apartment; everyone who visits parks, playgrounds, and public buildings; and everyone who uses furniture and utensils in house, school, or office. It includes every rider in automobiles, trains, and airplanes; everyone who looks at advertising and buys packaged goods. Everyone is somehow a consumer of art, is affected by it, develops likes and dislikes toward it and standards of value in judging it. Most of these persons, of course,

have no particular interest in "fine" art, in the refined and specialized products of painting and sculpture. Some are distinctly scornful
toward them, but this may signify only that they prefer another type
of art, such as the plain, informal, and "natural."

The producers of art are fewer in number, but by no means so few
as they are commonly supposed to be. They include not only painters
and sculptors, but also thousands of workers in many industries—not
all the workers, but those in any way concerned with affecting the
visual appearance of products and services. And these are only the
vocational, professional artists. Millions more practice some art or
craft in an amateur way. Children from nursery school onward now
construct pictures, clay models, and handcraft materials. Many un-
paid and amateur artists are recognized as outstanding in their fields.
Every amateur photographer, or hobbyist who "makes things," is to
some degree an artist. Psychologically, it is not even essential that the
art produced be technically skillful. Children's art is often quite lacking in this respect, by adult standards. The impulse to produce art
of some kind, to express oneself in some art medium, is almost as
universal as the use of art produced by others, if not equally so. Just
as everyone uses words, and thus produces rudimentary literature, so
everyone selects and rearranges, partly on a basis of their visual appearance, the objects presented to him for purchase, use, and further
observation. To assemble the elements of a costume, of a home or an
office interior usually involves some rudiments of artistic arrangement, along with more purely utilitarian considerations. The "con-
suming" of art thus includes "creative" phases, in the form of active
selection, reorganization, re-emphasis, and adaptation of given materials to a new situation, partly on a basis of their visual appearance.
True, such rudimentary types of artistic production involve little, if
any, special technical skill and perhaps no manipulation of a recognized art medium. It is well at times to make a clear distinction between artists in a broad sense and those in a narrow sense, between
good and bad or mediocre art. But to see the psychological significance of the activity called "art," we should not set it apart too
sharply from activities that differ only in the medium employed or
in the degree of technical development.

2. *The educational importance of aesthetic standards*

As there are many producers and consumers of art, so there are also many critics of art and theorists on the subject of beauty and artistic value. Most of them, of course, have not studied the subject formally and do not realize the assumptions involved in expressing critical opinions about art. Many outside the field of art like to re-peat the old saying, "I don't know much about art, but I know what I like." Sometimes these same individuals really believe that they know a good deal about art or at least about art values, about what makes a picture or a statue good or bad. Confidence in one's judg-ment of art values is often greatest in those who have little direct experience in that realm. As a rule, it does no harm, but it some-times does very definite harm when the dogmatic critic is a school principal, a superintendent, or otherwise in educational authority. As such, he may ridicule and tyrannize over art teachers who wish to have their children study or experiment with new and unconven-tional types of art that he does not understand or like. Men who would hesitate to express opinions in other technical fields with which they are unfamiliar often become surprisingly self-assured in evaluating art. Since the field of art itself contains all shades of opinion, such an administrator can nearly always find persons in the neighborhood, claiming to be art authorities, who will support his repressive attitude. In recent years the hand of such administrative domineering has fallen heavily on attempts to modernize art educa-tion by allowing older students to experiment in unconventional forms and by showing them examples of Post-impressionist art. "What's that supposed to be a picture of?" and "Are you trying to make these children into crazy modernists?"—with such remarks, the teacher is gradually frightened into conformity.

It is not part of our present discussion to defend modernism, or any particular styles in art. But it is relevant to urge upon adminis-trators and other persons of influence in education the duty of study-ing the subject of art values open-mindedly before becoming actively partisan. This subject in its most theoretical form is called "aes-thetics." But without delving far into theory, the layman can at least read a little of both sides of the case in current works of art criticism dealing with modern tendencies.

Great disagreement exists among artists, art critics, and theorists as to what constitutes good art. There is nothing new in this; such disagreement has always existed. It is well known that most of the artists whom we now recognize as great, and whose styles have become traditional classics, were met at first with violent attacks—often plausibly reasoned out—by conservative critics. Nor is visual art peculiar in this respect. Wide disagreement on values exists in regard to music and literature, and in regard to politics, economics, and morals. Some conflict and change of standards are signs of health and progress. But the clash of styles in painting and sculpture, and to some extent in architecture and furnishing, has been especially active in the last few decades. It has been vigorously publicized, and has attracted many of the lay public to take sides. Its causes are numerous and complex. One is that during the nineteenth century many strange, exotic, and primitive styles of art were introduced to the Western world by travel, anthropology, and archaeology. They commanded attention by their forcefulness, and by the passionate admiration of them on the part of some artists and critics. Their aims, qualities, and claims to aesthetic value were often markedly at variance with those of late Greek, Roman, and Renaissance art, on which our traditional rules and standards had been based. Yet they were increasingly imitated and adapted, gained popularity, and helped produce new contemporary styles that violated classical canons of beauty. Machine industry, new materials and techniques, and social and national upheavals also contributed their devious influences, stimulating but bewildering in their variety, and hard to reconcile with older principles.

One result of controversy and confusion in the world of art has been to produce a spirit of vagueness and uncertainty in art education. No longer quite confident of the old rules and "art principles," the art teacher has nothing very definite to take their place. With so many different artists, styles, and methods to choose from, he is sometimes overwhelmed by the task of choosing among them. Moreover, as we have previously noted, the whole subject of art education in this country is relatively new and unorganized. Hampered by far-reaching dissension in its own field, it has had to feel its way and struggle for a definite place in the school and college curriculum.

In contrast with the representatives of other subjects, especially the exact sciences, art teachers often seem to the administrator to be tiresomely incapable of making up their own minds as to what they want to teach and how, or even as to what materials and equipment they need to teach it with. The administrator, however well intentioned, often has no course but to put the whole matter aside and postpone the development of art instruction until the art teachers can decide what they want to do and can present some definite, convincing case for doing it.

A little more attention to fundamental aesthetic issues on the part of both art teachers and administrators might go far to improve this situation. Not that such issues could or should be finally solved and complete agreement achieved, for that is not to be desired in a democratic society. But it would help, first, to bring a realization of what the essential differences are, and, second, to show how much agreement already exists on the aims to be sought in both art and art education. It is easy to exaggerate the differences by stressing heated argument over a few controversial moderns and primitives. Aside from these, there is now almost universal agreement among artists, critics, and scholars on the artistic merit of most of the past traditions and individual artists emphasized by current art histories. Discussion goes on about the exact relative importance to be assigned to Giotto, Titian, Tintoretto, and El Greco, for example; but no responsible critic today denies that all these artists possess elements of greatness. The same is true regarding Greek, Hindu, Romanesque, and Gothic sculpture and architecture, Chinese and modern French landscape, Persian and Japanese decorative arts, and so on through a long list.

No aesthetic theorist denies, in general, that a good work of art will possess some unity and some variety, will achieve some harmony between material, form, and function; and so on. Dispute arises chiefly when we come to the specific implications of these principles; for instance, just what "unity" implies, and how much of it is desirable in a particular case. No one who has studied the old masters can deny that all of them to some extent alter or "distort" natural objects, including human anatomy, in the process of artistic representation; that, in fact, it is impossible to represent nature exactly as it is, since every artist must select and rearrange for himself. But dispute arises over just how much alteration, and what kind, is agreeable or disagreeable, justified or unjustified, in particular cases. No one questions that decorative design and utility, visual appearance and associated meanings can all be valuable in art at certain times and places.

As to art education, no one denies that some technique and direction are valuable for a prospective artist and also some freedom to work out his own ideas. The dispute is over what compromise between the two should be worked out for students of various age levels, and what kinds of technique and direction are most valuable in the light of all the educational goals to be considered. Intelligent solutions for these disputes can be achieved only by clear analysis and careful experiment over a long period of time. They must be constantly revised in the light of new conditions. It is not necessary, then, to decide all the moot points of aesthetic theory before going ahead with the development of art education. Many of these points can be handled most advantageously by showing the student frankly that different schools of thought and practice exist in these matters, and by helping him to work out intelligent opinions about them on a basis of study and experience, not of snap judgments.

3. Current "art principles"; their uses and dangers

Teachers of art sometimes oversimplify the problem of aesthetic value by excessive reliance upon a few concepts known as "art principles." Besides "unity and variety," these include "rhythm," "proportion," "balance," "dominance and subordination," and a few others. Some of the textbooks used by art teachers lay these down as rules of good art, and as yardsticks by which to measure the value of art, including the work of children as well as adult artists. Accordingly, many art teachers use them in class as a sort of Decalogue of Aesthetics, and as if they solved all evaluative problems.

The main trouble with these so-called "art principles" is not that they are definitely wrong or false, but that they are so vague and abstract as to mean very little in practice, or rather to mean whatever each individual writer or teacher wishes them to mean. The current definitions of them are so broad and general that almost any work of art can be shown to possess them to some extent, in one way or another. It is impossible to estimate that extent or to compare two works of art as to their conformity to a certain "principle" without giving to the principle some special interpretation that makes it easily recognizable, perhaps measurable. For instance, "good" proportion may be defined in terms of some particular mathematical ratio between the sizes of parts. Then, however, the principle is likely to be so narrow as to be very debatable. Past works of art, commonly recognized as good, can always be found that do not conform to it. Creative artists, for the most part, pay much less attention to these rules than do teachers and their more docile students. In art education, their excessive use often indicates a desire to reduce all problems as quickly as possible to some simple, stereotyped formula. There are not a few teachers, unfortunately, who continue throughout a long career to base their teaching upon a few impressive catchwords learned in their period of training. Others, more eager to be modern, make the same mistake by scanning each new art teachers' magazine for some new, simple formula to apply in their class: for the latest "method" by this or that writer.

Some of these formulas have a certain measure of truth and educational usefulness. They save the teacher and class from too much aimless groping. They call attention to some particular kind of art, or way of producing art, that is good in its own way, as far as it goes. The evil in their use arises when they are applied in an absolutistic spirit, rigidly and exclusively, as a substitute for studying different kinds of art, and for open-minded thinking about art; for analyzing the specific aims and qualities of each particular work of art in terms of what it is trying to do and of what it is expected to do under the particular conditions. The situations for which art is produced are so infinitely variable, the types of person who will make and use it are so variable, the ideals and styles of art in different times and cultures are so numerous and changing that no brief set of "principles" can possibly serve as an adequate yardstick of values. When such a set, narrowly defined, is imposed upon art students or seriously relied upon as a test of art ability, it becomes definitely repressive and harmful.

This does not mean that there are no standards of value in art, that any work of art is as good as any other, or that the task of evaluation is doomed to failure. Economic and political science cannot yet give us a simple yardstick for deciding what is a good law, a good form of government, or a good business practice. Democratic peoples are gradually evolving a general philosophy on the subject, but it is often hard to see its implications in a special case. Much experimentation and research are necessary, in the light of changing social conditions. The same is true of art values. There is much enlightenment in the old principles of aesthetics, as explained and illustrated by wise philosophers. From studying them we can derive suggestive hypotheses, not empty catchwords or arbitrary rules. Then it remains to develop and revise them in the light of all the new needs and situations that art is trying to serve today. For this study we need not only psychological information about the human beings who make and use art, but also detailed information about the kinds of art being produced, and how they work in contemporary society.

4. Scientific approaches to aesthetic value

For further study by advanced scholars, it is well to realize how the study of aesthetics is being approached today in the light of both sociological and psychological considerations. Through studying social history and the differences among past and present cultures, we are coming to realize how art has been a phase of all cultural development. We learn in what ways the various types of art have expressed their social, political, and economic backgrounds; how art has interacted with these other phases in cultural history, being influenced by them and exerting a profound influence upon them in its turn. We come to see modern tendencies in art, not as whims or aberrations of individual artists, but as intimately bound up with vast undercurrents in civilization. We become aware of the enormous variety of types of art that have been produced throughout the history of civilization, each with its own peculiar aims, functions, and standards of value. We see that each type has had certain reasons and certain justifications for its existence. As a result, we become less sure that our own personal tastes or familiar traditions represent immutable laws of good art for all the world. We look for common, broad principles in all of them. Finally, we ask in what ways it may be possible for education to help work out for our own time and culture those forms of art that are most suited to it and most conducive to social welfare.

The psychological approach to aesthetics and the problem of value in art proceeds from the recognition that valuation itself is a psychological process. Individuals are born with certain capacities for desire, pain, discomfort, and enjoyment. Experience conditions and redirects our impulses, responses, and attitudes from primary objects of physical need to secondary, remote, cultural objects, producing what we describe as "tastes" and "standards" of value in art, ethics, and other realms. Innate endowment and cultural influences thus co-operate in determining what each individual's tastes and standards shall be. Sometimes works of art are liked and are judged good or beautiful mainly upon a basis of their immediate effects on our sense perception and feeling; at other times, upon a basis of their expected future uses or consequences. These and a few more broad generalities are fairly clear, but they leave much room for future investigation of details, especially as to how individuals come to differ in their tastes and standards. Most of the terms commonly used in describing value and valuation are extremely vague and hard to define, such as "pleasant" and "unpleasant." They undoubtedly refer to some actual types of experience and underlying physical processes, but we know little about them.

Psychological investigation in itself will never succeed in proving that certain kinds of art are really good or beautiful and others the opposite, or that certain standards of value are true or binding. For psychology is a descriptive science and does not in itself try to set up aims or standards of value. There will always need to be added a more normative approach, and this the traditional subject of aesthetics has undertaken to provide. This approach can make use of data from other fields, such as history, sociology, and biography, to discover the specific effects and functions of various types of art in a civilized society. But psychology does throw much light on the problem of aesthetic value and does aid us in forming judgments intelligently, if not with absolute certainty. It will contribute much in practice if it shows us the actual genesis in human motivation of those traditional rules and standards of art that have claimed to be absolute and universal. It will not limit itself to the study of liking and disliking, but will show as well how various types of art have the power to impel various types of attitude and action and to function in many other ways in human behavior and experience.

5. *Methods and difficulties in the psychological study of aesthetic phenomena*

What has been done in the psychological study of aesthetic phenomena, and how can further progress be made? The first question can be answered quickly: very little has been accomplished by modern scientific psychology toward analyzing and describing, in any fundamental way, the processes involved in creating and experiencing art. Voluminous reports of the experiments and researches since the time of Fechner (who inaugurated experimental aesthetics in the eighteen seventies) have produced verified, accepted results only when they dealt with relatively trivial and external aspects of these processes. The essential inner nature of artistic and aesthetic experience is still obscure and open to speculative theory. Philosophical, literary, and introspective analyses often seem enlightening and plausible in certain respects, but turn out to be vague, abstract, and disputatious.

Aesthetics, which undertakes to explain the general nature of art and beauty, has been recognized as a distinct subject only since the eighteenth century. But philosophers since the time of Socrates and Plato have theorized about art; hence the history of aesthetics as philosophy of art can be traced back through many centuries. All sciences and fields of rational investigation can also be traced back to the parent stem of Greek philosophy. But the mathematical, physical, biological, and social sciences have broken away from it to some extent and achieved increasing power to stand on their own feet through objective methods of observation, experiment, and measurement. Aesthetics is apparently in process of doing so, but the transitional phase is long and difficult. It had perhaps to wait until general psychology had become at least partly scientific, changing over from its status as "philosophy of mind" to the experimental approach of Wundt, Helmholtz, and other comparatively recent students of mind. A half century or more of scientific psychology has succeeded in building up a considerable framework of verified knowledge about human nature. Within this framework, and with tested laboratory and statistical methods, it would seem that psychology could readily go on to study the phenomena of art, for much of what it has discovered, especially in regard to sense perception, learning, and the physical basis of emotion, seems obviously applicable to art.

One difficulty is that the phenomena of art are especially complex and subtle, involving configurations of thought and feeling as intricate, shifting, and finely differentiated as any in human experience. Another is that they are in large part inward, implicit, occurring in the depths of personality; often not manifested in overt behavior and expression, or manifested in delayed, indirect ways that partly conceal their nature. Often the work of art itself is our chief or only clue to what went on in the artist's mind, or the critic's words are the chief clue to how the work of art affected him. These are both difficult to interpret and not always to be taken at face value. A third reason is that the phenomena of art tend to arouse emotion and hence are hard to study objectively. The same can be said, of course, of attempts to study political, economic, and moral phenomena scientifically.

Opening any recent textbook of general or genetic psychology, one can see at once that by far the greater amount of space is devoted to relatively simple phenomena within each main division. There is much about the behavior of infants and animals, little about that of philosophers, scientists, and artists. The simpler manifestations of muscular control, of sensing, remembering, imagining, learning, and problem-solving are described and illustrated. How these function in the complex situations of art, religion, science, and political life is only briefly hinted. The case was exactly opposite in the old speculative "philosophy of mind." There the higher thought processes were emphasized, because they seemed most important. Modern psychology is more conclusive as far as it goes, but it will not have replaced prescientific psychology entirely until it likewise deals directly and fully with the more complex mental processes, including those which operate in art.

Will the general psychology of the future, then, include chapters on the psychology of art? Not directly, perhaps, for art may rather be considered a problem of applied psychology. In studying works of art, we immediately come into contact with specialized phenomena. Art itself, considered very broadly, is almost a universal human phenomenon, occurring in all cultures; but civilized art products vary greatly from one age and culture to another. The behavior, methods, and expressed attitudes of artists also differ widely in various cultural settings—for example, according to whether the artists work in the service of religion or of secular patrons, whether they use hand or machine methods, and whether the culture favors individual originality or strict conformity to convention. Thus it is a dubious step to set up such a concept as "the artist," and ask how he creates, as if all were of one basic type, or to assume that "art creation" or "art appreciation" is a single, constant process, similar under all conditions. Much of what is called "the psychology of art" is an account of certain behavior traits in a restricted, contemporary group of people, acting according to the customs in vogue at the time. It is comparable to "the psychology of advertising," of fencing, or of card playing. Such studies are not properly a part of general psychology. There is little danger of confusion when they are labeled so as to indicate frankly their limited scope. But too often psychologists observe a single group of children in one town or the behavior of a few college students and professors in one psychological laboratory, then imply that their findings are true of all children or of all humanity in every age.

Conversely, special cultural studies often do throw light on general psychology, however, by showing how given basic human traits operate in various special types of situation. It is rare, indeed, to encounter any mental phenomena that are not profoundly influenced by special cultural conditions, especially in the case of the higher mental processes of civilized adults. To progress into these realms, general psychology must examine many varieties of behavior under special cultural conditions, compare the behavior of people in different cultures past and present, and seek to find common, basic tendencies among them. Thus so specialized a field as the psychology of art, or even the psychology of modern concert goers and museum visitors, may be a source of information for general psychology. Light might well be thrown upon the higher processes by making use of such sources.

With a still broader outlook, the psychologist may undertake to study not only fine art and the special modes of civilized behavior toward it, but also aesthetic and artistic experience in general. For these are by no means limited to recognized art products and techniques. People experience many things as beautiful or ugly in addition to works of art. They observe, and respond emotionally to the perceptible forms of nature, of other persons, of cities, factories, machines, and other utilitarian objects. They react to the products of scientific as well as artistic thinking. What are these modes of response? In what ways are they similar to the experience of art, and in what ways different? Such phenomena are more universal than responses to art (in the narrow sense), and the study of them is more definitely a part of general psychology. Moreover, as we have noted, the professional artist is not the only one who arranges details into organized forms in such a way as to make them more satisfying to visual perception. Everyone does this to some extent. Everyone dreams, imagines visual forms, and builds fantasies expressing his desires, hopes, and fears. The life of fantasy in general, whether as idle reverie and escape from reality or as instrument to practical effort, is known to be closely bound up with the creation of art. It occurs there, but it also occurs apart from all relation to art, and its study is properly a part of general psychology. If the investigation of those types of phenomena needs a distinguishing label, or recognition as a branch of general psychology, it is perhaps better described as "aesthetic psychology" than as "psychology of art."

The opinion has already been expressed that the attempts by experimental psychologists to study aesthetic phenomena suffer characteristically from their limitation to the laboratory environment. This criticism is peculiarly applicable to recent American psychologists. By contrast with such Europeans as Freud and Jung, they fail to realize the importance of cultural history, biography, literature, and art as sources of data for generalizing about human nature. They tend to ignore all the opportunities for observing human nature in action outside the scope of their own laboratories and questionnaires. What little can be observed within this limited scope is, in the case of art at least, pathetically bare and fragmentary. It is hard to produce or experiment with the phenomenon of genuine art appreciation under laboratory conditions, and nearly impossible to do so with artistic creation. Of course, it is easy to get people to "go through the motions," but the result is likely to be an empty imitation. The laboratory situation, by its very nature, inhibits spontaneous imagination and emotion. The extreme subdivision and simplification of problems that is necessary for exact experiment and measurement substitutes artificial arrangements of a few lines, dots, or colored papers for the rich complexities of art, and artificially simplified questions of yes-or-no preference for the intricate relativities of aesthetic taste. Behavior in the laboratory is not necessarily like that in the outside world; indeed, it may be the direct opposite.

In reacting against the extremely unscientific speculation and introspectionism of early psychology, some psychologists have gone to an opposite extreme in exaggerated confidence in quantitative methods, with a tendency to distrust and exclude all observation that cannot be made under exactly controlled conditions, or at least expressed in quantitative terms. The result is sometimes to neglect consideration of inner mental experience and of complex, variable behavior under actual life conditions; sometimes to produce specious "researches" that claim to have measured these realities and that are convincing only to like-minded laboratory devotees. Recent attempts at the psychology of art have suffered from both these tendencies.

Genuine progress requires, in the first place, a deeper understanding of scientific method on the part of psychologists, including the fact that it is not necessarily quantitative, at least in its early and transitional stages. When the data are too complex and variable to be measured at once, much can be done through a gradual introduction of other phases of scientific method, as is common in anthropology and other social studies. Observations and hypotheses from all available sources, whether made under controlled conditions or not, can be assembled, compared, and tested out as far as possible through mutual checking of results among workers. When some of the phenomena are obviously inward experiences, inaccessible to behavioristic observation, more introspective methods must be used or none at all; but these methods also can be checked and controlled to an increasing extent through systematic co-operation.

In the second place, psychologists who wish to study art and other complex mental processes must become more widely educated in the humanities. They must learn more about actual works of art, about art's place in cultural history, about the biographies of artists, and about expressed responses to art in the form of critical writings. They must learn to interrelate these with the more exact findings of laboratory psychology, so that each can verify and augment the other. They must realize the potential value of researches that lie somewhere between exact science and the older introspective, speculative, and literary approaches in method and degree of conclusiveness—

researches that strive gradually toward science and do not expect to reach it at one bound.

Attempts to theorize about aesthetic psychology sometimes begin with works of art and people's responses to them. Here is a picture, and here is a person looking at it; the picture is a stimulus, and the person responds. How does he respond? What responses, inward and outward, does the picture arouse? The picture is a complex form, and the observer's total response is also complex, a highly differentiated gestalt or configuration. But how trace it further? Whether by questioning and introspection or in some other way, the psychologist usually hopes to analyze the response in terms of the basic functions of general psychology: of perception, emotion, volition, and so on, or whatever substitutes for these terms are in vogue. When instincts are in vogue, he hopes to trace the complex response back to original instincts; when conditioned reflexes are in vogue, he hopes to trace it back to these, and thus to explain it. This approach is on the whole analytic, from a complex to supposedly simple elements. It is a common approach among writers whose principal training has been in the arts and art criticism, rather than in scientific psychology.

Authors of textbooks and systems of general psychology usually proceed in an opposite, synthetic direction, beginning with the basic nerve centers, functions and mechanisms, the learning process, and so on, hoping to arrive toward the end of the book at some account of how these elements combine into complex types of behavior. Such culminating chapters are usually rather brief and perfunctory. If the author has committed himself to a rigorously scientific point of view, he has little to offer but reports of a few scattered researches on color preference and the like, which obviously do not cover the complexities of aesthetic experience and art. As one approaches these, the phenomena become not only more complex but more variable as well, so that no text of reasonable length could hope to describe even the main types of configuration. But if it could describe even one example of a complex aesthetic response in terms of the primary functions with which it began, it would at least have shown how to bridge the gap between simple and complex, basic function and configuration in adult, civilized experience. This gap is never really bridged, although it is often concealed in the effort to present a systematic text.

Psychologists impressed with gestalt principles tend to avoid the whole problem of linking up simple with complex, through insisting that the whole (the complex configuration) is different from the sum of its parts, or from the individual "basic functions" as conceived in any artificially simplified, isolated way. They attempt to present various typical configurations in behavior and to point out some of their recurring characteristics. Gestalt psychologists have so far done little with art or aesthetic phenomena and have restricted themselves on the whole to fairly simple configurations. Their most valuable work up to date has been in describing certain types of visual perception, mostly of objects other than complex works of art. The gestalt approach has not advanced very far toward describing or explaining any total aesthetic configuration because of its fear to analyze it into much simpler elements. It is even more opposed to attempts at synthesis of complex configurations out of supposedly simple elements. But how can any phenomenon be described or compared with another except in terms of some simpler constituents or factors whose proportion and arrangement determine the nature of the complex phenomenon? Admittedly, all conceptions of psychological "elements," such as "functions" or "instincts," are abstractions. None ever operates alone or remains entirely constant, and none has ever been satisfactorily defined or described. But all psychological advance must somehow proceed in terms of showing the relations between relatively simple and constant factors and relatively complex, variable ones. New conceptions of the former will have to be invented if the old ones are too misleading. Usually the new are very much like the old. In spite of much denunciation, the old concepts of "will," "instinct," "appreciation," and so on keep reappearing in slightly different terminology. The terms make little difference if the facts are correctly reported. Some psychologists are overquick to brand others in the field as "dated" or "old-fashioned" if their terminology is that of yesterday. It prevents them, for one thing, from appreciating the valuable insights into complex mental processes achieved by earlier writers.

Whichever course is followed at the start, analytic or synthetic, it must be followed through to the other end if real understanding is to be achieved. Probably both must be followed to some extent. In the process, we shall learn how to describe both the basic factors and the complex resultants more accurately. Certainly, the concept of configuration is useful in aesthetic psychology, and so is the implied warning that configurations in aesthetic behavior are enormously variable, not to be hastily "reduced" to a few simple formulas.

In the old, purely speculative type of aesthetic theory, one stumbling block has been overemphasis on verbal issues, with interminable debate over the proper definitions of "art," "beauty," and other abstract ideas. Such issues often distract the inquiries of psychologists as well. There is great need of an authoritative, accepted set of definitions for use in discussing the phenomena of art, but it is hard to get one because of the various controversial meanings attached by different writers to different terms. It helps considerably if each writer, whatever terms he uses, defines them clearly and holds to these definitions consistently.

Another perennial stumbling block has been the tendency of aesthetic theorists to adopt some one simple concept or formula and put it forward as all-explaining. Empathy, wish fulfillment, expression, communication—these and many others have held the spotlight for a few years or months, until the next appeared. There can be, of course, no one simple explanation for phenomena so widely variable as those of art.

Closely akin to this error is the tendency to adopt one extreme position or the opposite. For example, there has been endless argument in the field of art, as in every branch of psychology, as to whether special abilities are acquired or hereditary, produced by nature or by nurture. Is artistic genius inborn? If so, is education powerless to produce it, or even to know what means are best for its development? This view is common among artists and art critics who like to believe that genius is altogether mysterious and unaccountable, beyond the reach of schoolmasters. Is genius due to environment, and can proper conditioning accomplish everything? In that case, a great responsibility seems to lie upon education. But as usual, when either set of extremists is backed against the wall, it has to admit that both heredity and environment are responsible; that both interact to produce genius and lesser abilities, as well as specific varieties of taste and creative impulse.

ᐦ 6. *Determinants of art ability*

The many extreme and one-sided theories advanced in recent years, if taken all together, would supply a useful set of hypotheses. There is probably some truth in all of them, and there is no need for selecting any one as all-sufficient. In other words, there are many different *determinants* of art ability and of other aesthetic phenomena. Some may be classified as mainly *hereditary,* and others as mainly *environmental.* Among the former, some pertain to *human nature in general* and are relatively universal, such as the basic functions and the processes of maturation and learning described by general psychology. They are common to all normal individuals regardless of cultural environment. Then there is the possibility of inborn racial differences in equipment. This question is fraught with emotional dynamite among the theorists who maintain and oppose doctrines of racial superiority and inferiority. But that evaluative issue need not be raised at all. As the Negro differs from the white in pigmentation and shape of hair, does he also differ in nervous or glandular structure that might affect his behavior in realms of art? Little is known about this matter, mainly because of the difficulty in studying racial factors apart from environmental influences. There are hereditary determinants peculiar to certain *family strains,* as in the Kallikaks, the Adamses, and the Bach family of talented musicians. But again, what part of the final results is due to family heredity, and what to family environment? Finally, there are apparently inborn differences in *individuals* within the same family; for example, genius and mediocrity among siblings brought up under similar conditions.

Environmental determinants may be similarly distinguished. Some are *physical,* geographical and climatic. They include the differences between one locality and another. Some art historians have stressed this factor, as in attributing differences in pictorial and architectural style to the fact that one style arose in a sunny climate, another in a cold and cloudy. Certainly the presence or absence of materials, such as stone and wood, has had an influence on art forms. But to what extent does climate influence the personality of the artist?

Other environmental determinants are *social* or *cultural.* Here again they differ as to breadth of scope. In some respects all dwellers in the modern Western world are subject to the same cultural influences—to machinery, printing, and science—as contrasted with dwellers in medieval Europe or present-day Tibet. These are *major* cultural determinants. There are also *national* and *local* differences in culture, and these operate as determinants of artistic results. They involve language and special traditions. In what ways does the American environment in general predispose a child to different tendencies from those of France or Germany? That of New York City as compared with a small southern town? Marxist art critics stress the importance of *social* and *economic* class influences. What difference does it make whether a child grows up on a level of luxury, of modest comfort, or of bare subsistence? No doubt class distinctions in the old world are on the whole more fixed and radical, more loaded with emotional attitudes, than are those of America. But in any locality, it often seems that an artist's aims, interests, and antagonisms are largely attributable to the fact that he thinks as a proletarian or as a property owner. Some environmental influences are peculiar to a certain *type of school;* for example, to a free progressive school as contrasted with a strict military academy. Some are bound up with a certain set of *companions,* as a gang or snobbish clique. Some are centered in the *family;* in the peculiar drama of personalities provided by father, mother, brothers, and sisters. This last type of influence is heavily stressed by psychoanalysts and child psychologists. It involves the Oedipus conflict, sibling rivalry, and parental overprotection or neglect.

Obviously, these various types of influence overlap and merge in ways not clearly distinguishable. They affect not only the artistic and aesthetic sides of personality, but the whole personality and social culture as well. To study them adequately would take us far outside the usual scope of psychological investigations and into realms more commonly regarded as sociological, economic, and historical. Yet it is hard to see how general psychology can go very far toward understanding the civilized adult mind and its development without considering them. Here, as elsewhere, the old subject demarcations are breaking down, and discovery must proceed by co-ordinating many lines of inquiry. Aesthetic psychology by itself cannot go far toward understanding the nature and genesis of behavior in the realm of art. For if any outstanding fact emerges, it is that such behavior is not an isolated phenomenon, but intimately bound up with the development of personality in general, and with the interplay of all cultural factors.

Merely to list the diversity of influences at work upon the civilized child must make for some modesty on the part of educators. For it is obvious how few are the factors subject to control in the schoolroom, how restricted are the opportunities for even the wisest teacher to control the child's development or to experiment with the factors that determine it. We often assume that the responsibility for satisfactory development rests largely with education in a narrow sense and that this responsibility will be met by devising proper methods of instruction. No one knows at present just how true or false this assumption may be, but certainly the cause is not helped by ignoring the complexity of the problem. We can at least go on to see how well the school can carry out its part in relation to the others; and perhaps that may help to modify the other influences. Certainly, educational psychology is beginning to influence the family environment and the attitude of parents toward their children. The school transmits many cultural influences to the child, including national and local traditions, which it can select and interpret as it thinks best.

7. Individual aesthetic development

Art teachers are coming to realize the need for a psychological understanding of aesthetic development—of how children's ability to create and appreciate art grows from one age level to the next. They are trying to reorganize the course of study in art so that it will fit in with this development rather than be imposed in an artificial order conceived by and for adults.

In the past, the facts and skills of art have usually been presented to students in some artificial order. The cultural heritage of past art has been presented partly in historical, chronological sequence. In this case, it conforms partly, though not wholly, with children's growth. Moderately young children can be easily interested in primitive art and life, and children a little older, in that of Egypt and Greece, but the development of their interest and ability to understand is not an exact recapitulation of art history as a whole. Young children are also interested in certain phases of modern art that they can understand and enjoy. On the other hand, certain phases of primitive and ancient art are too difficult for them or are alien to their interests, as, for example, religious and sexual symbolism. To present the heritage of art mainly in chronological order does not fit in with normal individual development; it postpones the modern too long and fails to convey important aspects of early culture that only older students can grasp.

Another way of presenting art is in theoretical, synthetic order: to proceed from simple "art elements" and "principles," such as line and color, rhythm and balance, to complex works of art. But this procedure is too abstract and formal to fit in with the development of children. Power to grasp abstract elements and to be interested in them comes rather late in the child's mental growth, not at the start. Both these ways of organizing subject matter are more suited to older than to younger students. The old, academic way of teaching artistic techniques is similarly formal. It begins with supposed fundamentals of technique, such as drawing from a three-dimensional object in realistic detail, or copying a line drawing by some adult; in any case, with activities that young children do not ordinarily enjoy or do well and that fail to exercise their strong potential art interests at the time. (In much the same way, the conventional teaching of musical technique often begins with finger exercises on some difficult instrument.)

If we can work out some order of gradation in art studies that will be closely co-ordinated with children's natural growth, we may hope to gain the motivation of spontaneous interest as well as the many other values that come from properly adapting the content of instruction to stage of maturity. We need answers to the following questions: What can children on each age level be reasonably expected to do, learn, and enjoy in art without undue pressure? What tasks in art are suitably difficult—not too hard or too easy—for the normal child of each age? What kinds of art are most likely to interest children of each stage and to help them progress to the next stage of development?

Some educators in the progressive and free-expression group have gone to the extreme of abandoning all definite gradation and direction, all planned, systematic courses of study, relying on student initiative to guide the sequence of steps. This has led to significant experiments, but in the higher grades it seems to result in much waste of time through aimless trial and error. Older students, even the more independent, usually desire to be helped in learning something fairly definite in the way of techniques, information, and understanding. They enjoy following a definite series of steps that seems to "get somewhere." Adapting a course of study to the basic processes of growth does not necessarily mean letting children take the lead in directing their own studies or letting them do at each moment what they wish to do. Teachers who possess a scientific understanding of personality development should be better able than the child himself to understand what the child needs and fundamentally desires or will desire, what problems lie ahead of him, and what he needs to learn in order to cope with them. They will not ignore the child's present conscious impulses, but will so interpret them as to help him to realize his best potentialities and to prepare himself for adult social living.

What is "natural" or "normal" development? It is a name for an abstract and somewhat idealized conception of the more universal and inwardly determined phases of individual growth, as distinguished from the more peculiar and apparently accidental traits that individuals develop under peculiar environmental conditions. It is, of course, recognized today that the two factors, nature and nurture, cannot be clearly distinguished. In talking of natural development, psychologists are not trying to imagine how individuals would grow if entirely uninfluenced by particular environments. Their conclusions must be drawn from observing how people develop under particular cultural conditions, usually those of modern urban civilization. In talking of normal development, they are not implying that there is any one right or ideal way of growing. The "normal" is not necessarily the best conceivable, and moralists, educators, or eugenists may try to conceive of a still better, supernormal way for the future. But "normal" is not exactly the same as "average." Most of the children in a given region may be obviously stunted by faulty diet and living conditions. By studying how children grow under fairly adequate (not necessarily ideal) conditions, the scientist builds up a theoretical concept of normality. An account of normal development will be highly generalized, a sort of skeleton outline, stressing phases of growth common to all or to most individuals. However, it may mention some of the general ways in which individual differences develop through various combinations of inborn and environmental determinants. It may mention how deviate types of individual (some of them appraised as subnormal or supernormal) sometimes arise through departure from the normal process.

American psychologists have as a rule been cautious about generalizing on "basic human tendencies" or on "types of personality." Their accounts of development have been comparatively objective and verifiable, but somewhat superficial from the standpoint of those interested in the inner life of imagination, desire, and feeling. European psychologists have speculated more boldly from philosophic and literary starting points, often proposing theories of normal development and character types that, though dubious and unverifiable, deal more directly with problems of major concern to art and aesthetics. Thus the psychoanalysts, especially Freud, Jung, and Ferenczi, have proposed theories of individual development and of the formation of personality types, neurotic and normal, that have direct bearing upon the development of aesthetic tastes and creative or expressive impulses in children and adults. Especially noteworthy in this connection are Ferenczi's theory of the development of the sense of reality and Freud's theory of successive transfers of the libido through various bodily zones and types of desired object. Psychoanalysis also offers a suggestive theory of fixations and regressions as neurotic deviations from normal personality development. Graphology, the study of handwriting as a clue to personality traits, is in better repute in Europe than here. It is significant for art in that handwriting is closely related to line drawing. Such theories and approaches should not be quickly dismissed as unverified, for a tremendous mass of clinical and other evidence is claimed for them. They should be tested further on this side of the water to determine what they may contribute to the psychology of art.

An account of normal development will include the order and approximate age levels (allowing for the well-known principles of the distribution of traits) at which important physical and behavior traits appear, including the ability to learn various skills when opportunity and social stimulus present themselves. As cross sections of the process, there should be made composite, generalized descriptions of the normal person of each age level (again with due recognition of the usual range of sex, individual, and perhaps racial and cultural differences). An individual could then be classified tentatively as "normal," "advanced," or "retarded," either on the whole or in certain particulars. Tests of mental age and of intelligence quotient are based upon such a concept of normality, derived through comparing the ability of many children of different ages to perform a varied set of tasks. There is of course much danger of oversimplification in erecting such a concept of normal development and normal age-level abilities. We may be led to ignore important individual differences or differences between our own culture and others, so that what seems to us a basic, universal tendency may be only a limited culture pattern. But there are ways of guarding against this danger, especially through widening our field of vision with more case studies and more ethnological comparisons.

What art teachers could use to very great advantage would be a description of normal development and age-level traits with more explicit emphasis than heretofore on the interests and abilities and other traits most directly involved in activities dealing with art. In short, it would be highly desirable to have a measure of *aesthetic age,* analogous to mental age, by which we could determine whether a child was normal, advanced, or retarded in those characteristics and abilities most active in the production and appreciation of art. We frequently make judgments of this sort without scientific accuracy, and it would seem that science could help us to refine them. For example, it is regarded as childish or infantile for a civilized adolescent or adult to prefer dolls, games, songs, and stories suited to early childhood or to be able to draw or model only crude schematic representations. There are, in other words, certain types of taste in art, and in toys and games involving art qualities, that are associated roughly with certain age levels. When an individual deviates markedly from them, down or up the scale, he is considered as retarded or precocious. Similarly, there are certain types of art product, in drawing and other media, that are regarded as natural and normal for children of a certain age, but as retarded or as precocious if made by a child much older or much younger. Furthermore, it is believed that neurotic, arrested, or distorted modes of development may manifest themselves in behavior toward art, as in markedly feminine tastes—love of dolls, dresses, and delicate textiles, quiet games, perfumes, and the like—on the part of an older boy. But such symptoms must always be analyzed in relation to the prevailing culture pattern, which may (as in the Orient) approve them for the masculine boy or man.

It is often hard to link psychological accounts of the general characteristics normal for a certain age level with behavior and ability in specific art situations. There is great need for closer co-operation between psychologists and art teachers on this problem. Psychologists could help by using the forms, materials, and activities of art more frequently as stimuli and test devices; even for problems of general psychology they might often be as suitable as any others. For example, power to perceive complex form in art is some indication of an individual's perceptual powers in general. Art teachers could assist by consciously thinking out their curriculum in terms of the psychological processes, skills, and motivations involved.

A psychological account of development, in so far as it is restricted to the more basic and universal human traits, will tend to minimize reference to specific art works, styles, and techniques, for the reason that such phenomena differ considerably from one cultural group or epoch to another. It need not, however, exclude all specific art or other cultural situations or the behavior traits thereby induced. In fact, it requires a few of them as illustrations of how basic traits manifest themselves in the normal person living in a social environment. A fully worked-out description of normal development should include some reference to how people develop habits of appreciation —tastes, standards of value, habits of perceiving, using, and enjoying objects of art and other aesthetic phenomena; how persons of a certain age, a given sex, and so forth, tend to some extent to resemble each other in some of these respects and to diverge in others. It should include some reference to how people develop "creative impulses"—tendencies to construct forms and express ideas in some way that can be broadly classified as artistic. (This includes practically everyone beyond infancy.) It should include typical similarities within the chief age, sex, and other groups, as well as accounts of the genesis of individual differences through various combinations of determinants.

The desired psychological account of development in the field of art will naturally draw many of its data and examples from art situations of our own time and place, but it will seek to bring out for emphasis the more universal types of product and behavior. For instance, city boys of today may like to play with and to draw toy airplanes and machine guns rather than toy chariots and battering-rams, but the tendency for boys to play with some kind of miniature weapon and vehicle is fairly universal. The wooden sword, the doll, the little clay animal, the schematized line drawing of a human figure, the beaded necklace—these occur in some form in all cultures and periods. In short, when we survey the behavior of present-day children in relation to art, some part of what we see is cultural and transitory—perhaps a momentary fad; another part is a manifestation of more deep and universal motivations. Genetic psychology should seek to discover and emphasize the latter, in so far as it aims at comparative universality in its account of human development. For this purpose, there is need of wide interests on the part of the psychologist to take in data regarding the behavior of children and adolescents in other times and cultures.

As we have noted in regard to other problems of aesthetic psychology, the main requirement is to bring psychology and art into closer contact. This can be approached from either aspect, but in either case the task requires some familiarity on the part of investigators with both fields. Unfortunately, the number of persons who receive training in both is very limited; the pressure toward specialization is still too great.

One can approach the question of aesthetic development, first, from the standpoint of psychology. There are numerous partial summaries of genetic or developmental psychology in its broad outlines. So far there is none, however, that adequately combines experimental research of the type favored in America with the psychoanalytic and other theoretical approaches. It still remains for each investigator to make his own synthesis of what he will accept from the many proposed accounts of the psychological development of children. When he has done so, he can use it as a set of hypotheses for interpreting children's behavior in relation to art and for conducting new experiments in that field.

The art teacher can use such an account in selecting art materials and activities for each age level that seem to meet the general needs of that level. He can derive many hints as to specific art activities from the general traits of muscular strength and co-ordination, intelligence, power to learn motor and linguistic skills, attention-span, emotional control, personal relationships, and so forth, that psychologists regard as normal for each level. He can be ready to recognize and to deal suitably with individual differences and with common deviations from the normal, such as maladjustment and accelerated or retarded development, prescribing in each case the proper artistic diet so far as educational conditions permit. He can understand the function of art in education more thoroughly by seeing it against the background of an inclusive educational process.

The other approach is through an open-minded, inductive study of children's behavior in relation to art, their tastes in art, and their own productions and performances with art media. A substantial beginning along this line has been made in the United States and in England. Much work in this field, however, has suffered from serious limitations and false assumptions. (1) The tremendous amount of significant factual research conducted in Germany, Austria, and France between 1918 and 1933 has been largely ignored. Many thousands of children's drawings, some made by the same child over a period of years, have been collected and carefully analyzed; the results have been published in numerous books and articles mostly still untranslated and not easily available to English-speaking readers. (2) There has been a tendency to assume without justification certain adult standards of value of correctness in children's art products and preferences, and to appraise them by these standards instead of observing them objectively. (3) Excessive reliance has been placed on questionnaires of preference, which are easy to give but often superficial and inconclusive. (4) The American work has been too much restricted to drawings and other pictures, instead of being widened to include the whole range of forms, among them craftwork, toys, and games, that function as art in the lives of children. (5) Finally, there has been a persistent tendency to generalize on the basis of inadequate data—the cases available for direct laboratory study in a certain year and locality—without consulting the wealth of data on children's art and aesthetic behavior available in the history and literature of various peoples.

In spite of these five limitations, a body of information is slowly accumulating that permits us to classify children's art, especially drawings, according to types normal for various age groups. The broad division into stages of drawing (the "scribble," "schematic," and "true to appearance" stages) is being refined in terms of intermediate, transitional types, of narrower age and sex groups, and of individual differences. Children's preferences in art, many of them long recognized in an unscientific way, are being more precisely analyzed and correlated with other psychological factors. Studies are being made of intelligence in relation to art ability, though as long as art ability itself is so dimly understood, so incapable of measurement, no definite correlation with intelligence tests can be expected.

8. Social aesthetic development

Closely related to the problem of individual development in art is that of social or cultural development, as evidenced in the history of art and civilization. There are obvious resemblances between children's behavior and primitive behavior, and between children's art and primitive art. Children like to see and make pictures of primitive life, to hear stories about it, and to imitate tribal people (in this country, American Indians) in their play. Even without explicitly assuming a recapitulation theory, education often tends to act in accord with one, to feed children a heavy diet of primitive art and try to make them produce it. This procedure has its values as a corrective against academic methods, but it involves a misunderstanding of child psychology when carried too far. It is difficult to generalize about the relations between two kinds of development, each of which is only slightly understood at present. But the following brief comparison, showing some of the differences and some of the resemblances, may be hazarded.

"Primitive art" is a rather vaguely defined concept that ordinarily includes art produced under tribal social conditions at any period from prehistoric to contemporary. Strictly speaking, it should not include that of early empires and city-states, like the Egyptian, Sumerian, or Mayan, after these peoples had advanced to urban civilization. Primitive art thus *differs* on the whole from modern children's art in many ways, especially in the following four: (1) Being made mostly by adults, it tends to express certain attitudes, interests, and motives that are typically adult, including those connected with adult sexuality. Modern civilized children and their arts are on the whole more naïve, ignorant, and repressed in this respect than are primitive children; hence, more unlike adults. Civilized children are made to differ more from adults than primitive children in many respects, in the effort to postpone sexual activity. Primitive children also tend to mature earlier in other respects through being less sheltered and having to care for younger children. (2) Primitive art expresses a primitive (tribal) social order, including certain character-istic institutions, beliefs, and attitudes in religious, political, eco-nomic, and family relations; for example, totemism, exogamy, fet-ishism, and magic. It also deals with the physical environment and equipment of such life, with the nonmechanical, with wild nature, or with primitive farming. Children's art in modern civilization tends to express and represent an urban, mechanized environment. (3) Modern children's art, through school influences, is affected by recent adult art, and by special educational methods including those of art education. It tends to use the materials of contemporary adult art and to approximate the latter's techniques. It tends to adopt stylistic traits and formulas and to choose subjects that are not spon-taneously childish. Modern education tends to accelerate children's intellectual and emotional maturation in certain respects (other than the directly sexual), to hurry children into many adult interests, at-titudes, and techniques, including those of art. Art museums, stress-ing adult art, contribute to this effect. (4) Young children's sche-matic drawings are composites, assembled by combining more or less completely outlined parts. Paleolithic art often uses a continuous, flowing outline, showing grasp of the total contour of the figure as a whole, even in active movement. The young child's drawing is usu-ally a rather loose assemblage of more-or-less separate memory im-ages, which are added together without definite fusion into a single complex unit. Neolithic adult drawing regresses on the whole toward extreme schematicism. It resembles that of young children in some ways, but springs from a different motivation and mentality. It is associated with the origin of linguistic symbols, abbreviated pictographs.

On the other hand, the following *resemblances* are to be noted be-tween primitive art and modern, young children's art: (1) Both are often comparatively simple and lacking in subtle differentiation of parts and qualities. However, some tribal art is complex in certain respects—for example, the design and symbolism of a Chilkat blanket. (2) In pictorial representation, both tend to show such fea-tures as flatness; lack of three-dimensional modeling with shadows; lack of perspective; distortion of spatial, anatomical, and other rela-tions and of natural shapes and sizes; the use of strong contrast of bright colors when possible; and strong rhythmic repetition of shapes and color areas.

What appears to the civilized art critic as "distortion" or "conventionalization"—in other words, lack of conformity to the usual appearance of things—probably springs from similar, though not identical, sources in primitive and modern children's art. It is not merely a failure, through lack of skill, to represent things accurately, but is also due to an emphasis on what seems important. Neither the primitive adult nor the young modern child sees any reason for representing the exact appearance of any single object. He is more concerned to set down his concept of the main, distinguishing features of each type of thing that interests him. A modern woman has a dress and long hair; a man has trousers, short hair, and sometimes smokes a pipe. A dog is horizontal, not erect, with short legs (at first an indefinite number, from two or three to a whole fringe) below its body. Both the primitive and the young child at first set down their concepts, in comparatively simplified, schematic form, of the few main types they have mentally and visually distinguished, such as man, house, tree, horse, and, today, automobile or airplane. Their representations include typical movements as well as shapes.

As adult art becomes more civilized, its concepts are multiplied, refined, and subdivided. The development of an individual artist from childhood to maturity involves similar changes toward greater power to represent individuals and groups in a unified and realistic way. Some adult artists, to be sure, are deliberately unrealistic, and sometimes imitate primitive art for decorative or other reasons. The drawing ability of most adults is arrested at a childish stage. As a rule, not until comparatively late in either individual or cultural development is there much interest in representing subtle details in the appearance of a particular person or thing. Nor is there much interest in design, aesthetic form or composition for its own sake, though such attributes often develop along with representation. Young children, looking at an adult modern picture, are not likely to be much interested in formal aspects or in small details of individual representation, but rather in general types of object and situation. These a child wants to learn about, not from impersonal curiosity, but as they may (or might conceivably) affect him personally. He likes to enter vividly into a story picture, through identification and projection, and to use it as an aid to active fantasy-building. This applies both to the pictures he makes and to those he notices by other artists. In all these respects there are parallels in primitive adult art and behavior toward it. But the term "primitive" covers so many varieties that no exact analogy is possible.

There has been much research on this problem in Europe, but much remains to be done. If we are on guard against oversimplified recapitulation theories, we can well afford to consider the many suggestive hypotheses regarding individual development that arise from a study of social development.

As to art education, there are important implications. It should take account of the peculiar functions that picture-making, picture-appreciation, and other art activities naturally play in the mental development of children. These functions include the forming of intellectual concepts based on visual and other sensory experience, as we have just seen. Psychoanalysts would counsel us also to pay close attention to the function of art in the child's fantasy life, both as means of escape from reality and as means of effectively dealing with reality. In any case, the art teacher is wise not to hurry the child artist or appreciator into adult attitudes toward art, but rather to let him derive from it what he needs at each step on the way.

9. The evaluation of children's work in art

In psychological studies of children's art, it is usually advisable to exclude so far as possible all evaluative questions and assumptions—for example, whether a child's taste is good or bad, his drawings beautiful or ugly. Failure to do so has vitiated many researches in the field in spite of an imposing array of statistics. However, the practical problem of evaluating children's art does remain to be faced, if for no other reason than that of administering grades, rewards, and special opportunities in school. And the theoretical problem of what standards should be used in judging children's art must sooner or later be faced clearly by art critics and teachers, if not by psychologists. We cannot go very far in talking about "ability" without making evaluative judgments. A narrow special skill or performance, like making exact free-hand copies of a line drawing, can be measured objectively. But when we talk about "art ability" or "powers of appreciation" in general, we usually imply power to make or enjoy good art. Most applied sciences assume certain goals to be good; medicine, for example, assumes health as its goal. Science need not ignore evaluative problems entirely, but should try to distinguish them from descriptive ones and recognize its limitations in dealing with evaluative issues. It can throw much light on them even if it cannot settle them finally.

As to children's art, much depends upon whether or not we assume certain universal standards of value to be applicable alike to the art of adults and children. If we do, the task of appraisal becomes simple and dogmatic; we appraise a child's drawing on the basis of its approximation to what we consider good adult art. We appraise his taste from a standpoint of adult "good taste" as we conceive it. If we take a more relativistic view, in accord with modern trends in education, the task is harder. Then we need to consider what values art may have for children themselves. Of course, children do want to imitate adults in some things, but not in everything at once. There is danger in art, as elsewhere, of forcing and overaccelerating their maturation and thus of causing them to miss not only legitimate pleasures of childhood but also necessary steps in the development of abilities.

Psychological accounts of the normal development of children's art abilities—in drawing, for instance—may easily be made into a basis for evaluation. This is done by comparing a child's chronological age with the developmental stage of art that his product exemplifies. Thus it is now becoming possible to say that a given ten-year-old child can make drawings of a type that most children cannot make until twelve or fifteen years old. That may be taken as a sign of special ability as well as precocity, hence, as promising high art ability in later life, and, hence, as deserving present rewards and encouragements. There is no definite proof that such precocity is a reliable indication of adult ability, but the presumption is strong enough to act upon.

In such a case, the fact that the child's drawings are of an *older type* does not mean that they are necessarily *better*. It is not to be assumed that an adult type is the ideal of perfection for children. The young child's ways of producing art and his tastes in art are perhaps as right for him as the adolescent's are for the adolescent or the adult's for the adult. Furthermore, precocity of the sort just mentioned is not necessarily desirable or equivalent to total ability; it may even, at times, be an unhealthy symptom.

Again, *within each age-level type* there appear other variations that may be taken as criteria of value and ability. For want of a better word, we may call these for the present "qualitative" variations. Two children, six years of age, may both draw in a typical six-year-old way—highly simplified, flat, schematic, expressing general concepts rather than exact appearances. Yet the drawings of one will be inventive, full of imagined details and events, striking as designs, vivid in representing movement, interrelated as a group, while those of the other are bare and perfunctory, stiff, monotonous, awkward, unrelated. One seems animated, definite, effective in many ways; the other comparatively dead or vague and fumbling in every respect. Both stay within the limits of a single general type of form, yet the one realizes the possibilities of development within those limits more than does the other.

It is not easy to define such qualities as these in precise objective terms, or to prove that they do or do not exist in a particular case. Extreme examples, however, are obvious. It is not necessary to argue whether they constitute adequate standards of value; no brief list of abstract qualities will do so. The important thing to recognize is that, after children's art has been classified into a few main, developmental types of form, there still remains a possibility of wide individual variations within these types. Such variations are in a sense developmental also; they reveal different stages of development in certain abilities having to do with art. A six-year-old child can have most of the basic personality traits characteristic of his age and yet be more highly developed than another (by nature or nurture) in respect to certain component abilities, such as keen visual imagination, manual co-ordination, and power to translate mental concepts into objective forms through manipulating a medium.

Much the same can be said of adult art in various cultural stages. Some is primitive in type, some characteristic of advanced urban civilization, but within each type qualitative differences are found. Critics will distinguish good from bad primitive art; good from bad civilized art. Some primitive art is admired and kept in art museums; some adult art is rejected as mediocre. In other words, the difference between good and bad art is not the same as that between primitive and civilized art, or between childish and adult art. Flat, schematic drawings are not necessarily inferior to those with realistic perspective. Wide variations of development and personal style are possible within the former type, as in the case of much Egyptian painting by adult artists.

When art is taught for the definite purpose of vocational, technical skill, then it is reasonable to evaluate students' work on a basis of approximation to the adult skills and types of product desired; for example, those thought to be readily marketable. When art is taught as a part of general education, especially for younger children, exact evaluation is often less essential. When it is necessary, adult standards should be applied, if at all, with considerable modification. A premium should not be placed on conformity with adult taste or on perfection in the finished product. Habits of careful craftsmanship are desirable, but facile perfection and smoothness of finish in children's art is often less promising than vigorous, if clumsy, experimentation. Children should be encouraged to make and to enjoy the types of art appropriate to their level of general maturation and should be led gradually—not hurriedly—to those ahead. Within these youthful types of art form and behavior, the discerning teacher can look for those signs of alertness, sensitivity, inventiveness, and organizing power that distinguish excellence from mediocrity at every stage of development.

The present trend in general education, especially for the lower age levels, is to stress the importance of the psychological processes involved rather than that of finished products or set skills. In evaluating children's art work, as in the teaching itself, it is now considered more important to encourage the healthy development of personality, especially its aesthetic and artistic phases, than to secure a slick perfection in the artistic product or performance. We are less impressed than former generations were by mere precocity in a child; by the mere fact that he can do at an early age what most people cannot do until much older, if then. When such precocity comes more or less naturally, as it sometimes does, through inherent speed and vigor of maturation along a certain line, it should not be discouraged, but carefully nourished with concern for the young prodigy's general welfare. Child prodigies too often burn themselves out at an early age. Certainly, it is unwise to force precocity at the expense of health and adult achievement in order to satisfy the vanity of some parent or teacher by turning out a nine days' wonder-child. Works of art produced by children should, accordingly, be graded, praised and rewarded primarily as indications of healthy mental, emotional, and artistic growth and successful adjustment to life's problems at each stage, with reference to the peculiar problems of each individual child. They should not be graded entirely by comparison with any fixed, objective scale of supposed excellence in art; of supposed norms for adult art or for work on different age levels. The child's activity and experience in making the work of art, what he learns and how he grows in the process, is more important in the long run than the quality of any one product.

At the same time, one can go too far in thus emphasizing the process rather than the product, the general growth instead of the particular skill. Some respect for the quality and, if possible, the perfection of the product within intended limits is valuable for the mental growth itself. Supposedly creative or expressive activity without concern for the quality of the product is likely to degenerate into mere busy-work, trivial play, or egotistical posing. One cannot long remain devoted to a task whose outcome seems to have no importance, whose worth is solely in the doing. Such an attitude is too self-conscious, too vague and purposeless. Habits of carelessness in work, of leaving things unfinished or in a messy condition which could be avoided by a little patient effort, are not desirable traits of character. They lead in time to a sense of failure and inferiority. It develops one's self-respect to accomplish something as well as could reasonably be expected, and to have this accomplishment sincerely praised by experts. There is real value in setting up tentative goals and standards for the artistic product or performance whose achievement can be judged with some objectivity, as in the case of athletic or other technical skills. They should be hard enough to challenge effort and industry, but not too hard to be finished in the time allowed. It is for the educator to formulate them in a way which he believes to have developmental value; not as absolutes.

As one goes up the educational ladder, considerations of professional and vocational competence assume greater weight. Rightly or wrongly, it is assumed that the student's basic personality has been formed, and that—except in special cases of maladjustment—it no longer deserves pre-eminence among educational goals. Instead, the emphasis shifts to imparting specific knowledge and technical proficiency, in art as in other fields, which may be of value in a career. Here the student reared too long in overly "progressive" schools may be at a disadvantage. His personality is perhaps a little self-conscious from too solicitous nurturing; he is ill prepared for the rough give and take of a competitive world. Moreover, he may lack the self-confidence which comes from having learned to do and know certain definite, socially respected things well, and to earn a living by them if necessary. In the higher grades, objective goals and standards for the quality of the product or performance can and should be more explicitly specified. Practical, vocational reasons for them can be pointed out. At the same time, it can be recognized that such present professional requirements have no absolute, permanent authority. The original artist is still free to violate or transcend them in his own creative work if he wishes. If he can do so with constructive, significant results as a young student, the teacher should be free to treat him as a special case and to grade and reward him accordingly.

~◦⃘ IV ◦⃘~

CREATIVE ABILITY IN ART AND ITS EDUCATIONAL FOSTERING*

1. The meaning of creativeness: mistaken claims to it

The ideal of producing creative, original minds through public education, or at least of helping in their development, is characteristic of modern educational philosophy in America. It expresses our optimistic belief in social progress and in our own ability to accelerate and direct it. This optimism is perhaps uncritical in view of recent wars and economic troubles, but it has survived them with scarcely diminished enthusiasm. It is based on no very clear conception of what we mean by progress, especially in art, or of what sort of art we would like to see created. We realize that, so far, we have not filled many pages in the history of art, except perhaps with the motion picture and certain types of architecture. But we have a youthful confidence in the ability of our people to create worth-while things in this field, as in applied science and industry. As a democracy, we like to affirm, against the repressive systems of the day, our confidence that the masses can be trusted with freedom to think for themselves and to express themselves in art, and we have tremendous confidence in the power of education to remake the world and to produce the kind of people we desire. Among these will be individual leaders in art and other fields, supermen from all economic and racial groups, who will give personal concreteness to our progress and leaven the vast, impersonal standardization that characterizes so much of our social life.

Our own investigations of intelligence and learning ability should chasten this optimism a little, for they point inescapably to the limits set on individual development by heredity and inborn capacity. These would perhaps point rather to eugenics than to education as a means of producing mental superiority, but we are not yet ready for that mode of control. There are deterministic, old-world philosophies of history that would deny our ability to produce a really creative

* Published in *Art in American Life and Education* (1941), pp. 289-321.

period by trying to do so. Such periods, they say, happen automatically at certain stages in a people's development, when all biological and cultural factors converge to produce them, as in ancient Athens and Renaissance Italy. There are others, more encouraging, who maintain that cultural creativeness follows historically from political power and economic prosperity. If so, we have some of the prerequisites. Most of all, we seem to have one powerful new tool in scientific psychology with all its possible educational applications. That tool has been scarcely forged as yet, but we are impatient to try out its possibilities.

Let us try to clarify the problem a little by analyzing what we mean by creative ability. The words "creation" and "creative" are now much used by art teachers, and often in a rather vague, sentimental way that arouses suspicion in the scientist. They convey a eulogistic implication, as if the child who "creates art" were doing something much finer than merely drawing a picture. And yet so much ordinary student work is labeled "creative" by the teachers in charge that skeptical outsiders wonder if all of it can possibly deserve the title. Of late, the words have fallen into some disrepute for this reason, but still they stand for some important ideas that are difficult to ignore in working out a philosophy of art education.

Webster's *New International Dictionary* defines *create* as follows: "3. To cause or occasion; to form;—said of natural or physical causes and especially of social and evolutional forces; as, new environment *creates* new forms of life. 4. To produce as a work of thought or imagination, esp. as a work of art or of dramatic interpretation along new or unconventional lines; as, Irving *created* a new Hamlet." *Creation* is "1. *b*. Act of making, producing, fashioning, or bringing into existence, in general. . . . *d*. The presentation of a new conception in an artistic embodiment." *Creative* is "1. Having the power or quality of creating; given to creation. '*Creative* talent.' *Irving*." The religious sense, in which things are said to have been created out of nothing by a divine power, is not relevant to any sort of human art.

Evidently, two main ideas are implied here, one broad and one narrow. These are often confused. In the broad sense, any sort of production, or making, is creation, and thus all student art can be so described, whatever its quality. In the narrow sense, the term implies novelty or originality, as contrasted with the imitation of earlier products. In addition, it suggests that the work is somehow important and valuable; it would not be applied to something that was new in a merely freakish, trivial way.

Art teachers who use the term often have still another idea in mind. They mean that students' art is "creative" if it was spontaneously conceived and executed by the student, not done in accordance with the teacher's directions. Likewise, we sometimes contrast the creative adult artist with the mere artisan, however skilled, as one who conceives or thinks out the product, instead of following another's instructions in executing it.

If we wish a term for psychological purposes to include a wide range of phenomena—the making of art in general, whether important and original or not—it would perhaps be better to use a more neutral term, such as "art production." If we wish to narrow down the field, let us speak explicitly of "original" art production, and of "spontaneous" art production. Child art is often spontaneous (not directly influenced), but it is rarely original, in the sense of being new.

How much of students' art is to be called creative in the narrower senses will depend on the strictness of the standards we set for originality and spontaneity. This will also determine our answer to the question "How many people are creative, or can become creative, in art?" or in other words, "What range of creative ability exists in children?" There is no possibility of objective, quantitative answers to these questions, for they involve evaluation at the start. Anyone can produce some kind of art in a broad sense, even a person of very low intelligence and skill. But speaking strictly, the number of artists who are recognized by subsequent history as having made important, original contributions to art are few indeed—a handful in any generation. Historians argue for centuries over which artists were the really creative innovators. Their answers involve not only controversial standards of value and importance, but also factual questions of priority and influence.

No young child or his products has ever been so recognized, and it would be remarkable if any should be. There are many child prodigies in *artistic performance,* especially in music and acting, but few in art production or composition. Children's drawings often seem to promise marked originality in later life. Those of young children often delight us by a comparative freshness of imagination and technique, as if the child had looked at the world for himself, selected what seemed interesting to him, and worked out his own way of putting it down on paper. Their designs are often refreshingly unlike those of older, academically trained artists, involving forceful rhythms and surprising distortions. None is perhaps *exactly* like any other picture, old or new. Child art in general is certainly a contribution to human culture. But it is hard to find definitely original character- istics in the art of individual children—that is, any radically new and important quality or type of form that would justify us in calling it an individual contribution to the world's artistic heritage.

We sometimes go from one extreme to the other in talking of chil- dren's art. The old attitude was to judge it by adult, academic stand- ards, and thus to regard it as crude and lacking in all artistic merit. We have now discovered that it can please the adult observer in its own right, and that it deserves respect as an expression of a stage in development that is worth while in itself. It is not an unsuccessful attempt at adult art and hence cannot be fairly judged by adult standards. Moreover, there are reasons for encouraging young chil- dren to try out their own ideas in art and other activities. But to praise children's art in a wholesale, effusive way, in the same terms that we use to praise the work of mature genius, is to reveal a lack of standards for discriminating relative degrees of importance and originality.

There is much self-deception in the claims of progressive teachers for the utter spontaneity of their students' work. From Cizek on, the free expressionists in art education have ignored the constant, mani- fold influences that were playing upon the children in their charge. There are many ways of influencing students' art besides telling them explicitly "do it this way," or "copy this." No child who has lived for six or seven years in a world of cultural influences, including such popular art as magazine covers and cartoons, whose every thought is influenced by home and outside agencies, who goes to a school where certain kinds of art are praised and encouraged, can be called "spon- taneous" in any strict sense of the word. The most that can be claimed is a relatively high degree of freedom from definite influence during the immediate process of production. But anyone who ob- serves school art exhibits in one American town after another is likely to become first annoyed and then amused by the constant claims of originality and spontaneity on the part of proud teachers, in spite of the obviously stereotyped imitativeness of much of the work.

Furthermore, overemphasis by well-meaning teachers on the aim of individual originality may lead to undesired effects. The ninety-nine percent who can never be original creators may become discouraged and think of themselves as failures, missing the satisfaction and usefulness that should come with skilled craftsmanship and willing collaboration under the leadership of others. They may become self-conscious and conceited in the effort to express their own egos, turning out shoddy, "half-baked" products that are never frankly criticized in the school, and they may thus become doomed to a rough awakening later on. Real originality has often emerged without being sought, and even from environments and teaching methods that discouraged it, through long, patient study of traditions, techniques, and current practices. Admitting that such originality is to be desired and fostered in all who are potentially capable of it, we are far from sure that the best way to achieve it is through explicit preaching and unlimited freedom in school.

Adult artists, too, often make excessive claims of complete originality. They feel it as an admission of inferiority to recognize that they have learned from their predecessors, and especially that they have learned from their contemporaries. To the trained observer, their indebtedness is usually quite apparent. But the basic error lies in the implication that any artist or any work of art can be completely original. All artists build upon the past, upon the traditions and recent tendencies in their field. There can be no justifiable stigma in admitting such debts; and the most any artist should presume to claim is that he has made some slight addition of his own, some relatively new adaptation of earlier achievements to a new situation, need, technique, or material.

The notion of an artist as a unique, isolated genius, creating something *de novo* through a mysterious flash of inspiration, is itself a survival from the romantic tradition we inherit. It has cultural connections with extreme individualism and *laisser faire* in social thought. It ignores the whole drift of modern practice toward collective action. There is less and less place for the purely individualistic artist, the genius in a garret, and more for the man who can cooperate with others in a vast undertaking like the making of a cathedral, an airplane, or a motion picture, without worrying too much about his incorruptible originality. Of course, credit for really new ideas has its place, too. Patent and copyright laws try to protect and reward them, but find it harder and harder to do so in this day of adaptations and collective art production.

Painters and sculptors, and other practitioners of the so-called "fine arts," are especially prone to regard themselves as "creative," and to look down on mere craftsmen and performers elsewhere. One even hears of painting and sculpture as "creative arts," as if everything done therein were creative, and as if the making of a chair or an advertising poster were necessarily mere craftsmanship or commercialism. It is one of the commonest delusions of painters and their admirers that anything done in oil paint and which is not a direct copy of some other picture is necessarily creative and original. To be sure, it is probably not exactly like any other picture, but the difference may be only in details of subject matter. Anyone can paint or photograph a costumed figure, a scene, or a group of still-life objects that has never been portrayed before. But originality from the standpoint of art history and criticism implies far more than that. It implies a valuable innovation in manner of treatment; in pictorial form, composition, expression, or technique; in what the artist himself contributes through selection and reorganization of his subject matter. The claim to creative originality is specious if the subject matter, though in some details unique, is in all important ways like that selected by earlier artists, and if the mode of representation is conventional. This is not to say, of course, that an imitative picture is without value. It may give pleasure to many and good experience to the student artist. The danger lies in obscuring the nature of real originality, so that we fail to strive for it intelligently or to recognize it when it appears.

By discounting the snobbery of the "fine arts," we shall be readier to appreciate the creative elements that often occur in less genteel arts—in the handcrafts, industrial and commercial arts, utilitarian architecture, motion pictures, and even in popular and journalistic illustration. Creative originality in art is not limited to any particular arts, mediums, or techniques, or to people who call themselves "artists." The maker of a picture frame may be more truly a creative artist than the maker of the picture it encloses. The discerning critic who advances new points of view toward art, and even the discriminating collector who assembles a unique, suggestively organized collection, may be more creative than the majority of dabblers in a fine-art medium.

2. Is there a creative type of person?

Regardless of where it occurs, is there such a thing as a creative, original type of mind? If so, has it been possessed by the artists recognized as great innovators in the past? Is it a peculiar type of mental ability or mode of thinking, absent in ordinary mortals? We are entering into speculative problems here, and our answers can be supported only by slight evidence. In general, the present tendency is definitely to deny the existence of any quite unique ability or method, even in the very great. The more we learn about them, the more they seem in certain respects like ordinary people, motivated by the same desires, some petty and some noble; faced by analogous difficulties and dealing intelligently with some, ineffectively with others. Essentially, creative originality and the abilities that produce it seem to be different in degree, rather than in kind, from the mental characteristics of the mediocre. Judgments of greatness in art are made on the basis of the value of the product, not on how it was produced. For all we can see, the world is, and always has been, full of capable workers in art and other fields who possess tremendous skill, intelligence, and vivid imaginations, but whose products never achieve outstanding recognition. Other artists do gain recognition in spite of being very commonplace in most respects, like Cézanne, or psychopathic, like Van Gogh. Many show less than ordinary intelligence and *savoir-faire* in dealing with practical life problems and human contacts.

This surprising fact, and the conspicuousness of a few psychopathic artists, has led some theorists to maintain that genius and insanity are causally connected. There is no space here to discuss this theory in detail. But it may at least be noted that for every insane genius many others can be mentioned, like Bach and Titian, who showed no great abnormalities. Probably the percentage of definite neurosis among artists, great or mediocre, is no larger than among other people. Indeed, Freud has pointed out that the artist has peculiar opportunities for readjusting himself to reality through his art—through being able to objectify and use his fantasies in achieving success—and thus for correcting in part whatever neurotic tendencies he may have had in early life. Artists sometimes break down mentally or develop pathological traits in later life, but so do some scientists and businessmen. The artist often has the advantage that oddities of behavior are tolerated in him as a pardonable Bohemianism, thus producing less than ordinary conflict with society. At the same time countless artists, major and minor, lead the most conventional of lives, with no outward sign of abnormality or eccentricity. It may well be that the eccentric artist type is a product of special cultural trends or fashions rather than of anything more basic psychologically. Extreme differentiation of the artistic or aesthetic type from the practical is a sign of temporary cultural dislocation, of an artificial divorce between useful production and the pursuit of beautiful luxuries. It became a convention of the Romantic movement in Europe to think of the artist as an eccentric genius, living in a world apart, and not like other men. In the late nineteenth century the pose was fashionable, and many who were not seriously interested in art as well as some who were (Baudelaire, for example) cultivated its bizarre outward signs in costume and manner. At other periods, most artists have preferred to look and act like ordinary citizens.

On the other hand, there are reasons for believing that originality, especially in art, may involve some fairly distinct psychological traits. These are not necessarily differences in kind, but at least marked differences in degree and mode of development. For example, there is still debate among psychologists as to whether genius is the same as extremely high intelligence as measured by standardized tests. Terman has applied the term "studies of genius" to studies of children with unusually high I.Q. Others have insisted that genius, in the sense of creative originality, is something different from high I.Q. Highly intelligent children, at least as measured by our present tests, often fail to develop anything that could be called creative originality in later life. They usually become capable, successful, and respected citizens, but that is not the same thing. There is not sufficient evidence to show whether persons recognized as creatively original always have high intelligence. One may concede perhaps that the very greatest always do, and yet maintain that persons of moderate intelligence sometimes do decidedly original things.

The experience of teachers would often corroborate the hypothesis that high intelligence alone is not enough, though it is one prerequisite for great achievement. Every teacher of long experience has been disappointed by the phenomenon of students who apparently have all the qualifications for notable creative work—intelligence, information, technical skill, every home and educational advantage—yet who never go on to produce such work. Sometimes they even lose the desire to do so and settle down to lives of comfortable conformity, of mediocrity, as judged by their own youthful ideals and those of their teachers.

It may be that the reason lies partly in the realm of motivation; in what (to use the old-fashioned word) might be called the *will* to create. As yet, this factor is not measured by our intelligence tests, although every educator admits the importance of interest and effort. A mild, diffused type of interest and effort in school days is not enough, however. Neither is an attachment to one's adult occupation so halfhearted as to be easily distracted by competing interests. Drastic concentration and sacrifice of other interests are often necessary to achieve the heights of creative eminence. The creators have been willing to make this sacrifice when necessary, or perhaps have been unable to adjust themselves to life conditions so as to achieve other goals in addition to the one supremely desired.

History and biography have made us familiar with the story of the genius who fails to achieve success in money and its comforts, in health, in love and family relations, and in the approval of his contemporaries—at least in his early years if not through life. Whether he made these sacrifices voluntarily or involuntarily is perhaps not essential. He is frequently unable to avoid them and at the same time pursue his chosen course along creative lines. Perhaps that course took too much of his limited health and emotional energy, or led him to a stand too violently counter to approved conventions; in any case, the sacrifice was made. True, there are happier stories of men like Titian and Rubens, who achieved greatness without giving up many of the ordinary values of life. Such men are shrewd, versatile, and fortunate enough to ride the crest of a wave, and their kind of originality happens to be socially approved. But bitter struggle and sacrifice are by no means uncommon in the story of greatness, in art, science, religion, social reform, or any other field. We do not know exactly what conscious or unconscious factors impel some to choose sacrifice, but we do see the common spectacle of others, including extremely intelligent people, who do not feel called upon to make that choice.

It is not for the psychologist to appraise the wisdom of either course, but to explain both, if possible. Perhaps even the teacher has no right to condemn a student who prefers a happy, well-adjusted, useful social life to original creation. But let us not delude ourselves with the idea that no choice is ever necessary, and that originality is always easily reconcilable with social adjustment. The more potent the force of conservatism in any society, the more difficult the reconciliation.

How does the will to be original and to create in a particular field develop intensely in a given individual? To know that, we must trace his early history in detail, and as a rule its essential facts are inaccessible to the investigator. Psychoanalysis offers certain general hypotheses in terms of unconscious conflict and sublimation. It tells of how an early sense of guilt arising from the Oedipus situation carries over into later life; how the sensitive ego in adolescence and afterward needs to build up its self-esteem in some way; how this way may lead into neurotic symptoms, into overcompensation through egotism, conceit, cruelty, or pugnacity, or through sublimation into more or less approved channels, like those of art. This would perhaps help explain the discontent and restlessness, the egotism alternating with depression, the antagonism to conventional forms and people, that so often accompany genius. But even Freud admits ignorance of the fundamental reasons why some persons can adjust their conflicts only through crime or neurosis, while others achieve cultural sublimations. He hints that we may be driven back to inborn physiological differences for the final difference in power and mode of adjustment.

At least, the original genius would appear to be a person who has achieved a partial adjustment with his cultural environment, in that he has directed much of his libido into socially approved channels, such as art or religion. But he is not so completely adjusted as to seek conformity and immediate social approval at all costs; he retains a strong impulse to differ with his contemporaries, sometimes over trivial as well as important matters. He is often torn between the common desire for immediate social approval and a scornful resentment toward his contemporaries, which makes him disdain their opinions and dream of later approval by the judicious few, by pos- terity, or God; or he may try to find a lonely satisfaction in merely living up to his own standards. He usually maintains a rich fantasy life in dreams, waking reveries, or both, in contrast with the highly extroverted and adjusted person who lives more wholly in the ex- ternal present. But he is not content to relapse into excessive, idle fantasy, for he has a grasp of reality to the extent of learning to manipulate a medium, to express his fantasies objectively, and to become a force among his fellows. He can discipline and redirect his imaginings into paths of systematic construction. Within this general type, there is much variation. Some geniuses have a strong grasp on practical reality; some relapse at times into escapist fan- tasies and neurotic symptoms or struggle blindly against hopeless odds. Some are comparatively tolerant of old traditions and present practices, even regarding themselves as conservatives and finding the old forms flexible enough to admit progress. They are less discon- tented and exhibit less sacrifice and struggle; but even they have the will to persistent, concentrated work, and the desire to improve on the past.

The will to be original is not enough in itself, for many have it keenly and fail nevertheless. Mere radicalism, as antagonism to the conventional and a desire to improve things, is not enough. There, perhaps, is where intelligence comes in, as a power to discern what possible lines of effort are most promising, and to adapt effective means to ends in following them. But even general intelligence will not necessarily suffice. It must be directed and implemented with specific skills and information, as in some technique of art. Physical equipment, as in sensory and muscular powers, must be adequate for the task set, but intelligence shows itself in choosing a task for which one has the potential means.

Besides a general disposition to produce and alter things, it is characteristic of the original mind to develop an intense, persistent attachment to some particular art or vocation, to some particular medium, material, or instrument for expression and construction. He becomes fascinated by the look and feel of oil paints, brushes and canvas, marble and chisel, machinery, the piano, the written word, the stage, or the speaker's rostrum. Whatever his choice, he can never be long content away from it and must be somehow occupied with it, even when not actually creating anything new. Such devotion varies in intensity, of course, but it is often most intense in the most original and powerful creators.

However strong, this devotion entails a corresponding sacrifice of other interests, of the values that attract ordinary people. It can become so extreme as to seem exaggerated and obsessive to the latter. Even family ties and responsibilities may be abandoned, father and mother forsaken, one's own economic interests as well as social duties ignored, and the world counted well lost for the sake of one's chosen work. This, of course, is the exceptional extreme, but in lesser degree it is common. The gradual concentration of one who has found his work involves a constant and often regretful cutting off of minor interests that had been delightful during the rambling explorations of youth, but that seem now to demand too much time and energy. This is not to say that the creative mind becomes narrow in every way. It may expand to a universal perspective, like that of Dante or Shakespeare, in its range of ideas. But it tends to focus its mental interests upon a systematic process of thinking out and objectifying these ideas in some chosen medium. Versatile exceptions, like Leonardo da Vinci, are rare indeed.

One reason for stressing this concentration or channelizing of interest is that it helps answer the question we have raised as to why so many highly intelligent and capable persons, promising as students, never become especially creative. In some of these cases the essential reason is an unwillingness to concentrate on a single goal to the necessary degree. Such persons are perhaps too adaptive; they can become interested in too many different things; they can shift too easily to a new one if the first choice demands too high a price. They have more varied, more widely distributed interests; no one job seems important enough to deserve the sacrifice of the many other values and obligations of life. Much can be said in defense of this attitude; it may lead to a more balanced, socially adjusted, and healthy existence. But again, it is for the psychologist to describe and explain rather than to moralize about values.

Why does such intense and persistent concentration occur in some individuals? It is certainly not wholly inborn; at least physiological predispositions would appear to be much more general, though they may give a broad initial bent in some direction, such as visual, rather than auditory, art. We must keep in mind the great number of possible determinants of personality. Once more, the theories of psychoanalysis would suggest that such a powerful, often abnormal, concentration of desire must be traceable in large part to unconscious mechanisms. The material or special activity chosen must somehow have become symbolic in the psychoanalytic sense, and a sublimation that is necessary to the individual for reasons he does not fully understand. His own rationalizations, of course, may be quite misleading, and here is where the questionnaires of descriptive psychology so often go astray.

The phenomenon also suggests an answer to the question whether art abilities tend to be versatile or specialized. Some researches have indicated that high ability in one field usually goes with high ability in others, and that the one-sided genius is a myth. Such a conclusion has been based mainly on studies of children and of ordinary capable, successful adults. It may be true of these, but not true of the exceptionally creative. It may even be true of the latter, in the sense that they have many of the potential capacities necessary for success in any field. But in another sense they could not succeed in any other field, if they are so constituted as not to want to; that is, if their volitional and emotional drives have concentrated in such a way that no deflection is now possible.

It is another common characteristic of genius, though not observable in all cases, to form an intense, persistent attachment for some particular type of form or product, for some type or style of art, some one ideal, aim, and standard of value; for example, if an artist, he may be a passionate partisan of the romantic ideal and seek to embody it in everything he creates. To that extent, he tends to be intolerant or blind to the values of other and opposing types of art. Moral and political reformers often hold with bigoted ardor to a particular doctrine of the ideal state or the right mode of conduct. Their extremism, and the force and skill with which it is asserted, their consistent hammering away at one idea often enable them to make an impression on the world that more reasonable men, looking on all sides of the question, fail to make. This is especially the case in art, where success may depend not on truth or expediency so much as on the vividness and consistency with which a certain way of seeing things is expressed. It is less so in science and philosophy. There are so many ways of drawing a figure or painting a landscape, each pleasing and revealing in certain ways, and each perhaps as right as any other, that an artist equally interested in all may never follow any one very definitely. His products may become half-hearted, overloaded, or vague, eclectic, through his desire to combine too many values in one work of art. Great artists, on the other hand, are often narrowly intolerant toward other great artists, as were some of the giants of the Italian Renaissance. They are so intensely devoted to one way of doing things as to be irritated by any other.

Not that such an outstanding artist necessarily remains true to his first convictions or his first style of art. He may change radically in the course of his career, and either slowly or suddenly. Many original artists go through very different periods, in each of which they explore a certain approach with intense devotion. They may change to an opposite and previously hated style with little attempt at rational justification, being simply "fed up" with what they have been doing. But while in the grip of a particular attitude, they do follow it with intense conviction.

Again, such concentration and possible change of heart present to the psychologist interesting problems, as to their genesis and motivation. Let us note in passing but one educational question—namely, how far it is wise for the prospective artist to familiarize himself with many styles of art and to develop a catholic taste toward all of them. For the appreciator, there is every reason for so doing. And even for the artist, a wide acquaintance in art may provide valuable suggestions out of which he can select and reorganize for himself. So original an artist as Picasso (who, by the way, has gone through several radically different styles) is well versed in the history of art. He takes from it only what he needs at a particular time and usually produces therefrom a highly specialized, self-consistent form. But students often start their careers with some intense enthusiasm, then learn in college how narrow and "immature" it is, how much can be said on the other side, and how many other good ways of doing things exist. They gradually acquire a spirit of mellow tolerance and scholarly insight, but lose the creative impulse. Progressive education does try to keep alive this impulse, but there is little evidence so far that its methods will be effective. Its broad tolerance, its emphasis on a wide general education, the great latitude it gives students for experimentation may all operate to blur the student's vision and diffuse his enthusiasm. The stricter disciplinary methods of the past, which most great artists have undergone, may have the value of concentrating attention on a single line of approach, at least long enough for the student to grasp it clearly and to acquire habits of persistent work in following it. If he finds it too uncongenial, he may at least be goaded into a vehement counter-assertion, into an artistic revolt that is equally sharp and definite. Very liberal methods, in which the teacher carefully refrains from exerting any definite influence, often seem to turn out vaguely cultivated people who themselves have nothing very definite to say. This has been a weakness of complacent modern liberalism in general. It has helped open the door to fanatical extremists, who have captured mass emotion with their vivid and passionate advocacy of some particular course of action.

Before setting up "creative originality" as a goal of education, especially in art, it might be well for us to find out more about what it really is, what causes it, and how it behaves when it occurs. One may suspect that many teachers who praise it as a high-sounding slogan are thinking of something almost impossible: a sort of innovation that is always refined, decorous, and easy to get along with; that produces only beautiful works of art that please and inspire everyone and offend no one. They do not realize how shocking and unsettling extreme originality usually is. To be sure, they have read a little of the storms of abuse and ridicule that greeted Darwin in science, Beethoven and Wagner in music, Rodin in sculpture, Rembrandt, Courbet, Monet, and the Post-impressionists in painting; but these were far away and long ago. Of the men who shock and offend, like Freud and Havelock Ellis, Stravinsky, Picasso, and Frank Lloyd Wright, it is said that one cannot be sure whether they are really great or mere sensationalists who will be forgotten. But this is so of all geniuses in their own time. Teachers try to make students polite, respectable, and similar in tastes to themselves, not realizing that these qualities may be difficult to reconcile with high originality. There is more consistency in the Roman Catholic attitude, which condemns the tendency of modern education to glorify innovation and freedom of thought. If we do champion these traits in art and elsewhere, we should at least be prepared to accept the shocks and antagonisms they inevitably arouse.

Is it consistent to work for the ideal of originality in education and at the same time for that of harmonious personal and social adjustment? Only if we are prepared to qualify the latter and to admit that some harmony may have to be sacrificed in the interests of progress. The products of original minds must inevitably clash to some extent with accepted beliefs and practices. Even when the creative person has no desire for such conflict and is personally as mild and retiring as Darwin was, the intrinsic force of his ideas will produce explosive repercussions. Others will point out their negative implications if he does not, and will use them as weapons of attack.

Psychologically, we do not know how much inward neurotic conflict, if any, is necessary for artistic genius. Psychoanalytic theory would imply that a good deal is necessary. If so, when we try to promote normal, well-adjusted personality development in children, we may be unintentionally weakening the inner forces that make for creative genius. The answer may be, "well and good; let us have the former instead." Or, preferably, let us see whether a type of genius can be produced with the aid of proper education that can create in a more serene and reasonable way, with less inward conflict. Certainly, there is still no lack in the world of conditions that make for anxiety and conflict. If education can do anything to mitigate them, it need have no fear of doing too much. Liberal and progressive ideals of education have had too little time so far to work out really effective methods, especially in art, and in due time they may learn to avoid their present weaknesses.

Moreover, our chief concern in public education is not with the rare extremes of genius, but with more ordinary people. If we can succeed in developing a little more creative originality in the ordinary student, we need not fear the extremes of conflict that exceptional genius tends to involve. The latter is perhaps beyond our power to produce, and we have enough to do in encouraging a little more interest in art production on the part of great numbers of students. Incidental doubts and difficulties should not prevent us from going ahead to provide a few fairly obvious means to that end, such as a wider distribution in our schools of the basic equipment for art work in various media, of a chance to see good works of art, and of more time to spend on art under congenial conditions.

So far as our psychological understanding is concerned, there is a certain advantage in studying the extremes of genius, of superiority as well as of subnormality and pathological deviation. For all such examples help us to see in a magnified way, and sometimes in a detached, dissociated way, mental phenomena that occur to a less degree in the normal. It is useful to study genius, if only to see how its values can be cultivated apart from those traits that are considered undesirable. Certainly, there is need for more studies of genius in various fields carried out in the light of modern psychology. Freud's study of Leonardo da Vinci is a suggestive example, but it is limited to certain aspects of his personality and concerned with applying a special theory. Most of the data available are secondary and often unreliable, gathered from biographies and letters. Even the study of the artist's works is often misleading. But difficulties of this sort should not deter us from doing as much as can be done with so important a subject.

3. Creative imagination

Common usage of the word "genius," as expressed in dictionary definitions, emphasizes the factor of imagination in this type of personality. The most relevant in Webster's list of meanings is as follows: "6. Extraordinary mental superiority; esp., unusual power of invention or origination of any kind." Genius is contrasted with mere talent as "original creative power, frequently working through the imagination, in contradistinction to a faculty for effective dealing with existent material; as the intuitive and spontaneous, in opposition to the merely disciplined and trained; as the inexplicable, unanalyzable, and as it were inspired, over against what works in the main by rule and line." This would seem to contradict the popular saying that "genius is only an infinite capacity for taking pains," although such a capacity might still be needed as a means to effective accomplishment.

Discounting the mystical suggestion in such words as "inexplicable" and "inspired," we still have a valid psychological distinction. There is one kind of intelligent thinking that proceeds gradually, step by step, according to definite logical or technical rules, with each step fairly conscious and explicit. There is another kind that leaps through or over intermediate steps to a goal, to the hypothetical solution of a scientific problem or the image of a complete work of art. No doubt the intermediate steps are made somehow, but they are made with extreme speed and abbreviation and often in an unconscious or semiconscious way, as in dream or waking reverie. Past laborious struggles with detail are suddenly brought to fruition, blockings and obstacles suddenly overcome. Scientists have told of thus suddenly realizing the solution of a difficult problem; artists, of suddenly envisaging the total form they wish to produce. Such leaps of thought occur to some extent in all thinking, but in what we call "genius" they are more extreme and characteristic. The "creative flash" of original genius, which is recognized by common observation, is no less real because it is difficult to control in the psychological laboratory or to measure in standard tests.

There is a type of intelligent thinking that is effective in dealing with problems clearly stated in advance. This type is most easily tested in our standardized intelligence tests, so that those who excel in it receive high intelligence scores. But there is another kind of intelligent thinking, not so easily tested, that is likely to be impatient with artificially set problems; that prefers to set up its own problems and objectives; and that, impelled by strong inner motivations, dashes quickly to their solution. The quick, abbreviated thinking that is common in geniuses is by no means independent of discipline, technique, and ordinary step-by-step learning. But these come in advance, as necessary preparatory phases; later on, they enter as phases in detailed verification or technical construction.

Some psychologists distinguish between the "creative" and the "reproductive" imagination. "Imagination" in general is defined by Webster as the "1. . . . formation of mental images of objects not present to the senses." It would include the recall of images of objects previously sensed; and this process, identical with one kind of memory, is called "reproductive imagination." The other, called "productive, constructive, or creative," "starts with the notion of mental imaging of things suggested but not previously experienced, and thence expands, first to fantastic representation, or fancy, and later to the idea of mental creation and poetic idealization. . . ."

The fault in this distinction is that it tends to separate the two varieties too sharply. We rarely if ever imagine in a purely reproductive way. There is some "creation" (in the selection and reorganization of sense data) in all remembering and imaging and even in the process of sense perception itself. Every normal person learns to imagine objects and events he has not directly sensed, through mentally reorganizing details of his own past experience into combinations suggested by others. When we hear someone describe a journey to strange places, we are led to imagine places that are somewhat unlike any we have seen, although in doing so we recall and reorganize constituent details, such as colors, trees, and rocks that we have seen elsewhere before. All imagining is thus somewhat "creative" in a broad sense of that term. But it is true at the same time that some imagining tends to adhere, or tries to adhere, more exactly to the previous sense experience, as when we try to recall the exact words of an important conversation. Some imagining selects and reorganizes much more freely and extensively, as in dreams and wish-fulfillment fantasies or in reading a fairy story. Some individuals can perform the latter type of imagining more vividly and powerfully than others can. In contrast with the brief, fragmentary fantasy of a dull mind, the resultant forms may be unusually complex and systematic, as in imagining a whole novel or a picture of heaven. The imagery of other persons, not necessarily intellectually dull, is usually stereotyped, whereas a more original mind organizes unusual forms out of the common data of experience. They may be on the whole realistic, in accord with scientific accounts of reality; or they may be "fantastic" in the artistic sense, building up impossible, yet momentarily credible, worlds of spirits, monsters, and magic.

No one will know about these forms, of course, unless the imaginer also expresses them through a medium of communication, such as words or pictures. If these expressions have the power to interest and please other people, they will be called works of creative imagination in the strict and eulogistic sense. Thus we see again that the idea of creativeness can have a broad or a narrow sense, as applied to imagination. The latter implies an exceptional power to reorganize images into new types of form, as judged by other persons to whom they have been communicated.

Related to imagination is the little-understood process known as "empathy," which Webster defines as "Imaginative projection of one's own consciousness into another being; esp., sympathetic understanding of other than human beings." Briefly, its place in artistic creation is as follows. In varying degrees, artists tend to project their own experiences into an unfinished work of art. For example, the sculptor imagines his block of stone as possessed of inner life and muscular tension. Van Gogh projected his own emotional agitation into his paintings of trees, clouds, rocks, and houses. In other words, he expressed his feelings in his pictures, and such art is sometimes called "expressionistic." Children often have a vivid power to "make believe" that a doll, a drawing, or a clay model is living and doing things. But the artist goes further if he constructs a work of art so that observers are also stimulated to similar imaginings.

The theories of psychoanalysis have direct reference to the problem of the nature of creative imagination. Freud did not work out a very explicit, systematic application of these theories to the nature of art, nor have his successors done so. There is much to be done in this regard, for the general hypotheses are extremely suggestive and reinforced by vast amounts of clinical evidence. It is to be hoped that the assurance with which some present psychologists dismiss the works of Freud as outmoded will not long prevent an open-minded testing of the psychoanalytic approach to aesthetic psychology. Certainly, the more accepted schools of psychology have produced nothing that begins to promise so much enlightenment along this line; in fact, they have almost ignored the whole problem of creative imagination and of fantasy-formation in general. Freud's theory of dream and fantasy production, if true in general, must be true of much creative imagination in art as well. His account of dream images as symbols unconsciously devised to mask and compromise internal conflicts in the individual, and of folklore and ritual as examples of such symbolism in social culture, offers promising hypotheses for the analysis of civilized art. But most efforts to work out this analysis have been oversimplified and farfetched, consisting of superficial references to erotic symbols and wish fulfillments. As Freud himself made clear, the processes of symbolization are much too variable, indirect, and subtle to be explained in any facile way. Art teachers interested in psychology should read Freud and Jung for themselves, and not be content with popular misrepresentations of them.

The educational applications of these writings are also far from clear. For if creative imagination arises in large part from neurotic conflict, and if rational education tends to remove such conflict by bringing its sources into consciousness, much of the motivation of artistic fantasy (or at least of certain kinds of it) may be lost. Again we have the problem of whether creative originality in art can always be achieved along with a normal, happily adjusted personality. If so, how?

4. Component functions and abilities; individual differences

Whatever the answer, we may be very sure that it will have to be varied in relation to different types of individuals. It was stated above, and needs repeating, that there is no such thing as "*the* artistic type," in the sense of a distinctive kind of personality common to all practitioners of an art medium. Artists are as diverse as persons in any other great realm of human activity. There is no such thing as "the creative process," in the sense of a single, uniform mode of thinking and feeling by which all works of art are produced. Perhaps the nearest we can come to describing an artistic type is to recognize a sort of person who persistently seeks to produce objects and events which, through their sensory form, will interest other persons. But the artistic type is not necessarily creative or original. The visual artist likes to make forms appealing to the eye; the musician, to make forms appealing to the ear; the writer, to assemble words stimulating thought, feeling, or imagination. This is an obvious, external classification, and it includes numerous varieties of the creative process.

All these varieties are composite and diversified psychologically, in that they include the operation of many basic functions, such as perceiving, imagining, desiring, reasoning, experiencing emotions, and controlling the muscles of hands, voice, or limbs to manipulate some medium of expression. Now these same functions can be combined and used in any one of many different civilized activities; the same ones are used in art as in science, commerce, war, and sport. The most easily discernible difference is in the type of object produced, which, in the case of the artist, is primarily a stimulus to sense perception and imagination. None of the basic functions can ever be used in entire isolation. They can be co-ordinated into countless different configurations, some of which are momentary moods and attitudes, some, long-continued occupations, individual and collective.

Although they cannot be entirely isolated, the several functions do operate at different times with various degrees of emphasis or dominance. Sometimes we devote all our attention to seeing clearly, sometimes to hearing, sometimes to imagining, sometimes to reasoning, sometimes to directing the hand. The result in any case is a different

main type of compound behavior, in which many component functions co-operate in a certain general configuration. Such general
types recur in approximately similar form, and hence can be described by general psychology, although they admit of endless variation in detail.

Psychology is just beginning the task of describing these types of
mental activity in relation to various types of external situation.
When the task has progressed further, we may be able to use the
descriptions in analyzing roughly the activities of art production.
For example, it seems that every artist (like every other person) has
some moments in which visual observation dominates his behavior,
and other moments in which each of the other functions dominates.
In other words, while all, or nearly all, the basic functions operate
to some extent throughout the creative process, it has various phases
in which somewhat different configurations exist. These may occur
in any order. With the visual artist, there are phases of attentive observing—toward nature indiscriminately, toward some particular
object (such as a tree), or toward some work of art (such as a painting of a tree). There are phases when imaginative reconstruction
dominates, as when the artist, far away from any tree and perhaps
in a darkened room, tries to visualize his future painting of a tree.
There is a phase of attentive effort to manipulate the medium; for
example, to make oil paints look like the kind of scene he has in
mind. There is a phase of reflective thinking, criticism, and evaluation, when he stands off and tries to decide what is the matter with
his unfinished work, how it could be altered so as to improve upon it.

Such phases occur in any art or type of art to some extent. But
different arts and styles of art lead to stronger emphasis on different
ones. For example, if the art is representative and the style is realistic,
the artist will tend to emphasize comparison between actual trees and
his picture of one, so that the picture will resemble actual trees
and tend to arouse an image of one in the mind of an observer. If
the style is less realistic, he may devote more effort to imagining a
strange, fantastic tree. If interested in decorative design, he will
bend more effort toward organizing his imagery and the resultant
picture in terms of repeated lines and colors, and of unified patterns.
If making a statue of a god, he may have to compare his work with
authoritative conceptions of the nature of that god, and with his
own conception, rather than with any natural object. Some art has

a strongly intellectual content, conveying philosophic or scientific ideas in some concrete embodiment, as through symbolism and allegory. If the art is on the whole utilitarian and practical, as in the making of a chair or a house, the artist will probably try to imagine how his product will work under specified conditions: how strong, comfortable, and salable it will be. He may have to do more reflective, planful thinking along functional lines, and less observation of nature. But he will still use his eyes at times in observing other chairs or houses, and his imagination in visualizing the intended one. He may still include decorative design as one factor to be considered. In short, the artistic process tends to vary to some extent among different schools and periods of art, according to the aims and standards adopted, and according to the medium and technique used, though in all of them a few basic psychological functions and a few types of composite attitude or configuration tend to recur.

Again, the process will vary to some extent according to the individual personality and habits of the artist. Such differences, too, may be approached from a standpoint of component function and composite attitude. Some artists in any medium are more imaginative than others, spend more time and effort in trying to visualize an intended work of art before it is produced. Some do a great deal of close observation of nature or of other works of art; others, comparatively little. Some plan their works with conscious system and many preliminary sketches, thinking the whole thing out logically; others proceed more through spontaneous impulse and emotion. These likewise are differences that are not peculiar to artists but characteristic of human beings concerned with various matters. They provide the data for psychologists to use in distinguishing main types of personality and character. The artistic process, then, will vary according to the general type of personality to which the artist belongs.

Questions of *artistic ability* may also be approached from this standpoint. Each of the various functions and constituent processes, mentioned above as entering the production of art, may be considered in terms of ability, of the amount of power the artist shows in that particular direction. "Artistic ability" is a broad, inclusive name for the net result of all of them in joint operation. For example, some artists have unusually high sensory ability. This may again be differentiated, to the effect that some have unusually high powers of color discrimination; others, of space perception. Some artists have more ability to organize vivid, complex visual designs than others do. Some have more ability to imagine the strange and fantastic, whereas others can deal only with the realistic and actually observable. Some have more ability to plan intelligently; some, to criticize their own work objectively. Many can think more intelligently in a nonverbal situation, as in manipulating a concrete material, than in the verbal situations that our present intelligence tests tend to emphasize. Some artists can think intellectually, in terms of philosophic and scientific concepts, but find it hard to embody these in concrete images; some can do both. Some have more manual dexterity than others in the physical manipulation of the medium. (A heavy-handed technician like the early Cézanne, if strong in vision, imagination, and planning, may outrank many facile wielders of the brush.) Some artists have more determined will to create and be original than others do, more intense emotional devotion to certain types of form and subject. This, too, must be classed with the component abilities of creation—the ability to desire some kind of achievement strongly enough to impel the necessary work and sacrifice.

The total *character* of an artist and the net difference between one and another can perhaps eventually be analyzed in terms of such traits and abilities as these, with due attention to the relative strength and dominance of each, and to the peculiar configuration they assume at various stages of the artist's career. Discerning biographies of artists have approached such analysis, usually in nonpsychological terms, but with suggestive hints for scientific interpretation. Often our best clue to them is in the nature of the artist's works themselves. One picture has a strong element of color design, another of fantasy, another of philosophic implication. One utensil or building has elaborate surface pattern but little practical efficiency, another the opposite, and so on. We tend to assume, then, that the artist was comparatively strong in the modes of thought and execution necessary to the production of these traits in the finished product, and strongly motivated toward them as goals.

No doubt such an assumption is often warranted. But we must remember again that what appears in a given work of art is not necessarily the sole, original creation of the artist whose name it bears. He may have taken over and adapted certain elements from previous sources and have given them a new particular embodiment without having thought them out for himself or even thoroughly understood them. It is one thing to recognize the elements of form and cultural significance a work of art contains; another, to find out who really originated them. Often a religious or ethical concept is advanced by a thinker in that field, then translated by others into various art media. A picture may contain profound suggestions of sublime tragedy or poignant sentiment, even though the artist himself did not feel them very keenly. This is not necessarily a mark of insincerity in a derogatory sense. A playwright can express in words the emotional attitudes of hatred and jealousy and an actor can portray them without either of them feeling these attitudes strongly himself. Similarly, a painter can represent the facial expressions and gestures that tend to stimulate an emotion in others, without feeling it himself. He can express and represent madness, and yet be quite sane.

For such reasons it is necessary, in tracing the mental processes and abilities that led up to a work of art, to look behind the finished product. We may discover letters and comments of the artist or opinions of contemporaries, each of which is to be taken with a grain of salt, though contributing its bit to the mass of evidence.

In another respect, too, works of art are inadequate clues to the psychology of artists. It is hard to infer from the finished product just what steps were involved in its conception and execution. To what extent was it systematically planned? Or was it done on the spur of the moment? The final product may seem extremely casual, impulsive, free, and irregular, as in typical romantic art; and yet every detail may have been meticulously calculated for those effects. Here it is useful to study, if we can, the preliminary notes and sketches, in chronological order. Living artists are easier to study in this respect and deserve more attention from psychologists. For the training of young artists, information on these settings and motives of art production would be of great value.

Psychological research has much to do in studying the specific components of art ability, through comparison of individual cases and through measurement when possible. Some of these component abilities are much more easily measured than others. For example, the simpler kinds of sensory discrimination have been accurately measured. The ability to perceive complex visual forms, such as those of art, has been less explored, but it is not incapable of measurement. The ability to imagine vividly has not been carefully studied, except for the special variety known as "eidetic imagery." The ability to imagine complex forms, or unusual, original forms, has not received much attention. The Rorschach and other ink-blot tests supply a promising approach to certain types of imaginative ability, including the difference between stereotyped and unusual tendencies, but so far little has been done to distinguish between creative and pathological varieties of unusual response. Many manual skills can be accurately measured, but those involved in artistic technique have not been systematically approached. The emotional and the conative or motivational elements in art ability seem least accessible to experimental study and measurement.

In general, it would seem desirable to do more in the way of preliminary analysis of the field, of distinguishing tentatively the many different types of ability involved in art, before launching forth on ambitious programs of detailed measurement that may turn out to miss essential factors. Such fundamental facts as the compound nature of art ability and the general way in which component abilities are present in varying degrees in various individuals have not yet been clearly recognized. (It must be remembered that even the functions and abilities that we here designate as "component" or "basic," because of their recurrence in various configurations, are themselves compound, joint operations of many sets of nerves and muscles. There are no purely elementary functions, but there are degrees of complexity.)

Let us return to the problem again from the point of view of education. It was mentioned that art education has an unusual opportunity to deal directly and constructively with a number of important factors in the development of personality. In terms of ability, this means that it can try to foster, harmonize, and direct into socially desirable channels the various special abilities involved in art production. The objectives and methods of art education on each age level should be examined and developed from this point of view: how so to select and organize the specific materials and activities of art as to develop *all* the important component abilities to some extent. At present, the art course tends to exercise only a few of them directly, and even that is done without much psychological insight. College courses tend to overstress intellectual study and verbal memory; art academies, to overstress manual technique. All along the line, for both general education and professional training, more effort should be made to deal with those other mental and emotional factors the development of which is necessary for maximal creative and appreciative ability.

How can they best be dealt with? We do not know, but we can at least experiment consciously and systematically, through combining the approach of the psychologist with those of the scholar and the technician in art. Certainly, educational methods should be more carefully adapted to the requirements of different types of individual personality. To recognize these types is mainly a psychological problem. We cannot say in general how much intellectual training and information is conducive to creative originality. But what little we know at present about artists would indicate that some can profit by a great deal more intellectual training than others can; that there are intellectual, rational, planful types who can develop in this way without losing the spark of creativeness, whereas for others much intellectual study and rational analysis are uncongenial and even detrimental. We do not know how much discipline and definite guidance is good for the future artist; but, here again, certain types probably need more than others. Neither extreme free expressionism nor extreme academic discipline can be accepted for all cases; the two must be combined in varying degrees for various types of student.

It would be highly desirable in certain ways if we could recognize potential creative ability in art and other fields at an early stage of development. Democracy needs leaders, and mass education needs means of singling out gifted children for special opportunities. Leaders may arise from any racial, religious, or geographic group, and from any economic level. Special opportunities should be awarded without regard to these factors, though in ways to compensate for the disadvantages of unfavorable environment. At the same time, one may tremble at the thought of what would have happened to some geniuses of the past, had they been exposed too early to the spotlight of flattering attention or to the well-meaning solicitude of educational faddists.

We are still far from knowing the best way to treat superior children after we discover them: how much to segregate them; how much praise, freedom, and special training to give them. For the present, it is well to be cautious about premature devices for the selection and special nurture of children whom we believe to be superior in art. If better opportunities in art are provided for all children who desire them, the gifted may perhaps be counted on to make themselves known through better use of these common opportunities. At present, there is no brief, artificial test that can do more than hint at possible superiority. There is no set of measurable or easily recognizable characteristics in children's art that will guarantee later creative ability. Any that are singled out by present research must remain hypothetical until verified by adult achievement in later years. The judgment of art teachers is still mainly personal and subjective, with vaguely defined and conflicting standards. Of all available indices of potential creative ability, there is perhaps none more significant than *interest:* not mild or temporary interest, but the intense, persistent desire for art materials and activities that impels some students year after year to effort and sacrifice for the sake of working with them. If we can provide such students with a fair amount of opportunity and encouragement, we shall be reasonably sure of not failing in our first duty to the potential creators.

5. *Technical training in art*

The problem of technical training requires careful consideration in formulating a policy for art education. There is not only the general question of how much technical training should be required (as over against free expression), but also the question of what kinds to require.

Older students need and demand more technique, become dissatisfied with mere play, and want to know how to do a thing well (as judged by contemporary adult standards) if at all. They become more self-critical, impatient of awkward groping and mere self-expression; they delight in learning a technique for its own sake, as an interesting game. Almost any definite formula for drawing a figure or fastening two pieces of material together pleases them more than spontaneous experiment. To learn how to do or to make something difficult gives them an added sense of power and self-respect through control over environment. It helps them forget their anxieties and extrovert their attention. Technical training exercises limbs and muscles and is thus of use in assisting a balanced development of the whole individual. For such reasons, some amount of technical training in art processes is valuable as a part of general education, even for students who will never use it professionally. It is coming to be recognized as a desirable part of all liberal education, even on the college level. For the prospective artist, and as part of a vocational course in high school, art academy, or professional institute, it is paramount in importance.

But what is technique? It is skill in executing the details necessary for expert production or performance. It is learned ability, as contrasted with innate; it involves ability to profit by accumulated cultural experience. The technique necessary to paint a picture is not restricted to the hand alone. The hand cannot be separated from the eye and brain. Broadly considered, the technique of creating a picture includes skilled use of all the abilities involved in the process. It includes skilled vision, skilled imagination, skilled planning, criticism, and concentration of energies. As we have seen, the fault of most academic training in art has been that it neglects most of the elements necessary for a full technique. It fails even to realize that there is such a thing as the technique of artistic perceiving and imagining. It leads students too directly and constantly to the final stages of execution and expression, with too little attention to the preliminary phases of creative thinking.

For some purposes, however, it is useful to distinguish between these broader mental techniques and the specific kind of skill concerned more directly with the manipulation of a medium. This skill does focus ordinarily on muscular control through the hands or other parts of the body (perhaps the whole body, as in dancing or acting). It focuses on the actual putting on of paint or cutting of marble, on playing the piano or writing one word after another, as distinct from working out the thoughts and aims that should guide any such process. Even here, the mental and manual are intimately bound together, at least for the creative artist. Perhaps this is the main distinction between the artist and the mere artisan, the uncreative worker, however skilled the latter may be in a mechanical way. In the former, direction of the hands and outer medium is controlled by an inner, self-developed aim and vision, whereas the factory machine operator can at times almost let his hands work by themselves, without conscious control; the hack worker does what he is told to do and does not have to think out ends and means.

Technique for the artist involves not only trained nerve and muscle co-ordination, but also knowledge of the medium, its properties and modes of operation. He must know how oils or water colors will spread and mix; how jade will break if not properly cut; what chemicals to apply before firing to produce a red or a blue glaze. Part of his technique consists in remembering accumulated knowledge, such as that of science; and part in having it organized for quick, adaptive use in overt action. Part of his technique consists in a developed habit of intelligent thinking, of adapting means to ends. He must be able to think out what he wants to do and apply the means for doing it. Such ability is especially evident in the industrial arts, where it must deal with the functional effectiveness of utensils, but it applies to the "fine arts" as well.

To enrich his background stock of potential means, it is good experience for the student to do much extensive manipulation of materials and instruments in his art, even without any specific aim at the time; merely to "get the feel" of them and learn what they will do or not do if treated in various ways. Ideas for works of art often arise from such direct experience of the medium and its properties.

As a creative artist, he will not be restricted to seeking the same ends that other artists have sought or that he learned in school. He will formulate other goals, and consequently have to alter the methods he has learned. If his aim is relatively traditional, the old technical methods may be flexible enough to cover them. But the more original the artist, the more he has to devise new techniques as he goes along, or at least substantially revise and extend the old ones. If instruction is to stimulate creativeness, it should inculcate this attitude toward past and present techniques, as suggestions and starting points, not as final laws. Old materials have still unrealized possibilities. Through the acceleration of scientific technology, new materials and potential techniques are arising faster than the artists can effectively use them. Each year new machine processes, plastic materials, metals, dyes, colored lights, and so on are laid in endless profusion on the artist's lap. To the more adaptive artist, they suggest new types of art form. He goes ahead to learn their properties, and usually employs them at first in making types of form very much like the old ones; only later does the new medium stimulate more radical originations. This was the case, for example, with the motion picture, most of the early productions of which imitated stage plays and failed to utilize the peculiar advantages of the cinema for telling a story. Students who acquire one type of technique in any art too fixedly and unimaginatively are likely to be left far behind in today's competitive race. While applied science now provides new resources for the artist without his asking, there is no reason why artists should not be more active in asking science for desired assistance, as by envisaging new desirable art forms and letting science provide the means to actualize them.

Teachers sometimes speak of "learning the fundamentals" in an art, and doing one's experimenting or creative work later on. The "fundamentals" are certain technical skills, believed to be widely applicable. Academic art teachers have so regarded drawing from Greek and Roman casts, perspective, and life drawing, with emphasis on the correct representation of anatomy. These have been considered necessary preliminaries, not only for painting and sculpture, but even for architecture and the decorative arts. There is much to be said for this practice, and many highly original artists endorse it, but it has some debatable features.

Certainly, these studies and related skills are not fundamental in the sense that all modern styles of art directly involve them. Much modern art deliberately avoids or distorts naturalistic anatomy, perspective, and the classical type of light-and-shade modeling, and these are not involved in most oriental, medieval, archaic, and primitive styles. The idea that they are fundamental is in part a heritage from the time when little was known of any style of art other than the Greco-Roman and Renaissance. Today, one could argue that a quite different set of skills and disciplines is necessary if one desires to paint in the Chinese or Persian way or to model in the Egyptian or Cubist way. The Greek and Renaissance styles are still fundamental to our culture to a much greater degree than these others are, but less exclusively so in these cosmopolitan times. Since we have learned to respect other great styles, we are less confident that the traditional European style is the right one or fundamental to art in any absolute sense. It is becoming more and more advantageous for the modern artist in any medium to acquaint himself with exotic and primitive styles of art, both visually and, if possible, through some experience with their techniques. They are providing our day with a wealth of rich materials for the artistic melting pot, to be transformed into new modern styles. Leaders in the Western arts have long been making use of them with profitable results. Yet our art schools, on the whole, have yet to begin giving serious instruction in them, even from the standpoint of visual appreciation. In this respect, college and museum instruction, stressing art history, is farther advanced. Vocational courses for prospective artists must soon follow their lead toward greater cosmopolitanism, at least to the extent of offering advanced students an opportunity to learn something of the aesthetic principles and technical practices of exotic, archaic, and primitive arts.

Furthermore, it is a mistake to assume that students can acquire "thorough grounding" in a traditional European technique and then easily change over to something very different later on. Intensive drill in any particular technique necessarily involves a tendency to acquire certain habits of thinking, imagining, and creating associated with that technique. Along with manual skill and knowledge of a medium, the student may acquire a belief that there are certain right ways of using that skill and medium. He may acquire traditional aesthetic ideals, standards, and conventions of form along with the traditional technique, since the latter is never presented apart from them. If so, he can still free himself to some extent from them later on, perhaps through a rather violent reaction and exceptionally vigorous powers of original thinking. In music, a student who spends years in practicing Bach and Beethoven, Clementi and Czerny, is likely to acquire not only pianistic technique, but also a tendency to approach musical composition in the spirit of classical harmony and counterpoint. In visual art, a student who learns the technique of drawing through years of drawing in the style of Raphael will tend himself to see and imagine also in the style of Raphael. Only the more independent will avoid doing so. Often neither the teacher nor the student realizes that a particular style is being learned. He is so accustomed to seeing both art and nature from the standpoint of that style that it seems to him to be merely the "true" or "correct" way to represent nature, and hence as the necessary fundamental for any kind of art. The best cure for such narrowness is further observation of the many past and present styles of art other than those to which one has become accustomed.

At the same time, there are definite values in intensive, traditional training, whatever style of art one desires to produce later on. We have noted that there are values in following out clearly and consistently one particular approach to art at a time, to avoid the confusion and vagueness of too much freedom and cosmopolitanism. (Which approach is chosen first is perhaps not essential; but since the Greek is closer to us than the Chinese or Gothic, it is doubtless the one to emphasize.) One of these values is that of mental clarity and equilibrium—a matter of letting the student organize himself one stage at a time and absorb the vast cultural heritage part by part rather than overwhelming him at the start by too many complex influences and alternatives at once. Another value is that of acquiring systematic habits of continuous work.

This brings us to the question of transfer of training. Drawing skill acquired in making Raphaelesque pictures is not easily transferred to the making of Post-impressionist pictures like those of Matisse, based on the Persian style. But there is no doubt that some of that skill can be transferred; that the development of the skill is not inconsistent with some flexibility and adaptiveness. One at least knows how to handle a pencil or charcoal and approach the problem of dividing up a picture-space into areas. It is for such reasons as these that very radical artists often urge young students to begin with traditional training. "But," they sometimes add, "you don't need very much of it; you can learn all that's necessary in a short time and then go on for yourself." In other words, what is really fundamental for all drawing, transferable to any style of drawing and universal in applicability, is comparatively little and easily understood, though it may require long practice for proficiency in execution. Much of the work that art schools require as necessary grounding is really dispensable, since it consists in learning some particular style of art that the student may not want to use later on.

Where the exact truth lies in this issue is debatable. But it suggests an approach to the problem of technical training—that of analyzing the work to be required into different categories, from the standpoint of ends and means. The elements of training that can be shown to be most fundamental, in the sense that they promise to be most constantly and urgently required in any sort of art work later on, should be distinguished as clearly as possible from the elements that will be needed only by those who decide to practice a particular type of art. The three R's of the elementary school are certainly fundamental to general education, whereas the calculus and Egyptian hieroglyphics are not. Skill in drawing with pencil on paper is more widely useful for more persons in later life than is skill in arranging mosaics. Again, with any particular medium, such as oil paints, there are certain fundamental properties and procedures that artists in almost any style will find useful. How to prepare the canvas, to mix pigment with oil and lay it on so the colors will not run or change in unintended ways, to protect the surface with varnish without affecting the colors—these are comparatively fundamental and often rather quickly explained. Where an art makes much use of applied science, as do ceramics, industrial design, and architecture, there is more to be learned about complex properties and procedures. On the other hand, how to apply oil paints in the Impressionist, broken-color style is not fundamental to the art of painting. It is useful chiefly to those who wish to paint Impressionist pictures.

A technical course should include some fundamentals for all students, mostly at the beginning; and also a choice of several optional skills from which a student may select what he expects to need. Unfortunately, it is hard to get artists or art teachers to agree upon what is fundamental and what is dispensable. Each tends to regard his own pet practices and tastes as fundamental to all good art. They may agree that pencil-drawing is more fundamental than mosaic or enameling. But within a subject, such as "life drawing," "perspective," or "composition," what part of the work is really useful for any style of art, and what part is merely an expression of the teacher's own tastes? In figure drawing, such injunctions as "bring out the main masses" or "get the true proportions" are advanced as necessary laws, regardless of the fact that many leading artists, past and present, choose to draw the figures otherwise. Aesthetic standards are still so controversial, and art teachers mix them so unconsciously and dogmatically with technique, that we are a long way from agreeing upon technical fundamentals.

The applied sciences are much clearer in this respect and could well be emulated by art instruction. In the medical school, for example, students learn about "materia medica," the properties of various drugs. But they are not told: "Always prescribe strychnine." They are told: "If the condition is thus, and you wish to produce a certain result, strychnine is a way to produce it." This is technique, intelligently thought out in terms of means and ends. Art educators also must learn to think out their technical materials and methods in terms of general and specific ends. Some ends are very general and unquestioned, such as manual dexterity and (let us add) the various types of mental ability that have been noted. Some are optional, but widely useful because of frequent demand later on. The ability to draw active figures with realistic anatomy and perspective, for example, belongs in this intermediate category. Some are transitory fads or individual whims, such as a preference for dark and subdued, or bright, contrasting color combinations; for the geometric lines of Cubism or the wavy lines of *art nouveau*. The student can profit by studying and practicing many of these optional methods. But he should be led to regard them as useful means to certain types of artistic effect, not as basic rules. Thus he may be helped to acquire a really flexible technique along with intelligent habits of planning his work and with adaptability in contriving effective means to new ends.

AESTHETIC ABILITY: POWERS OF ART APPRECIATION AND EVALUATION*

1. *Educational aspects of art appreciation*

The appreciation of art is commonly contrasted with its creation. To use the language of economics, the artist, or creator, is the producer of art; the appreciator is its consumer, or user. "Appreciation" implies also that he is a discriminating consumer, who knows and enjoys real values in this type of commodity or service.[1] Since there are many more consumers of art than artists, educators are coming to stress art appreciation, especially as a part of general education. It is not necessarily divorced from the technical practice of art, however. Indeed, some amount of the latter is widely regarded as contributing to appreciation; and the artist is supposed to be able to appreciate aesthetic values, at least in his own field. But more attention is being given to the artistic needs of the layman, and to the value that art may have for his cultural background and leisure enjoyment.

The appreciation of art is also contrasted educationally with the history of art. College courses in art history try to stress objective facts: the sequence of major periods, styles, and outstanding examples of them; the lives, dates, and characteristics of leading artists, and the influences of one upon another. The scholarly approach to art tries to emulate science in excluding the writer's or teacher's personal preferences. No doubt there are evaluative assumptions even in selecting certain works and artists for emphasis and omitting others. But at least the scholar abstains from the sentimental rhapso-

---

* Published in *Art in American Life and Education* (1941), pp. 323-348.

[1] "To appreciate," says Webster, is "5. To be critically and emotionally sensitive to the esthetic values of; as, to *appreciate* Shelley's lyrics or a Beethoven sonata; to admire critically the artistic or technical excellence of; as, to *appreciate* a violinist's fingering." *Appreciation* is "1. . . . full recognition of worth; recognition through the senses, esp. with delicacy of perception . . . 5. Sensitive awareness or perception of worth or value, esp. esthetic value, as, his fine *appreciation* of painting." In education, it is defined as "6. The study of esthetic values (as distinguished from historical values), as in music, art, or literature."

dizing about beauty that often constitutes the bulk of popular lectures on "art appreciation." Scholarly professors of art history, indeed, incline to the view that appreciation cannot be taught any more than creative originality can be taught. The innately sensitive student of art will, they say, develop good taste as a personal characteristic, along with good manners and morals.

For children, however, and in popular lectures and introductory courses for adults, a less scholarly approach is considered legitimate. Here, too, the tendency has been away from mere emotional praise and toward pointing out why certain works of art are considered important. This is usually done through showing how they exemplify accepted standards of value or "art principles," such as rhythm, balance, and proportion. Progressive schools attempt to get children to express their own preferences in art and to discuss the reasons for them. All such courses in appreciation tend to include some amount of historical fact, even though not necessarily in chronological order. At least, an objective of such courses is to try to familiarize the student with a few main facts about artists and historic styles, so that he can recognize examples when he sees them. In short, the teaching of art appreciation is usually a rather superficial, unsystematic mixture of observation, history, and aesthetic theory.

How can the results of such instruction be graded, and how can any differences in "power of appreciation" among individuals be recognized or measured? It is fairly easy, of course, to measure knowledge of historic facts and ability to recognize artists' works. One can grade as literary compositions the essays students write about art and why they like or dislike it. But these obviously do not deal directly and fully with appreciative ability.

If the teacher is sure he knows what works of art are best, what the student ought to like, and why, it is also fairly easy to grade on this basis. But most teachers and art critics are a good deal less dogmatic about such matters than they used to be. Not only are aesthetic standards and the relative importance of artists in dispute, but it is also coming to be felt that there is no reason why children should always like the same kinds of art that adults do. Even for adults, some individuality in taste, some divergence from current authority, is recognized as valuable in a democratic society. Nevertheless, several alleged tests of art ability have been advanced and widely used that undertake to measure such ability on a basis of conformity to an established norm of taste. The psychologists who make these pseudo-scientific "tests" do not, as a rule, presume to decide what types of art are best, but they assume that somebody knows. Hence they proceed to ascertain the preferences of a number of established artists, teachers, and critics. Statistically treated, these will constitute a norm for judging other people as "high" or "low" in powers of appreciation, according as they agree or disagree with it. Another device is to alter or "spoil" certain works of art, and ask the subject whether he likes the spoiled or the original version better. This assumes, of course, that the altered version is really worse, for all persons at all times. That is again a debatable assumption, particularly because it still involves the old absolutistic attitude toward art value, which conflicts with modern trends in both aesthetics and education.

It is not at all necessary that we approach the question of appreciative ability on a basis of *what* people like in art, or even that we expect them to like the same things at all times. Certainly it is not necessary to assume they all should like the same thing, regardless of their differences in age and personality. *What* they like in art is perhaps less important on the whole than *why* they like it and *how* they come to form their judgments of value. The single issue of preference, of whether one likes picture A better than picture B, is far from being the whole of art appreciation. It is more important psychologically and educationally to find out what kind of total experience the individual is deriving from his contact with art, and what kind of subsequent experience and behavior it may lead him to. Psychologically, we should try to find out more about the nature and varieties of such aesthetic experience, under different conditions and for different types of individuals. This will disclose various types of specific ability, co-operating to make up the composite ability we roughly designate as "power of appreciation." Educationally, we should then try to find out how these can best be developed, along with other factors in the growing personality.

2. *Appreciative ability in relation to creative ability*

To some extent, the abilities involved in appreciation are the same as those involved in art creation or in any other complex psychophysical activity. Visual ability in general enters into many activities, and so does imaginative ability. This is another way of saying that persons who are capable at one activity are usually capable at many others also. A superior artist is likely to have superior potential ability in appreciation, whether or not he has tried to train it directly. In fact, few persons ever try directly to develop powers of art appreciation; they do so incidentally, if at all, in the course of other work.

One might infer that appreciative ability is nothing more than a partial approach to creative ability. Some theorists have declared that appreciation should strive to be as nearly as possible a reproduction of the artist's experience in creating the work of art. But these conclusions are oversimplified and misleading. The processes and powers of appreciation overlap those of creation to a large extent, but are not identical, and there is no reason why one should necessarily be a mere imperfect repetition of the other.

If appreciation is, and should be, merely a partial approach to artistic experience, then the best training for appreciation is perhaps a course in artistic technique, followed by practical experience in art production. Artists sometimes scoff at the idea of anyone who is not an artist being able to understand art as well as they do. "How can he know what it's all about," they say, "until he's gone through the work of doing it?" There are educators who sympathize with this attitude, and urge "participation in art activities" as the only road to appreciation. It is fashionable to quote the Deweyan maxim of learning by doing, with the inference that one can never learn to understand any human activity or its products without physically engaging in it. Must one then try to dabble in all the occupations and techniques whose products interest one or else give up the hope of understanding them? The idea is absurd and is never consistently followed out. We do not need to repeat the bee's experience to enjoy its honey, or the glassblower's experience to enjoy the glass.

The appreciator's experience lacks some elements present in creation, but it may develop others even beyond the point achieved by the creator. In looking at a child's drawing, for example, the teacher, by reason of his broader experience of life and art, can sometimes understand and appreciate certain qualities in it more fully than the child does. When we look at primitive or ancient art, we no doubt miss certain meanings and functions that have passed away with the early artist, but we can also appreciate its importance in the light of cultural history.

Undoubtedly, to have practiced an art is a help to appreciation in certain ways. One has associations of the feel of the medium. One knows from experience the difficulty of achieving certain effects, and so can admire their successful achievement. Children, especially, like to be doing things with their hands and grow impatient if asked to concentrate long on looking or listening and thinking quietly about what they observe. Wide experimentation in productive techniques is valuable in the early stages of general education. To specialize intensively on appreciation and criticism is a task for mature minds. But it is nonetheless possible and worth while. No one can go far in technical production along many lines. He may choose to practice one or two, but he must study the others from outside if at all.

It is extremely doubtful whether technical producers are as a rule the best appreciators or judges in their own fields. As to their own products, they are more than likely to be biased; also to the products of competing artists. The judicious outsider can achieve more perspective for a fair evaluation. Artists of the past were sometimes impelled by motives and emotions that have little relevance to us; they portrayed the kings they admired, the enemies they hated, the gods they worshiped. Is it necessary for us to reproduce and share these feelings or can we appreciate the lasting importance of the work of such artists in some respects more clearly by the fact that we do not share their purposes and attitudes?

In certain respects, it is even a disadvantage in appreciation to be much involved in technical problems. One is likely to regard the products so much from a standpoint of how they were made as to neglect other important aspects.

Perceiving a complex art form clearly and fully in all its subtle details and relations of design and meaning is a task in itself requiring training and experience. The development of such ability is one of the essential phases in the training of appreciation. Such ability is usually neglected in the technical training of artists; it is pushed aside by the more practical question of how to get results through an external medium. Trained appreciation involves techniques of its own, which are not dependent on skill in manipulating a tangible material. They are none the less important because perceptual and mental rather than manual.

As to the ideal of reproducing the artist's experience when we appreciate, it is easy to overestimate the quality of that experience. It was pointed out in the chapter on creative ability that a great deal of what the artist apparently "creates"—that is, puts down on canvas or otherwise embodies in a work of art—is really not his own creations. It is not necessary for the artist to understand or appreciate him, of the whole cultural tradition upon which his work is based. The element of real originality in all cases—even in the greatest artists of the past—is relatively slight by comparison. In the work of minor artists, practically everything can be traced to prior sources that the present "creator" has merely repeated with trivial alterations. It is not necessary for the artist to understand or appreciate fully the forms and ideas he thus repeats and adapts. If he is essentially an imitative mind, like most of the professional artists in any generation, the process will be rather superficial and mechanical. With some manual and technical skill, one can imitate or combine elements from a few great works of the past, and still understand or appreciate them little more than a camera would. To reproduce such a process of "creation" is a low ideal for the appreciator. Rather, he should seek to understand the full richness of the cultural heritage that enters consciously or unconsciously into each work of art, to distinguish also those elements of real originality that each artist has achieved, and to estimate them at their proper worth in the light of carefully thought-out standards. So regarded, appreciation can become to some extent creative in its own way; that is, it can involve an active, interpretive reorganization by each appreciator of the works of art he experiences, from the standpoint of his own mental background and ability.

From that stage, some appreciators will go on to a more fully creative response in the medium of verbal expression. The penetrating critic or teacher of art appreciation may be more genuinely creative than many artists if he makes an original contribution to social understanding. Such activity, however, passes beyond the limits of appreciation in a strict sense. Appreciation has values in its own right, even if it does not go so far. Indeed, extreme readiness to verbalize on one's reactions to art sometimes goes with shallowness and ostentation and is by no means a sign of profound inward experience.

3. The process of appreciation; the aesthetic and artistic attitudes

"Appreciation" is now used in a broad sense, as we have seen, which contrasts it with "creation" or "production." It refers to the whole process of responding aesthetically to art, nature, or other objects. "Aesthetic experience" is another term that vaguely covers about the same thing. Just what it means to respond in this way is a problem for investigation, but in common discourse certain general distinctions are recognized. Whereas the creative, or artistic, attitude emphasizes a disposition to change or reorganize outward things into a new form, to manipulate some objective medium of construction or expression, the aesthetic attitude minimizes this and stresses sense perception more or less for its own sake; that is, for the immediate interest of the process and of the external object on which it is focused. The artistic attitude is to a greater extent practical and purposeful, in that it involves an effort to adapt means to ends in achieving a future goal, the completed work of art. In aesthetic appreciation, the practical element tends to diminish or disappear, in so far as the individual's whole attention is fixed on the present object and the fantasies it suggests, not divided between these and some external aim to be striven for.

Of course, there are countless different ways of responding to art; some combine the aesthetic with the practical, as in the case of a collector who seeks to acquire a picture; some combine it with intellectual investigation, as in the case of an art historian or aesthetician who studies a picture. Appreciation can be combined with practical use, as when one enjoys the appearance of a cup, a chair, or a house while using it. It may involve verbal expression, as in speaking or writing an "appreciation" of some work of art, an explicit statement of one's own feelings and opinions toward it. But even this outward manifestation does not always occur. Appreciation can be almost wholly a matter of quiet contemplation, of direct sense perception along with various inward mental and emotional processes aroused by perception. Psychologists now tend to overlook this distinctively aesthetic type of response at this time when it is fashionable to lay heavy stress upon the active and purposeful aspects of behavior. The aesthetic type is no less real and important, though harder for behavioristic psychologists to deal with and often ignored in consequence.

The sense of relaxation and recreation that often comes from enjoying art is intimately bound up with the temporary escape it can afford from the ordinary tension of solving problems and achieving ends. Competitive struggles and anxieties force people as a rule to neglect present enjoyments in order to pursue elusive future goals. Those experiences are aesthetic when attention and interest are focused more completely on a present source of enjoyment, on intrinsic rather than instrumental values. Such a source need not be art; it can be nature or any kind of human product or activity. But art affords especially effective stimuli to the aesthetic attitude. One's attention does not need to be wholly on an object physically present; it can be on a fantasy suggested by the work of art, as in reading a story. The visible letters induce this fantasy, and the reader, if his attitude is aesthetic, simply contemplates this fantasy with no thought of doing anything in particular about it. The aesthetic attitude is in a sense compliant—not that one necessarily approves entirely of the work of art—but in the sense that one is willing to perceive and imagine more or less in accordance with its directions.

We must not say that aesthetic experience is wholly passive, however. One tends to be less active with the limbs and large muscles than when producing art or engaging in other practical activities, but one's sense organs and related nerve processes are active. To observe such an art as architecture requires a good deal of bodily movement, but in looking at a picture there may be no outwardly noticeable movement except that of the eyes.

4. Functions involved in appreciation

Although the word "aesthetic" means primarily a perceptual response, it cannot be restricted to perception without stretching that concept unduly. The aesthetic response is set off by visual or auditory perception, which itself includes some recognition of meanings, some comparison with past experience to interpret the causal, spatio-temporal, and qualitative data presented. It may go on to include extensive fantasy-building in response to the outer stimuli, as in seeing a picture of a battle or reading about one. In reading literature, the element of direct sense perception is restricted to interpreting letters and punctuation marks, and the major part of the response consists in organizing the images and concepts they suggest into systematic forms, such as narratives, descriptions, and conversations.

Psychologists once used the term "apperception" to denote a process in which the organizing of sense data in relation to previous experience is especially extensive and systematic. This term is still useful in describing responses to art and to complex verbal forms, whether artistic or not. All perception contains some amount of this, but in describing aesthetic experience it is especially important to notice the extent and order with which inner forms are built up more or less in compliance with the cues suggested by the outer form, the seen or heard work of art. Whereas the artist or the dreamer builds fantasies with comparative freedom (never complete, for he is impelled by inner forces), the person enjoying a story or a story-picture imagines more or less as he is directed. He may indeed launch forth upon independent reveries, but in that case he is no longer directly experiencing the work of art. His attitude is no longer aesthetic.

The apperception of art often involves some inference and reasoning, as in reading a detective story. In some types of art, such as religious symbolism, apperception involves understanding abstract ideas and theoretical relations. Even the understanding of a simple story-picture may require inference as to what is happening and why. Often the inference made is consciously false and illusory. In looking at a painted landscape, one tries to perceive the streaks of paint as trees, rocks, and clouds. Some types of art, those which depend more on the design and decorative qualities of lines and colors or of sounds, have correspondingly less tendency to direct the imagination or the reasoning of the beholder.

The aesthetic response usually contains an affective element also, which may vary in intensity from mild feeling tone to strong excitement. All the emotions of ordinary life may be stimulated by art and directed upon the art work itself or upon the images it suggests. All types of volitional or conative attitude can be aroused by art as a part of the total aesthetic response; for example, welcoming or rejecting; desire or aversion; impulses to possess, escape, or destroy. Aesthetic experience is not always enjoyable; it may involve displeasure at ugliness or evil as well as pleasure at their opposites. Whereas, in other attitudes, such emotions and volitions tend to issue in overt action, in the aesthetic they may or may not do so. Most often they are recognized by the individual as having no direct reference to the art work itself as a concrete object, but only to the images it suggests. Unlike the child or primitive, the civilized adult can usually inhibit with ease any impulse he may feel to caress or assault a portrait. He knows when there would be no possible, satisfactory outlet in present overt action. Hence the emotional and conative elements in his response may remain internal and rudimentary as far as action is concerned, though capable at the same time of great intensity and elaborate reference to systems of mental images and concepts. Of course, people often do respond to art with bodily action, immediate or delayed. Children and primitives commonly do so, and civilized adults do occasionally, as in dancing. Art can stimulate any kind of behavior. To respond with little or no immediate outward action is doubtless an artificial, culturally determined trait of civilized people. Even among these, some persons inhibit expressions of feeling more than others do.

Whether they issue in overt action and expression or not, the affective attitudes aroused by art include liking and disliking. These may be directed at something suggested by the work of art or at the work of art itself, in the latter case as a feeling that it is beautiful or ugly, good or bad. To call it "beautiful" is a projection of pleasant, admiring responses, affective and perceptual, on the object. One attributes these responses to their supposed cause, as if they were intrinsic qualities of the object. Unless one is theoretically sophisticated, one does not realize that the pleasant or unpleasant nature of the response is conditioned not only by the nature of the work of art, but also by one's own personality, one's previously acquired tastes or habits of liking and disliking. "Preference" occurs when two or more objects are presented for choice or comparison.

"Evaluation," in the sense of an explicit judgment of value based on general standards, is a kind of appreciation that requires intellectual development in addition to likes and dislikes. It may even be performed in a purely intellectual, deductive manner when the individual feels no definite emotional attitude one way or the other. This is often the case with sophisticated connoisseurs who evaluate by rule and principle rather than by spontaneous feeling and impulse.

Aesthetic appreciation thus involves a number of basic functions and attitudes that are much the same as those entering into the creation of art or into any other complex civilized activity. The difference between one such activity and another is a matter of configuration, of the relative emphasis or dominance of various component functions and their mode of co-operation in the whole process.

5. Varieties of aesthetic response and experience

So widespread an activity as art appreciation can be described only in a very broad and flexible way, since it varies greatly in different cases. Each aesthetic response is a joint product of many variables interacting at the time, including (a) the nature of the work of art or other stimulus; (b) the nature of the respondent or percipient, including stable and temporary traits; (c) the attendant circumstances.

The response tends to vary, as we have seen, in relation to the type of art that acts as stimulus; for example, music stimulates auditory perception primarily, while painting stimulates visual perception. Abstract textile design also emphasizes visual perception, but with comparatively little definite stimulus to imagination. Other forms, such as symbolic art and literature, offer explicit and detailed direction to imagination and reasoning. Again, some tend to suggest images and feelings of sadness and pity, as in portrayals of suffering; others, of joy or anger.

In addition, the nature of the response tends to vary in accordance with the type of individual who is responding at the time. Here we must have in mind not only the observer's general character, education, special training, and habits of preference, but also his mood and interest of the moment, eager and favorable or bored and indifferent. Further, the same person will respond to the same work of art in very different ways at different times, depending upon who else is present, whether the occasion is one of gravity or amusement, work or play, and so on. The emotion (if any) that he will feel *toward* the work of art may not be the same as the one the work of art expresses or the artist intended to arouse. For example, the artist may intend to arouse indignation in us through representing joy on the face of a villain; yet, as a result of our taste or present mood, we may be moved only to ridicule or boredom.

As an approach to understanding the nature of appreciation, we have been considering how the basic psychophysical functions co-operate in different configurations at different times. Appreciation and aesthetic experience, we have seen, refer to a certain general type of configuration, as yet dimly understood, and hard to define because of its inwardness and variability. In following this approach, we must be careful not to conceive of the basic functions as remaining individually the same in all configurations or complex processes. That would be to take an antiquated, atomistic view of their nature. True, there is such a function as visual perception that retains a few essential characteristics in all configurations, but in other respects visual perception or any other function is very different according to the total attitude and process within which it operates. It is not an independent, clearly delimited nerve system or process in itself, but is always bound up with others. Perception not only co-operates with memory, affect, and reasoning, but always contains some element of these other functions as well. In some types of total behavior, perception is more strongly visual than in others; in some more strongly affective; in some more strongly conceptual and inferential.

Each function differs somewhat, according as it enters into the aesthetic or some other type of attitude. We have seen that, in the aesthetic response to art, volition and emotion do not tend, as ordinarily, to issue in immediate overt action, but to be felt as inward likes or dislikes, pleasant or unpleasant-feeling tones that may or may not have even the slight outlet of facial or verbal expression. Perception likewise differs. In a practical, purposeful enterprise like hunting or commerce, it tends to be restricted and directed by the requirements of the end in view. Practical perception thus tends to be rather rigidly selective, ignoring features that are irrelevant to the present undertaking, and to stress the interpretation of sense data in terms of their probable causes in outer objects. The hunter interprets a mark in the snow as a deer's track. Aesthetic perception, on the other hand, as in contemplating a natural scene or a painted landscape, tends to be less rigidly selective and directive, more freely wandering, attentive to a greater variety of presented objects and qualities. It often involves a sort of voluntary illusion, as in the tendency mentioned above for an observer of a painting to perceive the paint as grass or trees. Also, it often involves greater attention to sense qualities as qualities, as greens or blues, light or dark areas, straight or curved lines, patterns, and designs. The perception of visual design often involves a voluntary disregard of the representative or causal meaning of sensory data and a focusing of attention instead on their immediate sensory aspects. This shift can never be complete. There is no such thing as purely qualitative perception; it is always mixed with some association and inference. But there is a difference in degree of emphasis.

The artist must often be practical in attitude rather than aesthetic. He must think of how to control his medium and achieve desired results; for example, how to lay on strokes of paint so as to make them look like a tree. The aesthetic observer is freer in this respect. He has no ulterior end to achieve; no task except to see, to understand, and, if possible, to enjoy. Hence he can let his attention wander more unrestrictedly over all the visible details of the scene or picture before him.

6. Component abilities in appreciation

As in the case of creative abilities, we can consider those of appreciation from the standpoint of the component functions involved in the process. As we have seen, these are basically the same as those in art creation or in any other complex human activity; but they vary in certain respects according to the nature of the total attitude and process. There is no one right way to appreciate, to look at pictures, or to listen to music, any more than there is one right way to create art—though the market is full of books and teachers who insist that their way is the only right way. The ways and techniques of appreciation are as diverse as the types of art and of human personality. In other words, no author has a right to urge people to notice only "pure form" and to ignore subject matter in pictures or to think only of moral effects or sociological aspects. The world of art is there in all its richness, for each to use and enjoy in the ways that seem best to him.

Nevertheless, we can say that certain ways of responding to art involve highly developed skill and understanding, while others do not. Some ways are superficial and fragmentary, involving the experience of very few elements in the work of art. A young child, or even a dog, may look at a painting by Rembrandt, but cannot perceive it fully or appreciate its qualities. Many adults look at art in ways that are superficial and fragmentary by comparison with the experience of a trained observer. The child or untrained adult may enjoy art very intensely in certain respects and thus deserve the envy of the jaded connoisseur. There is no special training that can guarantee such conditions of enjoyment as the basic health, vigor, and happiness of the individual. Some persons are highly developed in their intellectual responsiveness to art; some in their perceptual responsiveness; some in their emotional sensitivity. It is possible to develop one's appreciative ability in one or more of several ways. Those who desire a diversified kind of experience which utilizes the possible value of art in many ways will desire to develop and use many different types of ability.

One group of abilities is concerned with visual perception. We already have a key to them in what has been said about the nature of aesthetic seeing. Ordinary perception is likely to become strongly practical, through the pressure of gaining necessary ends. We learn to look at things mostly for their associated meanings (as in the case of letters, numbers, and other signs) with attention fixed on what they mean in relation to some practical interest. Intelligent laymen, confronted with a work of art, often approach it in the same spirit. They ask, What does it mean? What practical use has it? Now, these questions do apply to certain aspects of art. Some works of art do have utilitarian purposes, and some do undertake to convey meanings—religious, moral, patriotic, and otherwise. But there are other aspects of art that this approach tends to ignore. They are largely concerned with the values of direct sensory experience. Sometimes a work of art has little use or meaning save to present a design or texture of colors and shapes to the eye. Such forms have the power to arouse responses of interest and keen pleasure in the sensitive, trained observer. For him, they need not have any further use or meaning, but are worth while for their own sake, as musical melodies, harmonies, and rhythms are worth while. There is nothing especially mysterious about them, no hidden explanation. But to enjoy them, one must first be able to notice them; and it is just this ability that many educated laymen lack because long habits of practical perception have directed their attention elsewhere. This is especially true of busy people in our Western world, and much of our educational emphasis aggravates it. For this reason, it is important in teaching art appreciation at present to stress the technique of looking at things in terms of their directly visible qualities and arrangements, the technique of qualitative perception. One must develop the power to ignore, at times, the indirect uses and associations of things, in order to perceive more clearly their directly visible forms.

To do this well, some unhurried, undistracted calm and quiet are necessary. These are often hard to achieve under modern conditions, in education or elsewhere. But they are worth striving for.

Representative art, pictorial and sculptural, presents a difficult task in perception. For it usually combines some directly visible qualities of line, color, and design along with the portrayal of other objects, scenes, and persons. These may be interesting, too, and there is no reason to neglect them in the long run. But the usual tendency is to notice them only; that is, to perceive only the represented subject matter in a picture. Conscious effort and instruction are usually necessary to help students learn how to discern the design aspects in representative art. Their attention must be directed, in one concrete example after another, to subtle gradations of line, light, and color to complex organizations of pattern. When realism of anatomy and perspective is partly sacrificed to design, as often happens in ancient as well as contemporary art, the untrained observer is puzzled and offended. He sees only the negative aspect, the "distortion," and not the design for which it was produced. The tremendous variety of effects in visible form and design that art contains is quite unsuspected by the ordinary layman. He ignores them under his very eyes in walking casually through a museum or down a city street. It may require long experience under capable guidance to open his eyes to the rich world of visible form. And it is unfortunately true that not all professional artists or teachers of art have themselves learned to use their eyes in this way. When one does learn to do so, through careful looking at art, one is constantly struck by the similar visible qualities in nature itself, and in all the life about one, a fascinating world of shape and color that an overly practical civilization has tended to obscure from us.

To develop powers of sense perception does not mean, however, that one must neglect or repress imagination and understanding. These are different functions, and may be developed in their own right. They are called forth in response to certain elements in art, over and above the directly sensible. In all visual art except abstract decoration (and even there to a less degree) there are stimuli to make the beholder build up a fantasy of things and events not present to the eye. It may be of a comparatively static scene, as in a landscape or the interior of a room, of a group of figures in action, or of a long narrative. Arts that present a changing series of images, like the cinema, the theater, and the dance, are especially capable of telling stories.

The ability to imagine as a work of art directs us to is in part dependent on our general cultural background, our stock of memory-images, and our understanding of established symbols and meanings. Art suggests images at times by imitation, as in making paint look like grass; at times by arbitrary symbolism, as in words and signs like the cross or trident. By presenting sensory images in certain groups and sequences, the work of art influences us to call forth images and concepts from our own memories and to arrange them into forms we have never before experienced. These forms may involve not only sensory images, but also inferences and systems of reasoning. Thus we can follow an argument in a play or novel and apprehend its reasoning aesthetically without necessarily agreeing with it. In so far as ability to grasp the imaginative and rational content of art is dependent on one's general education, special training in art appreciation is inadequate to cope with it. This, incidentally, is one reason why art appreciation now suffers from the educational tendency to neglect classical, Biblical, and oriental culture. Students often cannot recognize the events and personages depicted, because they have never heard of them before. But, conversely, art appreciation can be made an occasion for familiarizing them with cultural traditions.

In addition, there is a fairly definite technique of responding to the associative content of art. It is dependent on the general power to link up ideas in new relationships, which is akin to intelligence. But it is not the same as intelligence in practical affairs, and one may have it without being very original. It is, in part, a sensitivity to outward cues, a quickness in grasping what the work of art is trying to suggest, a facility in organizing ideas in accordance with these suggestions. This may be called "aesthetic imagination" or "apprehension," in contrast with the more spontaneous and independent thinking required in creative work. Individuals differ markedly in their powers of "catching on" to what is intended. Some are slow and dull; others, bright. Some can grasp and follow very complex groups and sequences of ideas without losing track of subtle details or general outlines. High ability of this sort is required to follow a complex novel like *War and Peace,* with its many characters and vast march of events, or the symbolic and representative content of a great cathedral, as conveyed through the details of architecture, sculpture, and stained glass.

There are also differences of ability in regard to empathy, or the power to project oneself in imagination into some external object. Here the external object is the work of art, including the world of fancy it conjures up. Small children usually project themselves with ease into a world of make-believe; so much, at times, as to become more frightened or convinced of its reality than we intend them to. They forget themselves and become completely engrossed in the story or picture. More sophisticated adults often find it harder to forget their own self-conscious preoccupations and to enter vividly into the fantasy-world of art.

Knowledge about art can operate as a powerful aid in the apperception of particular works of art, through enabling us to recognize, classify, and analyze them conceptually. People who are ignorant of art history and theory sometimes feel that such knowledge would dampen their enthusiasm and destroy the fascination of art, through dissecting its mysteries. Yet it is doubtful whether anyone who has acquired it regrets the acquisition, and many feel that it multiplies the interest of art by endowing it with greater meaning. Certainly, there are persons, including capable artists, who know little about art from a scholarly standpoint and yet who can enjoy art with fine discrimination. Certainly, there are scholars of great erudition who cannot. Much depends on the extent to which such knowledge is linked with other abilities and modes of response. Factual information can be accumulated by itself, apart from perceptual and other direct experience of art, producing the dry pedant. A mass of verbal concepts can fill one's mind to the extent of obscuring the present object and diverting one's attention to problems of identification, date, and the like. These have a scientific value, but should not be confused with appreciation, as they often are by pedantic teachers.

However, information about art can be merged with other elements in a vigorous, diversified experience. It can be put into action as a means of understanding what one sees. All perceiving under civilized conditions is done with the aid of concepts, including verbal names for qualities, such as *red* and *blue*, *straight* and *curved*, *still* and *moving*. By their aid, we not only classify and understand what we see, in relation to our past experience and that of others, but we also are led to notice qualities and relations we otherwise would not perceive. Through scholarly education, one's conceptual apparatus can be developed to include names for types and styles of artistic form, their elements and modes of organization. It can include such historical concepts as Byzantine and Romanesque, Impressionist and Post-impressionist, Classic and Romantic; such aesthetic concepts as tragic and comic, design and representation, function and symbolism. If these are not mere empty words in the mind, but linked in memory with vivid sensory and other experiences, they can be used in encountering each new work of art. They help one not only to notice characteristics that exemplify these types, but also to interpret their meaning and importance in relation to a wider cultural background.

7. Taste and evaluation; the criticism of art

The affective phases of aesthetic response are more shrouded in obscurity. We have little specific understanding of why works of art move us to volitional attitudes of approval or antagonism, mild or violent. Certain it is that the reasons given to oneself and others, the plausible aesthetic and moral principles, are often not the real ones or the complete ones, and that these latter often lie deep in the history of individual personality. Taste in art is influenced by indirect association with one's personal joys, successes, conflicts, and frustrations that happened long ago and may now seem quite unrelated to art. We know also, mainly from study of neurotic symptoms, that the inability to accept and enjoy things that most healthy people like is often due to inward conflicts, repressions, and frustrations. To like very few things that others like, to be hypercritical and hard to please is often a sign of inward maladjustment and unhappiness. The individual is full of mental sore spots, and these are constantly being irritated by ideas and images that come to him through art or otherwise. He fails to recognize the inner cause of his antipathies and rationalizes them with faultfinding. An occasional violent prejudice in the normal person may result from such inner causes, and their correction makes him able to enjoy what he formerly could not.

Of course, one can never prove to another person that he ought to like what he does not. He has a right to his own dislikes, and will probably cling to them proudly, even though he sees other people enjoying what displeases him. Moreover, there is no reason for saying that people ought to like everything or all kinds of art. There can be no discrimination of values without preferring some things to others, and intense devotion to what seems best may involve intense dislike of what seems evil, ugly, or dangerous. The apparent ability to like everything may indicate a lack of standards or of any strong enthusiasms. Nevertheless, it often seems fairly obvious to the outsider that an individual is cutting himself off from real potential values for no good reason and merely through groundless prejudice or lack of understanding. A great many adults are reasonable enough to suspect this about their own lack of interest in art or their antipathy toward certain kinds of art. Some study art appreciation for this very reason, in the hope of expanding their scope of interests and learning to enjoy some of the things others have found worth while.

In dealing with young students, the educator is on firmer ground in trying to develop their taste for art and especially for more of the types of art that have been generally recognized as great. From his own and others' past experience, he is justified in saying about art, as he does about certain kinds of food, exercise, or mental discipline, "Try this again, even if you don't like it now. You may learn to like it, and be glad you did."

Of course, urging people to like things or preaching about our own likes is not the most effective way to get results. If the capacity to like is there, it may be sufficient to present the objects under favorable conditions, with a few hints as to their significance and what to notice in particular. Few things are more gratifying in education than to watch students develop, not only an understanding of great cultural achievements, but also a genuine interest in them and a desire for further experience of them. One has no right to hope that students will ever develop exactly the same tastes as one's own, but with due allowance for variation, one may hope that all will come to prize the central values upon which civilized people in all ages tend to agree.

Moreover, the wise teacher will not expect students to like all kinds of art at too early an age. The fact that some kinds are museum exhibits and interesting to mature scholars does not mean that they are, or should be, especially interesting to children. Like our foods, some kinds are especially needed by the individual at an early stage; others, at a later stage. Extreme precocity may be as unhealthy a sign in aesthetic taste as in other matters; it may be a sign of maladjustment. It is absurd to suppose that active boys and girls should prefer Gothic Crucifixions to athletics and dancing, or even to cartoons and motion-picture comedies. What they spontaneously like may turn out to have more genuine value for their growth in art and general education than what we mistakenly try to impose upon them. Certain kinds of adult art are too complex and involve types of motivation that are yet foreign to them. Certain aspects in adult art can interest young children, such as the obvious story element in pictures, and little by little, the more mature and difficult elements in a single work of art, such as a cathedral, can be gradually imparted to a growing mind; but not all at once. Research in art education has much to do in discovering what kinds of art, and what approaches to art, can arouse vital interest in children of various ages and types of personality. It is not enough to find what they prefer spontaneously, before educational influence. We must find also what they can become interested in by proper presentation and use.

The power to evaluate art is in part an application of general intelligence and rationality. Valuation in a broad sense occurs on all levels of mental development. It develops out of innate organic tendencies to accept or reject various types of stimuli, with accompanying emotions of joy, disgust, anger, or the like. Conditioning transforms these into more subtle, mixed, and complex attitudes toward many types of civilized objects that do not directly affect us physically, but affect us mainly through their associated meanings. Even the educated adult responds at times with simple, direct impulses of welcoming, escape, or attack. These are evaluative in a broad sense, as expressions of approval or disapproval, but they are not value judgments. The educated adult or older child is also able to express his likes and dislikes in words and to give explicit reasons for them. He may even be able to describe and defend his affective habits in the form of generalized, intellectual standards, theories of what kinds of art are good or beautiful, and why. Thus, evaluation on the higher mental levels is usually a combination of affective response with conceptual thinking. As we have seen, it may become almost wholly intellectual, a matter of applying aesthetic or moral principles deductively; in other words, one may be able to evaluate art in this way with great erudition and logic and yet have extremely meager aesthetic experience or appreciative power in a broad sense.

Reasoning may co-operate with sensory and affective functions in evaluation. This occurs when the individual is able to suspend judgment—that is, to suspend the first impulse to a "snap judgment" of like or dislike—and take time to perceive and understand the work of art as clearly and thoroughly as possible. No value judgment can be considered fair or rational that is not based on a moderately clear and thorough perception and understanding of the nature of the object. The ability to suspend judgment, to remain open-minded while exploring the facts of the case, is essentially intelligent, as opposed to crude impulse, prejudice, and dogmatism.

This is not to say that all appreciation or evaluation should be highly rational or thorough and painstaking. There is a place also for the quick, impulsive, and emotional type of response. Sometimes the situation is not important enough to justify detailed examination. Sometimes it is so obviously similar to others previously considered that one is justified in a routine appraisal. Life is too short to keep raising the same aesthetic or moral issues time after time. The power of intelligent evaluation consists in knowing how to think out a problem carefully and experimentally when conditions seem to call for it, as in making up one's mind about the inclusion of some new, controversial type of art in an educational program. In minor cases, one simply expresses one's feelings at the moment, in a word or gesture of approval or disapproval. A smile or a frown cannot be criticized on logical grounds as true or false. But when the individual goes farther and undertakes to judge a work of art as "harmful" or "lacking unity," then he is venturing into more theoretical issues about the nature of the object and its probable consequences.

Even generalizations about one's own likes and dislikes are sometimes subject to question. Parents realize that a child does not always know what he really likes, that he sometimes expresses dislike of a thing without really understanding it, that he would like it better if he knew more about it or were in a better humor. Likewise, the psychologist may have grounds for thinking that adults do not always accurately express their own fundamental tastes when they make a hasty, careless judgment, based on superficial observation. Still more, when the individual ventures into statements about the power of a work of art to please or displease, to benefit or injure other persons, the psychologist has the right to question the evaluation on factual grounds. Here, appreciation ceases to be a purely personal response and becomes a generalization about the effects of a certain type of art on human beings. The more one undertakes to verbalize and defend one's tastes in art, the more one enters the realm of aesthetic theory. Development in this respect requires the use of scientific methods, clear definition of terms, and verification of evidence. Most art appreciation does not seek to go so far. It remains somewhere between primitive impulse and scientific generalization. Art criticism of a literary or journalistic type is intermediate between the two. It is not merely personal appreciation; it is also an attempt to express the feelings of the writer about some work of art in explicit verbal judgments, with examples and arguments to defend them in a more or less logical way. It varies from the comparatively personal and subjective to the comparatively scientific and scholarly. Ordinary art appreciation, by educated adults, often leads to an informal sort of criticism, usually brief and casual. It can be pleasant and enlightening to exchange impressions of art with other people, in gallery, home, or classroom. There is no reason for disparaging such rudimentary criticism as inferior merely because it is undeveloped in accordance with scientific inquiry. It has its own values in education and immediate enjoyment, as an integral part of the process of appreciation. But we should realize how it involves abilities in reasoning and verbal expression, in which some persons are more capable than others. These abilities can be developed and equipped with requisite information through studies emphasizing the logical, psychological, historical, and sociological approaches to art.

8. Moderate relativism in evaluating art

Much of the confusion and disagreement involved in judgments of aesthetic value could be avoided by greater care in specifying the kind of evaluation one wishes to make, and by making limited, relative evaluations instead of sweeping and absolute ones. The common tendency, in appraising art, is to label it very simply and briefly as good or bad, beautiful or ugly, important or trivial, beneficial or harmful, pleasant or unpleasant. This evades the highly significant questions: "For whom?" "In what way?" and "Under what conditions?"

If one asks and clearly answers these questions in regard to the object of art under consideration, it usually turns out to be impossible to make a sweeping, brief evaluation, for the reason that the object is now seen to be good for some kinds of person, bad for others; good in some ways and under some conditions, bad in other ways and under other conditions. No one would think of evaluating other types of products so sweepingly—a drug or an instrument. Their goodness or badness is obviously relative to how and by whom they are used. Many works of art, especially in the handcrafts and industrial arts, are in part utilitarian devices, and their value thus depends in part on the value of the end they serve and how efficiently they serve it. Some works of so-called "fine art" also have instrumental functions—paintings as historic records, as religious symbols, and as military or advertising propaganda, for example. To evaluate them fully, one must consider such instrumental functions.

The effect an object will have on the observer, as beautiful or ugly, pleasant or unpleasant, also depends on a variety of interacting factors: on the conditions under which the object is displayed, and on the nature of the observer—his or her age, sex, native capacities, training, habits, and present mood. In relation to these factors, a picture may appear to be good for adults and bad for children, beautiful in drawing and ugly in color, appropriate for a theater lobby and inappropriate for a church or hospital. It may seem attractive or amusing on first sight, yet likely to grow tiresome if permanently installed; or unattractive on first sight, yet with qualities likely to "grow on one" through longer experience. A chair may please the eye because of its pattern and texture, and yet be uncomfortable, weak, or hard to clean—in other words, unsatisfactory in a functional, instrumental way.

Some works of art are effective and pleasing in many important ways, for many sorts of people throughout long periods of time. They are likely to be rated, on the whole, as higher in social value than those of more trivial, limited, and evanescent appeal. To make so broad a generalization requires a great deal of evidence, however, and will involve many debatable issues. Each object will reveal certain actual or potential values—some instrumental and some directly aesthetic—and certain limitations or weaknesses in relation to certain possible situations. It is difficult, and not especially important, to try to arrive at a total estimate of its worth. Long ago, debating societies gave up trying to decide whether fire was better than water. The important thing is to find out the specific properties, uses, dangers, and limitations of each.

An evaluation that is carefully limited, tentative, and supported with evidence is less likely to arouse disagreement than one that is sweeping and dogmatic. Two persons may seem to be in violent disagreement, one praising a work of art and the other condemning it, and yet they may be closer together than they seem to be. They are perhaps evaluating it from different points of view, for different sorts of quality or supposed effect, and the disagreement might be greatly reduced if each would explain and delimit his judgment.

9. Originality in relation to value in art

One of the commonest sources of misunderstanding in evaluating art is the question of *historical importance*, of *priority* and *originality*, as against imitativeness. Laymen in art are sometimes perplexed and antagonized when their sincere enthusiasms are brushed aside by some supposed authority on art, on the ground that what they like is "old stuff," or "just an imitation of so-and-so." If the layman sticks to his guns, he may answer with some reason that he doesn't care how original the object is, that it gives him and many others like him a great deal of pleasure and perhaps other values as well. The authority on art is likely to be judging the work, not in terms of its present power to be of use or pleasure, but in terms of its position in the history of art. He thinks in terms of the chronological development of styles and techniques, of the milestones in artistic progress, the outstanding innovations of each age and the men who made them. He appraises artistic value in terms of original contribution to the world's artistic heritage. Consequently, he looks down upon the legions of imitators who follow in the train of every great innovator. Seeing an Impressionist landscape in a shop window, he may recognize it at once as an imitation of Monet's style, with little or nothing added, and hence rank it low in value. In the same way, a trained music lover would condemn a newly written symphony, however agreeable to the ear, if it contained nothing but slightly modified, unacknowledged quotations from Brahms and Debussy. Accordingly, connoisseurs will praise in ardent terms the work of some old master in any art who represented a great advance for his day or of some contemporary who has introduced a novel effect. The layman tries hard, perhaps, but can find little of interest or value in either.

Each, the connoisseur and the layman, has some right on his side. They are judging art from two different standpoints; the one in terms of its historical importance, the other in terms of its ability to please or serve the modern observer. The connoisseur has no right to argue that all persons should enjoy the original work more or appraise it higher. As a matter of fact, some imitations are so nearly perfect as to deceive the most respected experts. Their aesthetic value cannot be far from that of the original, except as determined by the pleasure one may get from knowing (or believing) that one is looking at something authentic and historically epoch-making. Art authorities often form the habit of considering art so exclusively in terms of authenticity and historic importance that they are, in fact, unable to admire any work that does not qualify in these respects. But there is no reason why all consumers of art should be required to feel the same way. If they frankly and explicitly evaluate a work of art in terms of its power to please or serve them directly, here and now, they need not be required to take the broad historical point of view, and their judgments are not necessarily mistaken or inferior. The five-millionth reproduction of a certain utensil or automobile may be quite as useful and beautiful as the first, and (assuming the reproduction to be exact) so may the five-millionth reproduction of a certain painting.

The problem is quite different, however, when one undertakes to appraise a work of art or an artist in regard to the amount of credit that it or he deserves for creative originality or contribution to the social heritage. For this reason we are apt to admire an inventor's first model and perhaps to keep it in a museum of science and industry as a concrete example of progress, without implying that it has great value as a machine today. It is quite possible for a critic to assign great historic importance to a work of art, recognizing intellectually its value as a step in progress, without getting much pleasure or profit from seeing or using it today. In practice, however, the two modes of evaluation are likely to be somewhat merged in the critic's mind; on the one hand, as he looks at the object, he enjoys realizing how great a contribution it was; on the other hand, in looking at an imitation of it, his enjoyment may be diminished by the thought that it is only an imitation.

If we desire to think out our evaluations clearly, we must try to distinguish between such different grounds for praise or blame. Very often, of course, the two modes of evaluation lead to the same verdict; the historically important object is found superior as a present object of use or observation, a source of aesthetic enjoyment through its own form and meaning. In our age at least, the most capable artists do not often devote themselves to exact imitation or minor adaptation of others' works. The imitative work is apt to be also unskilled and unimaginative by comparison with the one it imitates. It deserves a lower rating for its own intrinsic qualities, without regard to its chronological priority. The connoisseur, in observing it, compares it with his memory image of the original work it imitates and rates it low accordingly. The layman has no such basis of comparison. He sees only what the present work contains, without knowing or caring that it is inferior to something else of the same kind.

While the layman's judgment has a certain validity in relation to his own present experience, it obviously has limited scope. He has not the right to extend his personal expression of like or dislike into a broad generalization about the object's general importance in the world of art or the artist's claim to social admiration and reward. Unfortunately, he often does just that. To justify such a broad evaluation, he needs some knowledge of past and present art and of the conditions under which and for which the present work was created, as a frame of reference for assigning the work its proper place in cultural history. He needs to know something about human nature and present society in general in order to say that the present work will, or will not, prove valuable for others besides himself.

It was mentioned above that modern civilization, especially in western Europe and America, sets a great premium on progress and originality in art as in other realms. In this we differ markedly from certain past cultures, such as those of Egypt, China, and medieval Europe. We profess a desire to encourage originality in mature artists and in students, even though in practice we do not always recognize or reward it. To admire an original product more than an imitation, even when they are practically identical, is one of our strongest social traits. This trait can be justified as conducive on the whole to further progress, although it is sometimes carried to an extreme of faddism, of ignoring the old, traditional values. On the whole, we are justified in praising originality in art; that is, in praising genuine, important innovation; not innovation for its own sake. We are justified in leading students to recognize and respect real contributions to social culture, past and present, to rank the original higher than the imitative work, and to prefer experiencing it when possible.

There is a great difference here between the frankly mechanical reproduction, such as a color print or phonograph record, and the "handmade" work of art that pretends to be original and is not. The student can enjoy the former as an honest, inexpensive substitute, in proportion to its exactness; it makes no claim to be creative in itself. The latter he can enjoy for what it is, though realizing that the present artist does not deserve full credit for it. It would be more honest, perhaps, if visual artists would somehow acknowledge indebtedness to their principal sources—say in a note at the bottom of a painting—as authors and musical composers often do in their texts and scores. Since this is not to be expected, teachers of art appreciation have so much the more obligation to help their students distinguish the original from the imitation. Under present cultural conditions such an ability is a necessary element in developed powers of art appreciation.

It should be reaffirmed that the principal thing to work for in teaching appreciation to children is not to make them like or dislike any particular kinds of art—even to prefer original art—or to make them use any particular standards of value. It is rather to help them experience art fully and vividly, under conditions favorable to use and enjoyment. For this, highly developed powers of intellectual evaluation are not entirely necessary. But those persons who undertake to criticize, teach, or direct the teaching of art professionally are under obligation to train such powers in themselves beyond the point strictly necessary for a layman's enjoyment. They should strive to clarify and support their judgments through especially careful perception and analysis of the factors involved in the interaction between works of art and human beings. These include both psychological and social factors in the individuals who create, use, and respond to art, and also factors in artistic form—the nature of the works of art concerned.

◈ VI ◈

ART AND WORLD-MINDEDNESS*

To be a citizen of the world, in the full and literal sense of the word, is still a dream of the future. There is no world state, no *civitas* of world-wide extent to which one can or should give allegiance today. "The parliament of man, the federation of the world," seem even farther away and more visionary today than when Tennyson wrote of them three generations ago. For in the meantime humanity has tried, with high hope, to create the basis of a world state, and in the last few years that hope has been disappointed.[1]

But there is another sense in which "world citizenship" means a state of mind. We can speak of it more clearly, perhaps, as "world-mindedness." In that sense, world citizenship is not only possible today, but is in some degree an actuality. It has existed for thousands of years, in the thought and action of a few enlightened citizens of every age who have risen above narrow group and sectional interests to achieve a broadly human point of view. There is a kind of world citizenship in the realm of ideas; of art and science, religion, philosophy and all constructive social effort. Its members are the true cosmopolitans. Wherever they meet, or read each other's written words, they quickly overstep the boundaries of language and nationality. They speak the universal language of world civilization and find a mutual basis of discussion in the interests of educated people; in the common task of opposing man's perennial enemies, ignorance, hunger, poverty and suffering; and in the creation and enjoyment of the arts. They overstep the boundaries, not only of space but of time, so that the meditations of an ancient Hindu, a Chinese or Egyptian

* Published in its original form in *Magazine of Art*, XXXI.10 (October, 1938), under the title, "Art and World Citizenship."

[1] The reference intended here, when the essay was first published in 1938, was to the League of Nations. Unfortunately, much the same comment can now be made on its successor, the United Nations. It has rendered valuable services and is far from being a failure; but the international rivalries which have grown up within and outside it have emphasized the dangers and difficulties of subordinating national independence to a powerful world government.

sage may be far more comprehensible today than the partisan rancors of some narrow-minded contemporary who lived a few years ago, or lives at present in another town. Ikhnaton of Egypt, Confucius and Plato, Epictetus and St. Francis, Leonardo da Vinci, Erasmus and Voltaire—men as different as these were all, in one way or another, world-minded citizens of the planet earth, and not merely of the town or country in which they happened to be born. Travel sometimes helps to produce the cosmopolitan mind; but not always. For some have it who have never traveled outside their own villages, and some confirmed globe-trotters remain provincials to the end of their days.

If the number of world-minded people could somehow be multiplied in every nation, so that each could have a sympathetic understanding of the others' needs, desires and peculiar folkways, the coming of an actual world state would no doubt be much accelerated. It would almost follow as a matter of course. For there are no problems of boundary, of raw materials or of tariffs too difficult to be solved by reasonable conference, if the will to solve them in that way exists. The primary need is for a universal will to world co-operation. And in the production of that will, the arts can and often do play an important role.

All great civilizations have left expressions of the ideal of a united, peaceful humanity under one rule and one religion. In Egyptian art we find the symbol of the overarching sky and the sun's disk high above, with mankind united in allegiance to one king. Of course, such conceptions of world citizenship have usually been coupled with the idea that all men should accept *my* king, submit to *my* form of government and worship *my* God with *my* kind of church and ceremony. Even the Christian church, strong force as it was for internationalism in the Middle Ages, was often intolerant toward other religions and toward other empires than the Holy Roman Empire. The nearest approaches to an actual world state have been made, not by voluntary confederation, but by those empires like the Roman and the British, which by force made many weaker peoples submit and accept the *Pax Romana* or the *Pax Britannica*. Perhaps (we say in discouraged moments) that is the only way in which world unity can ever be achieved. Certainly the history of attempts to induce free sovereign peoples to surrender their rights and privileges for the sake of unity, except in the face of a common enemy, has been a record of pathetic failures. But idealists never lose hope that such a world confederation will some day be made on the basis of voluntary agreement. They still have faith in more humane inducements than machine guns and policemen's clubs—in the forces of education and rational thinking. Among these, they look to art as a force for unity, through its power to express the ideals of unselfish harmony and beauty.

To what extent is this hope justified? Has art been a force for world citizenship in the past, and is it now? It would be pleasant if the answer were so simple, and if we could honestly indulge in a whole-hearted rhapsody in praise of art. But history shows the facts to be otherwise. Art is sometimes a force on the side of social unity, and sometimes on the opposite side. Like all the other great instruments of human living—like science, commerce and religion—art is a two-edged weapon. All these forces tend in some ways to unite people, and in others to antagonize them. In the history of civilization, art has sometimes made for peace and tolerance. Sometimes, and very often, it has made for narrowness and bitter rivalry; for greed, intolerance, and oppression. Art has been a means of expressing the hatred of one people for another; the struggle between social classes and religious sects. It has been a means of inflaming peaceful folk against each other, and a source of envious contention.

In general, the works of art produced by a people cannot rise very far above the average level of thought at the time. Artists are not a race apart, of supermen or pure idealists. Here and there, we can look back and pick out an exceptional genius, far in advance of his age. But on the whole, art expresses the mentality of its own age and culture. If religious bigotry and the desire for conquest are active in a nation, we may be sure that they will find artists to express them. If a dictator rises to power, whatever type of man he is, we may be sure that some artists, poets, and composers will be among the crowd that fawns upon him, flattering his pride with heroic statues, epics and triumphal hymns.

Let us not delude ourselves with the comfortable answer that all art so produced is bad art. Among the most respected classics in our libraries are the epics in praise of military conquerors and destroyers of liberty. Our museums are filled with idealistic statues of them.

The most skillful painters in China and Japan, in Bagdad and Mogul India, Florence and Venice, and in the capitals of modern Europe, have left us exquisite portraits of the bloodiest war lords of their day, whom we know to have been in many cases, the most consummate rascals.

The secular art and literature of all times, from ancient Egypt to the present, is full of the clash of arms and the praise of military heroes. Even religious art and literature abound in praise of those who have smitten down the enemies of the true God, burned heretics and witches, and put heathen infidels to the sword. Even supreme geniuses, like Dante, are not always above partisan bitterness. He could rise to cosmic visions of the universe; but he could also hate, with all the fury of civil strife, the enemies of his party in the medieval city of Florence.

The tremendous rise of nationalistic imperialism since the Middle Ages has been aided and inspired by artists in every medium. Not by all artists, for there have been voices raised in protest; but by enough to show that art is never wholly a force for unity. In recent years, Communism and anarchism have sometimes been expressed as idealistic philosophies, preaching a world-wide brotherhood of labor. But in practice and in the theories of actual leaders, they have emphasized another line of contention, in the class struggle between capital and labor. They have not been able to avoid nationalistic division, and we see them today as factors in the general scramble for political and economic power. They too have found artistic expression, sometimes of high aesthetic quality, as in the best Russian motion pictures prior to 1930. In these, as usual, art and propaganda, war and peace, expressions of hatred and of friendship were inextricably joined.

Has music been exempt, and always a charm to soothe the savage breast? Then let us remember that there have been war songs, and songs of triumph over fallen foes, as long as there have been songs of peace, love and friendship.

The production of art is often bound up with social injustice and oppression. If we look at the history of decorative art and architecture with an eye to its social background, the story is not a pleasant one. It would seem that, when we speak of palaces and gardens, of soft brocades and delicate enamels, we are entering a world of pure beauty where hate and suffering have no place. But who built these palaces and gardens, and who enjoyed them? How many slaves died wretchedly in building the pyramids of Egypt? How many serfs went without bread so that the lady of the manor could have silks and jewels from the Orient? The blood and hunger of workers run like invisible strands through the silks of Asia and the tapestries of Europe. True, this is only one side of the story. For craftsmen have at times been well paid, and lived in comfort. There are pleasant pages in the history of society, where industry brings its just reward, and where its profits are diffused to raise the level of a whole people. But on adjoining pages, we see the production of art bound up with extreme inequality of wealth—with utter misery at the bottom and fabulous wealth at the top. We see it flourishing because some leisure class could afford every whim, and could divert the energy of artisans from food for the masses to luxurious refinement for the rich.

Is this good or bad? As humanitarians we may deplore it; but as lovers of art we cannot wholly regret the conditions, unjust as they were, which made this art possible. Some economists would have us believe that these conditions are a thing of the past, since we are going from an "economy of scarcity" to one of abundance. Machinery and large-scale production, we are told, will do the work of slaves, and allow us all to have luxuries without depriving anyone of necessities. Let us hope this day will soon arrive; but it is not here yet.

What has this to do with art and world co-operation? Simply that it illustrates once more how art—in this case the luxury of beautiful possessions—can be a bone of contention among human beings. For such possessions do not rest easily in the grasp of their original owner. The thief, the robber baron, and the foreign conqueror cast envious eyes upon them. The hungry populace outside the garden gate looks in, and thinks how much has been spent upon them. At periodic intervals in history, it breaks through the gates and causes what we call a revolution. Then no art is sacred. Unless its own leaders are far-sighted enough to call a halt, the mob will seize and carry off what it can, then destroy the rest in a fury of revenge against the elegant fineries which have been produced at the cost of children's lives. What we think of as the most innocent and spiritual forms of art—the stained glass window, the altar, the carved figures of saints—all these are smashed with shouts of rage, as they were by the French Revolutionists, and by the embattled Puritans of England over a century earlier. The reason is that such things are associated by the revolutionists with an oppressive regime, in which Church and State have alike forgotten justice, and pursued instead the magnificent formalism of decorative art.

In this light we can understand why so many religious and moral leaders have preached against the love of wealth, including what we call decorative art. They denounce the glittering splendors of Babylon and Persia. They tell us to lay up our treasures, not on earth, but in heaven. They praise the simple life, ascetic and frugal, given over to things of the spirit. Often they denounce idolatry, and much of the world's great sculpture has consisted of these same "idols." Sometimes they directly oppose the artists of their time, as did Savonarola and St. Paul before him, who opposed the silversmiths of Ephesus. For such reformers see in what we call the decorative arts a source of greed, sensuality, and superstition, of eternal crime and killing.

I have presented the case against art for the sake of realism, and because we so often fall into exaggerated reverence for the very word "art," as if it were a synonym for all that is holy. As a matter of fact, it is human; and therefore by turns both good and evil.

It makes a great deal of difference whether art is *old or new,* from the standpoint of its effect upon social unity. When a war is over and peace declared, time begins healing emotional wounds. Many of the more extreme expressions of hatred are forgotten or pushed out of sight; with a little shame, perhaps, as both sides try to revive friendly relations. Songs, cartoons, and writings which were merely vindictive drop out of sight; those which have some artistic merit are looked upon in a new way, and praised for qualities which have little to do with the "late unpleasantness." Year after year, the survivors of the conflict, often slow to pardon old enemies, die off. The war itself, if its causes are really removed, recedes into the legendary past, along with the wars of classical antiquity. This has almost happened with our own Civil War. Descendants of both sides respect Grant and Lee; they sing both "Dixie" and "John Brown's Body." It does not happen at once, however. One is still wise not to sing "Marching Through Georgia" in the State of Georgia. It happened completely with our Revolutionary War, and with the Jacobite Rebellion of eighteenth-century Scotland. Prince Charlie has become a legendary figure, and the songs about him carry no sting. There is no partisanship, but a sense of our common heritage of old romance, when we "tell sad stories of the deaths of kings, and battles long ago."

It is the same with the statues and paintings of ancient war lords. We see them striding haughtily over the bodies of their foes, yet we feel no answering pride or anger at these bloody deeds. We know how brief their day of glory was, and how time has obliterated the wounds they made. Shelley wrote of such a statue:

> Two vast and trunkless legs of stone
> Stand in the desert. Near them, on the sand,
> Half sunk, a shattered visage lies, whose frown,
> And wrinkled lip, and sneer of cold command,
> Tell that its sculptor well those passions read
> Which yet survive, stamped on these lifeless things,
> The hand that mocked them and the heart that fed;
> And on the pedestal these words appear:
> "My name is Ozymandias, king of kings:
> Look on my works, ye Mighty, and despair!"
> Nothing beside remains. Round the decay
> Of that colossal wreck, boundless and bare
> The lone and level sands stretch far away.

The art of the past becomes a part of the cultural heritage of all human beings. As such, it tends to unify humanity, regardless of the old antagonisms which produced it. Indeed, the very spectacle of so many past disputes, of so much blood shed over quarrels which now seem unnecessary, makes thoughtful people think twice before engaging in another one. Perhaps, as some psychologists believe, art can even become an imaginative substitute for war, and a healthful outlet for some of the energy which, when maladjusted, produces war neuroses.

In all countries today, the treasures of past art become rapidly socialized. This is the case in capitalistic countries almost as much as in those which call themselves socialistic. Private art collections of wealthy men are left to public museums, often with the great houses which they occupied. Funds are left to purchase more works of art, including decorative luxuries which only aristocrats used to enjoy. Cathedrals, palaces, private parks and gardens are placed under government care and thrown open to the public. Though owned by one nation, they are really properties of all the world, for every traveler may enjoy them and carry home pictures of them. Literature and music of the past become even more completely socialized. After the copyright period, they are freely copied, translated, read, and performed in every country of the world. They cannot be stolen or hoarded. They form bonds of sympathy between the peoples who love them.

The heritage of past art is a powerful force to soften present rivalries. One who has learned to love the arts of Japan, of Russia, of Germany, of Italy—to think of these countries in terms of their music, their gardens, their temples, dances and paintings, their peasant costumes, has a hard time brushing aside these memories when a political dispute arises. The people of those countries feel much the same way about us, and about other countries, even though their governments are at the time shaking fists at each other. Much as propaganda offices may try to suppress these bonds of sympathy, to revile or exclude foreign culture and to force domestic taste into national channels, they meet with stubborn resistance. The love for American music and motion pictures, for American clothes and furniture, is a factor to be reckoned with by militarists who would make their people hate America.

Even in the class-struggle type of conflict, the traditions of art succeed at times in bridging over wide gulfs of sentiment. In Russia, those leaders who tried to force a sharp cultural break with the past were surprised and baffled to find that the public still preferred, on the whole, the kind of public buildings which the czars put up; and that it still liked to hear the music of Bach and Chopin.

Strangely enough, economic factors themselves often force the producers of art into a sort of internationalism; not on idealistic grounds, but on those of commercial self-interest. Many of us remember the early moving pictures, in which a Mexican bandit was the despicable villain; or in which a band of Chinese opium fiends kidnaped the heroine. Why do we see them no more? For one very good reason: the people of those countries refused to import our films as long as such misrepresentations continued. Producers are now very careful to ask whether a certain incident will offend the British market, or will have to be left out of the film when shown in India. It must not offend labor or capital, Catholics, Protestants or Jews. This is not altogether a good thing for art. Sometimes, when we try to keep from offending anyone, there is nothing left but insipid trivialities. On the other hand, the need to please an international market may favor a genuine artist like Charlie Chaplin or Walt Disney, whose films have universal appeal.

In the United States, much has been done by popular art to break down sectionalism and narrow local attitudes. Not only the movies, but the radio, television, popular magazines, art, photography, and even the much-condemned signboards on our highways have done their share. If not impeded by governmental restraints abroad, these popular arts may do as much for future world unity.

What has art done to express directly the ideal of world co-operation? Not as much as one might expect or wish. Art often does so indirectly, by rising above petty local interests to portray the basic themes of human life: love, birth, and death; man's enjoyment of nature, and his struggle to control it; his desire for immortality, and his visions of another world. Primitive folklore and mythology dealt largely with these themes. Greek art translated man's ideal of his own perfection into the visible forms of sculpture, even while Greek civilization itself was crumbling through its inability to achieve political union. Christian art has given visible form to the desire for peace and brotherhood, all through the ferocious wars of Christian history. But most of it pointed toward the hope of another and better world rather than an ideal state on earth. Philosophers like Bacon and More have shown us their ideal of a perfect earthly state. Many a wise man since has shown us how a world state could be organized and run, and has scolded us for not accepting so obviously sensible a course. Poets like Robert Burns and Whitman have voiced their love of all human creatures. Renaissance and baroque art, Christian and neo-pagan in subject, have left serene visions of life as it might be under the sway of love and reason; but too often they have little relation to the hard realities in the way of actual social improvement. Pictorial satirists, from Goya and Daumier to Orozco, have portrayed the horrors of war, the cruel egotism of militarists and the hypocrisy of those who profit by militarism. The painters inspired by Communism in and out of Russia (with Rivera as their best-known example) have expressed the new dream of workers and peasants of the world, happily freed under a perfect social order. But Communist art as a whole is still in the throes of class, factional, and nationalistic hatreds as bitter as those of other eras. Most of the pictures which undertake to portray or symbolize world unity are, it must be confessed, rather dull and pedantic—academic in style and banal in conception; of the type considered proper for college auditoriums and county courthouses. Most of the art, literary, musical, and visual, which the world agrees to call great, has *not* directly presented an ideal of world unity. Why is this so?

There are many reasons. But let us notice one in particular. It is an unfortunate fact that the notion of world co-operation is not, in itself, especially glamorous or exciting. It is much easier for an artist to excite us by talking about a clash of arms than by talking about peace and co-operation. The essence of drama, it is often said, lies in conflict. Peace and co-operation are all very well, but who wants to read a story or see a play about them? The same fact holds true of other arts as well. The music of Wagner and Beethoven excites us with emotional conflict. Castles and fortresses are exciting as architecture. Swords and armor fascinate the children in museums. But the instruments of world co-operation are humdrum desks and conference tables, statistical reports and tariff agreements.

Peace is not only prosaic, but often inglorious. We thrill to the memory of some great soldier who died with all his men rather than surrender an inch to the enemy. But peaceful co-operation is one long succession of compromises, partial surrenders of each national interest in order that an open break may be averted. Where are the epics and the monuments to patient diplomats and foreign secretaries who averted wars by months of tedious negotiation over economic details? Many received, not thanks at home, but insults, for the concessions which they chose to make in the interests of peace. The same is true of social strife between upper and lower classes. We have praise, too often, for the leader who incites our side to force, and stones for the one who proposes reasonable compromise.

It is hard, then, for art to add glamor and emotional appeal to so dull a theme as world-mindedness. Shall we give up the task, leaving all the glamor on the side of war and selfish nationalism? It seems to me that artists are accomplishing, in our own time and country, a task which is in some ways even harder. I am not thinking now of the fine arts—of the exalted painting and sculpture which fill our galleries. I am thinking of something much more humble and mercenary. This is what we call advertising and commercial art. We are too close to this development to see its full social significance. We rightly condemn a good deal of it for blatant insincerity and cheap sensationalism. But there is one thing to be said for it. The advertising artist sets out, in response to commercial inducements, to add visual and emotional appeal to any article, any service, which his patron has to sell. He achieves daily miracles, in our newspapers and weekly magazines, of throwing some aesthetic glamor on prosaic tools and industrial products—on articles of medicine and personal hygiene, which one would say could not possibly be so presented. This is the work of everyday artists, in the service of our competitive system of salesmanship.

A century and more ago, Auguste Comte, founder of sociology and truly world-minded philosopher, called for art to enter the service of humanity. As a psychologist, he recognized the tedious, even repellent nature of the tasks ahead on the road to social co-operation. He called for art to outgrow its primitive delight in violence and superstition; to ennoble and emotionalize the new ideal of humanity in poetry, music, visible form, and ceremony. His hopes have not yet come true. Art is a mighty instrument of social control, which we leave too often in the hands of selfish people with a war to stir up, or a piece of shoddy merchandise to sell. When shall we, as an organized people, put it seriously to work in the service of better aims?

Why have the League of Nations at Geneva, and the old palace of peace at The Hague, made so little hold upon the world's imagination? May it not be, in part, because they have been so lacking in the kind of appeal which art can give? Their meetings have, until recently, been housed in tiresome architecture, a weak imitation of older styles.

International activities are devoted largely to worthy but dull discussions of political and economic matters, to endless bickering and committee reports. There is no brilliant life around them, nothing remarkable for the traveler to see, or those at home to read about. Meanwhile the national capitals of Europe and Asia glow with life, with gay restaurants and music, with operas, theaters, and art museums, with athletic tournaments and sports. We take pleasure in visiting and revisiting them. The glamor of all the arts is cast, as a result, upon centers of nationalism.

World fairs and expositions are international centers of art and pleasure. But they are temporary and housed in national cities. Five years from now, or fifty, the noise of cannon may subside for a time, and the hopes of the world may turn again to the United Nations or some new substitute for it. Why should not world-minded citizens attempt to raise it, by the means of art, into a center of beauty and enjoyment, to which all men's thoughts can turn with pride? I have in mind a city which should be a true international capital of civilized culture, a permanent world's fair as well as a business office. It could be the property of an international organization, to which all nations contributed their best in friendly rivalry. It could have its great museums, of old and modern art and craftsmanship; its libraries, its palaces and pleasure gardens, surpassing in magnificence the forts and palaces of other days. It could be a center for international musical and dramatic performances, for scientific exhibits, for Olympic sports, and all other civilized enjoyments. Any nation could contribute to these, without first committing itself to fight or sacrifice economic interests in defense of a world state. Such a city of the future, I believe, will be a tangible foundation for world citizenship, an emotional bond between nations, and a potent symbol of their common cultural heritage.[2]

[2] The United Nations Building in New York, built long after this essay was first published, is a step toward such an ideal. In 1956, however, it still falls far short of the conception here set forth.

ART AND INTERNATIONAL UNDERSTANDING*

1. The arts in general education: an international project

The development of cultural interchange among all peoples of the earth is one of the principal aims of Unesco and the United Nations. It is intended to include the arts as well as scientific and other branches of civilization. So far, little has been done to achieve this aim as far as the arts are concerned, but there are a few encouraging signs. One is the project known as "The Arts in General Education."

At the second session of the general conference of Unesco, which met in Mexico City in 1947, the Director-General was instructed to assemble a committee of experts from various nations to recommend practical steps for encouraging the arts in general education on a world scale. Such a committee met in Paris in the spring of 1948. It recommended the establishment of a national committee in each member country, to facilitate cultural interchange with other countries in the field of the arts; also an international council or office in Paris to provide a central clearinghouse for world co-operation in this field.

Having adopted this set of proposals for administrative machinery, the Committee went on to discuss the kind of service or function which this machinery could most profitably carry out. Among the services most urgently needed, especially by teachers and students remote from the large metropolitan centers, are the following:

(a) information regarding improved methods for teaching the arts;

(b) circulation of exhibitions, not only of great works of art, past and present, but also of students' work illustrating various educational methods;

(c) information regarding sources of supply for materials to be

* Published in its original form in the 1949 *Yearbook of the Eastern Arts Association.* Abridged versions were also published in the Unesco periodical, *Arts and Education,* June 1949; *School Arts,* May 1950; and *Education in Art,* a Symposium, Paris 1953. As of 1956, the project mentioned has not yet been put into full operation.

used in teaching of the arts, such as reproductions, books, phonographic recordings, musical instruments, painting and modeling equipment, films, etc.;

(d) translation and publication of important books and articles in the field, most of which are not available for widespread use by teachers;

(e) encouraging the arrangement of international dramatic and musical festivals;

(f) encouraging the organization of international federations of teachers and other professional workers in the field, and international congresses for the exchange of ideas;

(g) assisting teachers and school systems in search of expert counsel on educational problems to secure it from the best qualified sources;

(h) aiding and encouraging the interchange of teachers and students, and the establishment of scholarships for research, especially for the purpose of observation and study in foreign countries.

It was decided that the term "arts" should be understood as including not only the visual arts and crafts such as painting, sculpture, architecture and pottery, but also music, creative writing, the theater, dance, and cinema. "General education" would be understood as covering all age levels, that is, the education of adults as well as children; it would include not only school instruction, but such agencies as museums, radio, television, films, libraries, publications, and folk arts.

In view of continued tensions and unsettlement in the world situation, and the fact that normal cultural interchange had not been re-established since the war, it was felt that constructive international measures along these lines were extremely urgent. The recognized power of the arts to promote emotional and other personal adjustment among individuals and peoples should be utilized as fully and promptly as possible.

The Committee's recommendations have since been approved by various national and international authorities in Unesco, but few steps have been taken to put them into effect. It is certain that something of the sort will have to be carried on, under one name or another, if and when the world enjoys a period of free and peaceful development. It will be expensive, but abundantly worth while.

2. *Interchange in the arts as a means to world peace*

The aim of Unesco as a whole has been stated as the building up of a mental attitude conducive to world peace. At present, as we live in the threat of another war, this aim appears as paramount, and all other aims as instrumental to it. There may be a time when peace among nations is taken for granted. The emphasis in world organization will then shift from mere avoidance of war, a negative aim, to more positive co-operation among all peoples.

Underlying the project for the arts in general education is a belief that the arts can and should be used as a means to international understanding and sympathy; hence to peace and active cultural co-operation. They can be used to reduce antagonism between racial, religious, social, and political groups, and to develop mutual tolerance and friendship. A second assumption is that the arts should be used in a systematic way, under official or semi-official administration. It is not enough to rely on the work of individuals or small groups, as in the past. They are too weak and limited; they do not utilize the potential social values of art to the full. In the third place, it is not enough to train and encourage artists themselves, or even to help circulate their works among the general public. One should go more deeply into the educational process; work with schools and other educational agencies in disseminating world art, so as to insure its reaching wide areas of population, children as well as adults, laymen as well as specialists, and in the most effective ways.

These assumptions are not as obviously true as one might think. Some kinds of art tend to unite people; others to divide them into hostile camps. There is militaristic art, intolerant, hate-inspiring art, as well as the opposite. The artist can try to glorify his own nation, race, religion, class, or section of the country by holding all others up to scorn and ridicule. This is often unconscious, as in the naïve conceit of the old missionary hymn, "From Greenland's icy mountain to India's coral strand." All distant, exotic countries, it assumes, are lands "Where every prospect pleases, and only man is vile." All we have to do is to "free them from error's chains," perhaps by subjugating them with the kindest intentions in the world. Practically all countries have produced art of this type. To circulate it now will not automatically increase good will on earth.

To gain that end, one must be selective: not circulate all kinds of art with equal vigor, but try to emphasize those kinds which will make for good feeling. There is plenty of good art, old and new, which stresses ideas and emotions that unite people: their common love for home and family, for children, animals, the beauty of nature, for courage and skill in doing things which improve man's common lot on earth. Most cultures, for instance, have legends about the early heroes who first brought man the useful arts—fire, agriculture, medicine, and building. It is mere common politeness in international intercourse to refrain from insulting our neighbors with art which vilifies them, as we would refrain if they came to our homes. It is equally wise not to force upon their attention art which gives an unnecessarily black account of ourselves, if we desire their good opinion. For home consumption, the frankest denunciation of our own social evils—and they are many—is salutary in the long run. But the neighbors may take us at our word, and think that is the whole story. Let us be tactful in expressing our attitudes toward them, and self-respecting though not egotistical in giving an account of ourselves.

The main point to realize here is that, if we intend to develop cultural interchange and teaching in the arts as a means to international friendship, we should study the problem scientifically, to learn from past experience and controlled experiment what kinds of art will best serve this end, and what ways of using them. This may lead to very different choices and techniques from those which we would use for other purposes.

New works of art will have to be produced, especially adapted to stimulate international friendship. A few attempts have been made along this line, but neither Unesco nor the cause of world unity has yet secured the active co-operation of artists on a large scale. They are therefore losing the help of a great potential ally. For centuries, kings and dictators, churches, propagandists, and now commercial advertisers, have realized the power of art to influence people's minds, for good or evil. Sooner or later, the tremendous emotional appeal of art will be systematically utilized in the service of world unity. Even with the best intentions, it is hard to secure effective co-operation on the part of artists. They are often highly individualistic, impatient of attempts to harness them in any official undertaking. Some of the best have narrow prejudices. Most of them hate wordy discussions about abstract issues. When they try earnestly to help, the results are often banal, preachy, or sentimental. There again, much study and experiment are needed to produce the best methods.

Friendliness between two peoples is obviously a matter of emotional attitudes. As in the case of individuals, it does not always depend upon having practical interests in common. It cannot be created by rational arguments alone. Emotional symbols can be a powerful cohesive influence. A common religion may provide them. When monarchs ruled, state marriages between two royal families provided symbolic bonds between their peoples. The British and American peoples have, or could have, many conflicting economic and political interests. Not only biological kinship, but common traditions, as in literature and drama, help strengthen the feeling that "blood is thicker than water," and predispose both sides to adjust small conflicts amiably. The French and American peoples are linked by the memory of Lafayette, the Statue of Liberty, and a common love for Paris, French fashions, wines, and perfumes. Great serious art is not necessarily the best bond; it often fails to touch the masses deeply. When ordinary people in both countries laugh at the same clowns, the same jokes and comic strip characters, weep at the same tragedies, admire the same actresses and athletes—when they have done so, not for a few years, but for many generations, an emotional atmosphere develops which is favorable to constructive negotiation on more practical levels. Unfortunately, that is not the whole story; otherwise the common love for German music might have prevented two world wars. But the arts are one potential instrument for peace which has never been adequately used, and at the present time we cannot afford to neglect it.

Every nation is pleased by having its products admired. In this, it is like an individual artist, child or adult. The psychology is very simple: it is a question of whether the sensitive national ego shall be enhanced and soothed by praise, or irritated by contempt. Of course, the praise must be sincere and discriminating; but when there are just grounds for praise, it should not be withheld. Professional diplomats and specialists on foreign affairs, like other practical persons, are all too apt to ignore the intangible, emotional factors which influence international relations. Too many of our diplomatic and business representatives abroad are insensitive to art and to the cultural climate of the places to which they are sent. Some of them live for years in a country without studying its language or learning to appreciate its arts.

Learning to like some exotic style of art may be the first step toward liking, or at least understanding and tolerating, the people which produced it. Often this first step consists in admiring some curio—some piece of carving from the South Seas, perhaps, as merely odd, grotesque, or fantastic. Next, we learn to appreciate its decorative appeal, its unusual design of shapes and colors. Most persons go no farther. But an increasing number of students wish to learn something about the cultural background of the art which interests them. The interpretations of anthropologists and foreign scholars, on the religious and other symbolism of art, are becoming more accessible to the general public. The final step may be a tolerant understanding of the whole culture and way of life from which the works of art proceeded. This does not imply indiscriminate liking and approval; one can still evaluate the foreign culture according to one's own standards, accepting some parts and rejecting others. But scientific understanding is at an opposite pole from blind, ignorant hatred of everything foreign, different in racial or religious origin, or merely "different."

Many an occidental student has been led to understanding and fundamental sympathy for the Chinese, Indian, or Japanese people through being first attracted by their decorative arts, their music, dancing, or literature in translation. We know also how much the young people of the orient are attracted by Western films, popular music, dances, clothing, and customs—a fact which their conservative elders deplore. And indeed, there are disadvantages in cultural interchange as well as benefits. What is accepted from abroad is not always for the best, from the standpoint of those who love the old traditions.

3. Planned, selective, cultural interchange as a social aim

Over and above its value as a means to political harmony, cultural interchange is valuable as a means to the continuous enrichment of human experience. Historians tell us that civilization started first in those regions where travel was easy; where the intercourse of different people led to a mixture of ideas and folkways; where it broke the rigid forms of custom, forcing people to work out new, compromise solutions, new syntheses of thought in art, religion, technology, and morals.

The stimulating effect of cultural interchange still operates. By learning of other cultures with different customs, different goals and standards of value, we become more conscious of our own. We become intelligently self-critical and open to change if there is reason for doing so. By realizing that other peoples are attaining values which we miss—as medieval Europe did through the Crusades and early explorations—we escape from narrow routines and reach out for those additional values. Once the habit of cultural importation is acquired, it goes on at accelerating speed. As scientists range the world for exotic plants and minerals, so artists, scholars, and importers of luxuries range it for exotic art in every medium.

The result is stimulating on the whole; it challenges the European artist to combine the values of exotic art with those of his own tradition. In the eighteenth century a French translation of the *Arabian Nights* strongly influenced romantic literature. Delacroix put Near Eastern color in his painting. Gauguin captured some of the spirit of Polynesian art and life. Rimsky-Korsakov and Debussy put oriental coloring in music.

To be sure, there are disadvantages and dangers. In present Europe and America, the imitation of exotic styles in art has led to a wave of eclecticism—of confusion and uncertainty from too much change, too many different stimuli. The main traditions of European art and thought have been partially obscured and rejected, for a time at least. Still more complete and overwhelming is the overthrow of traditional ideals and customs in the Far and Near East. The world teems with rival, struggling ideologies, in art as in politics.

Cultural diffusion is never a simple process or an unmixed blessing. When old patterns are broken, something is always lost. However faulty the old adjustment, it may seem like a lost paradise in the chaos which follows. The impact of a powerful culture on a weaker one is often to destroy the latter entirely. An anthropologist once said, "Wherever the white race has encountered a primitive culture, it has smashed it to bits, then laboriously tried to fit the pieces together again." To nurture the fine flowering of a weaker group, some seclusion and protection from invading forces may be necessary. It was only through a fortunate, temporary resistance to great neighbors such as Persia that the tiny state of Athens flourished for a while, only to go down at last before the Macedonian and Roman Empires.

Yet there is no going backward; cultural isolation is increasingly impossible today. No iron curtain can long enforce it. Even stubbornly exclusive Nepal is opening its doors.

Political imperialism is discredited, as a means of imposing one culture forcibly on others. But cultural imperialism is still alive, in the form of expensive propaganda by great nations in praise of their own arts and products. This has both good and bad effects. The United States has lagged far behind Britain, France, and Russia in thus actively spreading its influence. The spontaneous processes of world trade and travel are slow, and often fail to spread the best in each culture.

There remains a method hardly begun as yet—that of voluntary, systematic cultural exchange by free peoples, under official, international auspices. This does not mean that national or international governments as such would do the active work. There is much distrust of their ability or willingness to choose the best in their own cultures, or in foreign ones. They tend toward ultra-conservatism, favoritism, and timid compromises. In the United States, particularly, there is a tradition of leaving cultural matters to private agencies. This may have to be changed a little, in favor of some definite governmental aid and supervision. Some other nations, in which governments have exerted too much control over art and education, may need to change in the opposite way.

Such an undertaking assumes a hypothesis which seems reasonable enough to the modern liberal, but which is fairly new in world affairs. This is, that almost every contemporary culture has something of potential value for the others. It implies a willingness on the part of each group to learn from the others—a certain humility in cultural matters—instead of the old provincial assumption that one's own group is best in all respects. It implies a democratic attitude toward the right of small, weak nations and minority groups to be heard in cultural realms. Their contribution in these realms may be great beyond all proportion to their political and economic strength.

This does not imply that all cultures are of equal value; that each can make an equal contribution to world civilization. That would be a doctrinaire, unrealistic interpretation of democracy. To those who live in the great, advanced civilizations of both east and west, it seems evident that these have most to offer in the arts, and certainly in the sciences. It is not a question of inborn racial superiority.

Through good fortune or otherwise, some groups have gone farther in cultural evolution than others, and should take the greater share of responsibility and leadership for a while. Some cultures have produced little that can be admired by any civilized standards: for example, the inhabitants of Dobu, of whom Fortune and Benedict have drawn so unattractive a picture.

But the time has passed when any racial, religious, or political group can claim to have a monopoly on good art or on wisdom and success in meeting the problems of life. The African Negro tribes offer examples of sculptural design in wood and complex rhythms of drumbeats. The Zuni, of whom Ruth Benedict also writes in *Patterns of Culture,* give examples of serene and orderly adjustment between man and nature, the individual and society—an adjustment which is expressed in their arts and rituals. To admire these contributions and seek to incorporate them in our own way of life is not to revive romantic illusions about the "noble savage." We realize that every culture, including our own, has its faults as well as its virtues: its painful tensions and frustrations; its cruelties and failures to achieve the best mode of life which is possible under the circumstances. We are now making more objective, comparative analyses of different cultures, and can decide what we admire or disapprove in each. To make that selection wisely and open-mindedly is a task which calls for the best wisdom of this and later generations.

Some rudiments of planned cultural interchange can be observed on a small scale in many American cities, such as my own in Cleveland, Ohio. Cleveland is typical of many industrial cities in having a population of highly diversified national and racial origin, including large Polish, Hungarian, Czecho-Slovak, Jewish, Italian, and Negro groups. The older idea of the melting pot was to transform all such immigrant groups as completely and rapidly as possible into the Anglo-Saxon type of American. Children in these groups were often ashamed of their parents' old-country ways, and rejected their cultural heritage. Educators now encourage them to be proud of their national and racial backgrounds, to keep their artistic traditions alive, while absorbing at the same time the fundamentals of the American culture. The art museum and other institutions cooperate along this line by bringing exhibitions of painting, craftwork, music, dancing, and films from each of these foreign backgrounds. Each group is encouraged to take special pride in its own contribution, while taking a friendly interest in those of other groups as well.

The goal of selective cultural interchange is definitely not one of complete uniformity. No one wants a world where all peoples are alike. The thought is too dreary to contemplate, like that of a world in which both sexes dressed, behaved, and thought in identical ways. Variety is not only the spice of life, but a necessary phase in progress. Thoughtful Americans who travel in Istanbul, Bombay, or Shanghai often grieve to see American movies advertised everywhere, streets filled with Ford and Buick cars, American bars and dance halls, Coca-Cola signs, and huge stone blocks of pseudo-classic office buildings like the ones back home. It is not merely the tourist's lament at a loss of quaintness and color. We regret the apparent lack of indigenous creative power, which might resist the invasion of our popular arts, and compete with something forceful of its own, as in years past Asia withstood the influence of Greece and Rome, to evolve along its own distinctive lines. The victory is too easy; as lovers of competitive sport, we would enjoy more opposition. Americans, in spite of their frequent bad manners abroad, are on the whole rather humble toward foreign civilizations. They admire the great monuments of the past and the graces of modern living which they often lack at home. They go to learn and to have new experiences; accordingly, they feel let down when confronted with the inexorable march of American influence, good, bad, and indifferent.

Some uniformity and standardization are desirable. Mass production by machine methods has proven its ability to raise the economic standard of living, by providing satisfactory food, shelter, transportation, and communication in vast quantities at low cost. It raises new problems of controlling them in the general interest, but these can be solved. Science tends to standardize its nomenclature and certain routines, such as the cataloguing of researches. Even artists like to have standardized paints and brushes, pianos, paper, and ink. But there is always a danger that excessive standardization may stifle experimentation and improvement. Especially, there is danger of its interfering with the freedom of thought and of artistic creation. As large industry extends its web over publication, films, the theater, radio, and television, it often tends to discourage small, independent enterprises by making them costly and difficult, snarled in a maze of legal, financial, and trade-union restrictions. This is one reason why art lovers in highly industrialized countries look longingly at the so-called "backward" areas of the earth, where big industry has not yet triumphed.

In the old-fashioned, individual craftsman or ballad singer, in the folk arts of primitive peoples, they see the vanishing traces of the personal touch in art. What will happen, then, when the Western influence is spread still further, and given added impetus by the forces of world organization? Will it hasten to obliterate these last few traces, or will the Asiatic cultures develop new, strong, counter-affirmations of their own?

At the present stage, we hardly know enough about cultural dif-fusion to control it wisely. The scientific study of cultures is in its infancy. How can we know what elements in a foreign culture will be best for us in the long run, or what elements in ours will be best for that culture to receive? What we hate most may be what we need as a corrective. Our descendants may rejoice that we were unable to keep it out. Christianity was stoutly resisted by the early Roman em-perors and scholars along with other oriental cults regarded as bad for national morale. Historians are still debating its effect on the fall of Roman civilization. Exotic musical importations, such as the Gypsy music of yesterday and the African jazz of today, have often been condemned as vulgar by conservative critics, only to be praised and accepted by those of the next generation.

It is hard indeed to separate the good from the bad in any culture pattern. When we forbid a primitive tribe to fight or practice bloody, obscene rites, when we impose our own ideas of peaceful industry and good behavior, we usually end by destroying the whole primitive culture, including the arts and picturesque folkways we admire. The revival of Japanese arts in the early twentieth century—of the Noh play, the traditional music, costume, dance, tea ceremony, and all that connoisseurs admire, went hand in hand with the revival of Japanese militarism, repression of free thought, and dreams of world domination. Chrysanthemum and sword seemed to be inseparably bound together.

The story of the Forty-seven Ronin, celebrated in countless Japa-nese poems, plays, and paintings, is almost incomprehensible to the occidental, and even to the Chinese mind, in its absolute acceptance of the ideals of revenge and feudal loyalty. Much of our art is like-wise incomprehensible to foreigners, because of its peculiarly occidental motivation. A picture or a copy of a book can be exported, even imitated on foreign soil; but its full cultural associations cannot be transplanted or understood abroad, save by a few special scholars. Exchange is easiest between similar cultures, such as those of France and England, or China and Japan.

A particular culture, as anthropologists insist today, is a continuous whole, an organized pattern. It is not like a pile of gifts in a shop window, from which we can select what pleases us, and leave the rest behind. True, we can bring home an African carving and put it in a glass case. Our artists can copy it, and it may seem to take root in our own environment. But what has taken root is the mere external shell, not the processes of thought and feeling which led to it. In emigrating to our land, in being adopted by our culture, the work of art changes into something different from what it was. Likewise, when we ship Mickey Mouse or the latest comic strip to Lapland or Siam, we never know how it will be interpreted. In a recent American film, the item which aroused most excitement in some foreign countries was not the main story, but the sight of a bottle of milk being left unguarded on a doorstep in the early morning.

These considerations are not arguments against trying to develop cultural interchange, but against being too rigidly selective or self-confident about it. They indicate the impossibility, at the present stage, of predicting just what results will follow from any particular step. We should not be too sure that we know exactly what is best for all the rest of the world, or that all they need is a good shipment of European and American art, with materials and directions for reproducing the same. On the contrary, we need an attitude of willingness to learn, to study other cultures on the part of those great nations which now exert most influence in international affairs. Let them seek the guidance of expert anthropologists, art scholars, and educators on the problems involved. Let them examine all their assumptions, to be sure their policies express a world point of view, and not a merely local one, whether of Paris, London, or Washington.

Even the belief in free exchange of ideas, and in man's power to improve his lot on earth by democratic, scientific, secular control is an unprovable hypothesis. It expresses, primarily, the attitudes and patterns which modern Western culture—especially that of France and the English-speaking countries—has developed during the past three centuries. Some writers argue, in opposition, that extreme open-mindedness and eclecticism are signs of old age and weakness in a culture. In the world views of medieval Christianity, of orthodox Buddhism and Brahmanism and of many other religions, there is much to deny our optimism as to progress by naturalistic, rationalistic methods. For those who preach a radical, mystic, or ascetic withdrawal from the natural world, for those convinced of their divine mission to rule the world by force, all this palaver about cultural interchange must seem utterly useless and worse than useless. But the faith in democratic, rational methods is not limited to a few occidental liberals; it finds a warm support in progressive leaders everywhere, and they can find many historic sanctions for it in their own traditions. Unfortunately, they have to battle for it against the new tide of communistic regimentation, as well as against older forms of tyranny. Even though we cannot, strictly speaking, prove the value of systematic cultural interchange on a world scale, it is worth trying as a logical extension of the democratic ideal, and one which has never had a chance to show its worth.

At the same time, it would be naïve to expect that active unrestricted cultural exchange will be welcomed with equal enthusiasm by all nations. There are rocks ahead. Some who endorse it nominally now will protest when they realize its full implications. Just as American isolationists denounce the importation of "un-American" ideas, so other countries denounce the importation of American culture as a flood of crude, vulgar materialism, immorality, and gangsterism. Even the educated oriental still regards us, on the whole, as a people of engineers, gadget-manufacturers, and dollar-chasers. He has yet to be convinced that we have any art or philosophy worth recognizing, and will not be overwhelmed with joy at the prospect of additional floods of objectionable paintings, books, and films with official backing. Let us hope he will modify this verdict a little on fuller acquaintance. It will take many years to work out a philosophy which is fully acceptable to all the major civilizations of the earth, let alone the innumerable minority groups. All that can be said at present is that no responsible leader in Unesco desires to force on any nation foreign ideas or works of art which it wants to exclude. We may hope for a maximum of freedom. But if objections arise, there is nothing to prevent any nation from setting up its own censorship in governmental, church, or professional hands, to decide what shall come in and what shall go out. Every nation today is glad to accept something from the outside world, and hence can profit by help in getting it. Beyond that, let it open its doors as gradually as it wishes.

In administering cultural interchange, international agencies can avoid a great deal of trouble if they will abstain from officially endorsing particular artists or works of art. Much less should they assemble and circulate official exhibitions, sets of books, and so on. Such choices should, as a rule, be made by nongovernmental, professionally qualified groups and individuals. The function of Unesco officials should be to open up and facilitate the flow of cultural traffic, as policemen regulate the cars in a street, without vouching for the goodness of any particular car or its riders. They can throw their influence in favor of art which seems beneficial to world co-operation in general. But they should not presume to set up exact aesthetic standards. They must patiently endure seeing much bad art circulate along with the good, for the sake of the process as a whole. If they try to impose their own standards, except in very broad and general ways, they will bring down a storm of protest on their heads from persons who have different standards, and endanger the whole program.

4. Building world arts into the educational process

By far the most important part of the work must be done by each nation and community. It is for them to bring these resources within reach of individual students and the public. Indeed, much is already being done by each of the leading Western nations. They hardly need outside help themselves. An international project is a chance for them to help less privileged countries. But the problem of art in general education is not only an international one. Each community by itself can go ahead, if it will, to develop more world-mindedness through the use of art. Much has been done, but even the richest nations are not yet making full educational use of the treasures of world art which they possess.

The agencies concerned with diffusing world art, as we have seen, include not only schools and colleges, but libraries, museums, motion pictures, radio and concert bureaus, periodicals and many others. We shall consider here only schools and colleges, and only their work in general education; not the training of professional artists, which is another large problem in itself.

What would it mean, then, for a school system to develop a thorough, systematic program for the arts in general education—one having for its aim the production of world-minded citizens, in possession of the best in all humanity's artistic heritage? Needless to say such a large-scale program would be hard to work out at present; it would conflict with too many other interests. But there is something to be gained by seeing it clearly as an objective. Let us try, then, to formulate a few tentative principles for the development of world arts in general education.

The curriculum in general education should provide some instruction in all the principal arts, and in the principal styles and periods of each art. It is not enough to rely on English and a little European music, with a little drawing in the lower grades, to carry the burden of man's aesthetic education. More than passing attention should be paid not only to English and American literature, but to world literature in translation, including some primitive folklore and the masterpieces of oriental poetry. The student should have some direct experience, not only of painting and sculpture, but of architecture, city planning, the handicrafts, landscape architecture, photography, motion pictures, the dance, theater, costume and interior design. He should have some acquaintance with oriental and primitive music, as well as with the European classics; with some of the best music of India, China, Japan, the Near East, and Africa, through phonograph records.

All this may seem a staggering amount to put into our already overloaded curriculum and educational budget. So let us hasten to add: the schools and colleges do not need to do it all themselves. They can make much more use of other institutions which are willing to co-operate, such as museums, orchestras, radio, television, and films. The schools' task, in large part, is not to duplicate such agencies, but to co-ordinate its work with theirs. It should incorporate museum visits at strategic points in the school year, and link them up systematically with classwork. Where the school is far from a museum, it can borrow good circulating exhibits from the larger centers.

No school, of course, should try to teach all arts on all grades. They should be taken up at different times, on different age levels. For example, city planning involves sociological considerations, and some maturity of mental outlook. Hence, it is suited to study on the higher

levels. Some arts need only occasional notice; others, such as literature, deserve attention year after year, by all students.

Various approaches should be made in the study of each art: some
active participation, some observation, some criticism, and some history. Young children need much participation, and are bored with
too much looking, listening, or talking. Older ones can concentrate
more, at times, on abstract problems.

There should be no sharp line between art in general education
and art as vocational or professional training; the one shades gradually into the other. At present, there is far too wide a gulf between
them in many countries. It is often hard for the student to take a
balanced course involving several arts along with other subjects. He
must specialize too soon, and too narrowly, as by attending an art
academy where nothing else is taught. There is great need for the
general, liberal approach; but it should be closely co-ordinated with
the vocational, to allow for a gradual narrowing down of interests.
At the start, all should have a wide sampling of studies, with a moderate amount of art. Some will gradually increase the amount of art
until it becomes a field of concentration; others will gradually abandon it. For utmost flexibility in a school system, it should be easy for
the older student to transfer from one school to another where the
emphasis is different, as well as from one course of study to another
within the same building. A wrong choice early in the game should
not be too hard to correct.

Where can the study of foreign arts be most effectively introduced?
All along the line to some extent, but in different ways. The very
young child, say of kindergarten age, is not much interested in
nationalities or styles. He can enjoy a Chinese brush drawing of a
bird, without caring about how it differs from an Audubon bird.
The interest in national costumes and folkways, including styles of
art, develops gradually during middle and later childhood. Some lose
it; others retain it to the level of advanced scholarship.

There is greatest freedom for introducing foreign arts where the
approach is entirely or largely one of appreciation, history, or theory. It is hard to learn to play, dance, compose, or paint well in an
exotic style. It is much easier to appreciate foreign arts, not profoundly perhaps, but with pleasure and profit. Some attempt at practice of exotic styles of art is a valuable part of general education. It

is common in the schools, as in putting on a stage production of *Scheherazade*. But it is not worth carrying very far except for those who are willing to study some one art intensively. The discriminating, older student will soon tire of dilettantism in the practice of the arts: of dabbling clumsily in many different styles and techniques. But everyone of college age and capacity can develop a basic, layman's ability to appreciate all the main traditions in the principal arts without much risk of shallowness, or of serious interference with his vocational studies.

The training of the professional artist is beyond the scope of this essay. But it can at least be noted that some acquaintance with exotic styles is of increasing value to the artist in every field. There is perhaps a danger that too much diversity of training may confuse his own creative efforts, make him too eclectic. But no artist can entirely escape the flood of foreign influences pouring in upon each country today. One task of those who train prospective artists in each field is to help them assimilate these influences without confusion, to keep their individual balance in a changing world. This task will be easier if foreign ideas and styles of art are presented to the student, not all at once, but gradually, from early childhood, in such a way as to help him relate them to his native traditions.

In this and other ways, general education in the arts on the lower grades should be of value to the few who choose an art as a professional career. Thus the general approach should lead smoothly into the professional approach, even though not primarily adapted for prospective artists.

In both general and vocational education, receptiveness to foreign cultures can be carried too far. It does so when elements of value in the old native tradition are rejected and lost through extreme adulation of exotic influences. This often happens when a people is conquered or otherwise subjected to overwhelming influence from a more advanced and powerful neighbor. On the other hand, conquered peoples have exerted great cultural influence on their political and military conquerors. Colonial and trusteeship policies in the care of weak and supposedly backward peoples should stress the preservation of local arts and other valuable cultural traits.

In its own school system, each people has a primary duty to select, preserve, and impart the best in its own cultural tradition, including its arts. In that way it can make its own best contribution to world civilization. Its secondary duty is to select and impart to its own people what seems best in foreign cultures.

Each country in future will have to face more consciously this task of selecting the best elements in all cultures, and merging them into some new, harmonious pattern of its own, which shall be favorable both to individual personality and to international co-operation. Through international agencies, if wisely and tactfully conducted, study and experiment along this line can be scientifically guided, active, free, and impartial.

VIII

SELECTING AND TRANSMITTING THE WORLD'S ARTISTIC HERITAGE*

It is commonly recognized that the arts comprise one of the most important parts of the world's cultural heritage. Without some knowledge and experience of it, no one can be broadly and liberally educated. As compared with past productions in scientific, political, and many other modes of thinking, past art contains a large proportion of material which is valuable today; worth looking at, reading, or listening to; not outgrown or obsolete. The history of the visual arts alone provides the most extensive and concrete of all frameworks for the history of civilization. It provides the most tangible and sometimes the only surviving data from which an ancient culture can be reconstructed. It provides a revealing expression of modern culture in all its periods, and in its leading racial, national, and local manifestations.

These facts present a large and important task to those in charge of determining the content of a liberal education. That task is not being undertaken consciously and systematically today. It is to *select and organize the artistic elements in the world's cultural heritage for transmission to youth.* As the world shrinks in size through faster communication and travel, the cultural heritage of each nation, each racial and religious group, is made available to all the others. Innumerable local cultures are being poured into one human civilization—through translations of literature, phonograph records of music, photographs, films, reproductions of visual art, interpretive books, articles, and lectures. This process of cultural fusion, which has been going on slowly for centuries, has been greatly accelerated in the last few decades. It has placed a tremendous burden on the educational system of every country which tries to be broadly humanitarian and cosmopolitan in its outlook. The recent influx of cultural products in this country has been so vast, so diversified, so

* Published in its original form in *The Journal of Aesthetics and Art Criticism,* III.9–10 (1944), under the title "Art, Aesthetics, and Liberal Education."

chaotic and piecemeal in its order of arrival on our mental shores that our schools and colleges have not been able to digest it for educational use. Some of it is great, some trivial; some easily understandable and usable, some utterly remote and foreign to our point of view. Schools that try to absorb it are apt to find their curricula so overcrowded with new "units" and "projects" on this or that nationality or part of the world that basic subjects are slighted and children's minds confused. Other schools frankly turn their backs on world culture and on the problem of liberal education, concentrating instead on locally demanded vocational skills and information.

Exotic imports in the cultural realm are apt to offend conservatives at home, and arouse isolationist hatred. There is a stubborn effort by some countries, and some groups in every country, to exclude the flood of foreign traditions and return to provincial isolation. A bigoted nationalism, aided by unhealthy social conditions, can build strong dikes against world culture. But these cultural dikes cannot be maintained much longer in any part of the world. The future civilization of every national group will be increasingly international, while at the same time each group rightly tries to keep alive and make available to others its own most cherished traditions.

There is now a concerted effort to make our youth more aware of the cultures of Latin America and of China and India—a vast undertaking which we have hardly begun. Such efforts are often impelled and prejudiced by political events, military and commercial alignments. When it is expedient to make friends with Latin America, there is pressure to advertise and perhaps to exaggerate its cultural achievements. When Germany and Japan became our enemies, there was pressure to ignore or disparage their whole cultural contribution for centuries past. As against this, German *émigré* scholars have enriched our culture with a flood of books in English, emphasizing past German accomplishments and ways of thinking. Thus fluctuating currents in political and social life affect the process of cultural assimilation, with results which eventually sift down into school textbooks and popular journalism. In a democracy, the process of cultural importation is comparatively free and haphazard, as distinguished from the rigorously planned governmental control of dictatorship.

Without sacrificing any of this freedom—in fact, with the utmost free trade in matters cultural—it should be possible to make the process a little less haphazard, a little more intelligently thought out.

No individual and no professional group can be entrusted with the whole task of selecting what is best in the cultural heritage. That is a never-ending process, which each generation must undertake anew in the light of its own best judgment. There are no definite, accepted standards; the standards themselves are part of the changing cultural heritage, and often conflict with each other. Those of us who accept a relativistic, naturalistic philosophy of value in aesthetics will not presume to evaluate art and artists in any final or absolute way, for we realize our limitations. But that does not justify us in evading the task of evaluation entirely, and assuming a mask of neutral objectivity. Even those scholars who make the greatest pretense at pure, objective fact-finding do evaluate, though perhaps unconsciously and without acknowledging their assumptions. They do so in the very act of including some artists, some types and examples of art in their books or courses, and omitting or minimizing others. Such inclusion and emphasis are tantamount to saying, "These are the important things, most worthy of attention." The praises and preferences of the expert are followed in innumerable textbooks and classrooms. Such cultural evaluation is important enough to be performed explicitly, systematically, in concrete detail, by the best experts available and with full defense of each judgment so far as reasons can be given. The student has a right to such reasons, and should not be put off with pontifical dogmatism to the effect that "one just feels these things; they can't be put into words."

The task of *selection for educational purposes* is not one of saying, in a general way, "This is good; that is bad. This is great; that is trivial." The transmission of culture to the next generation has to be adapted to different age levels, from nursery school to graduate school. One must ask not only what is best from an adult standpoint, but what is best for children in each grade of school. What can they grasp and assimilate? What will interest them and stimulate them to further growth and effort? What will follow naturally after what has gone before, and prepare them for advanced studies? What will have the desired effects upon them, emotionally and volitionally as well as intellectually, toward making them the kinds of person we want to produce? Differences in sex and intelligence, in special aptitude and type of personality, must also be considered if we expect to plan the curriculum wisely. In the upper grades of elementary school and after, vocational considerations enter with increasing force, making

us subordinate the values of liberal education to the practical needs
of making a living or running a home. To what extent can both sets
of values be combined?

Each of these questions bristles with theoretical difficulties. Little
or no research has been done on most of them in relation to the arts.
Few expert opinions are available, for the scholars in art have not
often considered them. The school administrator cannot postpone a
decision, however. He must determine the curriculum as best he can,
with his limited knowledge of each field of learning. He must order
textbooks written and purchased in quantity; allot so many hours in
the schedule for each unit of study. Often subjected to selfish and
irrational pressures, uncertain of his ground, he must live up to his
educational ideals as best he can.

Besides evaluation, there is need for *summary and condensation;*
for brief descriptive *interpretations* of each important realm of world
culture, so that the high spots can be touched upon in the brief span
allotted to each in a crowded curriculum. Scholars are apt to look
condescendingly upon the task of "popularizing" culture, and to
speak loftily of "Cook's tours" through learning. But a brief introduction, when there is time for no more, is better than nothing. And
there is room for great wisdom and skill in condensing huge masses
of material; locating their essential values in a few typical poems,
pictures, or phonograph records. First-class selections and summaries
can help to clarify the thinking of scholars, as well as to inform the
public. The schools need expert help in summarizing the latest discoveries about each great historic period in civilization. They must
disregard its minor works and emphasize its outstanding examples—
its Parthenons and Mahabharatas—so that hurried students will not
be overwhelmed by minor details. It is for the experts to build a
bridge of understanding between the modern student and each remote culture by interpretation and comparison, pointing out the
motives behind each type of art—the religious, moral, and social
viewpoints needed for its appreciation.

In particular, they can try to show the student what is living or
worth reviving in these ancient and exotic cultures, as distinct from
what is thoroughly and deservedly dead. This is no place for pedantic
scholarship—for reviving a trivial artist, with many footnote references, merely because no one has recently mentioned him. The modern student, especially in the United States, is skeptical about ancient

history—and this means everything before World War II. He has seen all too clearly the downfall of old-world cultures, including some which prided themselves on a high state of civilization. He is thrilled by the power of modern technology and impressed by the difficulty of learning it, of finding a place for himself in the postwar world. He has little time for mere antiquarian browsing. If asked to spend time in studying an ancient product, belief, or custom, he is impatient and prejudiced in advance. He wants to be shown exactly how it can be used today; what he can learn from it that can be applied in modern life. The most narrow-minded will accept only what can be used to make money in their future jobs. But there are many who will go a good deal farther and look respectfully at the ancient or exotic if shown how it can be somehow applied in our own culture—perhaps as a guide to wise daily living; as material for decorative ornament, or as a setting for some play or film. A deeper understanding of how old wisdom and beauty can be used today comes only after long study, long comparison of old and new. In this we gradually learn, for instance, how Plato expressed some ideas better—more concisely and penetratingly—than any subsequent writer has done; how certain important values in Bach, in Sung Chinese painting, or in Persian rugs, can be found nowhere else. We may or may not regard them as better than modern art; fortunately, the choice is not necessary. But they are worth while experiencing for their own sake, in addition to modern art. Moreover, they can help the student understand modern art, by showing him the stylistic traditions, including exotic and primitive revivals, on which it is based.

It should not be supposed that the cultural heritage is exclusively ancient and exotic, or that the artistic content of a liberal education must emphasize the far away and long ago. It is well at times to emphasize tradition, for it is all too liable to be pruned away in these impatient, practical days. But what happened yesterday, the latest product of a contemporary artist, is as much a part of our cultural heritage as the pyramids of Egypt. It is a part of the educational task to appraise and select the *best in contemporary culture;* the task of the cultural historian does not cease when he has told the story up to twenty years ago.

Nor is the cultural heritage entirely composed of finished works of art, to be passively admired and investigated. It also includes a vast repertory of *skills and techniques; of instruments and processes,* many of them in the field of art. For the present-day student who can apply them to advantage, they are hints for active use. Many old techniques and materials have been surpassed by modern ones, in art as elsewhere; but there are notable exceptions, and the modern artist often profits by reviving an old device. As a rule, the ancient artist's best gift to the modern one is no secret of technique or material, but one of form and design, of insight into human nature, or of mental and emotional attitude toward life and the world. Many such values are lost in each generation as it rushes into new, alluring paths. In the next, discerning leaders look back again and try to recapture what has been lost, perhaps to combine it with recent achievements. Of such action and reaction new developments in art are made.

The huge task of selection and summary is not waiting for aestheticians to undertake it, but is being done by countless writers and teachers in each special field of art and education. To a large extent it must be done by specialists. To the authority on sixteenth-century Italian music we listen with especial respect in selecting the greatest works and composers of that period. Each art and period has its own authoritative scholars. But when the question arises of what relative emphasis shall be placed on one period, one art, one national culture as compared with another, we must turn to those who have surveyed and appraised more extensively. And someone must piece together the scattered articles and books by specialists, into some brief, coherent forms which teachers can use.

Here American scholars, on the whole, have been overcautious, overtimid about generalizing. They have accepted too completely the assumption that one cannot be a sound scholar without specializing intensively on some minute spatial and temporal division of history. They have failed to realize that one can, paradoxically, specialize on generalizing; that to do so is the essence of the philosophical attitude. This type of scholarship, if aware of its limitations and willing to make use of the findings of specialists, can be as sound and rigorous as the narrower type. A map of the world, or of world culture, can be as scientific as one of a small region, though less detailed. Specialization, if pursued exclusively, achieves only a heaped-up mass of unorganized details. To bring out its full significance and usefulness, it must be constantly supplemented by the synthetic, extensive phase of thinking. German scholarship in the arts as in other fields, while at times minutely intensive, has been less timid about philosophical generalizing, and its scholars have been on the whole more broadly trained. We may not accept all their theories or judgments of value, but can well afford to emulate their courage and ambition in attempting large-scale, systematic summaries of human culture.

Some of these should be technical and erudite, for the advanced student; others simple and popular. If informed and careful scholars will not write the latter, someone else will, for the public now demands it. Most schools can make a place for a small unit on oriental civilization, and no more. If the best authorities will not boil it down into tabloid form, some hack writer will do so and will thus help to determine what shall be the cultural heritage. While the specialist hesitates and inveighs against "mere smatterings," the book markets are flooded with outlines of this and that: short cuts to knowledge and appreciation; world histories of music, the theater, painting, architecture, gardens, textiles; surveys of Greek, oriental, and medieval culture in their intricate complexity. Reviewers find mistakes; pundits grieve at omissions and dubious generalities. But, more and more, competent scholars are writing these surveys and doing better jobs of it, using secondary sources where they lack direct knowledge, or employing collaborators to cover some area on which they feel too little informed. The major gulf at present is between the occidental and the oriental inheritance. Few writers feel competent to survey and appraise them both in a single work, to show their interrelations in a single world history of civilization. Sometimes one finds the orient touched on in a single, unrelated chapter, to satisfy the new demand. Eventually, more balanced, integrated accounts will be given.

From the educational standpoint, something more is needed than books and articles *about* art. Books are needed which can give the reader at least a secondhand experience of the *works of art themselves,* by photographic reproduction, detailed analysis, and guidance in finding original examples elsewhere. In addition to books, however well illustrated, there is need for more, better, and less expensive color-print reproductions, colored lantern slides, phonograph records, films, and anthologies of world literature in translation. What is needed from the experts is, first, advice in selection; and, second, a simple but adequate conceptual framework, both historical and theoretical. Without going into exhaustive detail, this should help the student find quickly the distinctive and important features of each work of art, and their mutual relations in the whole fabric of world civilization. Books to be read independently will be of less direct value here than museum guidebooks, concert program notes, and pamphlets to accompany phonograph record albums.

There are many ways of organizing and presenting the cultural heritage. One of them is basically *chronological and genetic,* and leads to the subject known as cultural history, or history of civilization. It should include not only the history of all the arts, but that of the social, economic, religious, intellectual, and other factors which have interacted with them and helped to determine their nature. If we try to cover world history, Eastern and Western, it becomes almost impossible to proceed in continuous chronological order. One must skip around: follow Roman history for a time, then go back and pick up the Chinese or Indian story for a time, and so on. But chronological order can dominate on the whole. Writers who prefer a somewhat smaller field can mark one off on the basis of a single art or group of arts, or of a single division of history. For example, they can write on a subject like "music in Western civilization," or "Far-Eastern architecture." Even a relatively limited field such as this is extensive and involved enough to require considerable philosophic scope.

Another mode of procedure is that of *comparative aesthetics and critical theory.* It attempts rather a *morphological* basis of arrangement than a chronological: one based on recurrent types and principles of structure in art. It brings out the main factors in artistic form, such as representation, decoration, and symbolism; color and line in painting; melody and rhythm in music. It analyzes and classifies works from all periods in terms of types and styles, showing recurrent and distinctive features in different arts, periods, and cultural stages. This approach is more difficult for the student to follow than the chronological, and is less popular.

No sharp distinction is possible or desirable between the historical and theoretical approaches. To an increasing extent they are being combined, and the difference is one of degree, as to which mode of organization dominates. Of the two, there is more need at present for the theoretical approach, for it has lagged far behind the historical. There is great need of clarifying and systematizing our concepts of form and style in art, both for teaching purposes and for historians themselves. Many of these show their weakness in general theory by using descriptive and critical terms loosely, and making unsupported evaluative assumptions.

More important than the distinction between history and theory is that between *specialized and philosophical, intensive and extensive.* History can be either, and theory can be either. Historians have not been alone in leaning too far toward specialization in recent years. Aesthetics has done the same, and so has philosophy itself— both forgetting their traditional function of helping to co-ordinate knowledge and thinking in all other fields. Too many aestheticians have withdrawn into hair-splitting verbal analysis, ignoring the world of art and of human beings who make and use art. Aestheticians of this type can never take a leading role in liberal education or in cultural progress. They must come out of their libraries and observe more extensively in all the arts.

Aesthetics, thus revitalized, should be given a more strategic place in the curriculum of the liberal college in future—not off by itself in an inaccessible side alley, reserved for the few who specialize in philosophy, but at the heart of a co-ordinated program in the history, theory, and (for some students) the practice of the various arts. Detailed courses in the visual arts, literature, and music should be linked together chronologically by courses in general cultural history, and theoretically by courses in comparative aesthetics. The students who take such a co-ordinated course in the arts should also take basic courses in philosophy and science, including logic, psychology, and social science.

As a definite subject, aesthetics will be studied mainly in the higher grades, in college and graduate school. To study it in a systematic, technical way requires many previous courses in the subjects just mentioned. At the same time, steps in that direction can be taken all along the line. Even young children in the primary grades can be led to compare works of art and to discuss their preferences. Older ones take courses in art and music appreciation, which help to draw together their studies in various fields, without introducing more technical terms than they are capable of handling. A great deal more can be done on each grade of a liberal education, toward organizing with as much theory as necessary the various detailed studies of the arts and their cultural backgrounds. The lower down we go on the ladder of grades and age levels, the less we find the evils of departmental specialization. The first few grades present their share of the cultural heritage in a much more unified way, without the artificial division into subjects and isolated fields. From junior high school onward, the student needs more urgently the help which comparative aesthetics might give, in reintegrating what man has put asunder.

Such integration does not imply an attempt to eliminate all differences, to reconcile all conflicts of ideals, tastes, and attitudes. Some writers have proposed that a new, harmonious world culture be developed by selecting philosophic and ethical beliefs on which all can agree, or by selecting and combining the best elements in oriental and occidental culture into one consistent whole. This is going too far and too fast. Some gradual reconciliation of opposite beliefs and attitudes will certainly occur as we learn to understand each other better. But other diversities will last a long time, because they involve contradictory answers to the same religious, moral, and aesthetic problems. It would be impossible and in many ways undesirable to produce a uniform world culture. Educational integration does not imply either abolishing or concealing such differences, but stating them clearly and fairly as such. We should not assume that our own solutions are always the best or (as some Western scholars do) that they are always the worst. It is too often falsely assumed that the orient has a monopoly on "spiritual values," while the West has only material technology to contribute. Both can contribute in both realms.

In art, the infinite diversity of forms and styles is a source of never-ending interest and instruction. To integrate them educationally is to present and interpret them so that their similarities and differences can be grasped clearly, both as historical facts and as suggestions for creative experiment in future.

IX

METHODS IN THE PSYCHOLOGY OF ART*

Contemporary writing on aesthetics and art criticism is full of casual psychologizing—of generalizations about the psychology of art and aesthetic experience, most of which make no pretense at scientific verification. Recent developments in general psychology, and in special fields such as psychoanalysis, are quickly applied to support aesthetic theories. Since the rapid advance of psychology as a science, writers in aesthetics as in other fields have come to think, to a large extent, in terms of psychological concepts and to seek aid from psychology in interpreting their own phenomena.

At the same time, there has been comparatively little effort, outside the German-speaking countries, to deal directly and systematically with the psychology of art as a subject in itself, or as a definite branch of psychology. Many specialized researches have been conducted, but, with the exception of A. R. Chandler's *Beauty and Human Nature*,[1] there has been no recent attempt in English at a comprehensive synthesis of present knowledge and theory on the subject.[2] Excellent as far as it goes, Chandler's book is devoted mainly to "experimental aesthetics" in the narrow sense—that is, to statistical and laboratory experiments involving quantitative measurement. There is need for a more extensive synthesis, which will bring in the

---

* Published in its original form in *The Journal of Aesthetics and Art Criticism*, VI.4 (March, 1948), pp. 225–235. Part of this article was read at a meeting of the Art Department of the National Education Association and published in its *Bulletin*, Vol. VII (1941). Thanks are extended for permission to reprint it with revisions and additions. The present version was read at the 1947 convention of the American Society for Aesthetics in Baltimore.

[1] (New York, 1934).

[2] Some of the books whose titles seem to promise such a synthesis are brief surveys, intended as introductory texts for the beginner, rather than as treatises on an advanced level. See, for example, R. M. Ogden's *The Psychology of Art* (New York, 1938), and N. C. Meier's *Art in Human Affairs: an Introduction to the Psychology of Art* (New York, 1942). On the other hand, V. Löwenfeld's *The Nature of Creative Activity* (New York, 1939) is a detailed, technical report of a specialized scientific research, but does not live up to its comprehensive title.

results of other lines of investigation as contributing to the psychology of art: e.g., those of anthropology, cultural history, psychoanalysis, individual psychology, and child psychology. There is need also
for more discussion of aims and methods, and for the planning of a
concerted approach.[3]

The psychology of art is usually considered as a branch of applied
psychology, not in the sense of being devoted to practical uses, but
in the sense that it studies the application of general psychological
functions in a special type of activity and situation. This type includes artistic creation and appreciation, and may be briefly described
as "behavior and experience in relation to works of art." As a subject, the psychology of art is an outgrowth of the older subject known
as "aesthetics," which in turn was derived from philosophical specu-
lations on beauty and art. Long before the rise of experimental psychology, aestheticians in England, France, and Germany theorized
on the nature of perception, taste, imagination, emotion, pleasure,
and the "sense of beauty" in relation to art.

In 1876, the German psychologist Fechner proposed that a scientific approach to aesthetics be substituted for the old, abstract, speculative one. He proposed an empirical study of observable data, and
a procedure based on experimentation and quantitative measurement. He studied, for example, what types of geometrical shapes are
considered most beautiful by various individuals, without assuming
in advance that any one type was actually most beautiful. Fechner's
approach to aesthetics had great influence in the development of
general psychology on an experimental basis, although the interest
of most psychologists quickly turned away from art and aesthetic
preference. His approach to aesthetic phenomena has been followed
by a number of later psychologists, but without far-reaching achievements.[4] The phenomena of art and of responses to art are on the
whole so complex and variable, so hard to observe objectively, that

[3] Chandler summarizes the methods of the psychology of art in a short para-
graph on page 6 (op. cit.). The psychologist may rely, he says, on the writings of
historians and critics, or "observe the effects of art on the public and his
friends"; he may examine his own experience introspectively, or conduct
psychological experiments.

[4] The experimental methods used by Fechner, Witmer, Angier, Legowski,
Thorndike, and others are described by Chandler, op. cit., Ch. III.

the strictly quantitative or psychometric approach has been decidedly limited in its power to deal with them. This approach to aesthetics has somewhat undeservedly monopolized the name "experimental aesthetics," for it implies that "experimental method" is restricted to quantitative laboratory procedure, whereas many other approaches are experimental in the broad sense.[5] Nevertheless, the Fechner tradition has survived as a somewhat distinct branch of aesthetics, strongly psychological in viewpoint, and devoted largely to studies of perception and preference. These processes have been studied, sometimes in application to works of art, more often in application to highly simplified forms such as isolated rectangles, dots, colors, and musical chords. There is great difficulty in transferring conclusions, drawn from experiments with the artificially simplified type of object, to the infinitely more complex world of art.

Works of art themselves can be studied from a psychological viewpoint, as products of human mentality and stimuli to various types of overt response and inner experience. But workers in the fields vaguely designated as "experimental aesthetics" or "the psychology of art" have rarely undertaken detailed studies of the various types of form in art, of their cultural genesis, or of their connections with personality traits. The direct, intensive study of works of art has been left on the whole to art critics and historians. In Germany, all these related fields, when approached from a scientific standpoint, have been grouped together as "general science of art" (*allgemeine Kunstwissenschaft*).[6] Naturally, the methods used for examining and interpreting works of art have to be somewhat different from those used in studying present human behavior. They tend to involve more use of historical, biographical, and sociological material. Such studies may all be considered as "psychology of art" in a broad sense, but they lead the student rather far outside the usual limits and methods of experimental psychology. In the United States, they are usually classed within the field of aesthetics.

The psychology of art has never been a major concern of psychology, but interest in it is growing in proportion as art itself becomes

[5] Cf. Thomas Munro, "Scientific Method in Aesthetics," *Toward Science in Aesthetics* (Liberal Arts Press, New York, 1956), pp. 5, 14.

[6] As in Max Dessoir's important work, full of psychological insight, on *Aesthetik und allgemeine Kunstwissenschaft* (Stuttgart, 1923).

a more vital concern of modern life and education. Teachers are coming to face the problem of trying to develop abilities in the field of art creation and appreciation, especially in children. They find that little is definitely known about the nature of these abilities, or about the processes involved in learning within the various arts.

Germany and Austria long and capably maintained the lead in both the philosophic and the scientific approaches to aesthetics and the psychology of art. This leadership lasted until a year or two after 1933, when cultural activities in central Europe entered the period of eclipse. In particular, the years between 1918 and 1935 were a time of prolific advance. Substantial works were written on the psychology of art in general, on children's art, and on art education. Unfortunately, a very slight amount of this material has been made available to American teachers and scholars. Ignoring the achievements of recent foreign science inevitably results in wasted time and energy on this side of the water. Much time and effort have been wasted by American psychologists of art through ignoring German contributions to the field. The tragic fact now is that many of the most important books and articles published in central Europe, and great masses of concrete data, such as children's drawings, are no longer available at all. In many cases, they have been destroyed.

Many books and articles in German which deal indirectly or incidentally with the psychology of art are fairly well known in the United States. They include writings on psychoanalysis, gestalt psychology, cultural history, phenomenalism, logical positivism, psychological tests (e.g., the Rorschach), child psychology, and educational method. Less attention has been paid in this country to the fewer German works which deal directly and explicitly with the psychology of art as a subject in itself. These works, and the long tradition of previous research on which they are built, provide a substantial body of knowledge and a conceptual apparatus which could be extremely valuable to American psychologists.

The outstanding German treatise on the psychology of art is the monumental three-volume work by Richard Müller-Freienfels, former editor of the *Zeitschrift für Aesthetik*. It is entitled *The Psychology of Art (Psychologie der Kunst,* Teubner, Leipzig, 1923). A smaller work by Paul Plaut is also notable from the standpoint of methodology: *Principles and Methods of the Psychology of Art (Prinzipien und Methoden der Kunstpsychologie,* Urban and Schwarzenberg, Berlin, 1935).[7] As the title indicates, the latter book is more restricted to a discussion of methods, whereas the Müller-Freienfels also undertakes a detailed explanation of the subject matter itself. This subject matter, in brief, is the nature of the arts and related types of experience. Art, of course, can be studied from many different viewpoints, including the historical and the sociological. The psychological viewpoint emphasizes the relation of art to the general framework of human nature, its functions and their development, including individual differences as well as general human traits. It studies not only the processes of artistic creation and appreciation, but also the nature of the work of art itself as a configuration of stimuli which tend to arouse various types of complex response in different individuals.

A third important work is that of O. H. Sterzinger, entitled *Foundations of the Psychology of Art (Grundlinien der Kunstpsychologie,* Leykam, Graz, 1938). This emphasizes the nature of form in the arts, whereas the other two emphasize the processes of creation and appreciation.

I will not undertake to summarize the theories or experimental findings of these writers, but will consider only the question of *methodology,* as discussed by Müller-Freienfels and Plaut.

It has been characteristic of American works on the psychology of art to follow one extreme approach or another: to be either frankly unscientific, literary and personal, or to be rigorously quantitative, admitting no grain of evidence for consideration which cannot be objectively verified and measured. Each of these approaches has decided limits, and when the investigator confines himself exclusively to one or the other, the results are sure to be one-sided. Unfortunately, those who approach the problem from the laboratory viewpoint do not always realize their own limitations, and sometimes claim to have solved perennial problems of the inner imaginative and emotional life of man by means of a few superficial experiments. European psychologists in this field are not unversed in statistical and laboratory procedure, but the best of them have a breadth of cultural background, an acquaintance with the philosophic and criti-

---

[7] I am indebted to Dr. Edward N. Barnhart, now of the University of California, for having called Plaut's book to my attention, and for help in translating it. Also, I am indebted to Dr. Leopold Levis for most of the translations from Plaut and Müller-Freienfels.

cal as well as the laboratory approaches to art which prevent them
from relying too heavily upon any one approach or overestimating its
results by comparison with the great amount that is yet to be done.
To contradict the popular assumption that German scholarship is
always pedantically oversystematic—that it follows out a single formula to the end without regard for facts or expediency—I have found
in the three books mentioned above a flexible disposition to make
the most of whatever tools are available for approaching a very difficult set of problems. The strength of German writing on psychology
of art has lain essentially in its ability to combine several approaches
to the same phenomena, to use each for what it will accomplish, and
to realize its limitations; to maintain a clear, broad conception of the
field and its problems, then attack it in a diversified, co-ordinated
way.

It is easy enough to find American and British psychologists who
have used each of the following methods by itself, especially in general psychology. In some cases, they have been carried farther here
than in Germany. But I have not found in this country (a) a combined, systematic application of them all to the psychology of art and
aesthetic experience, or (b) explicit consideration of them as abstract
methods, capable of such application in future.

Müller-Freienfels discusses method briefly at the beginning of each
of his three volumes, especially the first and third. He distinguishes
five principal methods, with two or three minor additions. These are
"the experimental, the questionnaire, the psychoanalytical, the pathological, and the objective-analytical methods." He points out the
values and limitations of each.

1. The *experimental* method was long unproductive in this field,
he says, because people used it to ascertain the absolute or universal
pleasantness of certain spatial forms, colors, rhythms, etc. Little in
the way of general laws could be derived along this line, but experimental research entered a more productive field when it undertook
to study individual difference. It succeeds best when it ignores the
central aesthetic problems of emotional response, and emphasizes
instead the apperceptive conditions of aesthetic experience. "The investigations of color and sound effects, apperception of space and
time (rhythm), association, mental processes and the like may serve

as examples of experimentation which contributes to psychological research in art."

2. The *questionnaire* method Müller-Freienfels considers "of perhaps even greater importance than laboratory experiment, which can be employed in only a limited way," although it has the drawback of being hard to control. It affords, he says, a much greater possibility of doing justice to the field of investigation:

The technique of this methodology has lately been improved in a subtle manner, with the result that many an apparent disadvantage now turns out to be advantageous in some other way. Thus the fact that the subjects are without professional training may ensure their unprejudiced behavior. The oral as well as the written questionnaire may have particular advantages. Several pioneers who have worked with this method agree on the vivid interest which the subject showed toward those investigations. I see also a great advantage in the requirement of exact questioning; some of the forms worked out for the purpose of such inquiries are valuable introductions to the field of psychological and aesthetical problems. . . . Valuable examples of such questionnaires are those on musical enjoyment or the participation of motor experience in the various mental functions.

In the United States, the questionnaire method was overdone a few years ago, especially in educational psychology, and this produced a reaction against it which is perhaps equally excessive. Overzealous graduate students imposed on the time and patience of busy experts, asking them to fill out long and often insignificant questionnaires whose results never justified the pains. However, there is no doubt that a brief, intelligently phrased questionnaire, dealing with specific points and not vague generalities, can bring in valuable information which is hard to obtain otherwise. In American aesthetics, the questionnaire has not been excessively used.

3. While the questionnaire method extends in width, says Müller-Freienfels—

the method of *individual psychology* strives for depth. As individual-psychological I designate that method which investigates the particular nature of an individual not only in regard to his difference from, or resemblance to, others, but for his own sake. . . . For some time valuable biographies and monographs about individual great artists have moved along this line—of course, mostly without a conscious methodology. If at all guided by psychological viewpoints, such writings are interested almost exclusively in the artist's *creative work*. This, however, is only a part of the task. What is required, is a psychological analysis of the nature of *enjoying* art. There is still much more to be done in this respect. The peculiarity of receptive behavior in great artists and critics would have to be investigated quite systematically and put in relation to the other parts of their personality.

Müller-Freienfels recognizes that a general problem and mode of approach exist which are broader than any theory or technique—namely, the problem of analyzing and describing the nature of an individual personality in all its uniqueness of configuration and behavior. One can psychoanalyze the personality of the individual artist or appreciator without following any of the special theories or techniques associated with the names of Freud, Adler, Jung, Stekel, or others.

Included within such psychoanalysis, broadly conceived, is that of the personality of the investigator himself. "It is an entirely wrong opinion that *self-observation* has exhausted all possibilities. On the contrary, it must be emphasized with all energy that even recognized psychologists are surprisingly clumsy in this regard. Self-observation is not easier but more difficult than most other methods, since it becomes possible only through a comparative use of observations of others."

Research in individual psychology, says Müller-Freienfels, becomes fruitful only if different individuals and groups are compared. This task he calls the "differential" method. It synthesizes the results of individual psychology by classifying resemblances and differences in the behavior of individuals. Thus *classifications of psychological types* are evolved. Recognizing the difficulty of working out a valid typology, he nevertheless regards the problem as one that must not be evaded.

4. The approach which Müller-Freienfels designates as "pathological" (i.e., that used by psychopathology), he classifies as a special form of individual psychology:

For all kinds of psychological exploration, pathological cases often present surprisingly elucidating, magnified examples. . . . The artistic predisposition to special intensity is often found among pathological people. Therefore, the artistic temperament will frequently be better understood if one knows how to interpret certain pathological symptoms. The special sensitivity of the artist, especially excitable imagination, enhanced eroticism, and many other factors can sometimes become understandable through the observation of the mentally diseased, although it is, in my opinion, entirely wrong to place creative talent and insanity in close proximity. This method has, up to now, been applied exclusively to artistic creation, whereas it may also be applied to the enjoyment of art.

5. Last of the principal methods is one which Müller-Freienfels designates rather vaguely as the "objective-analytical" method. It involves the study of works of art of all periods and peoples, in the attempt to ascertain the mental states and functions which caused them, and which they tend to produce:

Everything available besides the works of art themselves must be used— literary documents and any other evidence. It may be very informative to know the way in which earlier periods enjoyed architecture aesthetically. It is important to search, in all expressions of the mental life of a group or period, for some common spiritual attitude. This may manifest itself in political, economic, and scientific thinking.

In addition, Müller-Freienfels mentions an "ethno-psychological" approach, which considers art as an expression of collective rather than individual life. It emphasizes the study of primitive races and of cultural evolution. He mentions, finally, that "the psychology of art is also enriched by the exploration of the *child's* mental life, since some artistic phenomena may be observed in early stages of development. However, one has to be very careful in the establishment of analogies between children's art and primitive art. Of particular value in this field are detailed investigations of children's drawing and modeling, and of the speech and literary activity of childhood."

Most important of all to Müller-Freienfels, and the approach on which he bases all his writing, is what he calls the "comparative" method. It consists in the interrelating of all the others. In America, this would be considered rather a philosophic than a scientific method. Our scientists still shrink from extensive generalizing, as a rule, except in popular textbooks; and, unfortunately, our philosophers are often too unfamiliar with the empirical facts of art to undertake genuine syntheses.

The work of Paul Plaut, cited above, is briefer and devoted more strictly to the subject of method. His conception of method in the psychology of art naturally overlaps that of Müller-Freienfels to a large extent, but he uses a somewhat different terminology.

Plaut lays considerable emphasis on what he calls the "psychographic" method. He attributes the concept of psychography to Walter Baade (1908) and W. Stern. The former understood by it the description of the psychological characteristics of an individual by the methods of natural science. It involved collecting and organizing factual material, without preconceptions as to the nature of personality. Stern defines psychography, in contrast to biography, as "that method of research into individuality which proceeds not from the unity, but from the many-sidedness of the characteristics present in the individual, and arranges these according to psychological viewpoints." A "psychogram" is the application of the psychographical method to some particular personality. A "biography," on the other hand, tends to be in large part a work of art, although modern biographies utilize scientific knowledge.

The terms "psychography" and "psychogram" have not come into general use in America, and our writers prefer to speak of "case histories," "case studies," "individual profiles," "diagnoses," and the like. Whatever terminology we follow, the important point here is the need of factual, descriptive analyses of individual persons. When these are made of living individuals accessible to our observation, the study can presumably be more scientific; otherwise, it must be more a matter of indirect inference. Be that as it may, one of the central problems of the psychology of art is certainly that of elucidating the nature of individual artists, and of showing significant relations between their personalities and their products. This can be undertaken in a comparatively literary way, or with the utmost care in checking facts which is possible under the circumstances.

Plaut goes on to illustrate in detail the steps involved in working out a psychogram—especially, the preparation of classified lists of characteristics in terms of which the individual personality is to be analyzed and described. He points to the danger of assembling a multitude of detailed traits and yet missing those basic essentials which determine the uniqueness of a personality. Biographical investigations, heredity questionnaires, school questionnaires, and experimental researches are used to assemble information. "Psychopathography" is a special form of this same approach. It is here, perhaps, that American psychologists have become most familiar with the idea of scientific individual case studies, as in psychiatric diagnosis.

Plaut follows Emil Utitz in distinguishing psychography from "characterology." The latter is understood to mean "personality as seen from the viewpoint of striving." It is of no importance to characterology to show as large a number as possible of qualities, but rather to discover the essential traits or dispositions which determine the whole direction of growth and effort. Plaut admits the increasing danger of subjective interpretation as one looks for such "essentials." But there is no doubt that laboriously detailed case studies often "miss the woods for the trees."

Under the heading of character types, Plaut discusses "graphology" as a method. Here again it is rather surprising to the American reader to find reputable scientists treating with all seriousness an approach which our psychologists usually dismiss as pseudo-scientific, along with palmistry. Before dismissing the subject too hastily, it might be well for us to examine with more care the great mass of data which European research has assembled under this head. If any significant connection can be established between handwriting traits and personality traits, the fact will of course be very useful in the psychological study of artists, past and present. Handwriting is often one of the few direct bits of evidence which we possess in the case of persons long dead. Where the artist is a draftsman or painter, there seems to be a special likelihood of connection between the type of line which he uses for drawing, and that which he uses for writing. Doubtless the scientific study of graphology has itself been held back by the lack of adequate concepts for describing personality traits.

Plaut includes "psychoanalysis" and "individual psychology" under the general heading of "characterological" methods. His emphasis on individual psychology, under one name or another, is similar to that of Müller-Freienfels. It stands out in marked contrast to the emphasis common in American psychology. Here we tend to ignore the individual with his internal complexities, and to emphasize rather the statistical study of large numbers of individuals, as in attempts at validating tests of art ability. Incidentally, it is notable also that German psychologists seem very little interested in the whole question of standardized tests or measures of ability, in art or elsewhere. Nor have they recently shown much interest in any sort of collective rating, vote, or consensus of preference in the realm of aesthetic values. Perhaps our interest in these matters is an expression of our own democratic faith.

Plaut goes on to summarize the "experimental" approach to the psychology of art in two chapters: one on "methods of applied psychology," and one on "musical experience as a psychophysical problem." Here he illustrates various alleged tests of talent, especially in music, and statistical studies of children as measured by them. Some of the experiments deal with the ability of children to recognize, remember, and sing directly melodies which they have heard. Others inquire whether the subjects prefer original or "spoiled" versions of a piece of music. Others question the child on associations which various pieces of music arouse in him, and classify the results according to age and personality type. Similar investigations are cited in the field of children's literary composition and appreciation, and the principal studies of children's drawings are briefly reviewed. The "psychophysical" phase of experimental research is illustrated chiefly by measurements of variation in pulse, respiration, and circulation, as a result of music stimuli. Neurotic and normal, old and young, male and female groups are compared in these respects.

Finally, Plaut includes, as Müller-Freienfels does, the "ethno-psychological" and "sociological" approaches to art. He pays tribute to Wundt as the founder of ethno-psychology and illustrates its methods with experiments on the drawing ability of contemporary primitives. These are compared with ancient primitive rock drawings and with drawings by modern civilized children. The psychological approach to art is shown to overlap the sociological one, in that the latter merely adds considerations of *time* to the psychological viewpoint. In other words, the sociological view considers behavior in relation to certain particular periods and movements. It leads to theories of *type,* analogous to those of individual psychology. That is, cultural epochs are compared much as individuals are, and described in terms of their distinguishing characteristics as found in art and other modes of expression.

Certainly, these and other European writers have not said the last word on the psychology of art or on its methods. Hitherto, no American works have appeared which equal those of Müller-Freienfels and Sterzinger in scope and system. For American students of the psychology of art, the situation now calls, first, for a more careful study of the principal European contributions, and, second, for an equally thorough restatement of our own aims and methods in the light of them.

X

ART TESTS AND RESEARCH
IN ART EDUCATION*

1. Some proposed tests and their fallacies

Recent research in art education has been much concerned with the problem of tests and measurements. The success of objective tests of aptitude and achievement in other branches of education has encouraged similar ventures here. Several such tests have been worked out on an elaborate statistical basis, backed by institutions of high standing, expensively printed and offered to the teaching profession. Others are on the way. Some are scales to measure drawing and other constructive abilities; others are "preference tests," designed to measure ability to judge art values. The latter usually present two or more variations of a certain art form, such as a landscape, vase, temple, costume, or chair. The person tested is to grade them in order of merit, or to express his preference among the alternatives. His answers are scored according to a supposedly correct list, and his judgment is thus "measured." The "correct" answers are usually decided on, first, by taking some art works of more or less established reputation and then making copies in which details are altered so as to violate accepted textbook rules of good art. A reproduction of the original is assumed to be better than the "spoiled" variants. Second, these alternatives are submitted to numerous persons, including presumed experts on art, such as teachers, established artists, critics, and the like. A consensus is worked out, usually with greatest weight given to the opinions of the experts. If these disagree much on certain alternatives, other examples are substituted until there is considerable agreement. That agreed-on scale of preferences is then taken to be the correct scale for measuring the judgment of other persons.

The false assumption here is obvious: that consensus of opinion, even among a group of supposed authorities on art, is enough to

* Published in its original form in *Western Arts Association Bulletin,* XVII.6 (December 1, 1933).

establish an objective, reliable scale of art values. Few people with
any knowledge of aesthetics would come out flatly with such a propo-
sition. But in the language of the researcher it is covered over with
a mass of statistics and plausible verbiage. Lip service may be paid to
an open-minded, relativistic attitude, and caution expressed as to the
finality of the results.

Dr. McAdory announces the following modest aims for her test,
on the first page of her monograph entitled *The Construction and
Validation of an Art Test:*

It was the purpose of these studies to construct a reliable instrument for
the determining of the consensus of agreement or the order of preference
of given subjects and art elements by experts, and for estimating or measuring the differences of agreement of groups and individuals. There are
two underlying assumptions on which the items of the art test were constructed: first, that objective things can be ranked in order of artistic
merit by a consensus of any group of people; second, that as far as any
social group is concerned, its individual members can be ranked according to the degree of their agreement with the consensus adopted.

Nobody could quarrel with these avowed premises. Certainly,
people can express their preferences in order of ranking, and a consensus of agreement can be determined among those rankings. This
will give no ground whatever for saying that the consensus of opinion
is correct, or that the works of art actually correspond in order of
merit to the order of preferences expressed. But before very long we
find Dr. McAdory scoring people according to "their deviations from
the correct order"—that correct order being the consensus previously
established. Different sorts of people are said to "rank higher or
lower" according to the extent to which they agree with the consensus. And in the last chapter, we find this claim explicitly made:
"The test can be used as an instrument for measuring both individual and group ability to distinguish degrees of artistic merit." If
it is so used, it is used without any justification whatever.

The same fallacious reasoning underlies the Meier-Seashore *Art
Judgment Test,* published by the University of Iowa's Bureau of
Educational Research and Service. In a circular advertising the test
this definite claim is made: "It does measure the critical factor—aesthetic judgment, which is basic and indispensable." In the *Program*
of the Western Arts Association an advertisement asserts: "The

Meier-Seashore Art Judgment Test will correctly evaluate a pupil's artistic capacities, his aesthetic sensitivities, his critical capacities."

Such claims are quite unwarranted by the facts. The test does not measure aesthetic judgment, in the sense of measuring whether a person's judgment of art is good or bad, right or wrong. It measures only the extent to which a person agrees with some of the persons whom Professors Meier and Seashore previously consulted. To claim, as further confirmation of the test, that officials and celebrities in the art world are rated highly by it, is merely arguing in a circle, if the original consensus was based largely on the taste of persons of this type and the textbooks written by them.

To assume that a reproduction of a picture by an established artist is necessarily better than an altered variant of it is also unwarranted. Not only may essential values of the original, such as color and scale, be destroyed in reproduction; in trying to make "spoiled" variations of it, the draftsman often unwittingly succeeds in transforming an academic banality into something more pleasing, at least to persons of radical taste, for its odd and irregular form. A picture which violates textbook canons such as "balance" or "true perspective" may achieve different kinds of value, more attractive to those who like primitive, exotic or modernistic art. I do not say they are right; but the question is debatable in spite of any vote or conventional textbook. One used to traditional styles may perhaps feel a shock of unfitness and surprise on first seeing strange variations of them. But that sort of strangeness and even of disunity are not inconsistent with artistic merit. It is by just such variation of old traditional forms that the evolution of styles in art often proceeds.

If tests of this kind are used in any way which puts a premium on attaining a high score in them, such as receiving promotions, high marks, scholarships or positions, or any other special opportunities or encouragement, the result may be definitely pernicious. They will operate simply as one more means of standardizing public taste—a process which is going on fast enough as it is. They will work to discriminate against the individual, young or old, who for any reason whatever tends to deviate from the established conventional taste of his time. In art if anywhere, conformity to the mass is not necessarily a virtue.

2. *Tests of art appreciation*

After this criticism of existing art tests, it may seem that I am
opposed to all attempts to grade students' art work, or to study the
subject statistically. On the contrary, I do not side with those who
would eliminate all grades from art instruction. Nor have I any objection to statistical research within the field of art when it is done
judiciously, with a proper sense of its necessary limitations. Both are
useful and can be rightly as well as wrongly done.

In practice, we cannot escape appraising students' ability and
accomplishments in art, however much we might like to. As long as
any kind of scholarships or awards in art are to be given out, we must
decide in some way who seems most worthy to receive them. The
whole modern educational setup of schools and colleges, credits,
courses and diplomas, depends on some kind of grading. If any one
thing is holding back the extension of art instruction in high schools
and colleges, it is the failure of those in charge of it to work out satisfactory modes of evaluating students' work for credit. Works of art
are constantly subjected to criticism outside of school, and it is mistaken kindness to train a child to think that his tastes and his productions are somehow sacred and above all negative criticism. Not
only the subject of art, but all education and all democracy are
vitally in need of more active and intelligent evaluation, to select
potential leaders from the mass. We cannot perform this with scientific objectivity. But instead of going to the other extreme, let us do
more rather than less grading. And when we grade, let us not be
content with arbitrary, undefended judgments, but rather persist in
trying to think out and express what our standards are, and the reasons for them. We can do a great deal to make our grading more
thoughtful, fair, informed and reliable, while recognizing that it
must contain a certain element of our own personal and cultural
taste.

In my own teaching, both of children and adults, I look for certain fairly definite abilities which may be classified under the general
heading of "appreciation." I am not primarily concerned with what
students like or dislike, find beautiful or ugly in art, or with how
they may rank works of art in order of preference. These questions
are, I believe, much overrated in importance at the present time.

A person's expression of preference for one picture may be quite insignificant and misleading as an indication of his ability to appreciate art. One person may rate picture *A* higher than picture *B* as a result of thorough and sensitive grasp of it; another because of some trivial detail or accidental association. Two persons may differ in their total net appraisal, because of quite legitimate differences in interest and personality, yet both may be on a par as connoisseurs. A child's expressed preferences in art may be due to all sorts of hidden variable factors: to prior instruction, home influence, happy or unhappy associations, and the like. All his attitudes are more or less unstable and quickly impressionable. A child of great aesthetic sensitivity may, for one reason or another, develop a strong temporary aversion toward a certain kind of art, or toward all art.

I believe that it is more important to stress, both in teaching and in testing, the ability to perceive form in art, to grasp relations between visible details, to understand associated meanings in relation to design, and to evaluate a work of art intelligently through comparing it with others and relating it to human needs, including those of one's own personality. If a student can do these things, I care little whether his likes and dislikes in art are the same as mine. If they differ, I know that he has a right to his opinion, that it is based on a genuine, thorough experience of art and not on some nonessential. These abilities are all present to some extent in young children; they are capable of gradual development and training. Whether they can be quantitatively measured to any great extent I do not know, but it would be a worth-while job for someone to try. Anyone who tries it, however, should keep certain precautions uppermost in his mind. In the first place, he should seek to analyze broad, complex abilities like the ones just mentioned into narrower constituents, or into fairly specific, controllable applications of them. Ability to perceive form in art can be divided into ability to perceive different kinds of form, such as linear pattern, color arrangement, arrangement of masses in deep space; and these in turn into still more special abilities. The more we thus subdivide the field of aesthetic behavior, the more it becomes capable of exact observation.

But one can never be sure that the whole is equal to the sum of these parts; in other words, that after studying all the specific constituents which we can discern in a complex process like perception of form in art, we have grasped the nature of the whole. It is therefore especially important for the investigator not to claim to have studied more than he really has. Our situation here is analogous to that of all mental testing in the early twentieth century. Then psychologists were claiming to have devised tests for "intelligence," for "sanity," for "character," and the like, just as some are now claiming tests for "art judgment." Now mental tests as a whole are much more cautious in their claims. We have specific tests for certain aptitudes and abilities; we claim for them some power to predict success in doing a certain thing under present school conditions. Even if we average together a number of separate ratings, we are hesitant about claiming to have measured intelligence, sanity, or character. These specific measurements do throw considerable light on the broader questions. In practice the difference may be negligible, but in science we must distinguish as sharply as possible between inferences which are amply justified by the data and those which are mere presumptions or working hypotheses.

Another precaution is similar: not to make broad generalizations about all humanity, all children, or all children of a certain age, on the basis of inadequate data. Large numbers of cases are no guarantee of safety, even if one has tried to make a random sampling of individuals from different sources. I may study the reactions toward art of thousands of persons, students and teachers, from different parts of the country, and find certain striking resemblances. I may think these are universal traits, common to persons of certain age or educational levels everywhere and always. Yet as a matter of fact they may be due to some special and peculiar social conditioning. Most of the teachers may have been trained at a few closely related training schools, where a particular method of teaching art is in vogue; most of the students may be working under these teachers. Or outside of school, the influence of some popular mode in newspaper cartoons, magazine illustration, advertising posters, dress or house-furnishing may be at its height. Through large-scale rapid communication, such fashions in art now spread like lightning throughout an immense population, to vanish as fast as they came.

Such facts make it increasingly hard to distinguish aesthetic tastes which are superficial and ephemeral from those which are more deeply grounded in our culture, and harder still to be sure that we have found anything basic in human nature. Any research in the nature of mass observation—questionnaire or vote—is apt to be ancient history by the time the returns are tabulated. A very few cases which can be thoroughly investigated and watched under controlled experimental conditions may yield more valid results. Nevertheless, it may be worth while to study ephemeral or specially conditioned social traits in the aesthetic realm, frankly recognizing them as such, if only to take stock of ourselves as we go along, and to learn more about the influences which produce our fast and sweeping fluctuations of taste. Much of the research which has been carried on in connection with art tests would have been quite sound and valuable if it had been so interpreted—that is, if it had been content to tell us that certain kinds of person showed certain tendencies in aesthetic judgment. This, of course, would have involved an abandonment of the claim to set up a normative test for correct art judgment in general.

What help can research give us in the practical business of grading students' art appreciation work? There is very little help to be had from votes of preference, since they give no ground for rating the dissenter high or low. At most, they can serve to call our attention to the student of exceptional tastes, so that we may inquire what has made him depart from the mass. There is more help to be expected from detailed, descriptive study of various specific abilities involved in art appreciation. It will not of itself give us a scale of values, but it can illuminate the whole problem of grading by showing us more about the nature of the process we are trying to teach and grade; furthermore, it may show us what degrees of ability along certain lines are usual at different age levels, without special training or as a result of certain training. Hence we may be in a better position to know what to expect of our students. I would very much like to know what can fairly be expected of a ten-year-old child in learning how to grasp a complex pictorial or architectural form, including the design and some of its cultural meanings. What constitutes average and what exceptional ability for such a child?

There is no space here to discuss the details of method in research. Educational psychology has developed many which are applicable to our field, with modifications to suit the peculiarities of aesthetic phenomena. I see great possibilities in systematic use of the process of ranking, if it is properly used—that is, the process of having different individuals arrange a number of art objects in order on the basis of some definite criterion. The criterion does not have to be so broad and vague as "art value," "beauty," or "what I like best." It can be more specific, such as "extent of color-contrast," "clarity of space-relations" and the like. Such ranking stimulates careful, systematic perception, comparison, understanding, and application of aesthetic terms and principles. The results are not only revealing in each individual case, but capable of statistical comparison and correlation, to show the specific ways in which individuals and types of individuals behave, resemble, and differ from each other in responding to works of art.

3. Tests of creative ability in art

The situation is similar with regard to grading the quality of students' own art products. We must not expect, in the near future at least, any reliable test or scale for measuring creative ability in art. That ability, though perhaps less mysterious and incomprehensible than we sometimes suppose, cannot at present be objectively recognized or measured. But certain kinds of research could throw considerable light on the nature of creativeness among children and aid us in judging it fairly.

The wrong way is to arrange a "drawing scale" of pictures of a man, a face or some other object, rated in order from very bad to very good, and then propose that children's drawings be graded by their resemblance to one or another of these examples. It makes no difference how the scale was devised, or how elaborately defended by statistics. The thing is wrong in principle, since it assumes that there is a definite order of values among ways of drawing an object. That the "best" examples are most realistic, or were made by old masters, art academy professors, or salon prize-winners, are sadly inadequate grounds for assuming them to be best. At the lower end of such scales there is usually little room for dispute (since the examples consist of more or less formless scrawls). Among these, superiority consists merely in evidence of a little more control of hand-movements. But toward the other end of the scale the relative values always become increasingly debatable; this example is good in certain ways, that in others. There are any number of good ways to draw a man or a face, each of which may be best for certain purposes. The child who cannot or will not draw realistically, who produces drawings like the "mediocrities" of the scale, may be groping awkwardly toward some highly personal kind of caricature or stylistic simplification. From a creative and pedagogical standpoint, such an effort may be more worthy of praise than the finished skill of the expert. No single scale of ranked examples could possibly be made which would allow for such cases.

If we wish, on the other hand, to measure some definite, narrow kind of skill, such as the ability to copy accurately from memory a linear pattern one has just seen, that is quite possible and worth doing. Perhaps that ability is a necessary condition and test of all "good drawing," but let us not assume it in advance or confuse the two.

In practice at the present time, I believe there is only one general way to grade students' art work fairly on a basis of creative ability. It requires that the teacher himself shall have learned to appreciate many different kinds of art, including the primitive, archaic, and exotic, as well as the classical; the childish, naïve, and unskilled as well as the expert. This will help him recognize many different kinds of value in students' work, and keep him from grading them all in terms of approximation to one kind of art or one narrow set of principles. He should not lay too much stress on mechanical skill, exactness in reproducing nature, refinements of detail or structural unity; these are sophisticated qualities whose presence in children's art is not always healthy, and whose absence is no fatal defect. He must look rather for signs, perhaps crude and groping, of vitality and vigor in line or color, a rich and spontaneous imagination, a direct, personal way of looking at things, the forceful and consistent expression of a particular theme in design or story, some power to communicate a vivid experience in terms of the medium. One cannot grade examples very closely in terms of such vague criteria, but it is usually possible to put in one pile drawings which definitely have "something to say," some "signs of life"—in another those which are definitely impotent, confused, weak, and meaningless, and in a third those which are somewhere between the two.

No one could recognize the subjective, personal, and unscientific element in such grading more than I do. Yet I insist, first, that it is a better way to grade at present than to employ some unjustified pretense at a scientific scale; second, that it is possible by means of research and careful thinking to increase gradually the reliability of the process. I believe that there is an objective element in the vague criteria just mentioned, and that it can be brought out more clearly through comparison and psychological interpretation of children's art products. Certain German psychologists have in fact made a good start toward doing so; they have published excellent books well documented with reproductions in color of children's drawings, analyzed to show significant qualities and in some cases a given child's development over a period of years. American research could do nothing better than to follow up this beginning.

I would say in general that any formal test of children's creative ability in art should be of the "work-sample" type. It must not call merely for preference, true-false answers, or even completion of incomplete forms. It must give the child a chance to construct a complete, independent form of his own, since his power to do this is one of the things in which we are most interested. Our problem, then, is first of all to make this work-sample test as revealing as possible; to make it bring out the child's best abilities. It is not enough to say, "draw something," for that is apt either to confuse and paralyze him, or to bring out some stereotyped copy of a newspaper cartoon. Nor is it enough to say, "copy this drawing," or, "copy this object from nature," for these would not test his imagination. I doubt if any one task, any one art product, will serve to bring out enough different abilities. We should call for several different tasks, each designed to involve one or more of the abilities which we consider essential to good drawing. The tasks should be fairly but not too specific, so as to stimulate a definite quick response and yet leave room for individual variation. They should require no highly specialized training or experience, in which some children might be at an unfair advantage. They should not be too easy or too hard to complete in the time allowed, by children of the age level to be tested. If we hope to study the results scientifically, the test must be somewhat standardized throughout, so as to eliminate irrelevant causes of success or failure. I mean, for example, that all children taking the same test should be given similar materials and conditions for work; that the same time should be allowed to all for a given task; that instructions for the task should be similarly worded for all, so that none will have more instructions to work with. Much standardization would be harmful at the present stage.

It may be objected that any kind of set task or controlled conditions, or even the presence of a crowd of other children, will militate against free creative expression. There is much to be said for this objection, and it brings out one of the great difficulties against which the whole attempt at scientific and institutional approach to the problem of creativeness must labor. There are doubtless many shy, inhibited, or slow-thinking children—perhaps the best artists of all—who could not do well in any sort of formal test. For that reason I would urge that no such test be made the sole or final basis of selection and grading in practice, and that great caution be used in theorizing on the results. In practice one should take into consideration the work done by a child alone, at home, or in school or museum under free conditions. But such work is questionable data for scientific study, because of the many unknown factors, such as outside assistance, which may influence it. After all this has been said, I believe that tests and test conditions can be devised which will give a fair amount of scope for most children to display the extent of their talents. Whether they can or not is itself one of the problems which research will illuminate, as we come to compare work done under such conditions with work done otherwise.

A question which at once confronts us as we start to grade the test papers is how to weight the various tasks in relation to each other. Any answer at present will be mere opinion, based on our views as to what qualities are most important in art. Some years ago ability to copy from another work of art would have been weighted heavily in awarding a scholarship; today one questions whether to consider it at all. In practice at the present stage, all we can do is to test a good many different abilities which seem to be more or less related to the production of art; then average them roughly together as wisely as we can. But from the theoretical point of view, it would be interesting to find how much correlation there seems to be between these different abilities. To find this, rank the answers to each question in a separate series, and find the correlations between the different series.

Much of interest will appear as one studies the different rankings in the light of biographical data. What kinds of art form do children of different ages tend to produce? What changes occur in the favorite subject as the child grows older? At what age does the memory drawing of the classroom begin to contain perspective and deep space composition? When does light-and-shade modeling appear in the drawing of the man? Do girls excel boys in making a decorative rug pattern? Do children of different racial origins differ as to their

use of bright-color contrast? What effects of previous art training, of
home environment, of economic status, of motion pictures, stories,
history lessons, and newspaper illustrations appear? These are samples of a host of questions on which some definite information is
needed.

How are the abilities involved in art construction, such as sensory
discrimination, visual memory, and perception of symmetry, related
to other mental and physical traits? How do art tests correlate with
other mental tests? With success in various school subjects? (There is
much informal debate at present about the relation of art ability to
general intelligence, with a wide divergence of opinion.) What relation have the tendencies in a child's art expression to his physical
and emotional growth and stability? What therapeutic value has art
study in nervous and character maladjustments? Such questions obviously require a fitting together of the data from art testing and instruction with those obtained by other agencies, such as school and
clinical records.

What we can learn about the children themselves from grading an
art test is only part of the problem. It is quite as important—perhaps
more so—to study the people who do the grading. Art jurors, not
only in schools but in museum and other public exhibitions and
contests, are usually protected from all embarrassing questions. Like
a Roman emperor at the circus, they are above all need to defend
their judgments. In practice, some amount of this arbitrary power is
necessary; otherwise decisions would never be made. But special research could throw considerable light on the ways in which our judging of art is done. A group of test papers of the sort we are considering forms an excellent basis for doing this.

The first step is to submit the same group of papers for grading to
a number of persons. One may pick all the judges from a certain
group, such as art teachers, or one may wish to compare the views of
different groups, such as artists and laymen. The grading should be
done, not in terms of per cent or any outside scale of reference, but
by ranking the papers in order of relative merit. It is well to have
each paper stamped with an arbitrary serial number or letter, and to
withhold from the judges the name and all information about the
artist. Then each judge can arrange the papers from best to worst,
according to his opinion. A list can be made of the papers in that
order, designating them by their arbitrary numbers or letters. For

statistical treatment, it may be necessary to translate such a series into one in which the papers are listed, first, in some arbitrary sequence (the same for all judges). Then, after each item, put a number signifying the rank in which it was placed by that particular judge.

No amount of research along this line will tell us what the true order of merit among the papers is, even though we find that all the judges or all the experts agreed perfectly on a certain order. But there are other things we can find out. For one thing, we can ask each judge to defend his ranking briefly in words; at least to state why he put the highest, the lowest and the middle one where he did. Such comments are apt to be somewhat inadequate, for most persons find it hard to express in words the reasons for their judgments. Nevertheless, they are often illuminating, and they bring us to an essential point—what standards are being used, and how they are being applied. The gist of the various statements can be noted and roughly tabulated; then one can go on to compare the standards professed by different groups of judges. Agreement in professed standards may go along with great diversity in ranking.

The rankings themselves provide more clear-cut and tangible data to work with. It is useful to inquire, for example, about the extent of agreement among all the judges and within various groups, such as teachers, artists, and laymen. This can be roughly measured by finding the correlations between the different lists. It is useful also to have the same judge rank the same papers on different occasions, and to find how these lists agree; in other words, to what extent the judgment of an individual is constant. It is sometimes surprising and a little disconcerting to a teacher to find how much his ranking of the same papers will vary on different occasions, for no assignable reason. Do we know our own minds in such matters?

Why is it useful to make such inquiries? Because the extent of actual agreement on art standards and their application is an important psychological and educational phenomenon in itself, aside from any question of what standards are the true ones. Nobody knows at present how purely individual, unique, and capricious our methods of grading are in the field of art instruction. It would be significant merely to find out what approach there is to a common group consciousness in regard to art values, and to what extent that consciousness varies among different subdivisions of the public. The educational world in general, and such officials as college entrance boards, deans and superintendents, would know a little better how to regard grades in art if they knew to what extent art teachers could agree on their verdicts. At present they are apt to regard the whole subject as one where every supposed expert differs from every other. If the situation is not quite as chaotic as this, the fact should be demonstrated. If we can then increase the extent of our agreement through discussion, we shall be in a better position to organize and develop the teaching of art in this country. I am not arguing for uniformity of taste or of standards; let us not discourage whatever sincere and well-reasoned variation exists among us. But if we can come together voluntarily on certain broad aims and flexible standards, that also will have its advantages.

4. Scientific method in research

Who can do research in art education? How much does it require in the way of laboratory equipment and statistical knowledge? The word "research" sounds rather formidable; the rank and file of teachers and supervisors are apt to feel that it is a specialist's job, and beyond their capacities. They are apt also to be unduly impressed by what laboratory psychologists tell them in complicated mathematical terms, even though the psychologist has little knowledge of the practice, history, or teaching of art.

Research in art education and aesthetic psychology may be pursued with any degree of scientific precision, any amount of quantitative measurement one desires, providing only that the method used is appropriate to the particular problem under investigation. Roughly speaking, there can be three main modes of research in this field at present, each useful in its own way. The first is to measure with numerical exactness whatever can be so measured, with the cautions discussed above. The second is to report informally on one's teaching experiences, on one's personal observations of phenomena which cannot be measured exactly. Perhaps we should confine the word "research" to something fairly rigorous and formal; but at the present stage of development such informal reports are often the most valuable of all. And, as I am going to show, they can be made a little more scientific without going to the other extreme. The third type involves co-operation among research workers.

Most informal studies in art education could profit by a little more understanding of the fundamental principles of scientific method, of the logical way to map out and control an experiment, to test and defend a hypothesis. Scattered memories and anecdotes may make entertaining and suggestive reading; but if a teacher aspires to contribute something a little more reliable, he must organize his teaching and his observation along some fairly definite line. Let him select a few clear-cut objectives which he will work toward throughout a certain year or series of years, and a fairly definite, consistent method and set of materials for achieving those objectives. After trying out these methods for a sufficient time, with a sufficient number and variety of pupils, let him tell the rest of us what he thinks his results have been and why. Many progressive teachers experiment too much, are constantly changing their methods, taking up each new device they read about, with the result that their experience at the end of a year or a lifetime throws no definite light on the value of any of these methods. Many claims to have discovered an important fact about children's preferences, or a fine new method for stimulating creativeness, fall to the ground because the situation has been incompletely analyzed from a logical viewpoint. We are not told, perhaps, whether the group of children was a highly selected one, so that home advantages or general high mentality rather than the particular teaching method used may have been the cause of success.

In a certain problem it may be quite unnecessary ever to work out a statistical correlation; yet it may be highly important for the investigator to have the principle of correlation constantly in the back of his mind. For example, one can be on the watch to see what other factors in children's lives appear most persistently to go hand in hand with interest in art. Does home encouragement seem to be a necessary and sufficient condition for the maintaining of that interest? Is there a correlation between such interest and success in other subjects? To show that a certain teaching method is to be credited with stimulating interest, one should be able to show that the interest rose and fell along with the extent to which that method was practiced, *while all other factors were kept comparatively constant.* Yet such a concomitant variation could never be exactly calculated, for there is no objective measure of interest in art. One can only observe the expressions on children's faces, the tones in their voices when one activity or another is in process; their eagerness to stay in after school, to come on Saturdays, to follow up at home jobs begun in the classroom; perhaps to walk several miles to attend a museum class, when carfare is lacking. Significant data in research of this sort are general health, vitality, and vivacity, an eager or bored attitude, a prolific ease or difficulty in production, shifting or fixed attention, the quality of art objects in the home, and others quite as intangible. Yet the scientifically trained mind can observe them with care and system, noting apparent connections among them, and trying to arrange things so as to bring out persistent correlations.

Simple statistical devices can sometimes be used to advantage in such work, without making a fetish of them. The careful investigator will keep mimeographed blanks for detailed case histories and day-to-day observations. He may tabulate, at the end of a year, the comparative frequency of recurrence of certain behavior traits. He may even show numerically that certain variables are more highly correlated than others, within the data thus far collected.

In short, I am trying to emphasize the point that research can best progress within our field, at the present time, through a *middle course* between informal, "subjective" observation and exact measurement; with a steady pressure toward the latter, but no disposition to hurry into premature attempts at exact science. This middle course is not now being followed to any considerable extent. Instead we find, as a rule, one extreme or the other.

Assuming a moderate amount of scientific method, there are plenty of vital issues in art education on which we can profit from investigation. No one knows what methods or materials are best suited to achieve the ends we desire. I suppose there is a certain amount of agreement in ultimate aims among art teachers who subscribe to a progressive philosophy of education. We want to stimulate and sustain an art interest in students of whatever age. We want them to enjoy and appreciate past works of art, and to make some kind of art expression for themselves. We want their art interest to last over through later childhood and adolescence into maturity, and not die out as usual at the age of eight or nine. We want their art activities to be not isolated skills but parts of a general healthy vitality and growth, mental, emotional, and physical. We do not try to make our students produce or like only a few narrow kinds of art, but to develop some catholicity of taste and versatility of expression.

Even though we agree on a few such fundamentals, there is infinite room for experiment on ways and means to achieve them. What should be the relation between this general aesthetic growth and the acquirement of specific techniques in art; between both and other subjects in the curriculum; between various age levels in art education, so as to produce continuous development? Some of us think free expression is best at all age levels, some favor introducing more set tasks and disciplines as the child grows older. Some of us favor a close relation between art appreciation and the practice of art, while some would conduct them separately. Some would emphasize painting and sculpture, some the handicrafts, and others the art element in modern industrial processes. Some would expose the child from the start to many different historical styles in art, some would bring them to his attention at different age levels. Some of us would teach the visual arts along with literature and music in close co-ordination, while others would teach them as separate subjects. Some of us favor the project method in art, while some would teach in chronological order. Some would merge the whole subject of art in an "integrated curriculum," while others would maintain its separate identity.

As to all these possible alternatives, there is no way as yet of proving definitely by any sort of research that one is better than another. Probably each has its values under certain conditions. But there is urgent need for the accumulation of definite, tested, controlled experience with them—not vague impressions and guesses—which will help us decide which ones are best for which purposes.

The third kind of research which I have in mind would be a more co-operative approach to these same problems, to be conducted by organized groups of workers in the field. Present research and experiment in art education is now too sporadic, isolated, and haphazard to get very far. Consider the way in which the exact sciences conduct their mass attacks throughout the world on problems recognized as crucial—the nature of the atom, of cancer, of biological inheritance. Vast problems are divided up; it is announced that certain individuals and institutions are working on certain aspects; the results, as they proceed, are made known to all the rest and constantly fitted together. Learned bodies of scientists sponsor such co-operation and supervise it by delegating special committees for the purpose. In the educational field itself, it is coming to be more and more the practice for a certain school or school system to be recognized as trying out some definite method or type of curriculum—the integrated curriculum, the social science emphasis, or what not. The results are more or less carefully checked up at intervals, and the whole educational world profits by them.

It would be well if a certain school, school system, or museum educational department would agree to make a fairly thorough trial, over a few years, of some one definite method of teaching art—let us say a comparative, joint approach to the visual arts along with music and literature. Let other places embark on similarly definite experiments. If there is some duplication, no harm is done; but let us try to see that a good many different methods and kinds of material are tried out. Then let the committee see that observations are kept and tabulated with some degree of care and uniformity, and that each experimenter is kept informed, through bulletins and monographs, of what the others are doing.

XI

CHILDREN'S ART ABILITIES: STUDIES
AT THE CLEVELAND MUSEUM OF ART*

1. The aims and educational background of the studies

In a large democracy, it is an urgent problem to select potential leaders in and through the educational process. Mass production, standardization, and leveling constantly threaten to dominate. In. art, as in other fields, high grades and promotions, awards and scholarship aids are to be administered. Democracy calls for the giving out of such inducements to the genuinely deserving, the potential leaders, from whatever economic, geographic, or racial group they may come.

But how can we discover the really talented, promising students in art, if possible, at an early age? In most other subjects, ability is more easily recognizable and to some extent measurable, especially when it can be manifested through correct inference or fact-finding, or (as in engineering) by tasks in which the standards of successful performance are clear and accepted. The standards of successful performance and creation in visual art are still obscured by wide disagreement among artists and critics. The standards of mature artistic value being themselves highly debatable, how can we measure the creative or appreciative performance of children?

Several alleged tests and measures of art ability in production and judgment have been available for several years, but none has been accorded general acceptance by artists or educators. Still, the idea remains tempting—of a test or scale on the order of the Binet and later tests of intelligence, aptitude, or probable learning rate, which would deal with ability in the visual arts. Combined with tests of musical and other types of art ability, it might even yield a measure of *aesthetic age,* comparable to "mental age," and a numerical quotient in relation to chronological age.

---

* This article is the introduction to a joint report, in which other sections were written by Betty Lark-Horovitz and Edward N. Barnhart. It was published in its original form in *The Journal of Experimental Education,* XI.2 (December, 1942), pp. 97–113.

No such goal was attained by the Cleveland studies, or even sought as a practicable end in view. The resources of the program were far too limited, and the theoretical difficulties too clearly recognized. A few groping steps in that direction were made. All the workers were clearly aware of the paramount danger in constructing an art ability test, and studious in trying to avoid it: namely, the danger of assuming in advance that one knows what good art is (or asking a group of supposed experts who claim to know), and then measuring students' ability in terms of approximation to that supposed norm.

Yet, while the difficulties in the way of a standardized test were obvious, another fact was equally so. Art education as an actual process made some sort of evaluation necessary. This had to be done and was being done in thousands of schools, in order that the machinery of promotion and graduation, prize-giving and job-giving might go on. At this end, one might say, "the subjective judgment" of teachers held sway; a process of arbitrary grading with undefined or vaguely defined, unsupported standards. At the other end lay the unattainable vision of a purely objective, scientific instrument for exact evaluation of work and measurement of ability. Was not an intermediate, transitional stage possible—some procedure a little more systematic than the ordinary ones, more clearly thought out in its criteria, more informed about the facts of art and of child development, more intelligent in its adaptation to new educational objectives? Would not this be of value to teachers, even though no claims were made to have jumped at one bound to the heights of scientific precision?

A few years ago, it was felt by many educators that the secondary school level had lagged somewhat behind the lower ones in adapting its methods and content to the psychological needs of students. The growing influence on youth of radio, periodicals, screen and stage was being discussed, and that of the art museum as an educational agency. Teachers were asking, for example, how museum visits and loan exhibits could be most profitably fitted into school work in art and other subjects; whether, for example, the study of old masters in art could be made conducive to original creativeness rather than to imitation. A museum which had some contact with students of secondary age thus seemed to be one promising place to study the evaluation of art ability and performance. The secondary level was to be emphasized, but not exclusively, since it might be illuminated by comparison with the earlier ones. The inquiry was not limited to any single problem, such as testing, but was open to any way of throwing light on children's art and art abilities.

2. Conditions under which the studies were conducted

At no single place, or type of institution, can all aspects of children's art be effectively observed; different ones have peculiar advantages and disadvantages. An art museum has some of each which the ordinary school does not possess. The Cleveland Museum of Art was considered especially favorable as a place for study, because of the unusual extent to which it had emphasized and developed educational work with children. Children unaccompanied by adults had been given free access to all galleries, with permission to draw, and free drawing materials. In well-lighted studios, water color, ink, and modeling clay could be used. Thousands of students, from nursery school through university and art academy, flocked to its classes. School teachers brought their own classes during the week, to derive illustrative material for their work in art, history, and many other subjects. On Saturdays, several hundred children came to draw, paint, model, listen to music and stories, hear illustrated talks, and watch plays, moving pictures, and marionette shows. Some of them attended special classes for children of members; others attended open classes, free to all, and still others attended free classes for those believed to have special talent in art. The racial backgrounds of the children were extremely diverse. For all, cultural development rather than professional training was the principal aim. Classes were graded according to age level, and met on successive Saturdays in various parts of the museum, so as to permit a varied round of activities. In many of them, an attempt was made to interrelate work in visual arts with that in music; and in all, to combine appreciation with creative production. Exact, unimaginative copying from nature or from other works of art was not encouraged, but students could use museum objects as materials and suggestions for adaptive modification. It was not assumed that such an approach to art was necessarily better than completely "free expression," apart from other art; but it was felt that such an approach was the peculiar opportunity of the art museum for experiment, with its wealth of art objects beyond the reach of most schools.

On the other hand, the museum was comparatively limited in its contact with individual students. A child came, perhaps, each Saturday morning for a season of twenty-five weeks. (Some attended a year-round class which met outdoors in summer.) Those who came during the school week, with outside teachers, could receive little individual attention during their short gallery visits. Attendance was voluntary at the Saturday classes, except in so far as parents exerted mild pressure. A considerable number of children came year after year, but others drifted in and out, "shopping around" among the city's varied week-end activities. Thus there was a fairly large annual turnover, and new students were constantly entering the upper age levels without any previous museum instruction. An easy play spirit had to be maintained, for its own sake and to hold attendance; anything like sustained, enforced hard work ran the risk of making students leave entirely. This militated somewhat against the giving of frequent, formal tests. Although the psychological staff contrived ingeniously to make them short and pleasant, weaving them into the regular art lesson, and although the teachers and students co-operated surprisingly well, nevertheless the fear of imposing too much on the all-too-brief time for regular work restrained the psychologists from pursuing many experiments up to a theoretically adequate stage. Moreover, age-level groups in the Saturday classes were not evenly distributed, or all large enough to provide sufficient data. The peak load was around eleven years old, although classes extended from six to sixteen; older students, especially boys, were much less numerous.

Another advantage of the Cleveland Museum was the fact that examples of children's drawing had been carefully preserved there over a period of twenty years. The development of several individual students was illustrated from childhood to maturity. Some of these, after going through art school, had become successful professional artists, teachers, and writers.

Out of the need to choose students for the "Special" or Advanced Drawing Class for talented children came the recognition of a problem: could this choice be made more scientifically? It had been made rather informally for years, on the basis of interest shown through coming to the museum and drawing, or through recommendations of school teachers. Each fall for years, such recommended children came for an entrance test, which consisted in making several drawings. Museum teachers picked out the drawings and the children they considered most promising, but wished to improve this arbitrary process, if possible. Also, they wished to learn more about children's development in art—its natural course in normal and supernormal cases, and the best ways of enriching it educationally.

The Cleveland Museum of Art was and is not primarily a research institution. It lacked staff and equipment for conducting psychological experiments. Through a foundation grant, these were secured in modest proportions; but it proved surprisingly difficult to secure properly qualified workers, with some training in art as well as in psychology, especially on the short-time tenure necessitated by terms of the grant. Workers came and went, and the work lacked continuity.

3. Progress of the studies

Various art tests were given in the first year to hundreds of school children. Supplementary data cards were filled out for as many of these children as possible, with facts as to school I.Q. and other tests, school record, home environment, etc. All existing devices for testing art ability in production or appreciation were studied and discussed; and several were given museum classes for comparative purposes. The detailed management of the project was given over to Mrs. Betty Lark-Horovitz, who had had experience in both art instruction and psychological research on children's art in the Vienna schools. Dr. Edward N. Barnhart of the University of California came as research associate.

4. The Seven Drawing Test

This test was an outgrowth of the regular museum entrance test for the advanced drawing classes. It consisted of seven drawings to be made by the child of different subjects, and was designed to bring out different types of drawing ability—for example, to draw from memory, from imagination, from another picture on view, and from a moving, changing object. One was to show some of the child's interests by allowing him freedom to choose a favorite subject. This test was first given by Mrs. Louise M. Dunn and the author in September, 1933. The children were seated in the museum auditorium, with empty seats between them. They were given identical sets of material: a piece of drawing board, a box of colored pencils, and a pamphlet of blank sheets of drawing paper, each set being serially numbered and each sheet numbered from one to eight. On the back of the last sheet was printed the following questionnaire, to be filled out:

1. Name
2. Address
3. How old are you? .... Date of birth
   (year) .... (month) .... (day) ....
4. School .... Grade ....
5. Where were you born?
6. Where was your father born?
7. Your father's occupation ....
   When employed ....
8. Where was your mother born?
9. Are you left-handed?
10. Who has encouraged you to draw or study art?

Standardized instructions were read by the examiner, as follows:

Preliminary Instructions; repeat as much as necessary:

1. "Do not mark on these sheets until you are told to do so."
2. "Has everyone a folder of papers, a cardboard, and a box of colored pencils? If not, raise your hand."
3. "Lay your folder on the cardboard so that the blank page with numbers is on top."
4. "Be careful not to look at anyone else's paper."
5. "Don't use any pencils except the ones you were given."

Questions:

1. *Favorite Subject* (time, ten minutes). "Answer the first question on page one. You can use as much of the page as you like. This is the first question. Make a drawing of whatever you like best to draw. It can be a picture of anything at all. Make a picture of whatever you like best to draw. The time allowed is ten minutes. Begin now." . . . "You have one more minute to finish this question."

2. *Drawing of a Man* (time, five minutes). "Now turn to page 2. *On this page draw a picture of a man. It does not matter what kind of man you draw, what he is doing, or how he is dressed." (Repeat from asterisk.) "You will have five minutes. Now begin." . . . "You have one more minute to finish this question."

3. *Memory* (time, twenty minutes). "Now turn to page 3.

Shut your eyes a minute. Try to remember how your classroom looks at school." (Short pause.) "Now open your eyes. *Make a picture showing just how your classroom looks while the children and the teacher are there." (Repeat from asterisk.) "You have twenty minutes for this question. Now begin." . . . "You have one more minute to finish this question."

4. *Imagination* (time, twenty minutes). "Now turn to page 4. On this page make a picture showing what you would like to do next summer. Shut your eyes again for just a minute. Try to imagine something you would very much like to be doing on your next summer vacation. Now open your eyes and draw." . . . "You have one more minute to finish this question."

5. *Decorative Design* (time, fifteen minutes). "Now turn to page 5. *On this page draw a design which could be used for a rug. Make a picture of the most beautiful rug you can imagine." (Repeat from asterisk.) "The time allowed is fifteen minutes. Begin now." . . . "You have one more minute to finish this question."

6. *Copy of Lantern Slide of a Painting* (time, ten minutes). "Turn to page 6. In just a minute you will see a picture on the screen." (Dim lights and show picture of Chardin *Still Life*.) "Now, while this picture is on the screen, make a copy of it on your paper. Make just as exact a copy as you can. The time allowed is ten minutes. Now begin." . . . "One more minute."

7. *Drawing from Moving Picture* (time, ten minutes—while lights are on). "Now turn to page 7. In just a moment you will see a very short moving picture of an animal in motion. This moving picture will be shown several times. While it is being shown, make a drawing of the animal which you see. Make it in any position you like. If you wish to make more than one drawing on this page you may do so. The time allowed is ten minutes. Now begin." . . . "One more minute."

This test was given to over thirteen hundred children: in elementary, junior and senior high schools, under conditions closely approximating those in the museum auditorium; to all the museum Saturday morning classes at least once, and to a selected group of the "Specials" or advanced students again after two years. It yielded a vast mass of data in the shape of over nine thousand drawings, plus supplementary information about the young artists. It consumed a considerable share of the staff's time and energy throughout the research, although each new test likewise yielded masses of children's art—easy to get, but hard and slow to interpret.

As a testing device, the Seven Drawing Test (given before the research began) was never regarded as a perfected instrument, worthy of being given out for general use. It immediately disclosed several faults, especially the following: (1) In drawing a man (question 2) children should have been told to draw the whole man; many drew the head only. (2) The moving picture used for drawing 7, of a horse in motion, had been too inferior in quality, too blurred and rapid, for many children to grasp it; yet to change the film would make comparison impossible. (3) The lantern slide of drawing 6 was in black and white, unsuited to the colored pencils and too complex in line and texture for young children to copy. Dimming lights to see the slide made it hard for them to draw. (4) The instructions for drawing 5 were so phrased that some children tried to draw an actual rug in perspective, missing the point of the question, which was to elicit an abstract, decorative design.

5. Other experimental devices

More fundamentally, it was realized that no single test, no set of drawings made on a single occasion, could give more than presumptive evidence of a child's probable success in art. Too many important psychological factors, such as motivation, work habits, and emotional stability, would not appear to any considerable extent in the results. For these, observation over a period of time would still be necessary.

The Seven Drawing Test was obviously faulty, but at least it had brought out a wealth of promising data. The staff questioned whether to lay it aside and work out other tests, in the hope of perfecting some of them, or to neglect the invention of new tests, but study the results of the faulty one as carefully as time allowed. Actually, they took a middle course, trying out several new devices, but not attempting to perfect any one of them. They hoped to build up a series, not of formal tests, but of devices for observing and experimenting on children's production and appreciation of art. These could be partly standardized into definite tasks to be performed at various times, under controlled, uniform conditions. They were aimed at stimulating significant responses from the child, which an intelligent teacher might find enlightening, even though not exactly measurable.

Several such devices were carried to various degrees of completeness, and tried out in museum classes by Mrs. Lark-Horovitz and Dr. Barnhart. The principal ones are as follows:

a. *Seven Drawing Test.*

b. The *Beautiful Page* experiment: an attempted improvement on question 5 of the Seven Drawing Test, in that it calls for abstract decoration rather than a picture of a textile. The child is simply told to make the sheet of paper as beautiful as possible, and that it need not look like anything else.

c. The *Story Completion* experiment: an attempt to stimulate imagination by telling part of a story, then having the subject complete it (*a*) in pictures; (*b*) in words. (This allows comparison of pictorial with literary ability.) A fairy tale and a fictitious news item, both with vivid imagery, were used.

d. The *Recorder:* a device for preserving a record of consecutive stages in the development of a child's drawing; showing to what extent and how he plans it systematically, rather than adding details at random. The child draws on a sheet of paper, under which are carbon paper and a roll of white paper which can be shifted at intervals by the examiner.

e. The *Machinery Drawing* experiment: a way of studying children's ability to learn and change their own ways of drawing as a result of observing pictures by others. (This is specially relevant to museum instruction, where children are led to appreciate art of all periods, and then asked to make works of art of their own, which will profit by that appreciation and yet avoid direct copying.) The group is first asked to draw a picture involving machinery of some kind; is then shown museum pictures involving machinery; and is finally (at once or on another day) asked again to draw machinery pictures, without having the museum examples to look at.

f. The *Bear* or *Visual Memory* experiment: a way of studying children's ability to remember and represent an object seen, after various intervals of time. A ceramic figure of a bear is shown from different points of view, then withdrawn. The children are asked to draw it immediately, then after several days, and again after several weeks.

g. The *Art Appreciation* experiments. In addition to the above ways of studying drawing ability, methods were developed for observing and comparing children's preferences for different types of art. Selected, diversified sets of pictures, textiles, ceramics, and other objects were shown to them with specified comments and questions; their answers were noted down, analyzed, and classified. The aim was not to decide or measure how "correct" their judgments were, but to find out how different types (as to age, sex, etc.) differed in their attitudes toward art.

h. The *Project Analysis Record Sheets* for use in school or elsewhere; some for students and some for teachers, as means of systematizing evaluation and records of progress toward chosen objectives. They are, in a broad sense, devices for observation, experiment, and evaluation.

These eight types of instrument (each of them capable of much variation and development) were all aimed at eliciting samples of constructive work or aesthetic response on the part of the student, or at recording and appraising extended programs of work. In addition, the task of interpreting results of the Seven Drawing Test required certain instruments of a different sort.

6. Evaluation in practice

Three kinds of problem confronted the staff. One, when the test was first given, was immediately practical. In a few days, before classes started, about fifty students had to be selected for the Museum Special Class of supposedly talented children, eleven through sixteen years of age. The selection was to be made in large part from the drawings of about two hundred children who had applied for admission. There was no time for detailed analysis or theoretical quibbles; decisions had to be quick and arbitrary.

Accordingly, three judges of reputation and experience with children's art were asked to make them. The papers were first divided into piles according to age levels. Beginning with the youngest, paper after paper was inspected by the three judges at once, and assigned by them to an A, B, or C group (good, medium, bad) within the age level. Thus, each age level pile was divided into three. There was usually swift agreement on the verdicts; a few were discussed at some length, or held in suspense until the rest had been judged and the degrees of relative merit seemed clearer. No one simple standard was used; the judges often remarked of a "C" paper that it was "weak," "fumbling," "stereotyped," or "had nothing to say"; of an "A" paper that it had "life," "vitality," "sense of humor," "distinctive point of view," or "decorative quality," "rhythmic lines," or "delicate textures." Fifty best were chosen from all the "A" piles, with approximately equal distribution. As a safeguard, any applicant not chosen for the "Special" class was allowed to enter an "Open" class, with no restrictions. There he was observed for months, and in some cases advanced to the Special class afterward; while some who had been chosen for the latter proved unworthy in the long run. Such a process of choice could certainly be called arbitrary and subjective, strictly speaking. But at least it involved explicit discussion of standards, a tentative attitude, and systematic comparison of the data.

7. The analysis of children's drawings; a manual for teachers

A second type of problem was to make the Seven Drawing Test, or some altered version of it, into a more workable tool of evaluation for the outside teacher. Ideally, it should be not only capable of yielding exact numerical scores, but also somewhat mechanical and automatic in operation; so that the ordinary teacher, not an art expert, could use it. These results might have been attained through the usual process of "validation"—submitting the papers to many judges, or repeatedly to the same judges, giving the test repeatedly to the same children, and preserving only those features in test and scoring which seemed most "reliable"—that is, which would yield similar results on repeated use. But the staff were convinced that such a test would be specious, merely one more neatly printed device for enforcing established, conservative standards, for glorifying conventional types of "good art," while missing or disparaging the unusual and experimental. At the same time, while avoiding excessive claims to accuracy, the test might perhaps be sharpened up a little for general use.

As a means to that end, the staff worked out a report which was published by the Cleveland Museum of Art under the title *Graphic Work-sample Diagnosis: an Analytic Method of Estimating Children's Drawing Ability,* by B. Lark-Horovitz, E. N. Barnhart, and E. M. Sills. This mimeographed volume of 143 pages, plus appended "check sheets," contains a manual of instructions for teachers to use in checking and diagnosing children's drawings, preceded by an introductory explanation of the various types of children's drawing by age levels. It is illustrated with black and colored photographic reproductions and line drawings of various types. It amounts essentially to a scale of graded examples, with verbal comments to point out their distinctive traits, by comparison with which the teacher may grade the work of her own pupils. It was worked out through a study of the Seven Drawing Test papers, with examples taken from them. Hence its proposed age-level norms are applicable, in a strict sense, only to drawings made under the same conditions (as to subject, medium, time allowed, etc.). However, its illustration and definition of types of children's drawing, and of specific traits therein, may be found more widely useful. This book was sent out to a number of teachers, some of whom used the manual and reported to the staff on their results. Certain drawings were sent around to be analyzed and graded by different teachers, with the use of the *Diagnosis.*

Most teachers are not at present sufficiently interested in the careful grading of students' drawings to be willing to take the time necessary for it. To distinguish types of art requires specific training, as it does to distinguish botanical or zoological types. Few classroom teachers and not all art teachers have had it. It cannot be made entirely quick, easy, and automatic without dangerous oversimplification. There are too many kinds of good art, by children as well as by adults; too many important individual differences; too many detailed characteristics worthy of note, for any simple scale of examples to cover them adequately.

The idea of a manual for use in grading pictures runs up against serious difficulties. One is that of nomenclature and definition of terms, in referring to type of art and elements in art. Aesthetic theory is still in a very primitive state on this matter; there is little or no accepted terminology for the description of adult art, of the masterpieces of art history. There is no recognized technique for analyzing and comparing works of art. If there were, it might be applied with modification to children's art. But whenever we try to analyze a child's drawing in such terms as "design," "realism," "rhythm," "balance," "proportion," etc., we discover radical differences among teachers and critics as to what these terms mean and what aesthetic values are to be attached to them. At least, the staff did try for some clarity and consistency by stating definitions for the principal terms. But outside teachers often could not understand or accept them, and applied the same term to a given example in widely varying ways. It is too much to hope that any single educational device can produce at a single step a generally acceptable technique and terminology for art analysis. That is a long job for aesthetic theory, which must be approached through study of old masters as well as of children's art. A good start was made toward it in Germany and Austria during the twenties; but it has had little effect on American education.

Well aware of this problem, the staff approached the task of analyzing the "Seven-Drawing" papers in a careful, indirect way. They had first to work out a definite method of analysis. This was done in the form, first, of a questionnaire or list of characteristics believed to be somehow significant in children's art, for the analyst to notice in the case of each picture.

On the basis of the questionnaire, a number of large blank charts were made: several for each of the first four drawings of the test, as executed by boys, girls, and various age-level groups. Large, representative samplings of the test papers were taken, mostly from the Seven Drawing Test, plus some from the Beautiful Page and other experiments. These were analyzed in minute detail, the results being entered and tabulated on the charts. This was the slow, drudging, time-consuming phase of the process, common to all inductive science.

The questionnaire, the charts, and the tabulation had one primary aim: to show the age level and sex distribution of specific characteristics in children's drawings. By this means, it was hoped, we could begin to generalize in terms of developmental norms. These would doubtless not be capable of exact numerical statement, but would consist of verbal description, illustrated by typical examples, of the kinds of drawing usual on each age level. There would be a range of variation on each level; certain characteristics being nonexistent among younger children, then becoming gradually more prevalent; others perhaps gradually dying out with maturation. With such an account of normal development, the teacher could compare the work of any particular child and find out to what extent it was normal, advanced, or retarded, both on the whole and in specific ways. The *Diagnosis* provided such an account, replete with illustrative detail, and as such provides a suggestive (though not an accurate) instrument for any teacher who wishes to take the trouble to use it. Its indications will be useful in proportion as the teacher takes care to set up the same conditions as those used in determining the norms.

8. Developmental stages in children's drawing

Substantial aid was provided for this phase of the work by previous European studies of children's drawing. Psychologists had distinguished roughly between the so-called *schematic* or conceptual and the *true-to-appearance* or visually realistic stages. Historians and anthropologists had gone on to point out resemblances between children's art and primitive art, and some had even suggested that children's artistic development involved a recapitulation of some of the main stages in art history, from crude schematism to the developed realism of the Renaissance, with its three-dimensional modeling and perspective. On the other hand, it had been pointed out that some very primitive art—by the Ice-Age cavemen—was not schematic but realistic in outline. Leaving aside controversial issues in psychology and cultural history, there remained a thoroughly documented, skeleton outline of the normal development of children's drawing ability, which apparently held true of children the world over.

This important conception of artistic development in the individual had never been subjected to verification in America, on a scale comparable to that of the Cleveland studies. It is one accomplishment of these studies to have confirmed, refined, and considerably developed this conception. It can be subdivided into intermediate stages, as follows: (1) the primitive schematic stage; (2) the full or developed schematic stage; (3) the mixed stage (intermediate between schematic and true-to-appearance); (4) the true-to-appearance; (5) the perspective stage.[1]

Not all individuals, even modern adults, pass through all these stages. Many of them remain on a schematic and therefore childlike

[1] These names are capable of further improvement. The fourth is "true-to-appearance" only in a limited sense, especially as to linear outline and modeling and texture. Full visual realism comes only with perspective and deep space representation, if then.

or primitive stage as regards drawing ability, or regress to one through disuse, although highly educated along other lines, and perhaps capable of appreciating art. But the evidence indicates that no individual can advance to a later stage without going through the earlier ones, in substantially the order named.

Development from stage to stage is apparently not dependent on specific training in art, though probably capable of being affected and somewhat accelerated by it. (Experimental data is lacking on this point.) It apparently tends to go on to some extent with little or no art instruction, and whatever teaching methods are used, as a result of general mental and perceptual development, muscular co-ordination, and observation of popular art. In estimating a child's artistic development, then, we are studying not only his specific achievement or acquired skill in art, but also certain indications of his general mental development.

9. Maturity, realism, and excellence

Can degree of advancement in realism be taken as equivalent to degree of excellence in a picture, and of superior talent in a child? Is a more mature or precocious child or picture necessarily better? These questions recall the old controversies over whether evolution is the same as progress; whether increasing complexity of structure and of civilization are necessarily improvement, or whether (as Rousseau argued) more simple and primitive stages are sometimes better. In many cases no dispute arises: the more mature child and picture seem possessed of all the other possible artistic virtues, and so are unhesitatingly put down as "superior talent." Insofar as this is true, one can use the scale of development as a scale of excellence; that is, as an objective indicator or correlative of excellence, even though the two are not synonymous. But it is not always or necessarily true. A highly realistic work may be found in some ways mediocre; a schematic one may be admired for its decorative or expressive qualities.

In art criticism generally, extreme realism is not considered equivalent to excellence or a necessary sign of greatness. Art history has not stopped short with the realistic modeling and perspective of the Renaissance. It has gone on to modern eclecticism, with its frequent conscious reversion to the decorative distortions and schematism of primitives and children; with deliberate sacrifice of realism to design, expression, and fantasy. Often in the past, sophisticated adult artists have made the same sacrifice, consciously or not—for example, in Byzantine mosaics and Persian miniatures. They have managed to find great scope for development on a level which a scale of stages in realism would describe as relatively childish.

To decide artistic standards and define excellence in general is a problem essentially outside the field of the psychologist, and of all descriptive science. It involves aesthetic and perhaps moral standards, as well as questions of general mental and physical health. But the psychologist can at least analyze its detailed implications. Is degree of maturation regarded as equivalent to excellence in other phases of child development? Certainly we do not always consider precocity a desirable trait in children—for example, in matters of sex. On the other hand, the question does not seem to arise in regard to intelligence tests, where a more mature status is an accepted sign of superiority. Of course, it is open to any school or teacher to adopt as an objective the development of adult ways of drawing. As a matter of fact, this was the main objective in teaching drawing until the time of "free expression" and "progressive methods," with their implication that children's ways of drawing had values of their own and were not mere crude approaches to adult art. The vast majority of people, art teachers included, still think of art value largely in terms of successful realism. If any judge or teacher still wishes to adopt the scale of normal development in drawing as equivalent to a scale of improvement, of increasing ability in general, then the *Diagnosis* will help him evaluate much more precisely and systematically than before.

However, the progressive art teacher, like the "advance guard" artist and critic, will not be satisfied with evaluating children's art entirely on a basis of increasing powers of realistic representation. He will insist, as did the judges above referred to, who quickly appraised results of the Seven Drawing Test, that one six-year-old drawing can be better than another, even though both are definitely schematic in type and show no signs of advancement to the next stage. Within each developmental type, in other words, there is room for considerable variation in detail, in mode of treatment, which many judges will regard as sufficient to determine a picture's merit. Such characteristics may even outweigh, in the judge's mind, degree of realistic advancement. He may admire a child's drawing as he does an African Negro carving—not with a condescending smile as if to say, "Pretty good for one so young, or for a mere savage"; but on its own merits as superior to the average adult, modern academic piece. Often it is the decorative, design aspect of the childlike or primitive piece which is often weak or missing in the academic one. Often (as remarked above) the judges were attracted by an effect of vitality, humor, or a vividly childish way of looking at the world and picking out what seemed important to the childish mind—a net effect of artistry through definite selection, emphasis, and reorganization from direct experience. It seems to manifest itself on any age level beyond early infancy, and not necessarily in proportion to maturity or amount of skill and information. In fact, too often it seems to decline as these increase.

Can these intangible, supposed signs of excellence be described in any objective way? The Cleveland studies have made only a slight beginning, not enough to provide anything like a definite scale or manual. They have called attention to the problem, at least, and have gone a step farther in roughly distinguishing between "developmental," "constant," and "rare" characteristics. In the last two of these categories, perhaps, remain hidden the elusive intangibles which future workers will regard as signs of superior ability regardless of age level. A "developmental" characteristic is one which changes according to age level. A "constant" characteristic appears with considerable frequency in about the same degree in all age levels. A "rare" one appears very seldom on any level. "True to appearance" is a developmental characteristic; "smooth areas" is a constant one; and "bold line" is rare. Such classification of specific characteristics was made on the basis of fewer examples than could be wished, especially on the higher age levels, and it is hoped that future study will revise and clarify them considerably. As matters now stand, our understanding of rare and constant characteristics is still vague and fragmentary. It has been hard to describe them without the use of evaluative, subjective terms. Our conception of their importance in relation to giftedness is subject to change in the light of new aesthetic theories.

The term "developmental," as used here, includes characteristics which tend to dwindle and die out with maturation, as well as those which grow. Both, it is felt, are somehow bound up with development in general. One of the most interesting disclosures of the "Seven-

Drawing" study is the way in which decorative characteristics in general, especially in use of bright colors and rhythmic lines, tend to die out as the child grows older. In the art appreciation study, also, these characteristics gradually lose appeal as reasons for liking a picture. The tendency in both cases is more rapid and pronounced in boys. More and more, with advancing age, the sensuous delight in color, line, and pattern for their own sake is sacrificed to the dominating interest in representing certain types of subject matter, and in doing so with utmost realistic accuracy. The organized grouping of details in a picture also seems to decline in favor of great realism and accuracy in a few details.

Here again, one must notice the apparent recapitulation of certain phases in art history: the decrease of decorative color and line which accompanied the rise of realistic art in the Renaissance. And again one asks, "What next?" If an individual's artistic development goes on, and does not atrophy through disuse in adolescence or before, where will it go after achieving full perspective realism? In the case of modern Post-impressionists, as we have seen, it can evidently go on to a sort of eclecticism, with possible reversion to certain aspects of the schematic stage, enriched by adult experience, and perhaps combined with realistic features. Our studies up through age sixteen throw no light on this problem. But such considerations do deter us from assuming that our present view of normal development tells the whole story.

Moreover, we may ask, suppose our survey had been made in ancient Persia or Byzantium, or even in modern Paris, would the same decline of decorative emphasis have appeared? Is what we have seen due to the local cultural climate, to America's artistic immaturity or Cleveland's, or to faulty art teaching in schools and museums? Is it due to naïve prejudice against decorative art as effeminate? Is it due to some more basic impulse toward realism, bound up perhaps with growing intellectual and scientific powers, which makes decorative beauty seem trivial and distracting? If so, to what extent should the art teacher try to fight against it and preserve a taste for design and decoration in the growing child? How can he present the decorative and formal aspects of art in ways more attractive to older children, especially boys?

At the same time, there is food for thought in an experiment which tended to show that preference or liking is not always favorable to active learning. Pictures which the children at first disliked often changed their attitudes more than ones they liked at first sight. Quick liking is sometimes a sign of familiarity, of having learned how to respond to that sort of thing. Dislike, on the other hand, may be due to unfamiliarity. If the first impulse to brush the thing aside can be restrained and followed up by careful study, the result may be profoundly unsettling and far-reaching educationally. We must not assume that children should be given only types of artistic experience which they accept easily and quickly. How many would go far in mathematics on that basis? We are sometimes justified in persisting for a time against apparent antipathy to a subject on the child's part, if we have good reason to believe he will see its value later. But when possible, it is well to put the dynamic of interest behind his scholastic efforts.

It was evident to the staff that merely grading pictures as more or less advanced or mature in type was not the same as evaluation, and was not a sufficient way of grading from the teacher's standpoint. To bring it nearer to the teacher's needs, the authors of the *Diagnosis* ventured out a little way from the safe shore of objective analysis, and onto the thin ice of evaluative standards. Among the various characteristics they labeled certain ones as "desirable" and others as "undesirable." Advanced representational stages were declared to be desirable "because there seems to be a strong inclination for children to strive toward a naturalistic representation of objects and figures. The tendency toward expressionism and abstract art, when it occurs at all, seems to grow out of the true-to-appearance drawing." "Outstanding color," "decisiveness and boldness of line and area," "subtlety of line," "clarity of outline," and "highly organized grouping" were declared to be desirable or superior qualities. On the other hand, "hesitating and weak lines," "ragged, smudgy areas," and "inconsistent use of medium" were called undesirable, signs of inferiority. Evaluative significance was thus given to "developmental" as well as to "rare" and "constant" characteristics. By individual diagnosis blanks, the teacher was aided to analyze a given picture, and to appraise it as "superior," "typical," or "inferior."

Probably no one interested in art criticism can read such a list without at once rising to challenge it with exceptions. Is boldness of outline always good? Do not some great artists use ragged, smudgy areas—and so on. Endless debate would certainly be possible on these points, for they merely carry over into children's art perennial issues in the aesthetics of drawing and painting. At the same time, there are other considerations to remember. Granting that a certain characteristic may be good when used in a special context by a sophisticated, adult artist, it does not necessarily follow that the same characteristic is a healthy, promising sign in most children's art. On the whole, and except for occasional atypical cases (which the teacher may evaluate as such), we may be justified by experience in regarding it as a sign of weakness. Occasionally, a great artist may affect a smudgy, fumbling, awkward stroke for a certain purpose, long after he has learned to draw firmly and clearly when he wants to. But if a child draws that way consistently, at an age when most children want to draw clearly and have a hard time doing so, the chances are that he is doing so through inability and not intention. No scale can be relied on completely, and the wise teacher will always supplement its use with a careful eye to the rare, atypical genius.

Moreover, there is no use trying to evaluate and be purely objective at the same time. The two are essentially inconsistent, and if the teacher wants a method of evaluation, he must be prepared to accept some trace of debatable standards in it. The psychologist renders no great service by remaining impeccably objective (if that were possible) and evading all the practical problems of educational grading. The important questions to raise about a proposed method are: "what standards does it imply or assume? Does it state them explicitly as such, conceding their debatable nature, or does it hide them under a mask of pretended scientific objectivity?" If it does state them, we can go on to debate them and decide whether or not to accept them. Evaluation becomes more intelligent, not by trying to avoid debatable standards entirely, but by realizing more clearly what one's standards imply, abstractly and concretely, and what arguments can be advanced for and against them. We are making a step toward objectivity whenever we define our standards in explicit terms, and analyze vague, general ones into specific characteristics. The importance of such analysis is indicated by Mrs. Lark-Horovitz's study of subjective judgments,[2] in which it appeared that judges professing similar abstract standards applied them with very different results.

[2] *The Journal of Experimental Education,* XI.2, p. 116.

10. Gifted and average groups compared

Yet another approach to the problem of evaluation has been made throughout the Cleveland studies. It involves detailed comparison between students in the "Special" classes at the museum, made up of supposedly talented, gifted, superior children from eleven through sixteen, and all others. The others included (a) children in the public schools, who had shown no unusual interest in coming to the museum or in taking special art work; (b) students in the museum's Saturday Open class for children, free to all and very diversified as to economic, racial, and educational family backgrounds; (c) students in the Saturday classes for children of museum members, coming from high economic and presumably cultural levels in the community. The *b* and *c* groups were not wholly unselected in relation to art, since either they or their parents had shown a definite interest in coming, and perhaps in paying to come; but they had not had to show any special art ability. In fact, any child in the open class who had long shown marked ability was likely to have been transferred from there to the Special class. Choices for the Special class were made either in this way or, as explained above, through the Seven Drawing Test. In either case, admission to it was based on the arbitrary judgment of museum teachers or judges appointed by them.

What right had we then to assume that the "Special" children were actually more gifted than the "Averages," or that any differences between them were associated with differences in art ability? None, theoretically; and all generalizations were made with this clearly in mind. But it is valid scientific procedure to assume something as a working hypothesis, and see where it leads. Also, lacking evidence to the contrary, it is reasonable to believe that supposed experts have some justification for their views; not to accept their judgment as final, but to examine it carefully as a hypothesis. In the same way, the findings of any art test at all, or any mode of judging talent, may be followed out hypothetically and themselves tested by experience. However implausible or unreasonable it sounds, the results may justify it over a long period of time. Such results—for example, a high percentage of successful careers in advanced art study and professional work—are the only real way of confirming the accuracy of any method for evaluating children's art ability. This way itself can never be final, for all judgments of later "success" in art are debatable, even for centuries after the artist is dead. But it is the only one we have. The chief trouble with most of the current art ability tests is that they conceal their assumptions, and the hypothetical nature of their findings, under a cloak of statistical claims to "validity" and "reliability"—terms which are popularly understood, unfortunately, to mean a great deal more than they imply in a strictly technical sense.

The "Specials," then, were a group of children who had been judged (rightly or wrongly) to possess superior talent. We assumed that they at least deserved special study, and set out to discover in what specific, observable ways (if any) they differed from other children in matters concerned with art. The answers would at least show more clearly what kind of children the judges considered gifted. At most, if the judges were right, we might know a few more observable facts about artistically gifted children. These facts might serve in turn as *indicators* of talent—as signs by which other presumably gifted children could be recognized. By a highly diversified set of tests or experimental devices—some analyzing work samples, some observing ability to remember visually, to learn a new technique, to defend preferences intelligently, and so on—we might approach the composite of diverse abilities known as "art ability."

Objective differences between the Special and the Average groups were indeed found in a considerable number of experiments. The Specials were on the whole a little, but not much, more intelligent than the Averages; on the other hand, some high I.Q. groups in the schools did very uneven work in the Seven Drawing Test. The Specials were considerably more advanced in developmental type of drawing than the Averages were. They paid more attention to artistic style, form, mode of treatment than the Averages did, both in their own productions and in judging other works of art, and were correspondingly less concerned with the nature of the subject represented. They were able to explain and defend their preferences more explicitly, with reference to the artistic qualities of a particular object. They identified themselves less with the subject or scene portrayed, and were more able to take an objective view toward the artist's accomplishments. They observed and learned more quickly, and retained visual memories longer; they were more capable of experimenting with a new medium and adapting their technique to its requirements.

Whether such differences are really typical of artistically gifted children in general is, of course, the crucial question. As mentioned above, that cannot be decided with any assurance unless and until we can compare the later artistic performance of the Specials with that of the Averages. More long-term observation of that sort is to be desired. In the meantime, wherever a group of children is selected as gifted in art, by any test or mode of judgment, it is worth while to study them carefully, in order to have the data in hand when their later performance can be appraised.

11. The meaning of "development" in relation to art ability

In a letter to me, Mrs. Lark-Horovitz summarized her impression of the Museum "Specials" as follows:

Our findings substantiate the fact that Specials are heightened Averages; that the top-group of Specials represent a still more heightened average (especially as to perception) plus certain intangible qualities—whether inherited or native or acquired—that are, as yet, unexplained. The main difference between the two groups is neither intelligence, nor of a developmental nature. It is the phenomenon that specially gifted children express themselves (and think primarily) in a *visual* medium: that is, they translate all their experience into this mode of expression; while average children lack this ability, even though their experiences are as powerful and their gift of expressing them as strong.[3]

In other words, there appears to be no radical difference in kind between the gifted and the average child in art, but rather a gradual stepping-up of a number of related abilities, plus a strong tendency to experience things visually, and even to try to suggest, represent, and symbolize other types of experience in visual terms. This itself might perhaps be called an ability—to interpret the world in visual images—but it also involves a direction of interest and motivation, each no doubt stimulating the other. The importance of interest in the matter has seemed especially important to me in observing chil-

[3] This refers primarily to children gifted in visual art; those gifted in music would presumably be more inclined to auditory thinking. (T.M.)

dren's behavior throughout the tests. I often sensed that many of the high I.Q. students tested in the schools were simply not interested in the tests or in art at all; that they felt a positive antipathy toward the more decorative, sensuous aspects of art; that this antipathy tended on the whole to increase with age and to be much stronger in boys than in girls. This accords with the obvious fact, so disappointing to art teachers, that large numbers of children who apparently show talent in art at an early age drop it as an activity later on. What may appear in tests and questionnaires as a decline of ability in art may be mainly a decline in willingness to use and exhibit what ability one has. The result, however, is eventually the same; since an ability unused or inhibited tends to atrophy.

Educationally, it seems important to decide, if possible, the question raised above: To what extent are these apparent declines in ability and interest, especially along decorative lines, due to cultural influences? If largely so, then we may hope to counteract them by building up more respect for art, including decorative art, as a respected masculine interest. If the cause goes deeper, the problem is harder. We must decide how much to fight against nature, the nature of adolescent development. Again, we should ask very searchingly whether art is now presented to adolescents, in schools and museums, in a way to attract the changing interests and abilities of that age level. There is no great difficulty in interesting adolescents in sports, moving pictures, clothes, and ballroom dancing, all of which possess features akin to visual arts, including the decorative. What have they which school and institutional types of art lack? Some of the answers are obvious, but what to do about it is not so easy to decide.

In the remark just quoted, Mrs. Lark-Horovitz states that the main difference between the two groups is not "developmental." Although the Specials are a little more advanced on the scale of successive types or stages, this does not seem to be the essential difference. "Developmental" includes diminishing as well as growing abilities, as we have seen, but this again fails to distinguish the two groups. The Specials do not lose their decorative interests faster than the others. Often they seem to hold them longer, especially when explicitly directed to such a task, as in the "Beautiful Page" experiment.

However, the other characteristics which do help to mark them off are also developmental, in another sense. One can say of a certain six-year-old that he has a good all-round development, although he is not at all precocious. He has not developed in any way beyond the typical six-year norm, but differs from certain others of his age in having developed just that far along more different lines at once. Development of the individual, in other words, is potentially a process of growth in many distinct though related functions, bodily structures, and abilities. No one grows equally fast or far in all of them at once. Some go ahead precociously along certain lines, and are arrested, slow, or even regressive along other lines. Now the ability to draw in a visually realistic way, rather than schematically, is apparently an ability which increases rather steadily among all children under present educational conditions. It seems, therefore, to be intimately bound up with the process of maturation, and is therefore called "developmental"; perhaps a better word would be "maturational." The other kinds of characteristics (here called "constant" or "rare") do not seem to vary definitely with age. But, at the same time, they may be more highly developed in one individual than in another. Nearly everyone has a highly developed desire for sweets at an early age, and in some it remains constant all through life. Some have a highly developed musical interest at an early age; no doubt partly due to innately high development of the auditory nerve systems. In some the high though early development is in visual alertness. Later experience and learning may in a sense develop these early traits by redirecting, complicating, and refining them, while in another sense—that of relative strength or sensitivity—they do not develop, but appear as markedly in childhood as they ever will.

Essentially, then, it is not mere precocity in visual realism that we must look for as a sign of artistic talent (though this may well occur as one indication), but rather such characteristics as perceptual, imaginative, emotional alertness, directed by preference into visual experience and manipulation of visible materials. Such signs will never appear abstractly, in a vacuum, but only in some concrete activity or production. Hence the need for "tests" to call out such behavior. But we must read between the lines of their results, not judging them for obvious signs of maturity, special training, or sophistication. Rather we should look for signs of that vitality, sensitivity, eagerness, inventiveness, and organizing power which distinguish excellence from mediocrity on every age level and at every stage of cultural development.

It is possible that such characteristics, although "constant" or "nondevelopmental" in one sense, can be developed in another sense by proper educational and other influences; that is, stimulated into more active and harmonious exercise. Is not this the essential task of education in art and in other subjects? There would seem to be little value in merely hastening the progress toward visual realism, or other mature ways of drawing, any more than there would be in trying to accelerate physical maturation. It seems a better ideal to help each child achieve maximum fullness of experience, happy and successful living (however these are conceived) on each age level as he comes to it rather than hurrying on to the next. It would seem better to help him draw, think, feel, and play as well as possible in the six-year-old manner while he is a six-year-old. Accordingly, we should not put a premium on mere maturational advancement in drawing or any other ability. We should not, perhaps, even refer to the stages in such advancement as "the development of drawing ability," for that is too broad a term and omits the other phases in drawing ability which we are now considering. On the other hand, any attempt to retard artistic maturation artificially, so as to preserve the decorative charm of schematic art, runs the risk of unexpected repercussions on general mental development.

Much remains to be done in showing the deeper significance of the tendency in children's drawing toward visual realism. Its suggestive analogy to art history through the Renaissance has been mentioned above. More specifically, the schematic stage of early childhood bears certain resemblances to adult drawings of the neolithic period. Culturally, this was an age of great development in language, including the beginnings of written language. It was an age when humanity was struggling to form its basic set of concepts of the main types of person, animal, plant, inanimate object, action, event, and abstract quality. These emerge later on in Egyptian and Chinese pictographs. Schematic drawings, simplified and apparently crude, were an important means in this process of distinguishing main types and giving them written as well as vocal symbols. Visual realism was not essential at that stage, and would have been an unnecessary encumbrance. In young children, also, the period of schematic drawing is one of recognizing basic types and forming basic concepts. Schematic drawing is conceptual drawing, of the way a thing is understood to exist—of what seem to be its most interesting and important features—rather than of how it would look to a disinterested observing eye. Drawing, clay modeling, and other modes of representation play an important part in aiding intellectual and perceptual development as well as manual co-ordination.

12. Educational implications

What, then, should be the role of art education in early childhood? Has it not been an error to urge visually realistic drawing, from a model or otherwise? Would we not be further mistaken to favor such drawing by any scale or test which restricts the idea of "art ability" to realistic drawing ability, or to any other way of conforming to adult standards? The alternative is not to discourage precocity; when it occurs along with signs of health, well and good. But a paramount need may be to utilize schematic drawing itself, while it lasts, as an aid in certain phases of mental development. Indeed, schematic drawing can itself be developed into mature scientific diagramming, mechanical drawing, and other types of expository art involving conceptual realism, without ever yielding place entirely to visual realism.

An associated problem arises in the relation of children's drawing to their ways of appreciating pictures made by others. The present research and supplementary teaching experience indicate that young children do not prefer looking at the kind of pictures they make themselves. While making schematic pictures, they tend to prefer realistic ones. In some ways, they treat adult art as they do the whole outside world of objects: as something to be looked at selectively, in a childlike way, for what interests them. If asked to copy a realistic picture, they will do so with highly abbreviated schematism, and will either not notice or not be bothered by the discrepancy. They can enjoy and appreciate, to a limited extent, much more mature and realistic art than they can produce. Often they tend to look down on primitive art which is nearer their own productive level. They are not much interested in what the adult artist tried to emphasize or how he secured his realistic or decorative effects. They are more interested in the subject represented; they like to project themselves into the scene and perhaps identify themselves with one of the persons. Average older children maintain this type of interest, while Specials tend at an earlier age to adopt the more specialized technical and visual attitude of the adult artist. This of course has been stimulated in the Specials by teaching; but they respond to it more than the Averages do.

Again it would seem wise to consider these psychological hypotheses in working out our teaching methods. To what extent shall we try to influence all children toward liking contemporary nonrealistic art, or toward liking art for its technical and purely visual, formal aspects? Some, with special visual talents and development, may take to such experiences easily and heartily; and if so, well and good. But for the rank and file, and for all in early childhood, there may be psychological values which we do not now understand, in using art appreciation as a means to vicarious experience, to enriched and heightened conscious fantasy—not in isolation, but linked with other studies and practical experiences.

Any light on a student's level of artistic development, and on his peculiar interests and abilities, is of direct value in adapting educational methods and contents to the human factors involved. It brings immediate returns in more successful teaching, whether or not it can be mathematically expressed and verified.

Drawing is not, and perhaps should never be, a required subject for all secondary students. But art appreciation, properly taught, might well be advanced to that status. For young children, drawing, painting, and modeling are already so recognized in a great number of schools. They are not sufficient as media to exercise productive impulses in visual form, and should be supplemented by crafts, dancing, and theater, as well as by music and literature, to give adequate scope to art education in a broad sense. Accordingly, studies like the present one should be supplemented by studies in other arts, to raise there similar questions about normal and accelerated development and other signs of art ability. Children's drawings, however, will remain peculiarly worthy of attention, because of the clear, permanent, easily produced and handled evidence which they present. It is hoped that the present report, inconclusive as it is, will point a few paths for later inquiry.

FRANZ CIZEK AND THE FREE EXPRESSION METHOD*

It was largely with the aim of seeing Professor Cizek's class in operation that the writer went to the Vienna School of Arts and Crafts. The experiment being tried there in children's art education was something to be enthusiastic about, for many American schools observed had shown a glaring need for exactly what Professor Cizek stood for: more freedom for the child to look at the world and to experiment in congenial ways of expressing himself in some artistic medium.

The school was used to receiving foreign visitors, and was courteous and clear in explaining its ideas. Cizek himself was a man to command respect: assured, quiet, and intent in manner, he struck one as an intelligent enthusiast, quite confident that the road he had mapped out was the best one. He was a teacher, not a politician, and had lately been forced by intolerant superiors to abandon a modernist class of older students in favor of conventional craft training. The outside world had honored him more than his own country.

The small workroom, crowded with some fifty boys and girls from seven or eight years to fifteen, was a delight to watch. What could more completely justify a method of instruction, one thought, than the fact that it obviously gave children such a good time in the process? No one who has ever been present at an old-style-school art lesson and seen or suffered himself in the cramped, painful, and smudgy task of copying, could have failed to enjoy the spectacle of animated industry.

In the Vienna school it was a continued delight to look at some of the products: here was a carved wood frieze of boys playing football, in crisp, irregular rhythm; there a crowded street-scene, composed unconventionally but firmly in broad areas of pure color; farther on

---

* Published in its original form in the *Journal of the Barnes Foundation,* October, 1925. Reprinted in *Art and Education* by John Dewey and others (Merion, Pa., Barnes Foundation Press, 1929).

a group of fantastic birds against brilliant foliage. But gradually, with other pictures, came a sense of recognizing something familiar, and with it a few vague doubts. One picture after another was almost identical with those other pictures from the Cizek school which had been printed in colors and exhibited in America: groups of children playing and dancing with flying hair and ribbons, in posterlike blocks of color against flowery fields or elaborately decorated backgrounds. Then came reminiscences of Austrian handicraft, such as the familiar porcelain figure of a child with curly hair and flowers outlined in black—echoes of the romantic colored illustrations in *Jugend,* of Böcklin and Thoma, of newer expressionist grotesqueries that had become a current formula in German exhibitions. Even the striking obviousness of street posters blurted out here and there.

Was this the spontaneous personal expression of the students? A word with Professor Cizek and his assistant revealed their devout confidence that the work was absolutely uninfluenced. And there was no reason to doubt their entire sincerity. They moved quietly from bench to bench, looking on, giving no directions or authoritative judgments, now and then proposing a problem or dropping some half-humorous, encouraging remark.

The children had been given no opportunity to see outside works of art, it was asserted in reply to a question: reproductions of old or modern masters were never shown them. They were actually discouraged from visiting the Vienna museums, rich in works of almost every school, for these were expressions of other ages. The class of older students had sometimes been advised to see modernist exhibitions, of expressionism, cubism and futurism, so that they might learn to express the spirit of the present age—machinery, motion, construction, and power. Professor Cizek himself had originated a form of art in this spirit, which he called "constructivism" or "dynamic rhythm." His advanced class (now abandoned) had, it seemed, been taught not entirely by the free expression method, but with some definite pressure toward these modern forms. The products of this group were abstract and wholly different from the children's, but showed a marked resemblance to each other.

In short, it was obvious that in spite of the attempt at preserving spontaneity, several different types of influence had affected the work of both groups. The teacher himself, first of all, was doing more than he realized; in no other way could the marked likeness between the pictures, which stamped them at once as Cizek products, be explained. Just how this force had been exerted during the year, one could only guess at. But every teacher knows how eagerly pupils look for someone to lean on, for some advice or praise, some hint as to what to do next, and how easily any word, act, or facial expression on his part may reveal what he likes, or suggest some way of procedure. Try as he may to help children to be natural, he can only encourage his own conception of what children would naturally do.

It is another common experience of teachers that pupils imitate each other, and that no amount of praise for self-reliance can stop them. Above all, pictures exhibited on the walls are imitated, especially when thought to represent the teacher's preference. When, as in the Cizek school, work by former as well as present students is accessible to view, a strong factor is at work toward the continuing of stereotyped forms.

Finally, the student is sure to see current art outside the school, and to hear art criticism of a kind: the pictures at home, the comments about his own and other work, the shopwindows full of prints and paintings, as well as the magazines and posters above referred to. These are not all bad. The Austrian child, for example, has an unusual opportunity to see brightly decorative peasant costumes, embroidery, painted and carved wooden boxes and furniture. Even advertising reflects and cleverly popularizes, much more directly than in America, new movements in art. Any active and curious child, especially one who is himself trying to draw and paint, is sure to look avidly at such things about him, and no teacher can prevent their influences.

In view of these conditions, the ideal of keeping a child's imagination in a state of absolute purity and freedom is from the start impossible. The very attempt at such an end is evidence of the false psychology which has affected much writing on art education: of the old belief that some "self" within the child is bursting for expression and release, and that all outside forces tend to repress and enslave it.

Yet the persistent attempt to shut out influence is sure to have some effect. For which types of art are easiest to keep away? Not the vulgar of the street, nor the childish type of the schoolroom, but the great traditions of the past and the best work of the present. Not readily accessible, less ostentatious than the visible clamor around, buried in frozen disorder in the museums, good works of art may never catch a child's attention or be understood, unless the teacher points them out and invites him to see how they differ from things of a more obvious appeal. Failure to do this can have only one result: that the bad influences have practically no competition.

Their effect on the children is of course very gradual. A more detailed inspection of the Cizek classroom revealed a fact already observed in similar American schools—that in general the most original and appealing designs were those of the youngest pupils; the older the child, the more his picture tended to be sentimental, conventional, and weak in visual form. A question to the teacher in charge revealed the further significant fact that the older students tend to drop out and abandon the class, which is held out of regular school hours. After its twenty years in existence no prominent artist could be named who had received his early training at the Cizek school.

What is the reason for this disheartening failure of precocious talents to develop, after a splendid start? The answer given at the school was the force of economic pressure, the demands of college and vocational training. This is doubtless true in many cases, but is it enough to explain the situation? Would not a determined interest survive these obstacles, as many artists have in the past survived them? The problem recalled a remark heard last winter from an American boy of considerable talent in modeling, who had left it to spend his spare hours at mechanical engineering. The art classes had been fun, he remarked with a superior air, but were just "fooling around"; he wanted to "learn something" and "get somewhere." A few years of undirected toying with art materials had been enough to exhaust its attractiveness as a game, and he had come to demand something more substantial to bite down on mentally, some intellectual food for his growing curiosity about the world. For this next step in development the free expression method had no help to offer him—nothing but the vague advice to keep on being himself and doing whatever he wanted.

The old academic method also tends to be restrictive; not, as the free expressionists suppose, because it imparts traditions, but because it imparts too few traditions, and too little of each, so that the only ones to be followed (usually the Greek, Florentine, and Dutch) seem to have absolute authority. Indeed, the restrictions of the Cizek method and the old academic method spring from the same source.

The Cizek plan, far from achieving its end of freedom, robs and restricts the student when it shuts out all but a few influences, and
these few none of the best. Both methods fail to aid as they might
the growth of real creativeness, because they fail to present a sufficient
variety of artistic forms and techniques. A broad study of traditions
is thoroughly compatible with individual experiment, and in fact
makes original choice and reorganization almost unavoidable. At the
same time, unlike the free expression method, it provides the student with the artistic heritage of the past, without which his interest
in art materials cannot long be sustained, nor his use of them become
mature and rational.

❧ XIII ❧

ARTISTIC DEVELOPMENT AND
LOGICAL SYNTHESIS*

One who looks over American school art work is still impressed with the far-reaching influence of the late Arthur Wesley Dow, of Teachers College, Columbia University. East and west, in state and city school boards, in conventions of art teachers, his name was long a rallying cry for the liberal factions, usually far in the minority, that struggled for advance toward modern methods of instruction. Many of these teachers and supervisors studied directly with Professor Dow, then went back to their home states to champion his ideas against the inertia of politics-ridden school administrations. To such lonely and hard-pressed missionaries, the memory of their leader is an almost sacred symbol for truth and progressiveness in general, and some of them regard his teaching with a veneration that is not always conducive either to clear understanding or to open-minded criticism.

If it is true that the school art situation cannot be understood without reference to Professor Dow's influence, it is doubly true that his writings cannot be justly estimated without reference to that situation as he perceived it. His lifework was a struggle against the academicism which he saw throughout the field, and his own ideals were always presented in sharp contrast to it. What was this old regime, and what did he offer instead?

A future historian may perhaps look tolerantly on the early stages in American public school art work. Its leaders had a difficult task in gaining for art any recognition at all in the curriculum, against the vigorous protest of hard-headed farmers and businessmen, who thought anything beside the three R's a wasteful indulgence in frills and fancies. If admitted at all, it had always to conform to popular standards. Thus picture-study was made a vehicle for patriotic and moral lessons; drawing and painting consisted in trying to reproduce a box in true perspective, or a spray of flowers in pretty tints. Many

* Published as "The Dow Method and Public School Art" in the *Journal of the Barnes Foundation,* January, 1926; reprinted in *Art and Education,* 1929.

teachers, of course, were almost totally untrained either in the technique or appreciation of art; they were few and overworked; hence their methods had to be capable of easy, standardized application to large classes, with clear-cut standards for grading results. Books of motives for decorative pattern were given out to them, simple, stereotyped lotus flowers, fleur-de-lis, and other conventional forms. Minute directions were prescribed for conducting an art class; in some cases, for example, each child was to have a sheet of paper printed with dots, and move his pencil in unison with the rest, three dots to the right, two down, and so on until a cat or house was outlined.

More or less pardonable as such expedients may have been at first in frontier communities, they could only disgust a man of Dow's intelligence and European training, especially when he saw them entrenched and perpetuated, long after the need had passed, in wealthy and cultivated cities like Boston and New York. Attempting to influence certain federated groups of art teachers toward liberal ideals, he found them narrow-minded, without genuine interest in either art or education, hand-in-glove with dealers in textbooks and art materials, who found ways to checkmate any forward-looking proposal. Against reactionary school boards everywhere, his pupils and their liberal allies are still struggling.

Dow was far from unsuccessful in gathering about him groups of devoted followers, from his first efforts in Boston in 1889, through his years of teaching at Pratt Institute in Brooklyn, at the Art Students' League, in summers at Ipswich, Massachusetts, and from 1904 until the day of his death in 1922, as head of the department of Fine Arts at Teachers College. No small part of his influence at all these places was due to a personality that drew affection and sympathetic response to his enthusiasm, as well as respect for his clear and sensible thinking.

The method elaborated in these years of teaching was first conceived in Boston with the aid of Ernest Fenollosa, then in charge of the Japanese collections in the Museum of Fine Arts, and was expressed in Dow's widely-used book entitled *Composition*.[1] Polemically, the idea most insisted on there is the falsity of the academic division of art into representative and decorative, both conceived as imitation, the one of natural objects and the other of conventional

[1] Ninth edition, New York, 1923. See also *Theory and Practice of Teaching Art* and *Constructive Art Teaching*, both published by Teachers College.

historic patterns. On the contrary, said Dow, both aspects should be sought together, natural objects being taken as themes for creating new, beautiful forms. Instead of the old copying method, he proposed instruction in the principles of design or composition, which he redefined and listed under the headings of Opposition, Transition, Subordination, Repetition and Symmetry. Each he illustrated with many examples chosen with catholic taste and an eye to underlying resemblances from the Greek, Oriental, Gothic, Renaissance, and modern traditions, from textile, pottery, furniture, and architecture as well as from painting and sculpture. This approach he believed would involve "a new classification of the world's art, cutting across the historical, topical and geographical lines of development . . . with many examples differing as to time, locality, material and subject, but alike in art-structure." The elements in art he classified as line, notan (dark-and-light), and color, and went on to show how the principles of harmonious composition can be realized in each, and in combinations of them.

So stated in general, these principles are unexceptionable, and there is no doubt that their adoption and study would provide a considerable advance over many of the methods now in use. But some significant things have happened in the fields of educational and aesthetic psychology since Professor Dow formulated his principles, in the light of which his way of presenting the subject to students requires considerable modification.

Toward Post-impressionist art Professor Dow, though tolerant, had no positive sympathy. Teachers today are trying more strenuously to encourage individual variation and originality in creating new designs, an aim which Dow recognized in general, but for which there was little place in his rather standardized system of procedure. There is greater attention also to the problems of stimulating the interest of children in art work, and correlating it with other phases of their mental growth. In view of these ends, pupils are led to choose subjects for visual expression from their own experience. By the project method and other devices their initiative is encouraged, and art work made a process of gradual, continuous enrichment of everyday life. They are following no rigid order of progress, and are using color from the start, not beginning with abstract lines—a step whose propriety Dow admitted in the case of young pupils only, and which he never incorporated in his own method.

Along with these changes, Professor Dow's successors have found it possible to retain and reapply a large part of his method, especially the insistence on principles of design. But his own writings give little indication that in recent years he had reconsidered the method in the light of newer psychological tendencies, especially the Deweyan conception of education as natural growth. The order of steps which he prescribes is one of abstract logical classification rather than of the necessary sequence of steps in mental development. Without applying her criticism explicitly to the Dow method, Miss Belle Boas (a former pupil, later Director of Fine Arts at the Horace Mann School) put her finger upon its essential practical weakness: "A course of study in spelling doesn't arbitrarily begin with words of one syllable in the first grade to progress to complicated six-syllable words in the high school, but rather follows the growth in the child's vocabulary as he finds his spelling complexities grow through his needs."[2]

Dow's method begins with what is logically simplest, the basic elements in a work of art, such as lines, dark and light spots, hues and intensities, and with the general definitions of the principles of design. From these atomic elements he invites the pupil to put together a beautiful form, leading him on in strict logical order from simple to complex—first straight lines, properly spaced, then curves, then two values of light and dark, then three, four, five values, then one hue in two and three values, two hues, and so on, until a form as complex as an ordinary painting is finally reached. This is a "natural method," says Dow, "of exercises in progressive order, first building up very simple harmonies, then proceeding on to the highest forms of composition. . . . It offers a means of training for the creative artist . . ."

To a mature and scientific mind such synthetic production of art is theoretically interesting, and to a teacher it may be helpful as a reference map of the field. But to propose it as a method of creating beautiful forms is to reveal a decided lack of familiarity with the psychology of artistic creation. New and vital plastic forms are rarely if ever conceived through such a course of plodding synthesis, but rather all at once as a new vision, the product, largely impulsive and automatic, of many experiences in looking at nature and art with a selective and reconstructing eye. The memory of elements and principles may come in to refine and proportion, after synthesis or

[2] *Art in the School,* 1924, p. 20.

along with it, each of the various phases of intelligent organization occurring now and then, in no fixed order, as the trend of the situation indicates. This does not mean that rational analysis and synthesis, with use of general principles, have no place in art education, but that the primary concern of the teacher is to secure vitality and freedom for perception, emotion, and imagination. Intelligence can liberate and harmonize creative impulses, but it can never build out of bare logical concepts a form touched with life.

The Chinese and Japanese artists, whom Professor Dow constantly holds up as examples, sometimes adhered strictly to certain fixed rules, and their works, pruned down to the last degree of subtle economy, provide him with many instances of design from a few means, such as two values of gray. But what we prize most in these works is the inventive imagination that worked through the rules (often religious tenets) to some unique and striking result. When the rules alone are grasped, the products are as mechanical and lifeless as the pictures in the Japanese manner by Dow and his pupils, which are scattered as models through the book.

Aside from educational method, there are serious misconceptions of visual form involved in Professor Dow's analysis—some of them springing, perhaps, from his preoccupation with Japanese styles. Had his feeling for Venetian painting, for Renoir, Cézanne and contemporary movements, been as appreciative as for the Japanese print, he would have seen more clearly the possible functions of color, merged with line and light, in building up structure and organizing a picture with pervasive atmosphere. Instead, he conceived of design in basically linear terms: "A picture may be said to be in its beginning actually a pattern of lines." On the line-idea "hinges the excellence of the whole, for no delicacy of tone or harmony of color can remedy a bad proportion."[3] This misses the fact, all-important in painting since the Venetians, that color can be so merged with a linear pattern (not superficially added to it) as to transform entirely the nature of that pattern and the rightness of its proportions.

To the Japanese, whom he praises for thinking of painting as "the art of two dimensions," may also be due his tendency to conceive design as flat, and his failure to grasp the function of solidity and depth in painting. For a painter to work for roundness and solidity, he thought, was to imitate natural objects and to encroach on sculp-

[3] *Composition*, p. 44.

ture; light and dark were of value chiefly as contrasting areas on a flat surface rather than as means of modeling. Such a defense of exotic style was no doubt salutary at a time when many academic painters knew only the European. But to ignore the building up of designs of solid objects in deep space, and the relation of color thereto, is to ignore the main achievement of European painting from Giotto to Cézanne, and to leave one's account of pictorial design sadly incomplete.

Although neglecting one of the most important elements in pictorial space, the third dimension, Professor Dow declares the final criterion of harmony in design to be Good Spacing. Yet he leaves its meaning undefined ("The mystery of Spacing will be revealed to the mind that has developed Appreciation"), and gives little reason why the selected examples of good spacing are good.

In short, Professor Dow's "synthetic" presentation of design fails in several ways to become genuinely or completely synthetic. It is of doubtful utility as a help to any creative synthesis, because, as noted above, it is foreign in its method to the process of artistic imagination and construction. Leaving out organic color, depth, and solidity, it is incomplete as a theoretical account of the important elements in visual design, and such elements as it gives are left more or less in isolation: there is no indication how these elements are completely merged in the color-line-and-light forms of modern painting. Yet, for all its inadequacies, it deserves respect as a landmark in American education, for its clear statement of a method still far in advance of those used in many schools, and for the example it offers of a sensitive and penetrating mind at work upon a generous variety of artistic forms.

✤❀ XIV ❀✤

ADOLESCENCE AND ART EDUCATION*

1. Present difficulties and some superficial remedies

There has long been a vague impression, on the part of individual teachers here and there, that art instruction on the secondary school level is not succeeding as it should. Several recent conferences among school and museum educators have made this sense of dissatisfaction conscious and explicit. As to the fact of comparative failure, there seems to be fairly general agreement; as to its causes and possible remedies, very little.

At the Cleveland Museum of Art, educational work with younger children and that with adults are both in a much more flourishing condition than work with adolescents. It is comparatively easy to attract young children to attend voluntary classes at the museum, both for art appreciation and for work in drawing, painting, and modeling. Adults of various types form another active section of the museum public. As might be expected, the most numerous among these are mature women, who come to the museum individually or in clubs to attend single lectures, courses, and gallery visits. Business and professional men come in good numbers to attend evening lectures. University students, graduate and undergraduate, come for special courses on art history and appreciation. Women still make up the greater part of these university classes, but the last few years have brought a notable increase of interest in art among men students also. Between the younger and the older age levels, there is a notable gap in the art museum public. Around the age of thirteen or fourteen, many children cease coming to the voluntary classes which meet out of school hours. Students of secondary school age are not often to be seen among museum lecture audiences.

In junior high schools, and still more in senior high schools, art is often omitted or given a very minor place in the curriculum. When

* Published first in the *Bulletin of the Worcester Art Museum,* XXIII.2 (July, 1932), pp. 61–80.

248

given at all it is likely to be of a vocational and commercial, not a cultural, nature. Very few classes from high schools come to visit the art museum, as compared with those from elementary schools, even allowing for the difference in total school enrollment.

In quality the drawing and painting of high school students, whether done at school or at the museum, tends to be inferior to that of younger students. It is usually more imitative, stereotyped and weak, less vigorous and individual, than the work of children aged seven or eight years. This happens even in the case of very talented individuals, who show great sensitivity and creative power up to the age of twelve or thirteen, then lose interest in art, and most of their former ability to create and to enjoy it.

The trouble is thus not limited to museum educational work. It is obvious also in the majority of public and private high schools throughout this country. If we are thinking, not of technical training in commercial and industrial art, but of art as a phase of liberal education, then the fact is plain to any observer that art has not yet become a vital or important part of the American secondary school curriculum.

Let us consider on a broader basis, then, some possible reasons for the present failure of art instruction on the adolescent level. Several partial causes may be pointed out at once. In the first place, the need of earning a living, or of preparing for it by studies of direct vocational value, comes to bear upon the vast majority of children during this period. Secondly, the select few who are going on to college must get ready to satisfy stringent college entrance requirements. These leave little time for subjects not recognized for college entrance, and since art is not yet generally recognized, it tends to be crowded out of the secondary curriculum. Indirectly this affects the use of leisure time also, for the required studies are difficult enough to demand about all the energy which a student can spend on cultural pursuits. Instead of keeping up his art interest, at least as a minor avocation, he is forced to more distinctly recreational amusements in his leisure time. To remove this particular obstacle, attention is now being given to the problem of assigning more college entrance credit for work in art.

It is often difficult, also, to arrange the complex high-school schedule of hours and subjects so as to permit visits to a distant museum. This difficulty, too, can usually be overcome where the will exists.

Even where no museum is available, the new, improved color prints now supply excellent materials for picture study in the school.

Another widespread obstacle is the surviving prejudice of many educators, as well as of the general public, against art as a frill, a trivial and rather effeminate luxury. This attitude is gradually disappearing of its own accord and giving way to the belief that some aesthetic training is a necessary phase in all liberal education. But it still militates against art in backward communities and, even in highly cultured ones, tends to restrict art to lower grades of school, because of the belief that older students should take up more serious and important subjects. To some extent, too, the feeling that art is a subject for girls still exists and prevents boys from choosing it even when it is available.

Having men as teachers of art to students of high-school age, both boys and girls, makes a considerable difference. Aside from what is taught, or how well it is taught, the mere fact of having a man as teacher tends to dispel the notion that art is an effeminate subject. It must be remembered, too, that adolescent girls as well as boys are sharply conscious of the age difference between themselves and younger children. They want it to be evident that their activities are radically different from those of their juniors. The very fact, then, that both art work and women teachers are associated in their minds with young children tends to prejudice the adolescent against both. To hold the respect and interest of the adolescent, it may be necessary to devote some pains to making their art work seem, as well as be, very different from that of lower groups. This applies to choice of materials and activities as well as to manner of teaching.

2. The deeper problem, and a psychological approach to it

All these are simple and fairly obvious measures for dealing with the superficial aspects of a very complicated problem. They may alleviate, but cannot fundamentally correct, maladjustment between the adolescent mind and the established institutions which it has to encounter. The failure of the art museum to meet the needs of adolescence is only one small detail in this widespread maladjustment. Secondary schools are commonly charged today with being the weakest link in our educational chain, from many points of view. If attendance at them were as voluntary as it is at the museum, and spontaneous interest the only motive drawing children there, the failure of these schools to sustain vital interest might be quite as obvious as that of the museum is today.

Progressive methods have in recent years begun to make the elementary school a congenial place for the young child. But they have not yet made any appreciable headway toward producing high schools in which the adolescent boy or girl can feel at home. What the adolescent wants to do, think, and feel is too inconsistent with what the conventional adult thinks he ought to do, think, and feel. Our established institutions are still antagonistic to his basic impulses and interests. Outside the school, his behavior may be at times so unconventional as to alarm his elders. But this only aggravates the conflict between his repressive schooling and family discipline, on the one hand, and, on the other, the thousand forces, both inward drives and external influences—the ferment of new radical tendencies in civilization—which reach him in spite of all attempts at censorship. If the school, the family, the museum, and other formal agencies of instruction ignore the latter, his real interests will inevitably turn elsewhere, as they are now doing.

Aesthetic education in particular, dealing as it does with the likes, emotions, and imaginings of individuals, is in vital need of being well adapted to the growth and variation of individual personalities. The need is much greater here than in the more impersonal, factual, and logical studies of history and science, although even there it exists. Yet art educators have not yet succeeded in working out, even in theory, a real continuity of program to extend through all age levels, based on the psychology of individual development. They have not yet escaped from the old conception of their subject as a fixed discipline, a body of facts and technical rules to be imparted in a uniform way. Instead, each age level should be considered psychologically, by itself and in relation to the rest, and provided as far as possible with a set of materials and activities which will attract, develop, and exercise the natural basic interests of the child of that age.

I have seen very progressive and intelligent high-school art teachers make the mistake of trying to impose a fixed method or a taste for some one kind of art which appealed to them as adults: for example, to make all the class paint still-life compositions in Cézanne's late manner. Now this manner was an expression of Cézanne's highly specialized interests in middle age. It has influenced art, and it has a strong appeal for the modern adult of specially cultivated taste. But none of these facts makes it necessarily congenial to adolescence. The high-school class will obediently try to imitate it if told to do so, but the result will be, as usual, a poor imitation of Cézanne, and not a good expression of the adolescent mind or of the individual student.

If there is any thoroughgoing mode of approach to the problem, it seems to me to lie through the avenue of psychology. We must observe and understand more clearly the peculiar interests and abilities of adolescence, and consider how the study of art could be more sympathetically adjusted to them. In a general way, nearly every modern educator accepts the philosophy that educational procedure should be adapted to the basic, natural interests and capacities of the child; that such basic interests should be appealed to and utilized as dynamics to spontaneous effort, in such a way as to induce a voluntary, active assimilation of the cultural heritage and a well-balanced development of all innate powers. We know fairly well, moreover, what are the basic interests of adolescence. It is in the concrete application of our high-sounding modern philosophy to the facts of adolescence, and to the actual methods of secondary teaching, that we neglect—or fear—to draw the obvious logical conclusions.

There are three characteristic traits of adolescence which I wish to consider in this manner, showing specifically what it would mean to find an outlet for them in the study of art. One is the increase of *intelligence* to a point, late in adolescence, which in certain respects is never exceeded in later life. Another is increase in consciousness of the *self* and of *individual motivation,* both in oneself and others. A third is the rise of *sexuality.* Let us consider, briefly, the meaning of each and its bearing on aesthetic studies.

3. Growth of intelligence

The fact that intelligence keeps on developing, throughout most or all of the adolescent period, points rather obviously to the conclusion that the study of art on this level should involve more reflective thinking than on lower levels. But just what does this mean in terms of teaching methods?

For very young children, activities related to art need not and cannot involve much systematic reasoning or planning. The spontaneous impulse to play with different materials, to feel their sensory qualities, to manipulate them this way and that, provides a dynamic strong enough to carry them through the time available for art. This curiosity and thirst for sensory experience carries over into art appreciation, where there is an immediate response to the stimulus of line, color, and shape. In almost every young child, there is also an easily aroused desire to set down his experiences and imaginings in the form of graphic illustration. But as the child grows older, these motives are not enough. He demands more and more to know the reasons for things: why certain things are worth doing, why he should be asked to learn certain facts and to like certain kinds of art. True, bad teaching often fosters a passive attitude in children throughout high school, and the habit of expecting to be told exactly what is what. But such teaching, making no demand for intelligent thought on the part of students, is one of the very reasons why they become so often bored with school work. Every subject, including art, can be taught as a mass of dead facts and routine tasks, or as a set of purposeful activities, giving scope for the conscious adapting of means to ends, for logical inference, and for the constructive use of information.

In art instruction, a greater emphasis on intelligent thinking could be carried out along several different lines. The first of these is purposeful planning of *projects* involving art construction. The project method, as everyone knows, has revolutionized and invigorated American teaching on the elementary level. In high schools, it is generally neglected in favor of academic studies. There is no necessary conflict between the two methods. Where the project for lower grades is largely play, with some planning but little need for technical knowledge, the high-school project can be made to call for serious research, and to incorporate information learned in academic studies. Each successive age level can be made to demand more skill in difficult craft techniques and more systematic mapping out of the various steps in an enterprise, more conscious adapting of means to ends. Knowledge of art history can be utilized, not only in the common and superficial way—such as looking up historical details to get an accurate setting for a play—but more profoundly, to see how the older schools of art solved their own aesthetic problems, and to derive therefrom suggestions for dealing with one's own, perhaps in a very different way.

Craft work, involving manual co-ordination, controlled by a definite aim whose importance is seen, has special value at an age when the student is apt to feel awkward and loose-jointed. In many of our academic high schools, the purely intellectual studies are so overweighted as to leave little time for applying intelligence and careful observation to the control of nerves and muscles.

Another line is to encourage the *criticism* of works of art, including those of old and modern masters, and also the efforts of the child himself and his fellow students. By criticism, I mean especially the process of explaining, analyzing, and appraising particular works of art in relation to general standards of value.

It is quite possible—in fact customary—to teach the appreciation, history, and practice of art without any systematic effort to develop the student's powers of criticism. Technical skill can be imparted as if there were only one right way of producing art; historical information and a set of ready-made judgments of value can be taught without ever asking the student to think out for himself why a certain work of art is better than another. The result is mechanical routine and rote memory, both devoid of appeal to the intelligent student and of little use in training him to discriminate the good from the bad in later life. Even the subject of aesthetics can be taught as a body of abstract, *a priori* theories, of little help in solving particular issues in art.

As a substitute, I propose that the training of critical powers should be one of the dominant aims of art instruction on all levels. It is a process which can be continued from early childhood through graduate school, in application to different materials, and with changes of method to keep pace with the growth of mental ability.

The very young child, of course, cannot be asked to use big words or to follow long chains of logical inference. But he can be encouraged, almost as soon as he begins to speak, to express his preferences among different objects of art and craftsmanship; to give reasons for them; to notice and point out the qualities which distinguish one object from another. These are the rudiments of criticism. From that stage on there can be a steady and gradual progress based on increasing ability to observe and compare complex and subtle relationships in art and to think in terms of abstract ideas and general principles.

Aesthetics, as a subject highly generalized and philosophical, belongs on the collegiate rather than the secondary level. But the secondary student can properly be expected to understand the principal issues in current art criticism, the various aims which have guided different artists and schools, and the chief disputed standards of artistic value. Any general course in art should include periods of open-minded classroom discussion, in which the students can talk over the reasons for their tastes, likings, and opinions, and possibly revise them through comparison of views.

A third opportunity for the exercise of intelligence can be found in the study of *art history from a broadly cultural viewpoint*, in relation to social, intellectual, and religious factors. For the elementary school, these relationships are too intricate to be grasped in more than a very superficial way. The advanced university student, on the other hand, often wishes to pursue some rather specialized approach to art and to other subjects. The first year of college and the last year or two of high school will, I believe, come to be recognized more and more as the proper time for orientation courses of a broadly cultural nature, involving aesthetic as well as scientific and social contents. By this time, the student should have both the mental grasp and the background of information necessary for a first synthetic view of human culture as a whole. Before going on to specialized studies, he should certainly have this opportunity. If rightly presented it will attract and exercise his powers of comprehension in a way the present secondary curriculum fails to do.

4. Consciousness of self, and of individual motivation

The "self-consciousness" characteristic of adolescence involves something more than the tendency to embarrassment and brooding introspection which we associate with that word. It involves also— and to this the embarrassments and broodings may be largely due—a heightened awareness, keener than the young child's, of individual differences among people. In adolescence one is hypersensitive, in perception as well as emotion, to one's own peculiar characteristics: to one's physical appearance, attractive or otherwise; to one's own states of mind—pleasures, discontents, and yearnings, the world of inner dreams as contrasted with the overt activities in which (perhaps unwillingly) one must engage. The adolescent is quick to notice small details in the appearance and behavior of other persons and to compare them with his own; he studies facial expression and conversation, trying to read them as signs of inner thoughts and motives, and especially of the attitude of people toward himself. Lack of experience may often cause him to magnify and misinterpret these signs—to attribute a casual remark or smile to some inner attitude which does not exist. He may, in other words, be a poor judge of psychology, having little understanding in theory or practice of what is really going on within himself and his friends. Nevertheless, he is intensely concerned about the phenomena of individual motivation, eager to observe and explain, in no disinterested scientific spirit, but from an eagerness to understand and improve his status in the esteem of others.

Along with this interest in observing personal traits, there tends to arise a desire to assert oneself, to *become* a personality distinct from others—especially from parents and teachers, the former arbiters of one's conduct and beliefs. At first this declaration of independence is likely to show itself, not as the desire to create a really original personality (in the weaker character it may never become so) but as a mere *transfer* of admiration and emulation to a new set of persons: to the sophisticated boy or girl a little older than oneself or to some famous athlete, actor, actress, or other hero or heroine, living, dead, or imaginary. This is the stage of "crushes," of treasuring photographs clipped out of magazines, and of reading avidly every shred of information about the personal life of one's adored.

From these significant facts, let us turn again to the study of art. What sorts of experience, in the realm of art, are most closely in line with these traits of adolescence?

In the first place, they suggest a study of the *personalities and biographies of artists* in relation to their works: of the feelings and motives, the personal relationships, which led them to produce the kind of works they did.

In proposing such a study, I am well aware of running counter to the present tendency of art critics to ignore biography and to stress the study of art forms apart from all associated facts. I am aware, also, that the study of artists' biographies is usually little more than a hunt for sensational episodes which may have little to do with the man's importance as an artist. Nevertheless, I believe that such study can be intelligently pursued, not for its own sake, but to illumine the meaning of the work of art itself. And I believe that it belongs peculiarly to the adolescent level, when students are vitally interested in the personal significance of things. The young child, with his simpler, more extraverted outlook, can more easily be led to contemplate form for its own sake, and so can the more specialized, mature student. The latter, if he wishes, can disregard biography as irrelevant to his interests and return to scrutinize the art work directly, for what it offers to the eyes. Associated knowledge, properly controlled, need not confuse perception, but can remain as a rich and illuminating background for it. Meanwhile, the adolescent's interest in personality is a door to experiences rich in themselves, which we have no reason to discourage. In practice, one of the best ways to interest adolescents in art is by way of the artist's life and character. Properly followed up, this approach can lead him to a new interest in the art work itself, as he finds it possible to sympathize with the artist's desire to create that sort of thing and to sense the difficulties he had to overcome in creating it.

A second suggestion to be drawn from the adolescent interest in personality and facial expression is the study of *portraiture*. There are, of course, many different ways of treating the human face in drawing, painting, and sculpture. One of these is to transform it into a decorative pattern of lines, planes, and color areas. This tendency, notable in Post-impressionist as well as in primitive and archaic art, should, I believe, be emphasized on the elementary level and again in the specialized work of mature students. But it is not especially congenial to adolescence. In a few cases, an interest in decorative form remains dominant and persists throughout adolescence. These are students of special talent for arts and crafts. For them, the instructor need only lead them into more and more difficult, complex, and subtle forms of decoration, and their interest in art will be sustained.

The majority of students, however, on approaching adolescence, come to regard the decorative emphasis as rather trivial. In them, the delight in purely sensuous and perceptive forms is gradually superseded by an interest in broader, more varied human meanings and relationships. For the present at least, they are more interested in a portrait for what it represents and expresses than for any pattern it may offer to the eye. To them it is the picture of a person, real or imaginary, and unless it suggests some definite kind of person, beautiful or ugly, seductive or ridiculous, masterful or weak, frowning or smiling, it has little to hold their attention.

The face which charms them need not be especially full of character: an older person may regard it as empty, vapid, expressionless or gushingly sentimental. Their conception of beauty is likely to imply an extreme regularity of feature which mature taste finds monotonous. Nevertheless, they admire such a portrait, not as a design but as the face of a person they would like to resemble or to have as a lover. In other words, the face is a human ideal, as the sculptured face of Apollo or Aphrodite was to the fifth-century Greek. Most adolescent children, asked to draw whatever they wish, will (unless previous art training has conditioned them otherwise) draw the profile of a pretty girl or of a handsome athlete. Next to these in popularity comes the caricature, usually in imitation of current newspaper cartoons, in which some eccentricity of physique or dress is shown with grotesque exaggeration. In all, the human face and figure remain the objects of paramount concern.

Any such spontaneous expression of an art interest is worthy of notice by the art instructor. It should be followed up, not ignored or brushed aside in favor of some other subject—a still-life group, perhaps—which the teacher considers more highly artistic. Whatever the subject, it can be utilized as a theme to be treated more and more artistically. It is better to start with one already congenial to the student's interest than to substitute another. However crude and insipid is the pretty girl face with which the student starts, it can lead him into a study of other and better conceptions of human beauty. Through training and practice, he may learn to conceive and express his own ideal in more mature and substantiated form. Likewise the drawing of comic or grotesque types, though at first crude and imitative, may be the starting-point for a study of caricature as a fine art.

In regard to art appreciation, these considerations suggest a study of great past achievements in realistic portraiture, and in idealistic portrayals of the human face. For the latter, Greek sculpture of the middle and late periods is obviously appropriate, and it can be followed up with a study of the human face in Renaissance and later painting. Realistic portraiture offers a field for the student of more psychological discernment, who is drawn by the subtleties of facial expression and physiognomy as indices of character. The names of Leonardo and Rembrandt, Tintoretto and Velasquez come to mind at once in this connection. Here the chief point to be emphasized is the meaning of slight nuances of line, light, and shadow in suggesting fine shades of difference in personality and state of mind. This study can well be correlated with that of characterization and word portraits in literature.

For caricature, we turn to Leonardo's drawings, to Goya, Hogarth, and Daumier. Through comparing them with ordinary newspaper cartoons and with his own first efforts, the student can be shown the difference between greatness and mediocrity in the same field. From the repetition of wooden, stereotyped banalities, he can climb to a grasp of terse and vivid graphic expression, based on keen observation of human idiosyncrasies and a whimsical or satirical exaggeration of them.

Another type of art congenial to adolescence is the representation of *dramatic situations* and figures in *expressive attitudes*. This of course is closely related to the study of facial expression. Children of all ages love to tell a story in pictures. The young child is easily satisfied with his attempts in this direction, even though they are not very expressive or true to nature. The decorative effort occupies a good deal of his interest, and his imagination makes up for all deficiencies in the representation of nature. But the older child has observed more, and is more conscious of his failure to represent convincingly the attitude or gesture he wishes to show. Decorative qualities fail to satisfy him as a substitute.

At this stage, many intelligent, self-critical students become discouraged and turn permanently away from art. The wise instructor will try to help them achieve the effects they desire. One of the best ways to do so is through a study of great masters in the representation of action. Once again, an excellent start may be made with middle and late Greek sculpture and with vase painting (not the early, which is more concerned with pattern). Athletic, military, and ceremonial subjects are especially appropriate. From these, one may go on to Renaissance and modern masters from Masaccio on, with special emphasis on Michelangelo, the later works of Raphael, Tintoretto, Poussin, Rubens, Goya, and Delacroix. Such studies can well be correlated with literary study of the mythological, Biblical, and other stories which these painters illustrated. Too many present-day students are lamentably ignorant of these great stories and the characters in them.

Observation of nature and drawing from the living model form a valuable part of the study of graphic illustration. But it is a mistake to hold the student down to accurate representation of anatomy. The actual appearance of things gives material and a starting point for artistic construction, but no more. Vivid portrayal of action, suggestion of the essence of a dramatic incident is usually best attained through considerable selection, elimination, and even distortion of the actual appearance of human figures. The chief aim in graphic illustration should be to learn how to emphasize essentials, to make every detail function in suggesting the particular action intended, and the state of mind that motivates it. Some fidelity to natural appearance is a help in this; too much is a drawback.

In general, it should be stressed that the emphasis on human associations need not and should not involve a sacrifice of design. In the masters just mentioned, as in the best Chinese and Japanese brush drawings, graphic expression is always combined with rhythmic organization of form. Decorative values need not be entirely lost sight of while other values are being grasped. One of the most regrettable features of present art-school teaching is the separation between "design" (conceived as utilitarian form or abstract, decorative ornament) and the representative arts of figure drawing, illustration, perspective, and modeling (conceived as arts of reproducing the appearance of nature). As a result, the latter are reduced too often to mechanical copying, with no realization that figures can be vividly expressive, more or less true to nature, and at the same time organized into complex decorative designs.

Properly taught, the emphasis on human associations which is here proposed for adolescence can be made to enrich the student's conception of plastic form, not to compete with it. As he learns to grasp the subtle and intricate associations which visible forms can suggest, he should be made to realize how these visible symbols can themselves be arranged into patterns which enhance and concentrate their visual appeal.

5. Sexual development; primary and secondary sex interests

As everyone knows, the rise of sexual powers, desires, and feelings is beyond all others the dominant change which occurs in adolescence. There is no possibility of doubting this fact, or the attendant fact that sexual development has far-reaching effects throughout the personality of the individual, influencing directly or indirectly many or most of the interests, thoughts, and activities of the adolescent boy or girl.

It seems obvious that so fundamental a change must be taken account of in any rational system of education, and that educational methods must in some way be adapted to it. Yet the whole question, with all its attendant problems, is timidly evaded by most writers and authorities in charge of secondary education.

Especially in the subject of art, where themes related to sex have perennially played a major part, the question cannot be omitted from any frank and thorough educational discussion. To do so is to limit one's thinking to superficialities and to miss the crux of the present difficulty.

As to the relation of education to sexual impulses, two extreme attitudes are possible: one, that of rigorous medieval asceticism, which would imply an active opposition to these impulses, and hence a policy of suppressing and concealing all their manifestations in art. The other would be a free and complete encouragement of such manifestations. In between are infinite possibilities of moderate compromise. The present actual policy in secondary education is not always actively ascetic, but rather one of ignoring sex as far as possible. The public high-school curriculum is rigorously pruned of everything in art, literature, history, biography, or sociology which might tend to raise disputed issues or to satisfy adolescent interest in the realm of sex.

At the same time, liberal educators on the secondary level, as on others, profess the modern ideal of adapting education to human nature, of appealing to spontaneous interests, and of letting normal tendencies in growth determine the phases of the educational process. Let us see what these principles would consistently imply.

First of all, it is necessary to describe more fully some of the psychological manifestations of adolescent sexuality. We can then inquire as to their bearings on the study of art.

On the physiological side, the changes characteristic of puberty are commonly divided into primary and secondary. The former are directly connected with the maturing of reproductive organs and functions. The latter are less closely connected, yet are parts of the sum total of characteristics which differentiate the sexes and operate indirectly in determining sexual attraction. Examples of these are the general changes in bodily contour, in hair, voice, and carriage.

Psychologically, in the field of interests, desires, feelings, and behavior traits, this distinction between primary and secondary may also be drawn. As to the former, I mean that the normal adolescent child becomes increasingly interested in—is drawn to contemplate and be emotionally concerned about—primary physical sex characteristics in himself (or herself) and in members of the opposite sex. Through ignorance or repression, this interest may not be consciously recognized and may show itself as anxiety, fear, or disgust rather than as admiration or attraction. Nevertheless, it operates in every normal individual, through symbols and indirect expressions if not frankly, and always in the form of heightened emotional sensitivity and perturbability under the stimulus of sexual images and ideas.

By secondary sex interests, I mean the multitude of other tendencies in behavior, thought, and feeling which develop meanwhile, not directly concerned with the physiology of sex, yet distinctive signs of approaching maturity and of increasing sex differentiation. Many of these are related to courtship, flirtation, romantic love, and other milder forms of sex relationship. Some of these, like increasing attention to personal neatness and adornment, are shared by both sexes, but the girl's taste in dress becomes more distinctly feminine. In manner, the girl develops modesty and coquetry; the boy a greater tendency to "show off" before the opposite sex by feats of physical skill and strength, witty repartee, and leadership among his fellows.

In both sexes, adolescence tends to bring a heightening of all emotional activity, of imaginative powers, of aesthetic sensitivity to the glamor and beauty of all existence as well as to its misery and ugliness, which may never be reached before or afterward. This is the period *par excellence* both for aesthetic appreciation and for creative power in art. When in love, as the old saying reminds us, everyone is a poet. How lamentable, then, is the failure of our schools and museums to take advantage of this period of enormous aesthetic vitality! The one age level which above all others should be sympathetic to art now seems farthest alienated from it. In some way, a great potential dynamic is being lost. Can it be redirected into the study of art?

6. Primary sex interests in relation to art

An obvious effect of growing concern about the physiology of sex is growing sensitivity to pictorial and sculptural representations of the nude human figure. In literature, this primary sex interest may find its object in erotic narratives and lyrics, in religious or sociological discussions of sexual morality. In music and dancing, certain rhythms and movements also stimulate and partly satisfy this interest. All these forms of expression are therefore naturally congenial to adolescence, although more or less rigidly tabooed by its parental, religious, and educational mentors. In the strictly reared adolescent, acquired inhibitions and ignorant misconceptions of fact repress and confuse these natural responses, producing an emotional conflict in which satisfaction may be partly or wholly outweighed by shame or embarrassment.

With repeated contemplation of the living nude model or its images in art, such anxiety symptoms gradually tend to disappear, unless the student is repressed to a neurotic degree. Instead, a positive interest and attraction survive, which may be partly erotic and partly sublimated along artistic lines, through emphasis on accurate observation, technique, and criticism.

The opportunity to observe and draw from living nude models of the opposite sex is still rarely offered in high schools, though common in art academies. Even in the former, however, where the teacher has been tactful and has maintained a calm attitude of serious study, it has been quite possible to secure a similar attitude on the part of students. So far as I know, however, the experiment has been restricted to private progressive schools, with a selected type of student. It would doubtless meet with more difficulty, both in parents and in students themselves, if attempted in large public schools.

Where such a result is possible, it has the advantage, from the standpoint of art instruction, of utilizing the fundamental dynamic of adolescent interest which we have been discussing. From the standpoint of self-control, as well, there is something gained when a student has learned to observe nudity in the opposite sex directly and frankly, and to regard it in the spirit of the serious professional artist.

Against these considerations, however, others will be raised by the conservative. In the first place, it will be said that such visual familiarity tends to stimulate sexual impulses, and thus to aggravate the conflict between youth and traditional morality. In the second place, it will be urged by art teachers themselves that the calmly aesthetic attitude toward nudity is too difficult for the adolescent to achieve; that the major interest will inevitably be in the subject represented, and not in artistic form.

A detailed discussion of the moral issue would be out of place in the present article, and we must leave it with the simple recognition that a conflict may exist between the claims of aesthetic development and of conservative morality. Psychologically, however, many authorities deny that familiarity with the sight of nudity necessarily produces an erotic attitude. Where such familiarity has existed from early childhood, we are told, it arouses no highly emotional response later on.

If this is true, in so far as art studies can help supply this familiarity even *before* adolescence, they may help to avert the shock of a first observation at the most sensitive period of life. The students most affected and troubled by nude art in museums, the ones whom the museum instructor finds it hardest to teach, are those who come to the museum for the first time as high-school students, who have never seen images of nudity before save in a few shame-faced glimpses. Those who came first as elementary pupils have much less difficulty in preserving a calm and reasonable attitude later. From the museum standpoint, the earlier and more frequently they come, the better.

Not all students, of course, come to the museum or high school with backgrounds of ignorance and inexperience. Any modern urban population will provide many cases of precocious sexual experience, whose attitude toward nudity is rather one of blasé sophistication than of shocked embarrassment. Such precocious experience, however, acquired as it usually is in a furtive, bungling manner, is far from guaranteeing a genuinely humane and rational attitude in matters of sex. Without the beautifying influence of art, it is likely rather to be tainted by associations of shame, uncleanness, and concealment.

Both extreme conditions, and others in between, the museum instructor has constantly to deal with in presenting nude art to high-school students, usually with no way of knowing the history or attitude of any individual, and with little time or opportunity to straighten out tangled emotions and misconceptions. Their only outward manifestations may be suppressed giggles here and there or a stony unresponsiveness which makes the art lesson seem a failure for no apparent reason. Infrequent, unprepared contacts with sexual images are much harder for the adolescent mind to adjust itself to than either complete ignorance or complete familiarity.

As to the possibility of a thoroughly dispassionate attitude on the part of adolescents toward nudity of the opposite sex, we should frankly recognize the fact that under present conditions it is nearly impossible. Familiarity through repeated observation, and a persistent emphasis by the teacher on technical aspects, may develop it to some extent, but the erotic interest is too strong in the normal individual to be entirely sublimated. Yet the situation here is different only in degree and not in kind from the attitude of most adults toward nudity in art. Only the rare specialist, artist, or critic is able to forget entirely its erotic aspects and to contemplate it from a purely technical or formal viewpoint. For humanity at large, the erotic associations form a large part of its appeal. Yet this fact does not necessarily prevent one from also appreciating formal values and the difference between good and bad art in the treatment of this basic human value. Even for an artist, both types of interest can coexist, each strengthening the other. The erotic appeal, in other words, can be and is in all art schools tacitly utilized as a dynamic, an attraction, for leading the student to appreciate how this, like all other phases of human experience, can be treated well or badly from the standpoint of artistic form.

Let us go a step farther. Many liberal teachers at the present time will approve of children's drawing or modeling nude figures, just so long as the child shows no sign of doing so in an "objectionable" manner—that is, with any erotic emphasis on sexual parts or gestures. Were he to do so, his work would be promptly condemned as both aesthetically ugly and morally vicious. He must represent the nude, if at all, in a chaste, "classic" manner.

The thorough student of art history, and of other aesthetic traditions than our own, will realize, however, that the emphasis on sexual aspects in representing the nude is no isolated case of individual naughtiness. It is a common tendency in all primitive periods of art and in many highly civilized ones. Such emphasis, through exaggerating the size of genital organs and depicting erotic gestures, is there regarded as a quite legitimate convention of art—for example, to indicate royal potency, to symbolize fertility in a fetish, or to celebrate some religious ritual. Even the classical Greeks and Romans, though we try to conceal the fact from youth, often freely exaggerated sexual aspects in their painting, sculpture, and vase drawing. To insist upon the so-called "classical" style of representing the nude, and to ban all sexual emphasis, is to repress a perennial tendency in art.

Even under an ascetic moral tradition such as the present one, this perennial impulse has its outlet in what we call "pornographic" drawings, involving exaggerated representation of sexual images. In the medium of words, they have their counterpart in outspokenly erotic anecdotes, verse, and songs. Common among schoolboys of our own civilization throughout later childhood and adolescence, pornographic drawing is said to be comparatively rare among peoples with a more liberal sex morality. Rare, that is to say, in the form which it assumes among us: the crude, *sub rosa* sketching and scribbling on walls and in hidden places. Under different conditions, the desire for erotic visual experience can more easily be gratified both in real life and in works of art regarded as legitimate. Among us, it is the morbid, distorted, and (to most adults) unpleasant outcropping of a persistent human impulse toward graphic expression. What gives it these unpleasant qualities is not necessarily the frankly erotic themes with which it is concerned, for such themes are to be found in great works of art, but the way in which they are treated—usually stupid, awkward, and stereotyped, shame-faced and furtive. Nevertheless, they deserve consideration by the psychologist and the educator as something more than morbid phenomena. For one reason, they constitute a wholly spontaneous, unforced attempt at graphic representation, which is enjoyed for its own sake both by its creators and their school-boy public, probably far more than the school art lesson. For a second reason, they are gropings toward a sort of terse linear expression, selective and emphatic, allied to caricature.

It is out of the question, of course, for any public educational institution in our time to tolerate or present for study by adolescent children any forms of art emphasizing frankly sexual themes, whether crudely or skillfully constructed. I mention them for theoretical reasons in order to clarify the triple relationship between adolescent psychology, art, and the social conventions which delimit educational methodology. I do not propose that public educators should now embark upon any course of teaching so inconsistent with present convention as the foregoing remarks may suggest, but only that they realize the nature of a maladjustment which under present conditions is largely incurable.

The essence of this maladjustment is that our educational system, by excluding and ignoring the aesthetic aspects of sex, not only loses the most fundamental means of interesting adolescence in art. It also (and this is vastly more important from the standpoint of character training) loses the power of art to rationalize, control, and beautify the sexual phases of life. Furthermore, these phases and their expression in art will not be entirely repressed, whatever attitude the schools may take. As a result, they often issue in early adolescence in the form of a crude pornography which is trivial and contemptible, to say nothing of the manifold neuroses which more complete repression may produce. Throughout adolescence, they are catered to after school hours by sensational journalism, stage, screen, and dance hall, which mask a hectic and unhealthy eroticism under hypocritical pretenses of morality. The great works of art, which might show them that the theme of sex can be finely treated in art and in life, are never brought to their attention, and few discover them by accident.

Each school and museum must decide for itself what small distance it can go, if at all, toward reaching through art the primary sex interests of adolescence. One obvious step in that direction would be to stress, for students of this age, the great past schools of painting and sculpture in which the nude figure is represented, either naturalistically or idealistically. Standard examples would readily be found in late Greek, Roman, and Renaissance sculpture, and such moderns as Rodin and Maillol; in Greek and Roman painting (vase and mural); in Renaissance painting from Botticelli on; in modern masters of figure painting such as Rubens, Rembrandt, Poussin, Fragonard, Ingres, Goya, Courbet, Renoir, and Degas; and in selected works of oriental sculpture and painting, especially of India.

Modern Post-impressionist painting and sculpture, like that of the primitive and archaic periods which have influenced it, I consider (in this regard as in portraiture) less suited to adolescence than to childhood and maturity. Its radical distortions of anatomy for the sake of design tend to weaken erotic as well as other forms of associated interest. Adolescent taste in nude art, unless specially condi-

tioned, runs to fairly naturalistic but somewhat idealized representation. Its interest in its subject matter is so strong, as a rule, as to
prevent a preference for types of art in which the figure is much distorted or regarded as an object of no more intrinsic concern than a
still life or a landscape. This is the fact under present conditions;
greater freedom to observe the body in actual life might very well
operate to satisfy the subject matter interest elsewhere, and release
attention to dwell upon the formal and decorative aspects of nudity
in art, including the Post-impressionist type. Nevertheless, it would
still be true that both the young child and the sophisticated adult
could do so with less conflict of interest.

To a certain extent, the choice of subject matter just indicated
would probably augment the interest in art appreciation among students of this age level. But too extreme, abrupt, or tactless an emphasis on sex would only alienate the students themselves, as well as
their parents and the public. We must accept the fact that no practicable solution of this problem under present conditions can be more
than a fragmentary compromise. Our folkways run too sharply
counter to much that is basic in human nature. They are relaxing
a little, but very slowly.

For the theoretical conception of a more complete adjustment
between adolescent psychology and aesthetic training, we may find
suggestive examples in the history of other civilizations—for instance,
in the visual and literary arts of India, especially its Kama-Sutra,
which presents a complex traditional art and aesthetic of love as the
proper study of adolescence. But any such solution belongs to another age and social system, and as such provides no ready-made
answer to our own problems. These must be gradually solved in their
own terms, and with regard to different conditions.

7. Secondary sex interests in relation to art

In considering this phase of the subject, one can think more easily
in terms of practicable teaching methods. For in our civilization the
secondary sex interests are much less inhibited by convention from
recognition and exercise. Thus the art instructor can more freely set
to work from a psychological starting point, to choose materials and
activities in which these interests can find satisfying outlets.

As to the psychological facts from which to start, however, the problem is in some ways even more complex. The primary character-istics of sex are comparatively universal, fundamentally similar in all normal human beings in spite of the superficial effects of a particular group morality. The secondary characteristics vary much more widely from group to group and time to time, fluctuating in the winds of transitory custom and fashion, and subject to great individual varia-tion. It is difficult to describe exactly the secondary interests and tendencies of adolescent boys and girls in general. Any *a priori* ex-pectation may be set at naught by some local wave of fashion which completely overwhelms, for a time at least, what we suppose to be a fundamental sex trait.

The feminist movement, post-war confusion, and the blending of national folkways in modern cosmopolitan cities—all tend to compli-cate the situation. The Victorian girl and the young English gentle-man may have been ideals not always realized, but they were none the less sufficiently accepted as ideals to determine educational policy, including its aesthetic phases. There was no doubt whatever, for example, that fine embroidery and the making of wax flowers were eminently suitable for the young lady, and an ability to speak tags of Latin verse for the young gentleman. Now all that has passed, and nothing definite has taken its place.

Even the value of training for domestic tasks, such as cooking, sewing, and the care of children, is rendered dubious by the rise of feminism, with its insistence on the right of women to avoid these tasks and to enter the same occupations as their brothers. In one decade, the manners and fashions of the adolescent girl are ostenta-tiously boyish, and the "flapper" type is in vogue, and in the next, they swing again toward a modified version of Victorian femininity. In one American city, the high school or college boy will scorn to show interest in any form of art, for fear of being thought effeminate; in another, the study of art history and the hobby of painting or print-making is suddenly taken up by student leaders, and a small aesthetic movement begins.

In all this change and variety it is hard, indeed, for the observer to discern any stable sex characteristics. If the educator were to try adapting his program to the manifest interests of students, he would have to cater each year to a new set of fads and whims, from ukelele-playing to contract bridge. An educator conscious of the dignity of his calling may of course prefer to ignore these ephemeral interests, and to teach fundamentals of permanent value, cultural or vocational, whether the student likes them at the time or not.

I believe, however, that there is an intermediate and wiser course between these two extremes. It is one which many individual teachers pursue informally, and which could well be given formal recognition. This is to lay greatest stress upon the enduring values, the important facts in so far as we can determine them, but to show the relationship between these and the transitory fads and fancies which are uppermost in the adolescent mind at any given time. No matter how trivial the latter may seem to the serious adult, they will all be found on careful analysis to have some psychological and aesthetic significance: some reason for their spontaneous collective appeal at a certain time and place—a reason partly compounded of peculiar environmental conditions and partly of basic traits within the adolescent mind which co-operate to make that particular fad or pastime an engrossing, satisfying one. The student—always supposing that he has acquired some habit of intelligent thinking—can be led to analyze the nature of each current object of passing interest; to understand why it appeals and satisfies as it does; how the utmost value can be derived from it, and why it falls short, if it does, by comparison with more important things. The process is one of intelligent criticism in the light of standards of value, but applied to relatively trivial as well as great established works of art; it is a process of comparison between the two. The process can begin with either or with each at different times: with masterpieces and the principles behind their greatness, then compare them with popular attempts in a similar field, or begin with the latter, and lead the student from them to an appreciation of great comparable achievements. In either case, the object of spontaneous present interest will be there to animate the study, while deeper realities will also be there to make it seriously educative.

There are many difficulties in this form of education. It is hard to standardize; it must be constantly altered in details, and it makes great demands upon the individual teacher. The teacher must not only understand the great works and principles of which he speaks, but must be able to view the passing whims of youth with sympathetic discernment. Youth is rightly suspicious when its elders comment from the rostrum, however benignly, on its pleasures out of school. It senses that these pleasures will be judged by cold or moralistic adults, who never felt them or have forgotten how they felt; it is uncomfortable even when they are ingratiatingly praised. It will listen politely to the teacher's proof that something is great art, and something else very poor, then go out and enjoy the latter even more wholeheartedly. In such cases it is quite possible that the professors are wrong. They do not realize that a certain kind of art may be good for adolescence, providing exactly the aesthetic food and joy it needs at that time, and yet be mediocre by the standards of maturity. I am not saying that each period of life has its own quite distinct standards. Some works of art are good for any age, but each age has in addition its own peculiar needs. Too often we tend to forget these, and even become ashamed of them when we have passed to another level.

The teacher who would help youth toward a rational understanding of itself must, therefore, be able to demonstrate, in manner and in sympathetic understanding, that he is still able to appreciate fairly the things which it appreciates. If he nevertheless believes them inferior by higher standards, he must be able to defend his views on grounds which the young will respect; not through arbitrary rules or the prestige of authority.

As to the content of the sort of aesthetic teaching proposed, it is impossible to be very specific, for the reason that it should be constantly changed to incorporate the forms of popular art which are in favor with adolescent students at the time. It is the instructor's task to discover what these are. It is not hard to do so, for they are always more or less common knowledge. Students themselves will describe them readily enough if properly approached, for there is usually no reason to conceal them. One must, however, be cautious about believing that students always like what they say they like. In reply to questionnaires and in commencement balloting, they will quite honestly profess a love for the dreariest classics which the teacher has praised and which they have tried hard to enjoy. The truest indication is to be found in the ways they actually spend their leisure time. What plays and moving pictures do they go to see? What novels, magazines, and newspapers do they read? What phonograph records do they buy and dance to? What pictures do they cut from magazines or buy in reproductions and actually hang upon their walls? These are objects of spontaneous aesthetic interest; and it is these, I believe, which should be starting points for art instruction to adolescent students.

Beneath all the shifting of fashion in popular art, there do remain a few fundamentals of adolescent taste. The school curriculum excludes them from serious study. But they are all too well known to the purveyors of popular journalistic, musical, and motion-picture art. To these purveyors, whose attitude may be crassly mercenary and whose influence neurotic, we thus consign the function of actually training our children's aesthetic tastes.

These fundamentals are so familiar that it is almost needless to repeat them. Nevertheless, it is necessary to recognize them explicitly from an educational viewpoint and to urge that they be regarded seriously by teachers, not with amused condescension. I mean, for example, the obvious fact that adolescent children, especially girls, like highly sentimental love stories, dramas, and poetry, full of passionate yearnings and adorations. In one form or another, such art has a perennial appeal, in spite of the occasional blasé individual. Boys' taste at the same age runs rather to detective and adventure stories, full of dangerous exploits; but they, too, like love stories and to fancy themselves in the place of the successful lover. The more practical among them like tales of dramatic rise to riches through business shrewdness. Thus vicariously, the boy lives through art man's traditional roles of warrior, lover, and food provider; the girl that of the sought-after beauty.

In dancing and in music, modern jazz and sentimental tunes are highly congenial to adolescence, with their exciting and sensuous rhythms. The modern ballroom dance, with its separate couples rhythmically swaying and turning, borne here and there by the spell of the music, is much more adapted to the spirit of adolescence than the cold, set patterns and brisk movements of English folk-dancing, which appeal rather to childhood and maturity.

In a well-rounded aesthetic education, all these arts would be considered together. But we are here concerned mainly with the visual arts. The average adolescent taste will run to the more romantic and the picaresque in pictorial classics and in modern illustrative art, especially to works having a sentimental, adventurous, or athletic subject matter.

There are also several other lines along which secondary sex interests can find a more positive outlet in the study of visual form. One is in the study of clothes. Narrowly presented, as applied only to modern dress, it is of course a subject to attract girls rather than boys. If it can be extended to include textiles, jewelry, and perfumes; if it can be presented in relation to current style and smartness, and with no old-fogyish absolute rules about what should and what should not be worn, experience has proved it one of the best of all possible means of interesting the girl of high-school age in aesthetic studies. If it can be given a theatrical emphasis, in relation to stage and ballet settings, or a historical emphasis, in relation to the study of past epochs, armor and weapons, boys as well as girls will find it fascinating. The study of textiles leads easily into a study of either design and ornament or practical interior decoration; the latter of which interests more boys than might be expected, in view of the girls' supposed monopoly of the home-making instinct.

The manifest interest of high-school boys in architectural and mechanical design is related to their approaching manhood. These are arts in which the aesthetic element appears not as idle, sensuous enjoyment, but along with obvious practical utility, so as to draw the esteem of hard-headed men of affairs. Their successful practice demands not only a sense of design but a grasp of scientific construction. Any such study, which gives him a thrill of power and worth-while achievement, inciting him through appreciation of past efforts to emulate and surpass them, is an ideal one for the adolescent boy.

✦✦ XV ✦✦

MODERN ART AND SOCIAL PROBLEMS*

Two opposite policies are now being followed with regard to the place of art in general education. Their leaders tend to move in separate realms, and do not often join the issue clearly. I believe that American educators must work out a reasonable middle course, combining certain values in each of them. The conflict is not new so far as aesthetic theory is concerned. In essence, it is the old one between "art for art's sake" and "art for its social and moral significance." But, in the turmoil of the last few years, it has taken on new life and a new set of special implications.

On the one hand, we have the more established and firmly entrenched body of specialized art teachers, who have learned art as a subject by itself, a particular group of skills, rules, and historical facts, and who propose to continue teaching it as such. They have little interest in the relation of art to social problems. They are, at best, capable artists, scholars, and teachers within a comparatively narrow range. They disagree on certain crucial points: for example, whether art should be taught in the old, "academic" way, through drawing from classical models and learning the methods of the old masters, or whether students should be encouraged toward "free self-expression," experimenting with art materials and building up their own visual forms from imagination. Some of them insist upon "art principles" and rules of composition which others consider false and repressive; some of them insist upon memorizing facts of art history which others consider tedious and pedantic. Some of them emphasize experiments in abstract, semi-abstract, or "non-objective" form, as in Cubism and the paintings of Kandinsky. But they tend to agree upon the intrinsic importance of art as a product for its own sake. They agree that the creating and enjoying of beautiful or significant, symbolic forms is an activity worth while in itself as well as for its effects on personality and culture.

* Published in its original form in *Art Education Today* (New York: Bureau of Publications, Teachers College, Columbia University, 1938), pp. 49-64.

On the other hand, we have the group of artists, writers, and teachers who emphasize the relation of art to social factors. They minimize the value of aesthetic form for its own sake, or for the direct pleasure of observing it. They are not much interested in the directly perceptual aspects of art, or in those of its suggestive elements which deal with exotic and unrealistic fantasies. They tend to depreciate the importance of specialized art activities, including the traditional types of historical scholarship and technical skill, as well as the products of free expression. With certain exceptions, they tend to belittle the whole generation of Post-impressionist and Expressionist art which flourished in the early twentieth century (including Surrealism) as being effete, concerned with trivial matters of abstract decoration and with neurotic imaginings. Some wave the flag and call for more painting of the American scene, of American people and places, instead of the "sensuous" French painting which reflects interest in nudes, flowers, designs, and decorative color. Others take a consciously Marxian standpoint and characterize all these types of art as the expressions of a dying capitalist culture, seeking to glorify its old institutions and to gratify the luxurious dilettantism of its masters. Some apply Spengler and see in Post-impressionist art only the madness of a dying civilization, confusedly groping backward toward its own childhood in the imitation of primitive and barbaric styles. From this standpoint, even free expressionist teaching, with its adulation for the natural, the childish, the spontaneous and pure, the soul unspoiled by civilized art, is but a late and sentimental version of the same romantic regression.

The new group, however, is not necessarily Marxian or communist. It includes theoretical "rightists" and "leftists," admirers of fascism as well as of communism, and many who profess neither of these creeds but consider themselves moderates, liberals, or conservatives of the old school. They all agree in finding most significance and worth in art which deals clearly with social problems, which expresses an attitude on current social issues, which holds one side or the other up to praise or blame, which can arouse emotions of sympathy, ridicule, indignation, or enthusiasm for a social cause. They favor emphasizing its social aspects in teaching the history, appreciation, and production of art, with a view to influencing pupils toward a definite social attitude. In so far as they are consciously radical or conservative, they differ as to what social attitude should be imparted, and hence as to what works of art should be held up to admiration. Conservatives favor those which portray the American scene as prosperous, just, and healthy, with muscular, well-fed farmers and happy coal miners clasping the hand of capital. Radicals prefer pictures of labor as wretched, emaciated, clubbed by police, and oppressed by grasping landlords. They call for more social realism in the schools and are impatient with any subject which does not emphasize it. Art should deal, they say, with the contemporary scene, with labor and capital, poverty, crime, war, and social injustice. The conservatives usually have more influence in public and fashionable private institutions. The two groups feel sharply hostile toward each other because of this political difference. But their policy toward art and art education is essentially similar, since both stress the economic, political, and sociological implications and effects of art.

Many educators and writers who feel themselves definitely on the liberal side, in matters of general policy, cannot enjoy the vagaries of "modern art" or the subtleties of primitive and exotic art. One may say that they are incapable of appreciating aesthetic values. Be that as it may, these liberals now find themselves on the side of the Philistine scoffer at specialized art studies, the typical businessman member of a board of education, who sees no value in any study unless he can understand it and unless it has an obvious vocational or civic utility. I have heard more than one conscious liberal remark, with amused cynicism, that Hitler was right on at least one thing— a picture of a cow ought to look like a cow; all art should be such that the ordinary person can understand it. The wave of government-subsidized painting during the depression was almost all of this type. Sometimes it inclined a little toward radical protest, sometimes toward complacent approval of the "American system." But in either case it has usually been a fairly realistic, easily understandable representation of some phase in "the American scene," with strong emphasis upon social illustration.

There are many shades of difference between art which is mildly, vaguely sociological through representing some scene in factory life or patriotic history, and that which is explicit partisan propaganda. There is no way of drawing a line between what is propaganda and what is not, and the most effective propaganda is often indirect and subtle. Once an emphasis is established upon dealing in art from the point of view of the sociological aspects of American life, it will be difficult to tell the extent to which art and art education are becoming propagandist, whether for fascism, communism, or capitalistic liberalism.

Certainly the tendency toward making them propagandist has gained great headway in many nations of the world in recent years. There has been an extensive trend in countries under dictatorial governments, either fascist or communist, to make the arts serve as propaganda for the form of government, the party, and even the individual leader in power. Artists are being closely regimented as to both the subjects and the style of their works. They are under pressure to produce art which deals obviously with social and political themes, so as to strengthen the party in power and attack all possible rivals. In such countries, the teaching of art in schools and colleges is soon brought into line. Children of all ages are made to draw, paint, model, and present stage plays which glorify the existing regime and express its ideals and antagonisms.

The history of art and art education in Mexico provides some illuminating data in this connection. It is well known that Mexican painting enjoyed a notable renaissance during the twenties and early thirties under the leadership of Rivera, Orozco, and Siqueiros. There was a spirit of released creative energy in the country at large, and it showed itself not only in painting but in handicrafts, music, the dance, architecture, and other arts. It produced immediate results in art education as well, which as usual followed the main trend of creative art instead of influencing it. "Coincident with the reform of the pictorial movement in Mexico, initiated in 1921, led by the painter Diego Rivera, who had just returned from his long sojourn abroad, the Ministry of Education availed itself of the services of some of the artists to substitute, for the academic methods of teaching art in the official primary schools, others that would relate art to life and develop originality and creative ability in the children."[1]

The aim of "relating art to life," a highly vague and ambiguous one, was at first rather broadly and flexibly interpreted. Children and adults were aided and encouraged to create more or less as they pleased in painting, sculpture, and the decorative arts, choosing as themes the types of people and activity, work and play, which they saw around them. They were not required to express any particular

[1] Julio Castellanos, in *Mexican Folkways* (November, 1934), p. 5; (the periodical was published in Mexico City and edited by Frances Toor).

social creed, to praise or condemn any political or economic system. More naïve and spontaneous technics and modes of representation were encouraged, instead of the conventional European methods which had hitherto been imported to the School of Fine Arts in Mexico City from European academies. There was no doctrinaire extreme of free Expressionism, and the work of these naïve artists was in general based upon the older Mexican tradition, itself a combination of Indian and Spanish influences. There was much imitation, conscious or unconscious, of Rivera himself. There were differences of educational policy almost from the start. Adolfo Best-Maugard attempted for a time to use his plausible formula for design, but it was soon abandoned as "inadequate for developing the instinct and imagination of the child, for it did nothing more than imprison his personality within new molds."[2] Lozano, his successor, introduced somewhat freer methods: "He observed that the children worked better without copying, so he permitted them to draw and paint without models and limitations. They were to paint complete and not parts of compositions. Perspective was not subjected to previously fixed laws, but on the contrary the child was allowed to place the objects himself, to draw them sentimentally and to give them size according to their importance and interest to him. The themes to be drawn or painted were selected by the children themselves, thus making them observe their environment—home, school, country, etc. In this way were achieved works which expressed clearly their mentality and social class."[3]

Some of the best work of children and adults was accomplished in the Open Air Art Schools. These were founded by Alfredo Ramos Martínez. The first was established as far back as 1913, but the movement did not become important until 1925, when several such schools were opened. "Mr. Ramos Martínez' method was one of laissez-faire. He believed in permitting the children to select their own subjects and to discover the secrets of drawing and painting through their own experience. All that was required of the teachers was criticism and advice when the pupils wanted and needed it. . . . In 1926, after these schools had been functioning but a few months, Mr. Ramos Martínez took an exhibit of their work over to Europe. It was shown in Germany, Spain, and France. In Paris, Picasso, Matisse, Derain,

[2] Diego Rivera, *ibid.,* p. 14.
[3] Castellanos, *ibid.,* p. 6.

and others were frequent visitors at the exhibit, and in all of the countries, including the United States, noted critics filled pages of leading papers and magazines with their praise."[4] A Japanese painter named Kitagawa started one of these schools in Taxco, and his influence contributed an oriental note to the work of several of its pupils.

Students' work of this period was widely exhibited, circulated, and reproduced. It still gives Mexican art education a reputation which, unfortunately, it no longer deserves. The Open Air Schools have been closed (most of them since 1932); the leaders in the movement are out of office and in several cases (e.g., Martínez and Kitagawa) out of the country. The officials now in control of Mexican art instruction have a very different attitude toward it. This is hinted at in Miss Toor's article: "The Ministry of Education found that while these Open Air Schools of Art were giving the pupils an opportunity to paint and to paint well, except in the case of some specially gifted child, they were not preparing them to go ahead." Mr. Castellanos adds that Juan Olagúibel, who became director of drawing instruction after Lozano, succeeded in "making of drawing not only an artistic and manual recreation, but also a complementary subject to their other classes. For this purpose, he organized contests on social, hygienic, and other topics, and thus the children showed in their drawings whether or not they had understood their lessons."[5]

Mr. Olagúibel himself was frankly proud of his new policy in the section of Drawing and Manual Work. These subjects were now to be "integrated" with others. "The teaching of drawing and manual work," he wrote, "is not isolated and unrelated to the rest of the curriculum, but, on the contrary, is in perfect harmony with it. The instruction is occasional, the pupils drawing only when illustration is required in any of the classes. . . ."

Previously the methods used gave to the instruction of these subjects in the Primary Schools a purely artistic character, depriving the pupils of acquiring knowledge applicable to graphic or industrial expression. This does not mean that the artistic side is being neglected. It is one of the chief concerns of this Division that the future artists come from the primary schools. But we wish, by all means, to work in perfect harmony with the tendencies of the program of general subjects in the schools. The drawing lesson is always given in accord with projects that the teacher

[4] Frances Toor, *ibid.,* p. 34.
[5] *Ibid.,* pp. 7, 36.

may be developing at the moment in his group. In this way, the pupils do not change their environment rapidly; that is to say, they do not pass brusquely from one subject to another, but on the contrary, the interest and attention and even the knowledge assimilated is used in the drawing, so that the pupil perfects his graphic expression and understands and fixes more clearly the instruction that he is receiving at the time. The marvelous results obtained in the first cycle through concrete expression; that is, by the illustration of words, phrases, and oral sentences, are indisputable, and the same applied to history, geography and the natural sciences necessarily produces equally marvelous results.[6]

So far as I have been able to discover, the Mexican schools have produced nothing of consequence in children's art since that time. The theory sounded well; it was quite in accord with the pedagogical precepts dispensed at some of our best teachers colleges in the United States. One can only hope, but without much assurance, that the influence of American educational theory did not play too large a part in the downfall of Mexican art education.

During my visits to Mexico, I have heard statements of policy from the lips of officials in the education department which were pure Marxian dialectic, such as one might have heard in Russia in the early days of Soviet educational reorganization. I have also heard much admiration for the "integrated curriculum" of American schools, which so beautifully "ties up" art with social studies. Whatever the source, an exhibit of Mexican school art is now a melancholy spectacle. In spite of pious hopes, the "artistic side" of art is not only being neglected, but has almost disappeared. Instead, there are long rows of children's drawings and clay models which consist partly of crabbed, cheerless "illustrations" for some lesson in physical science, biology, or social studies; partly of dreary posters preaching hygiene; and partly of other posters which weakly imitate the proletarian class-struggle, social-conflict art of adult Mexican painters. Classes in industrial art are making perfunctory copies of standard patterns in leather, wood, and textiles. Murals of the most approved class-struggle type, by adult as well as youthful artists, are prominently displayed in some of the schools, replete with all the stereotyped figures of such painting: fat, avaricious capitalists clutching moneybags and trampling peasants; stalwart workers throwing off the yoke; and so on. I saw in the schools practically no examples of foreign paint-

[6] *Ibid.,* p. 9.

ing, old or modern, originals or reproductions. In such an atmosphere, neither Mexican children's art nor folk art in general can flourish.

The criticism of this regime is not made on the grounds of the particular social or political philosophy on which it is based. A communist (Stalinite or Trotskyite), a fascist, a royalist, or a capitalistic philosophy can be imposed with force on children's minds if the educational system is disposed to do so. I am objecting on the ground of what it does to children's art and to their personalities, by depriving them of the kinds of art activity which are genuinely congenial and appropriate to them. The Mexican policy of the twenties was congenial and appropriate, as its results showed; the present one is not. Rivera, whose art and personality inspired the first policy, is an admirer of the early phase of Russian communism. This appears in his paintings; but they are not mere propaganda. He is first and foremost a pictorial artist; his pictures stand the test in drawing, color, modeling, and composition, in the universal human feelings and the ancient Mexican traditions they express. Because of this very breadth, he is disliked by many of the new and feebler generation of Mexican painters, who denounce him from a partisan political standpoint while they continue to imitate his style. Now Rivera did not attempt to impose his economic or political views upon the Mexican children. Although a man of considerable learning in fields other than art, he did not urge that they spend their time drawing illustrations of dry scientific and sociological themes. He knew too well what children are interested in, and what they love to draw and make.

It would be going too far to lay the blame for this decline entirely upon any one man, or upon a single change in school administrative policy. The whole Mexican renaissance, which in a single generation produced magnificent results in many arts, is apparently coming to an end. There is no new generation of artists which seems capable of reaching the stature of Rivera and Orozco. Many troubles, economic and political, beset the Mexican nation. It is understandable that the government has asked for an emphasis on practical studies. It is understandable that practical officials should call the Open Air Classes a "waste of time," although their products sold for no mean prices.

There has often been a burst of creative energy in the arts, as in science, industry, and other walks of life, just before and after a liberating revolution. Later on, perhaps after fifteen or twenty years, comes the phase of settling down to hard institutional reconstruction, which is often bitter and repressive. This sequence of events occurred in both Germany and Russia after the First World War. Both nations experienced a wave of released, joyous creation in all the arts, in which the work of children had an important part. In both nations, this particular creative period then came to an end; witness, for example, the recent deterioration of Russian moving pictures. Instead, a period of forced, repressive unification is in process, in response to harsh economic and political forces. No doubt the native artistic genius of both countries, and of Mexico as well, is but temporarily dormant. In the meantime, however, a number of totalitarian, dictatorial regimes are repressing free imagination and rational criticism in the arts. The result, so far as we can see in the contemporary world, is to produce an immediate deterioration in the quality of art and education, although historical examples can be brought forward to show that extreme hero worship of a Caesar or a Napoleon sometimes leads to another kind of artistic advance. Any single change in the policies of school administration is probably a result or a symptom of this general cultural change rather than a force strong enough to bring it about. Nevertheless, it is worth noting, in Mexico and other places, how art has flourished when free to progress along its own lines; and how it has declined when forced into artificial, uncongenial channels.

In the United States, art is still happily free from dictatorship and from the more obvious, extreme forms of economic and political repression. Our schools are comparatively free from partisan propaganda and from indoctrination with any systematic political philosophy, except in so far as patriotic praise of our civic institutions implies tacit propaganda for capitalistic democracy. In this broad sense of the word "propaganda," there is no reason why it should be excluded from the schools, even if exclusion were possible. I am not proposing to insulate children or children's art from all social discussion or to keep them chemically pure and free from all outside influences. The wise course, I believe, lies somewhere between these extremes.

It may seem a far cry from mere "integration" of art with social studies to repressive imposition of a particular social ideology upon children's art. But the distance is not too far to be quickly and imperceptibly traversed. Once the crucial move has been made of forcibly "tying up" (the current phrase is unpleasant but revealing) children's art with sociological discussion, it is hard to avoid insinuating a particular set of sociological principles for them to illustrate. Every teacher is likely to be so thoroughly convinced of the rightness of his own principles, radical or conservative, that he feels himself as only conveying the truth, not propaganda, when he passes them on to students. If he is not much interested in aesthetic form or its enjoyment, it seems to him much more profitable for children to be expressing some admirable sentiment about peace, farm relief, a minimum wage, cleanliness, or traffic safety, than to be "wasting their time on useless decoration," or "escaping from reality" to a study of Greek sculpture. On the contrary, I insist that however righteous these causes and however right it is to study them during a portion of the student's time, they should be kept within bounds and not allowed to monopolize the curriculum.

In recent years, many liberal educators have fought for more emphasis on social studies and for more honest realism in them. As against the timid or prejudiced obscurantism which has prevailed and still prevails in many schools, I sympathize heartily with this effort. As against the old overemphasis on studies of the past, it is right to teach more about the modern world we live in. As against the old overemphasis on subjects which are ostentatiously useless, designed for aristocratic leisure, it is well to bring art education a little closer to earth. The new emphasis on realistic social and economic studies has not yet gone far enough in many schools—perhaps not far enough in most of them. In some, it has gone too far. It has gone as far as to throw out studies of great educational value, simply because they cannot be easily correlated with sociological projects and discussions. In spite of the present urgency of problems in this realm, it will be short-sighted educational policy to sacrifice everything to them. The liberal school has other duties, among them the fostering of a balanced development of children's abilities in many lines, including the aesthetic, the artistic, and the imaginative. This is hard to do through an art which has been subordinated to economics and sociology.

The present American tendency toward an "integrated curriculum," with much use of projects to combine artistic and other interests, usually involves this kind of subordination. Art is frequently crowded out, or becomes "the tail of the dog." To use another figure, it may be said that integration becomes the tiger upon which the smiling young lady from Niger (in this case, art) went for a ride. They came back from the ride, it will be remembered, "with the lady inside, and the smile on the face of the tiger." Now there is no essential reason why this should happen in a well-integrated curriculum. It might as well turn out, theoretically, that the lady swallowed up the tiger. Art is broad enough and powerful enough, if set free, to illuminate every branch of human thinking and experience. In a school where the artistic point of view is ably championed, integration might well result in bringing out the aesthetic aspects and artistic possibilities of every other activity, including the physical and social sciences, history, literature, athletics, dances, and personal relations. In such an integrated school, art would be the dominating subject. If it does not at least approach this, the fault lies partly with art teachers who fail to see the great possibility of integrated projects for their profession. But so far this has not often occurred. The people who organize integrated curricula, it appears, usually lack the necessary appreciation of art and its educational importance. Art teachers, perhaps, are too lacking in influence to speak up for their interests with authority. They should do so, for these are not merely selfish interests, but a serious responsibility for defending a vital phase in culture and personality development, which is slighted in present education.

The solution is not to return to the old subject curriculum in its entirety, with art as a completely isolated subject. This, indeed, has its advantages and is better than a complete loss of the artistic viewpoint. Then, at least, there may be a certain time in the student's week when he can enjoy some of the more peculiar, intrinsic values of art, without thinking of how they can be made to serve some outside purpose. But the old-fashioned type of school and college art, as a completely separate subject, is obsolete. The art teacher, if he or she is to exert a strong influence upon the whole educational program, must acquire a broader view of that subject in relation to others and to modern society.

We cannot go back to a narrow academic type of art teaching or to the free, intimate, and idyllic conditions of the Mexican Open Air Schools. They were a brief and beautiful product of revolutionary transition in a land very different from ours—a land composed mostly

of small villages, of peasants and handicraftsmen who had inherited
a fine decorative tradition and were already accustomed to simple,
direct artistic expression. Our goal should be to achieve results as
fine aesthetically, along with a more sophisticated, scientific general
education, under our own conditions of mass education and machine
industry.

I have no objection to the treatment of social and economic themes
by either adult or student artists. Art has a useful function to perform in these realms, by arousing people to protest against injustice
and by stimulating thought and advancing worthy ideals. Certainly,
also, good art has been produced in this way and is now being produced. Broadly speaking, all the great styles of art have been propaganda for something, whether Christianity, imperialism, or the Greek
view of life. Daumier made pictures which are good pictures as well
as good propaganda for social justice. Many notable artists have incorporated scientific observation and knowledge in their paintings
and statues—Leonardo, Dürer, Barye, and our own Audubon, to
name but a few random examples. If a child is genuinely interested
in one of these social or scientific themes and has something to say
about them in art, by all means let him do so. But there will be
many who are not so inclined; in fact, very few younger children will
be, unless strongly influenced in that direction. In our social order,
they prefer to draw animals, children playing, houses, trees, airplanes, and fairy princesses. These other children should not be held
back from their own congenial avenues of expression, however useless they seem to the nonartistic mind. Let us remember, too, that
repression can be exerted, not directly by forbidding the child to
create or enjoy in a certain way, but by depriving him of the necessary materials for doing so and by filling his time so full of other
things that he has no strength or enthusiasm left for doing so. He
may be looking at pictures a great deal, and making them; but if his
attention is made to focus almost wholly upon their illustrative subject matter and social functions, it will have correspondingly little
chance to focus upon the essentials of aesthetic form. His interest in
art as a whole may be killed by forced contemplation of a kind of art
which is (to him) tiresome and unpleasant, and by forced participation in uncongenial activities.

For the older student, especially in senior high school and college,
a certain amount of social illustration and even obviously propa-

gandist art on controversial themes can well be introduced for objective analysis and criticism. He can be shown how all types of theory, self-interest, and political movement tend to express themselves in art, how such art operates to influence the public mind, and how it can be (aside from the rightness of its social attitude) either very good or very bad as art. He can learn to guard against being the easy victim of emotional propaganda. In creative expression, if an older student feels strongly on a controversial social issue, I see no good reason why he should not be allowed to express his ideas and feelings in pictorial or literary form and to have his work criticized by the art teacher from the standpoint of its artistic effectiveness. There are values, even for somewhat younger children, in acquiring gradually a realistic idea of the world in which they live, including the fact that poverty, suffering, crime, and injustice still exist. Otherwise the school will be an ivory tower, and children will come out of it unprepared to face the realities of life.

This does not mean overemphasizing misery and evil. For very young children, and for the early adolescent, it may be definitely harmful to dwell intensively upon the evils and failures of present society. Such extreme frankness often results only in aggravating depression and discouragement at an age when such moods are all too common under the best of circumstances. The school should not allow the child, especially the young child, to be overwhelmed, discouraged, or pulled about by the violent forces which are at war in the present world. He should be protected somewhat, though not too tenderly, until his personality has had a chance to develop an equilibrium and protective mechanisms of its own. If the child's home environment is drab, sordid, and unloving, why bar him from learning through art that a better kind of life exists somewhere and may exist for him? Why deny him the chance to touch rich textiles and hear rich music? Why bar him from the chance to express his own fantasies and hopes for a happier world? Such enjoyments can be kept within moderate bounds; in most present schools there is small danger that they will interfere much with practical duties.

The real psychological problems of the child and the adolescent are not those of adult society. He or she is not yet as emotionally concerned with problems of labor and capital, international relations, and impersonal science as with certain much more personal relationships whose psychological significance we are just beginning to discover. Much recent social thinking has pointed to the fundamental importance of aesthetic and artistic activities as possible means of healing in part the evils of present society. The more far-sighted use of art for social reconstruction is not to sacrifice its essential values for some quick, superficial "integration" with anything else, but to let it work in part at least along its own lines.

XVI

THE ROLE OF FINE ARTS IN A LIBERAL EDUCATION*

1. Fine arts and liberal arts in a modern democracy

The conceptions of fine and liberal art have long histories, in the course of which they have changed considerably in meaning. The "liberal arts," as understood in ancient and medieval times, were not the same as "art" or "fine art" in the modern sense. "Art" in general meant any kind of useful skill, including agriculture, medicine, and war. We still speak occasionally of the "medical arts," but this sense is now uncommon. Art was not necessarily concerned with beauty, although the making of beautiful things such as pottery and painting was included. Among the arts, some were classed as "liberal" and others as "servile" or "mechanic." Only the former were considered worthy for a freeman or a gentleman of the upper classes to engage in. The servile arts, which administered to the physical needs and comforts of man, were not suited for a gentleman or lady, but were for slaves and servants. The liberal arts were primarily intellectual and literary. They included various kinds of poetry and also philosophy, logic, and the beginnings of science, such as mathematics and astronomy. Many of the arts we now respect, such as painting, sculpture and pottery, were regarded as beneath the dignity of a gentleman, largely because they required the use of the hands with brush or chisel. Pottery and furniture-making were ignoble also because they served utilitarian purposes. A lady could use her hands in making embroidery, but should leave the more useful kinds of sewing to her servants.

The liberal arts were conceived by Plato and other Greek philosophers as those which liberated the mind from ignorance and sensuality, which elevated the thoughts of man to spiritual and intellectual things, including the ideal world of goodness, truth, and beauty. Throughout the Roman and medieval periods, the aristocratic prej-

* Published in its original form in *The Bulletin of the University of Georgia*, LIV.4 (October 22, 1953), pp. 15-37.

udice against manual labor persisted, and painting and sculpture were usually considered as beneath the dignity of a gentleman. The liberal arts of the Middle Ages were largely tools of intellectual inquiry. Even literature was only given a doubtful and precarious place among them.

The old conception of liberal arts is still implied in our degrees of Bachelor of Arts and Master of Arts, and in the so-called "arts" curriculum which leads to them. Thousands of people secure these degrees every year, in American and foreign colleges, without studying any "art" in the modern sense. They do not have to study the visual arts, music, drama, or even literature beyond a few basic courses in English and perhaps one foreign language.

As to the meaning of "fine arts," there has also been a gradual change in modern centuries. In the Renaissance and later, a distinction arose between the "fine" and "useful" arts, on the ground that the former were devoted to the production of beauty and to giving aesthetic pleasure through sight or hearing. The useful arts were those which supplied the physical necessities and comforts of man. It was realized that beauty and utility are often found together in the same work of art and the same craft. A building, a garment, a cup, or a sword may be useful and beautiful at the same time. So there was no sharp division between the fine or aesthetic arts and the useful ones. However, many skills, especially since the industrial revolution, have been devoted to utility without any thought of beauty or decoration. A good example is the industry of coal mining. Such skills and industries were formerly classed as "arts." But more and more we have come to class them as applied sciences or branches of engineering and technology. In the same way we have ceased to speak of medicine, war, and agriculture as "arts" at all. They, too, are regarded as applied science or utilitarian technology. The word "art" has come to be restricted to those skills and products which have an aesthetic aim and value, whether or not they also have utilitarian values. Architecture and furniture combine a utilitarian purpose with the desire to please the beholder through visual beauty or "eye appeal." Music and poetry often have little if any utilitarian function. They sometimes do serve such a purpose, as when march music and work songs help in co-ordinating bodily movements; but usually poems and symphonies are composed for aesthetic reasons.

Sometimes the fine arts are said to include music, literature, and theater; sometimes they are restricted to the visual arts of painting, sculpture, architecture, and the minor decorative arts. These confusions persist in university catalogues today. What is or should be included in the "art department" of a university? Broadly speaking, music and literature are fine arts and should, therefore, come under the department of "art." In practice, however, college art departments and professional art academies are usually confined to a few of the visual arts. Film and ballet are visual but are usually taught elsewhere. The tendency now is to say "visual arts" when these are meant, and to say "arts" when music and poetry are included. The poet or composer, the teacher of music or drama, has a right to protest that his art is just as fine, as aesthetic and beautiful as the arts of painting and sculpture.

Modern democracy and applied science have given us a new conception of the liberal arts. We now have little prejudice against the use of the hands, especially in work involving technical knowledge and skill. We do not scorn useful labor. The work of a Thomas Edison, who used his hands in the laboratory to make useful inventions, is now respected at least as much as that of a philosopher or mathematician who does not need to use his hands except in writing. The visual arts are respected as much as music and poetry, in spite of their manual techniques. Some extremely practical educators look down upon them rather as useless frills, but even this prejudice is vanishing. Democracy has almost eliminated the ancient distinction between the arts of a freeman or gentleman and those of the lower classes. Today the liberal arts are conceived primarily as those which give a broad, well-balanced, humanistic education, and which help to liberate the mind from ignorance, superstition, and blind conformity to custom.

2. General and specialized education

The term "general education" is sometimes used today as roughly equivalent to "liberal education," although both have taken on special meanings. They are similar in that both imply a wide area of subject matter, as opposed to narrowly specialized vocational training such as a course in radio repair work. But highly specialized courses are not necessarily out of place in a liberal education, provided the whole curriculum does not specialize along one line. No one can rightly understand the character of modern civilization or of science and art without realizing how it does involve specialization along countless divergent lines, for the sake of more effective discovery and power. Some experience of precise, intensive, rigorous inference and control along restricted lines is an indispensable part of liberal education on advanced levels. Mere generality is not enough in itself; if all one's learning is in terms of generalities it can easily become vague and shallow. Mastery in any field requires an ability to go back and forth at will between generals and particulars; to base general statements on concrete examples, and to apply general knowledge in the solution of concrete problems. Liberal education at its best involves, accordingly, both extensive surveys and intensive seminars: on the one hand, broad orientation courses, theoretical introductions, chronological and geographical outlines which map wide areas and help the student organize details into patterns; and, on the other hand, concise researches which show him how to reach the utmost in precision within a limited area. General surveys are valuable at the beginning of a college course and also near its end; they should not be hastily brushed aside as "mere smatterings." Each student needs them especially in those fields which he does not intend to study thoroughly, so as to give him a "speaking acquaintance" with many fields besides his own. But within his field of concentration at least, he should experience both the extensive and the intensive approaches and the relation between them.

In art history, he needs a sweeping survey of the whole evolution of the visual arts in time, space, and cultural background; also, within that framework, a microscopic look at one or more selected areas of art—at certain pictures or buildings down to the minute details, at the men who made them, and the special occasions for which they were made. In the practice of art, it is well in the lower grades of school to try one's hand, voice, and limbs at a wide range of media and techniques—to paint, sing, dance, act, and versify as a child without too much critical self-consciousness. But after such a period of extensive sampling, the curriculum should gradually lead one to select and narrow down the range of execution or performance, so as to acquire high standards of quality and learn to do something really well. All of us have to narrow down in this way as the years go by, and drop many beloved occupations because we cannot keep them all up and still satisfy mature criteria of excellence in some chosen specialty. The four years of college are long enough to help the student make this progressive, gradual selection intelligently, in relation to his individual talents and ambitions.

3. Vocational and non-vocational education in a democracy

A little of the old, aristocratic concept of liberal art survives in the idea that liberal studies are not concerned with training one to make a living. Instead, they are to enrich and develop the whole mind and personality—to prepare one for a well-adjusted, valuable, and happy existence in society. The liberal arts in this sense are contrasted with skills which are taught for some immediate, salable, vocational use. But there is much overlapping between liberal and vocational studies on this basis, since vocational studies can also be of value for general mental development and adjustment. Likewise, any liberal study, any subject in the liberal curriculum, can help one to earn a living directly or indirectly, as in the case of a student who decides to teach philosophy or literature. We have no prejudice today against earning a living, or against studies which help to prepare for it. But liberal studies are expected to do something more besides; to enlarge and refine one's understanding of the world and one's discrimination of values; to make one a truly educated, balanced, and well-rounded human being.

The liberalizing of education is not entirely a matter of what subjects are taught. Just as any subject can be taught in a liberal way, any subject can also be taught in a narrowly vocational way. Mathematics and physics can be taught as mere tools for calculation and manufacture, or in such a way as to bring out their deeper cultural importance, as examples of human reasoning on a high level of development and as explanations of the world in which we live. Likewise, English composition, music, and painting can be taught either as mere salable, superficial skills, or with due regard to their deeper meanings and values. The teacher of architecture can merely show conventional ways to plan and construct a building or can show the wide bearings of architecture in social history and in the world today—the causes of trends in architectural style and technique; their effects on the lives of individuals, families, and communities; the basic ways of thinking out new architectural forms to meet changing social and psychological, as well as physical, needs. The teaching of many liberal subjects may make a college catalogue look respectable, but it is no guarantee that education in that institution will be genuinely liberal or humane.

It is now commonly recognized, on the other hand, that a liberal education can be well worth while from the strictly practical and professional point of view. In the long run, other things being equal, a man stands a better chance of success in medicine, law, or statesmanship if he has a broad and balanced training which will help him deal with educated people and keep up with new developments in his field. Specific facts and techniques, learned in school, often go quickly out of date; the man who keeps ahead is likely to be the one with a deeper grasp of ideas and methods, who can see his subject in relation to others and to civilization as a whole. Some of our leading schools of science and engineering have recently decided that a man will probably be a better engineer as well as a better human being if he learns something about other subjects, including the arts. They are bringing concerts, art exhibits, and lectures on humanistic subjects to the campus, and are including more nonvocational subjects in the curriculum.

We do not have to choose sharply, on the college level or any other, between a vocational and a liberal education. Vocational schools can include a basic minimum of liberal study. A liberal college, on the other hand, does not need to keep its students in a sheltered ivory tower. It can gradually prepare them to choose a career intelligently and to direct their studies more and more toward it in the upper grades, without entirely losing touch with other interests.

As to which subjects are inherently most liberal and humanizing, opinions have been changing steadily up to the present time. Plato recommended for the best youths of his ideal state some training in music and poetry as well as in gymnastics. Humanistic studies declined in the Middle Ages in favor of theology and related subjects. When they began again in the Italian Renaissance, an ideal of all-round, versatile accomplishment arose which called for some skill in the arts. A gentleman should be able, it was thought, not only to fight a duel but to write a sonnet, sing a song, or draw a picture on demand, as his contribution to the refined enjoyment of life. But the emphasis was strongly on literature and on the study of the Greek and Latin classics. Down to the present century, the tradition survived that a gentleman's education should include some Latin literature and history and, if possible, a "grand tour" of Europe to admire its monuments of art.

In our American zeal for democracy and practical studies, in our scorn for aristocracy and the old-fashioned classical education, we have swung too far in the opposite direction. We have almost eliminated not only the classical languages but much of the literature, art, and wisdom of the ancient world as well. In trying to keep religion out of the schools, we have produced a generation almost ignorant of Biblical literature, and hence unable to understand much Christian art. In stressing the realistic and practical, we have deprived our children of the treasures and delights of mythology and folklore.

Of course, there are compensations. The rise of the social and psychological sciences in the early twentieth century has given education, beyond a doubt, a much more true and realistic picture of ourselves and the world. The study of history has profited greatly by increasing reference to social and economic factors. But the arts and their tremendous role in cultural history were, until very recent years, passed over carelessly. The imaginative and aesthetic capacities of the ordinary student were neglected, as they had not been in the old liberal education.

Now we are coming to see, at last, that democracy does not require us to abolish or ignore those values which aristocracy enjoyed, but only to make them available to all, without regard to birth or wealth. Meanwhile, our understanding of the artistic element in modern life and in our cultural heritage has greatly increased. Hence we are able and willing to approach in a new way the problem of a liberal education on the college level. Without reviving what is obsolete in the old-fashioned classical, upper-class education, or losing the values of modern realistic and practical studies, we must contrive somehow to select and combine the best in both. Not content with this, we must make available to students the important new developments in the realm of art which were lacking in the old classical education. These will include a much greater knowledge of world art and culture, including the oriental and primitive; new technological skills and resources in the arts; a new respect for the visual and theater arts to correct the old overemphasis on printed words; and a deeper understanding of the value of all the arts for humanity.

4. The growth of the arts in American civilization

In recent years there has been a notable growth in the production, use, and enjoyment of all the arts in America. Foreign observers have called this a sign that America is "coming of age" culturally; that we are no longer a youthful country, concerned mainly with conquering the wilderness and with building up our agriculture and industry. We have crossed the continent with railroads and airplane lines; we have outstripped the rest of the world in our factories and farms, and we are now ready to enjoy some of the finer products of civilization, as well as to create them ourselves. We are freer than our pioneer ancestors were to engage in pursuits which are not required for food or shelter, but which improve the quality of experience and raise the mental level of American life.

Along with this general growth in the arts has come a great increase in school and college courses on the appreciation, history, and practice of painting, sculpture, architecture, furniture, textiles, ceramics, photography, and many other arts. The visual arts have been later in achieving a recognized place in the curriculum than music and literature, both of which were accepted many generations earlier. The growth in teaching of the visual arts has occurred on all age levels, from nursery school and kindergarten up through graduate school. In nursery school and the lower grades, some work in the visual arts has come to be a universal, basic activity. It is recognized as valuable to the young child in developing nervous and muscular co-ordination. As he draws and paints, he learns to distinguish the main types of visual object in the world, such as men, women, children, animals, trees, furniture, and houses. Expressing his emotions and fantasies in conscious, tangible form also helps him to achieve mental adjustment and control.

We are not yet at a stage where the visual arts form a continuous thread or phase throughout the educational process. Most students stop their work along this line at a fairly early age. If they pick it up again, perhaps as an elective course in college, they do so after a long interval, and hence miss the continuity of development which they might otherwise have had.

5. *The arts as an aid to the balanced, harmonious development of personality*

Every normal child is born with a highly diversified set of physical and mental aptitudes. He is born with a complex and sensitive visual and auditory apparatus, as well as with hands, arms, a voice, and other equipment. These can be developed along any one of a number of different lines, or can be left undeveloped. In growing up within his cultural environment, he has to develop along lines which are encouraged and required by his group. The result in our times is often an overspecialized, unbalanced kind of development. We are forced to use our eyes for reading the printed word to an extent which is often fatiguing. This is especially true for high school and college students. On the other hand, many of our potential abilities go undeveloped. We soon adopt a rather sedentary life in the school or in office work; we sit at a desk most of the day and do not develop our limbs as an athlete or dancer develops them, our vocal cords as a singer develops them, or our hands as a pianist, violinist, or painter develops them.

It is possible to imagine an ideal kind of development in which one would continue throughout life to use and train a wide diversity of functions, not separately, but as parts of a well-integrated, balanced personality. It would make for a wider range of experience and for physical and mental health. No individual, of course, could practice all the arts throughout life; but by careful selection a much more balanced development could be maintained than we attempt at present. Thousands of ailments come to civilized people because of the monotonous lives which many of them lead. Boredom and monotony result from the same narrow round of activities over and over in work and play. An ability to participate in some art, as in sports and games, helps to correct this to some extent. The need for such supplementary or avocational activity is growing steadily as leisure time increases. In the last few years, it has become usual for people in all types of job to take both Saturday and Sunday off, to quit work earlier in the evening. This raises again the problem of what to do with leisure time, and a ready answer is at hand for those who have any aptitude for the arts.

It must not be supposed, however, that the arts are necessarily mere diversions or leisure pastimes. For some, they are and should be. But in general, art as a main branch of civilization is not practiced merely for pleasure or amusement. It is one of the chief avenues by which the human mind expresses ideals, denounces evils, and plans improvements. The arts express not only trivial ideas but also the most sublime aspirations of religion, philosophy, and social reform; they portray ideal types of human being, both physically and mentally, conceptions of a better way of life and a more perfect social order. At the same time, we must not minimize the value of the arts in contributing a play spirit, a little gaiety and amusement into this world, which has plenty of trouble and frustration. Even art which is called "escapist," which allows us to forget for a while our anxieties, problems, and fears, which helps us to relax and forget our troubles at times, contributes to mental and emotional health. This can be overdone, of course; but in moderation it helps us to recuperate and come back to our daily problems with more strength than we would have had otherwise.

Another feature of the arts in a democracy is that they are not for the benefit of a privileged few. Just as there are many thousands of practicing artists in the United States today, so there are millions of people who enjoy, use, and own works of art. Radio and television have brought popular art in these fields into the smallest farmhouse. The popular illustrated magazine has brought reproductions of fine visual art down to the price range of everyone.

We are developing at the same time a broader conception of what it means to be an artist, or at least to practice some art. It is not necessary to be a professional painter, to dress in a smock and carry a palette, to wield brushes and oil paint, in order to be an artist. This is only one of the techniques which come within the realm of art. Every housewife who decorates her home and garden, every boy or girl at school who hangs a picture on the wall, no matter how crude its nature, is expressing himself or herself in art. The very choice and arrangement of clipped-out pictures from a newspaper or magazine is a kind of participation in art. It has been pointed out that the farmer expresses an artistic impulse in drawing careful furrows with his plow over the hillsides, and that the farmer's wife is an artist when she preserves her fruits and jellies in attractive and well-labeled jars and arranges them neatly on the shelves. The businessman who pays some attention to his office, the committee for village improvement which cleans up rubbish from vacant lots and improves the neatness of streets and parks, the city council which provides playgrounds and shade trees, eliminates slums, and provides public buildings for the use and enjoyment of all—these are all contributing to the production of art. They may do so as an avocation or as part of their civic duties after work. But art includes all these things; it is democratic today and becoming more so every year.

All of us acquire in our early years certain basic skills in expression and construction, such as those of reading and writing. Centuries ago, these were found to be so basic and universal that every child should be forced to acquire the rudiments of them if possible. Other skills today are desirable though not imperative. It is useful to be able to read a simple musical score and to sing in a group or to follow the score of music being played by an orchestra. Drawing is another skill whose potential utility is great. Whether we become artists or not, it is useful to be able to illustrate ideas with a quick sketch in conversation, either as a freehand sketch or as a simple architectural or mechanical drawing. The housewife who wishes to discuss furniture and decoration with an expert can express herself by making a quick sketch of what she has in mind. In the office or factory, the businessman can explain his ideas to a technical expert by a simple sketch.

Most of us do too much passive looking and listening in proportion to active performance or participation. As each new invention comes on the market—first the film, then the radio, and then television—we are tempted to spend more leisure time in an armchair looking and listening. The day is past when young people gathered around the cottage organ or piano to sing songs. Today we go by the thousands to a football or baseball game, or we listen to a symphony orchestra. This has its advantages from the standpoint of aesthetic appreciation, but it does not build us up into active, creative individuals, with our muscles and limbs co-ordinated and able to obey the dictates of our imagination. In fact, so much looking and listening tends to fatigue even further the same sense organs, especially the eyes which we use in our daily work. It is no real recreation or rest for a professional worker who has used his eyes all day in close work at the office to come home and use them again in watching a television show or in playing cards all evening. From the standpoint of physical and nervous rest and recuperation, what we need to do all through life is to bring into active play those sets of nerves and muscles, and those phases of our mental and emotional life which we do not have the opportunity to use in our daily work and business contacts. For this reason, it is worth while for the student to acquire in the course of his education some basic skills in the performance of a number of arts, so that he can come back to them, perhaps after an interval of years. Someone who has acquired a few rudimentary skills in drawing or modeling may have to drop them entirely for the closing years of college, for his military career, and perhaps for his early years of professional struggle—while he is trying to make a place for himself in a competitive world. But there may come a time when the pressure lets up a little and when he can come back to enjoy his hobbies. This is especially true when men and women retire. In our society, middle-aged women often find themselves with much time on their hands as their children become more independent. The man may keep on until his later sixties or seventies. But many a man is a pathetic object after his retirement, because he has never kept up with any avocation and does not know how to use his leisure time.

6. A liberal education for the prospective artist

The false idea that art is necessarily effeminate as an activity for men is rapidly disappearing, along with the other false belief that art is a useless frill in education. Both had an element of truth a few generations ago as applied to the actual status of art—especially painting—in this country. "Art education" then suggested, primarily, lessons in flower painting for young ladies, or Bohemian life in Paris. Both seemed at the opposite pole from the man's work of building and managing a new country. This conception of art ignored, of course, the robust and vital roles which art had played in the old world, and the masculine type of men who usually dominated it. A new conception is arising as the arts actually assume a more important place in American life and permeate every phase of industry from automobiles to television. Hundreds of new careers for normal, active youths are opening up; the financial value of artistic skills

and products is climbing to enormous totals. Art calls today, not so
much for the delicate dreamer of the romantic age as for capable,
intelligent men and women who know what they are doing, and
how to use the latest resources of technology in doing it. The arts
call today, not only for painters, poets, and composers, but for countless other types of worker, including executives and organizers,
engineers and skilled technicians, museum officials, teachers, and
critics.

New careers in the arts bring a greater demand for technical
training in them. Young men and women, some returning from
military service, are impatient to get well-paid jobs as quickly as
possible, to waste no time on general studies but to concentrate on
skills and knowledge of direct vocational use. Schools and academies
thrive and multiply with the aid of generous government funds for
veteran education. They offer to teach by day, night, or correspond-
ence every art from portrait painting to cartooning and interior
decoration, from pipe organ to "hot jazz" and tap dancing. Respected academies of art and music are under pressure from students
to cut out all the frills—in this case, general cultural subjects—and
give a degree or diploma as quickly as possible for nothing but
direct, studio practice of the art in question. Even prospective
teachers of the arts in public schools grumble at having to take
"academic" subjects and to learn the principles of education. It is
often hard to persuade a student to take a long, adequately balanced
course of study for a teaching job which is none too well paid; but
meanwhile overpopulated schools are clamoring for teachers, and
for speeding up the training process.

Since the close of World War II, there has been heavy pressure
toward specialized vocational training in the arts, apart from the
requirements of a balanced, liberal education. This pressure has affected not only independent art schools, but university departments
of the visual and other arts and teacher training. It is hard to oppose
this trend, and many radical concessions have been made to it
throughout the country. But some resistance is developing, especially
in well-financed liberal colleges and state universities where the size
of enrollment and tuition fees is not the prime consideration, and
where a respect for the liberal tradition still survives. Two strong
objections are being made to the wide separation of studio art in-

struction from the liberal college curriculum. Those who object do not deny the value of specialized training for those who already have a good basic education, or must forego it for urgent reasons. But they do insist that there is also a place for the combination of the two; that is, for the practice of the arts as an integral part of the new, liberal college program.

The argument deals, first of all, with the relatively few who will become professional artists or workers in some related field. For these there is serious doubt as to how far a purely technical, specialized course after high school will take them toward professional eminence. Is their case not essentially like that of the doctors, engineers, and other professional men who are discovering the need of more general education? Can an artist afford to be an ignoramus outside his own field at the present time? Will not a more general education and a more thorough intellectual grasp of his own field through study of its history and theory help him to go farther in the long run? It is hard to be sure of one's answer here, for many celebrated artists of the past and present have had little general education. Perhaps a little more would have made them better human beings, but one cannot be sure that it would have made them better painters or composers. In architecture, industrial design, and city planning, more general knowledge seems essential than in some types of painting and music. In general, it must be admitted that we know little at present about the factors which favor creative genius; hence the best policy at present is to offer various types of art education for various types of student, both the highly specialized and the balanced, liberal type.

We are on safer ground in considering those students who will teach an art in public school or college, or manage it in museums and other cultural institutions. Their jobs directly require something more than intensive skill and imagination in one chosen medium. As teachers, they must understand the mentality of students at a certain age, and how to fit their subject into a total curriculum. Thus there is a definite call within the wide, expanding field of art for persons of good general education as well as for the narrow specialist. To answer this need, we must do two things: (a) provide more instruction in the practice of the arts within the liberal college framework, and (b) provide more instruction in general subjects within the framework of the professional art school. This issue is being argued all over the country at the present time, and various workable compromises are emerging.

7. Practice in the arts as part of a liberal education

Are we leaving our theme of liberal education in thus considering the professional training of artists? No, indeed; let us remember again that a liberal education from the standpoint of modern democracy is not necessarily useless or unrelated to one's future work. Some college graduates enter fields for which they have no direct, technical training in college; others make professional use as teachers, writers, or otherwise, of the courses on history, literature, philosophy, or social science which they took as parts of a regular A.B. curriculum. By the same token, studio courses in painting or music are no less legitimate as parts of that curriculum because one student out of ten or twenty will choose a life work in that field. The essential question as to the rightness of including them in a liberal college is whether they also have a broadly educational function, not only for the few who become professionals but for the many who will not. Is some college experience in the practice of art a valuable thing for the majority of students, including the future doctors and housewives? It is not essential that it should be so for *all;* there must be some room for choice, and some will avoid all art as others avoid all mathematics, if possible. But are the arts roughly comparable to natural and social science in their broadly educational effect? Will they help to produce the kind of human being we desire to graduate from our colleges? The literary arts are not in question here, since their status is assured and strong; but can music and the visual and theater arts lay claim to value as liberal subjects, in comparison with that of literature? Perhaps not equal value as yet, for verbal expression is still more basic and universal in our culture. But in proportion as other arts exert a more important influence in our culture, it will be more and more necessary for the educated person to have some acquaintance with them.

It has been easier, along this line, to convince college authorities of the need for courses in the *history and appreciation* of music and the visual arts than that for courses in their *production and performance.* The former could be taught, and at first were taught, out of books and in a largely intellectual, verbal way, with much memorizing of facts; they were not too far out of line with other bookish subjects in the traditional college roster. Throughout Western history, it has been considered much more proper for the gentleman or lady to enjoy and patronize art, collect it, and learn a little about it than to make or perform it. For a respectable person to do this last, and for a liberal college to teach it, is still considered an innovation of doubtful propriety. The present task of art educators is to show that attractive construction and expression in the visual, musical, and theater arts can be a liberalizing, broadly educative experience for the ordinary college student who has no extraordinary talent and will probably not become an artist. This conviction is gaining ground so fast that studios and practice courses in the arts are springing up in colleges and universities throughout the land.

It is not always realized, however, that the mere building of costly, luxurious, well-equipped studios, theaters, and concert halls is no guarantee that the arts will be taught in a liberal way therein, any more than a long list of art courses in a catalogue is a guarantee. Studio work can be, and often is, mere manual or vocal training, mere unthinking drill or aimless fumbling under the wishful name of "creative expression." History and appreciation courses can be dry, superficial biographies of artists or mere practice in the recognition and naming of famous works of art. Both can be taught year after year with no realization on the part of teachers or students that they are missing essential aesthetic, intellectual, and other humanistic values. For the arts to be taught at all in the liberal college is something, to be sure; but the next and equally important step is to see that they are taught well.

To teach them well as parts of a liberal education is not quite the same as to teach them well in a strictly vocational art school. Some approach to professional standards of care and precision is necessary; habits of laziness and carelessness defeat all educational aims. But one must sacrifice some technical perfection in order to achieve the other value, paramount in the liberal college: that of making art activities contribute as much as possible to the total, balanced development of personality. The turning out of finished, completely trained professionals in the art world is not the responsibility of the four-year liberal college any more than it is in law or medicine.

More and more, we are coming to rely upon graduate work for intensive professional training. As the arts become highly technical professions with stricter standards of competence, they will require a fifth year, and even more, of work on the university level of those who are to assume directive roles in design and management. There will always be a need in the arts, as in other professions, for less highly trained, less ambitious persons to serve as minor craftsmen and technicians. And we have noted that in certain arts (not all) one can rise to eminence with little formal education of any sort. Since the training of artists is not our main concern in this discussion, let us return to the distinctive aims of art in the liberal college.

8. Psychological objectives of art education

These can best be approached from the psychological point of view, to which we have already alluded. On the college level, as on the lower grades, the "art department" is entrusted with stimulating and developing the student's visual powers and interests, mainly in the arts, but also in the perception of nature and the visible world in general. The music department is entrusted with fostering his auditory powers and interests in the realm of organized sound. These tasks would be relatively easy if the college could count upon every student's having had a continuous program of visual art throughout the lower grades as one phase of a balanced education. It could then go on to its proper task of applying already developed powers to the harder tasks of perceiving, understanding, creating, and performing complex and subtle forms. At present, it can assume no specific, previous experience of art and must begin with the A.B.C.'s of the subject, yet in such a way as to hold the attention of young adults.

This is not an easy task, but great progress can be made in a single year on the college level with proper materials and methods: with great works of art to look at and listen to, and help in the fascinating task of learning to appreciate them slowly, sensitively, and fully. Sight and hearing are refined and developed in that process, not as isolated functions or as used in ordinary tasks, but as applied to the significant, infinitely varied forms of art. This seems obvious enough as a major aim, but unfortunately it is often ignored in the effort to do other, easier, and less important things. A great deal of time can be spent in drawing, painting, or playing the piano with little development of visual or auditory powers if the emphasis is all on manual dexterity or on the execution of a few conventional techniques. A great deal of time can be spent in learning facts about the history of visual art or music, with surprisingly little direct looking or listening. That is the old, obsolescent approach. Better color-slides, films, and phonographs have now made a wealth of source material available. But it will not be used to fullest advantage until we think out the whole problem in psychological terms.

What are the mental, emotional, nervous, and muscular functions and abilities used in performing or producing in each art? The answer is partly but not wholly different for different arts, such as painting, musical composition, and ballet choreography. In each case, there is an intricate, dynamic co-ordination of sense-perception, imagination, feeling, intelligent control, and muscular co-ordination. In each art, studio activities can be planned so as to develop all these powers as much as possible, and not merely a detached, isolated set of them. This requires that, in all studio work, the college student be not only taught to do certain things, but to see and understand what he is doing and why—to see each skill and each step in relation to its larger context of activity and form, and to see the arts in general in their still larger cultural contexts.

Every high school and college which emphasizes a liberal arts curriculum should have not one but several studios, well equipped for the practice of various arts. It is not enough to have one large studio with all the students crowded together and performing the same tasks under direction. Ideally, there should be many small studios in which one or very few students can work without distraction along different lines. It is manifestly impossible for many students to practice on musical instruments in the same room. But students of painting, sculpture, writing, and other arts also need some privacy at times. There should always be an instructor nearby to explain the use and care of equipment. But qualified students should be free to work informally with art materials, whether or not they are taking systematic courses in art. Where such equipment is available, many will drop in to pass the time in an idle way and will be attracted to systematic study later on. It is a mistake to insist too rigidly in college that all study should be performed as part of a regular course of semester's length. We need more opportunity for informal, casual enjoyment of the arts, both in practice and in appreciation.

The past overemphasis of art-historical scholarship on factual memory and mechanical recognition of styles can be likewise corrected only by fuller psychological analysis of what is involved, humanly speaking, in learning to appreciate and understand the arts. Again the experience must focus on a much fuller, richer type of perception, an ability to see or hear, understand, and feel in sympathy with the total work of art as related to its larger context of cultural history. Historians have too long deluded themselves and others with the easy disclaimer that "appreciation cannot be taught." It can be taught, and only the indifference of many college art professors to the educational and psychological aspects of their work prevents them from seeing how it can be taught.

9. Social and cultural objectives of art education

The role of fine arts in the liberal curriculum can also be expressed from the standpoints of sociology and cultural history. It is hardly disputed now that the visual arts, music, literature, and theater comprise a factor of tremendous importance in our total cultural heritage. They are far older and more universal in human experience than the recent scientific and technological advances. Unlike much science and invention, they do not become rapidly and completely obsolete. Ancient Egyptian and Chinese art is still valid for us, not merely as a quaint reminder of the past, but for its perennial contribution—its beauty of form, and its peculiar insights into certain truths and values of life. A century and a half ago, the Western world was almost ignorant of world art, literature, and music outside its own limits, and even its knowledge of Greek civilization was fragmentary. We still teach comparatively little world literature in schools and colleges, although excellent translations from ancient, oriental, and primitive languages now exist. Until recently exotic music was almost unknown to the Western public, for it could not be written down in our notation. Now it is increasingly available in authentic phonograph records, in all its amazing diversity of rhythm, scale, pitch, melody, and often of symbolic meaning. It is primarily the responsibility of college art, music, and literature departments to select the best in this new flood of world art which is pouring in upon it, to interpret and reorganize it, and present it to the minds of American students. Yet how often the college teacher of these subjects, because of his own limited horizon, fails to bring these riches to his students, and instead plods drearily through some petty routine which he has learned in school a long time ago.

The value to students of acquiring the artistic element in their cultural heritage is both psychological and social. First, it helps to make their mental resources and abilities greater, and their experience richer throughout life. Second, it makes them less provincial, less bound by the sectional intolerance, prejudice, and hatred which give rise to wars. It helps to make them world citizens culturally, more aware of the values as well as the limitations of each culture, including their own. It helps to make Americans of every racial, national, and religious origin more respectful toward those of other backgrounds. It helps to fit the college graduate for life on a plane of leadership within his group, as a person of all-round competence who is capable not only of conversing but of exerting a constructive influence in many fields: in education and community life, as well as in his own home and profession.

These potential values of world art to the modern student are not always apparent at first sight. The layman hears a piece of Hindu music on the phonograph, or sees a Rajput miniature whose symbolic meaning is analogous, without much comprehension of their underlying meaning, their relevance to human situations and feelings with which he can sympathize. He feels only their strangeness, their apparent crudity and ugliness by the standards to which he is used, and he misses their excellence along quite different lines. Here is the task for discerning interpreters, especially on the college level, where difficult matters of religious and social background can be explained without excessive simplification. There is much in Western medieval and ancient art, and in that of our own country a hundred years ago, which requires expert help in understanding.

The value of world art, thus properly explained, is not limited to the connoisseur's delight in perceiving different forms of beauty. It goes beyond this, for those who can follow, into a fuller understanding of all human values, including the practical, moral, religious, and intellectual, in addition to the sensuous or narrowly aesthetic. In poems and novels, heroic epics and meditative lyrics, as well as in symbolic pictures, stone, glass, and tapestry, the world's great artists have set forth their conceptions of what is to be admired and sought in this world, and what detested and avoided. Every conceivable type of human being, and of feeling, deed, and motive of which man is capable has been portrayed in art, with or without explicit judgments on its worth and consequences; for us to contemplate, weigh against other alternatives, and use in framing our own set of standards.

There are techniques to be learned in the appreciation as well as the practice of the arts. No untrained person can walk into a concert hall, sit down, and grasp the complex form of a symphony by Brahms or Beethoven. No untrained tourist can walk into a French cathedral town and perceive the complex form of that great product of the Middle Ages, understanding its symbolism and seeing the relation of part to part—the stained glass windows, the wood carvings in the choir and altar, the relation of the interior to the exterior design, and so on. Art appreciation requires training the eyes and ears to perceive and enjoy specific qualities and forms in art, and developing standards to distinguish good from bad. A teacher of art appreciation today does not seek to impose fixed rules or laws of beauty and value in art. He tries to help the student to recognize the distinctive values in each art, those of each style, period, and individual leader. The result is to sensitize and broaden the student's background of experience and ability so that he will be ready to appreciate and enjoy whatever he encounters later on. This may be in travel abroad, visiting museums, hearing new works of music performed, or reading new books of fiction and poetry. The person of trained appreciation is ready to cope with them intelligently and without narrow prejudice.

Through comparing ourselves as individuals with the characters of fiction and drama, both good and bad, we decide what we ourselves want to be and want to avoid. We form our own personalities in the process of dealing with works of art past and present. The novel is one of the greatest ways of educating people in the psychology of personality and in the ability to make independent moral choices. Through persistent and open-minded contact with the literature of our own day we come to understand the problems and tensions, the conflicts and harmonies which exist in contemporary American culture. Our artists today are frank, sometimes to the point of savage caricature; they do not mince words in telling us of our own faults, of social evils and injustices. Social problems are dramatized in the arts of today. We may approve of one work of art and agree with one artist's attitude, and violently disagree with another. Students, in so far as they are mature enough, should be given the opportunity to become aware of the arts of their day and the main current trends in them.

There is no better avenue than art to the understanding of past and present culture. Through a better use of it, we can make the American civilization of the future into something greater than any which has gone before. We can try to include the best elements, the great contributions which Greece, Rome, China, India, and the others have made to the common fund of world civilization. A college student who has received a broadly artistic education will be more world minded in a cultural sense. He will have a cosmopolitan mind, not limited by the provincial restrictions of his native environment. This does not mean that he will be less patriotic or less devoted to his town, his state, and his country. He will, on the contrary, appreciate the best elements in his own tradition more intelligently and at the same time will be more able to understand other nations and parts of the world. As the United States is being forced into a position of world leadership today, it is more than ever necessary for us to understand the mentality, the traditions and cultural backgrounds of the people with whom we have to deal. It is shortsighted diplomacy for us to send out to Iran or India diplomats or businessmen who have no appreciation of the civilization of the peoples with whom they are to deal. Too often our representatives abroad are lacking in general education, especially in the arts, by comparison with the products of old world education at its best.

10. Wider uses of art in the liberal curriculum

The growing role of the arts in education is not limited to the giving of special courses on art. In the contacts which an art museum has with public schools and colleges, there is hardly a subject in the curriculum which cannot profit by the vitalizing influence of visual and audiovisual illustrations. Studies of history, such as the history of Greece and Rome, or of the Middle Ages, used to be almost exclusively out of books, with an occasional small illustration in black and white. Now the history lesson can be vitalized by a trip to the museum or by bringing fine reproductions in color to the classroom. These will show the children concretely how the people of past ages looked, what they wore, what they lived in, how they fought, what they made, and how they worshiped. The social sciences, in the study of various cultures, can achieve a vivid realism through the use of audiovisual illustrations. Teachers of English literature are using art materials as themes for essays and stories. Teachers of languages are illustrating literary examples with visits to museums and with study of the painting and architecture, the cities and palaces contemporary with these literary works. Music can be used in relation to architecture, armor, and costume. Music on phonograph records can give the student an impression of the sounds in a great cathedral, or in a Buddhist temple. Even the physical and mathematical sciences can be illustrated by examples from the realm of art. Architecture is full of forms from solid geometry—columns, pyramids, and domes; the proportions of great architecture are carefully calculated in terms of ratios, curves, and spirals. The physics of architecture is not separate from the art of architecture. The architect or the engineer today must consider the strength, rigidity, and elasticity of materials and the visual effect which the final form, say of a great bridge across the Hudson River, will have when completed.

Studies of cultural history are broadening out to include more and more reference to the arts of each period. History used to be taught largely in terms of the names and dates of kings and queens, of their dynastic successions, of their wars and treaties. The next step was to fill in this skeleton of dates and names with a fuller understanding of the role of social groups and forces, economic trends, the rise of the lower classes, the introduction of new methods of industry and commerce and travel. Now still another mode of enlarging the scope of history is making itself felt. We cannot claim to have taught the history of a period such as Greece, the Middle Ages, China, India, the Near East without giving a fair sampling of the visual arts and the literature in translation of that people. How much better we can teach a course on Egypt, China, or Japan if we include in it a film in color with scenery of the great temples, with views of the religious processions along the streets, and with records of the native music and singing.

To summarize, it may be predicted that in the near future a well-equipped university which undertakes to develop its program in the arts for undergraduate men and women, up to a level now common in the sciences, will have to include the following main approaches:

1. Some reference to all the major arts of the time and of cultural history, with due attention to film, dance, and other theater arts, housing, community planning, and other industrial arts, now often neglected by college art departments.

2. Different ways of studying these arts: (a) in the performance or execution of existing forms, as in playing the piano, acting in dramas, painting and designing in traditional styles; (b) experiment in creating original forms; composing and designing; (c) histories of the arts in chronological and developmental order; general surveys and intensive researches; with due attention to the historical interrelation of the arts, their cultural backgrounds, and the political, religious, philosophical, scientific, and technological factors with which they have interacted; (d) theory of art; aesthetics; philosophy, psychology, and sociology of the arts; on an introductory level as general courses in appreciation, the nature and function of the various arts, current trends and issues in art criticism, etc.; also, on an advanced level, as detailed comparative studies of form, style, symbolism, function, culture pattern, the artistic personality, the processes of creation and appreciation, standards and theories of value, and similar problems in various arts and their interrelations.

3. Due attention to the arts in courses given by other departments on related subjects; for example, in general or cultural history; in surveys of contemporary civilization; in psychology and psychotherapy; in the social sciences such as anthropology; in discussing programs for social co-operation on a regional or international scale, as in the United Nations; in technological applications of the physical sciences, such as the invention of improved materials and instruments for the arts.

4. As to equipment for such instruction, one must plan in terms of (a) studios, laboratories, theaters, and concert halls; (b) materials and instruments; not only the familiar ones such as paints and brushes, kilns, pianos, and costumes, but new and complex ones, such as motion-picture cameras and television equipment; (c) galleries for permanent and temporary exhibitions; (d) works of art, originals and reproductions to be placed in them; (e) other types of reproduction and devices for using them, such as colored lantern slides, colored

films, projectors, phonographs and records; (f) books and periodicals, pictures, and card indexes for research.

5. More important than all the rest, a faculty of genuinely well-educated teachers—all possessing the fundamentals of a liberal, humanistic education, but diversified as to special interest and training: some practicing artists, some historians, some critics, some aestheticians, some experts in the training of teachers.

This list of specifications is ambitious, to be sure, and is not yet realized anywhere. It will cost money, and the public must gradually be convinced of its value. But it is far from unattainable, and is not out of line with the vast sums now being spent for science. Different institutions will specialize to some extent on different arts and approaches to them; but if specialization goes too far, the student's grasp of the whole field will suffer. The approaches just listed will some time be regarded as the indispensable minimum for a well-balanced undergraduate program in the arts.

XVII

A PSYCHOLOGICAL AND SOCIOLOGICAL
APPROACH TO COLLEGE ART*

"The Princeton student," says Mr. R. L. Duffus in *The American Renaissance*, "does not learn 'appreciation,' for that, as Princeton looks at it, cannot be taught. 'Appreciation' is an expression of something inside the appreciator, the result of such thought and experience as he may have undergone, the reflection of the kind of person he is . . . . What can be taught is facts. Pictures, statues and cathedrals are facts."

I believe that this statement expresses the attitude of many, perhaps most, art historians in American colleges at the present time. There is much to be said for it. "Art appreciation" as usually taught has consisted of a mixture of sentimental effusion with a few arbitrary, conventional standards of value laid down by the instructor. To teach appreciation has meant teaching students *how* to appreciate, what they should like and dislike, how to respond emotionally to works of art. There is little sound scholarship or logical reasoning in such instruction. In reaction from it, the universities have wisely turned to scholarly research, and especially to art history, where there is abundant opportunity for constructive and verifiable work. They have tried to leave out the "subjective" factor of aesthetic value and to confine themselves to factual problems in the history of art. College art history in this country has produced a large amount of excellent research and a tradition of accurate scholarship.

I have no intention of minimizing the value of these achievements. Nevertheless, the historical approach should no longer dominate the field of college art. Good as it is, there are other good approaches which should be pursued along with it. From the standpoint of liberal education, there are others of even greater value.

The present method is far from being wholly scientific and objective. It contains a large admixture of aesthetic valuation, based on personal taste and conventional standards, along with its ap-

* Published in its original form in *Parnassus,* V.6 (November, 1933), pp. 27-30.

parently rigorous devotion to factual evidence. This element is implicit in the initial choice of subject matter for courses in art history, and in the emphasis laid on certain types of art. The emphasis now given to archaic Greek sculpture, for example, or the frequent ignoring of primitive Negro sculpture as mere ethnological data, not art, implies (right or wrong) a sweeping estimate of art values which the student accepts as gospel until the fashion changes. Examine almost any piece of writing by an American art professor. You will not read far before discovering, tucked away among technical terminology, words implying aesthetic worth or lack of it. This drawing is "weak"; that one is "more successful"; this statue is "well organized"; that one shows "a distinct deterioration from the earlier style." Such appraisals, often highly debatable and undefended, are woven inextricably into the texture of current historical argument in defense of theories of attribution and chronological sequence. Pictures, statues, and cathedrals are "facts," as Mr. Duffus remarks, but what the art professor says about them includes a large element of his own personal feeling.

There is nothing wrong in this inclusion of aesthetic judgments along with the study of art history. It is indispensable in any attempt to come to grips with the meaning and importance of art to human beings. What is to be deplored is the fact that such judgments are made only incidentally and carelessly, with a casual dogmatism that conceals and ignores debatable issues, confusing them with verifiable facts. What is to be desired is a more frank, direct, and systematic facing of the whole subject of aesthetic value in the study of art, including the question of general standards and variation in taste.

From a standpoint of liberal education, this evasion of aesthetic issues has an unfortunate result. Students are sent out into the world, their heads crammed with technical information about past art, yet poorly prepared for the task of comprehending or evaluating any unfamiliar forms of art, ancient or modern, for which their teachers have not provided them with a ready-made appraisal. The natural desire of students to debate aesthetic values is brushed aside as "a matter of personal taste." Their powers of critical appraisal are not developed through the rational analysis, application, and discussion of standards. Thus they are left helpless in the face of modern art experiments and critical controversies. Even as future art historians their training lacks a vital element. For the writing of significant art history in every generation is necessarily a process of revaluing the past, selecting and reorganizing data in the light of what seems most important at the present time, as well as of bringing out the meaning of past art in terms of its functions, aesthetic and otherwise, in the lives of people by whom and for whom it was made. If art is not appraised intelligently, it will be appraised with dogmatic prejudice, and the duty of college art departments is to see that it is appraised as intelligently as possible.

The present method of study fails to develop in students even the power of fully perceiving art, of using their eyes to grasp directly the whole organic structure of a form. They are forced to memorize a host of names and dates, of iconographical symbolisms, of minute peculiarities in the shape, materials, and technique of individual works of art. In consequence they acquire the habit of approaching all art in the spirit of pedantic dissection and classification. They are made to scrutinize works of art minutely, even with microscope and X-ray. But the aim of such observation is not to attain a clear, organic perception of the structure as a whole; it is rather to detect peculiar individual mannerisms, earmarks of technical construction, which may help to identify the provenance of the object. The ever-growing mass of memorized information and technical terminology comes like a screen between the student and the visible form of the object he is studying. As a result, many advanced students lack the ability to visualize, to imagine, and to look at an object directly for what it is. Verbal memory has replaced and destroyed the power of aesthetic perception. When such students write about art after graduation, the result is likely to be mainly a series of quotations from authorities, and of conventional textbook *clichés;* they are powerless to explain why an object is worth buying or looking at, or even to characterize it as a distinctive work of art.

On the plea of exact scholarship, students are discouraged even from making a broad philosophical approach to art history. Their essays must specialize, as narrowly as possible, on some small subdivision in the field, such as a contrast between two miniatures in a single tenth-century manuscript. They are told that only after years of such minute research can one venture to deal with broader questions, and that even then the true scholar will hesitate to do so.

Meanwhile they acquire fixed habits of seeing no farther than their noses, so that the time for trying to understand main trends of cultural history never arrives.

Some amount of specialization is of course essential, not only for advanced scholars but for undergraduates, too. They should acquire, not merely glittering generalities, but some exact information and a habit of rigorous attention to detail when necessary. My objection to the present method is twofold: first, that there is too much specialization in proportion to the time spent on co-ordination of the details thus acquired; second, that the specialization is wrongly directed. It is directed too much along chronological, technological, local, and nationalistic lines. The field of art is divided up, and research or essay problems are assigned, on the basis of centuries, countries, national schools, works and artists of a given time, place, and medium. Thus one man's field is sixth-century Attic vase-painting; another's is the Romanesque ivory-carving of northern France. The farther he goes in advanced work, the more he is made to concentrate upon some narrower division, to the consequent neglect of others. Now it is quite possible to specialize intensively on general principles—for example, on some recurrent aesthetic quality or tendency such as flat decorative pattern in sculpture; on mysticism or the grotesque. Art history is sadly in need of light on the ways and circumstances in which such tendencies recur, but they cannot be studied thoroughly without comparing examples from widely separate times, places, arts, and media.

Courses in philosophy, in aesthetics, and in general history are sometimes relied on to provide the necessary co-ordination in a student's course of study. But as a rule they make little contact with the subject matter of art history. Aesthetics as taught by a philosophy department today is usually an abstract, purely speculative subject, a review of classical and current theories of the nature and supposed laws of beauty and value in general, with little, if any, reference to particular works of art, and certainly no direct, extensive study of a wide range of concrete examples. Ask of a student in fine arts whether he can get from his philosophy professor any enlightenment on the relation of his field to the history of music and literature, any help in correlating wide ranges of historical data. The philosopher, who might traditionally be expected to offer such guidance, has in most cases suffered, like his colleagues in other departments, from

the vice of overspecialization. He has withdrawn into some tiny research in semantics or epistemology, or he is engaged in microscopic researches on the history of his own subject. The history
professor has his own small individual field, usually political or
social, and slights the history of culture. Music is studied by itself,
in an airtight compartment, as if its history and critical problems
had nothing to do with those of other arts. Literature is not only
studied apart from music and the visual arts, but is further divided
into national or language departments—Classical, Romance, Ger-
manic, English—which have little to do with one another. All of
these studies in the arts are of course widely divorced from the study
of psychology, logic, and scientific method, so that the possibility of
approaching their aesthetic problems in a scientific spirit is hardly
dreamed of.

In the future, I believe that a distinct department of *Comparative
Aesthetics* will be considered a necessary part of every university and
liberal college faculty. It will undertake the much-needed task of co-
ordinating detailed studies in all the arts, of comparing and interpreting them in the light of cultural history and aesthetic theory.
But I am here concerned, not so much with this broader task, as
with the visual arts alone—the "fine arts," as they are now inac-
curately termed in college catalogues. Since there are many visual
arts—"fine" and "applied," painting and drawing, architecture, sculpture, ceramics, textiles, glass, mosaic, furniture, and all other forms
of decoration and craftsmanship—there is ample scope within these
limits for a broadly comparative and philosophical treatment.

This treatment should be psychological as well as philosophical in
viewpoint. Most liberal colleges now accept as a dominant aim the
whole mental and physical development of the student rather than
the training of professional specialists. It would seem to be the function of an art department, then, to attend to the aesthetic phase of
this development, or at least to the visual element in it. This in turn
would involve, if the function were thoroughly carried out, not only
training in perception, criticism, and general interpretation of visual
art, but also more opportunity than at present for use of the hands
in constructive experiment with art materials.

I am not proposing, however, that college art be regarded wholly
as a matter of mental and physical training—of gymnastics, however
salutary. There should also be a subject matter to learn, a set of

facts to deal with by rigorous thinking; and the best sort of mental training will come as an incidental result. But to gain this result the subject matter must be properly presented. For this reason I would emphasize that the method proposed involves a study of facts, quite as objective and scholarly in aim as the present historical approach. The set of facts to be studied would, however, be differently chosen. In the subject matter of college art, I would include the main outlines of archaeology and art history, with less emphasis on a few isolated details than at present. I would add a study of the psychology and sociology of art.

To teach the sociology of art involves an explanation of how the arts have functioned in various cultures, advanced and primitive, and how they function in various countries today. Anthropology and cultural history are rapidly providing us with data for this approach in college courses. In it, the work of art is not seen in isolation, in a glass case or a photograph, or only in a chronological series. It is seen in its living context of social activities, as related to political, economic, religious, technological, and other factors. Such an approach throws new light on the genesis of styles: why the arts of one culture and period differ from those of another as they do. A natural sequel to the comparative study of art in various cultures (including our own) is the evaluative question of what the arts have contributed to human progress and well-being there, and of how they might contribute more in Western—especially American—culture today. Another phase of this approach is a study of the role of the artist in present society: his changing sources of patronage, his socio-economic status, his relations with governmental and other powers, his relation to social and political issues and to his local community.

To teach the psychology of art means in a sense "teaching appreciation" rather than excluding it as a purely personal matter. But it does not mean telling students *how* to appreciate, what to like, and how to feel about art. It does mean studying *what appreciation is,* as a psychological process; how works of art are actually conceived and executed, not how they ought to be; how people perceive, like and dislike, worship, use, and appraise works of art; how they resemble and how they differ from each other in these ways of behavior. These are "facts" quite as real as statues or cathedrals, and it is only in their light that the tangible artifacts take on human and historical significance.

The materials necessary for an adequate study of art have been rapidly accumulating. They have been developed separately, and the task of putting them together is still to be done. On the one hand we have a body of facts and theories about the nature of art, produced by the excavations of archaeologists, the explorations of ethnologists among primitive peoples, the exchange of art works and reproductions among distant civilized groups, and the attempts of historians, sociologists and critics to co-ordinate and interpret the results.

On the other hand, we have the body of knowledge and theory which psychology has developed about human nature, including its basic inborn mechanisms and their development through individual growth and cultural influence. The common human processes of sensation, perception, recognition, memory, association, emotion, volition, growth, and maturing, the conditioning of reflexes, the formation of habits and types of character, unconscious levels of thinking and feeling, the behavior of groups, rational inference, choice, and valuation—these and others have been described in their general outlines with some assurance, in spite of disagreement on details and metaphysical ultimates. All these processes enter into the production and appreciation of art.

Enough is now at hand, of the two necessary sets of material, to permit their correlation. That task is a logical next step, both for general psychology and for the subject of art. To anyone moderately acquainted with both fields, their mutual bearings are to some extent obvious on first consideration, and both fields are illuminated by putting them together. One has only to read through a textbook on general psychology or psychoanalysis with an advanced art class to realize at each step some significant possible application of psychological principles to works of art; to the motivation and methods of artistic production; to the methods and judgments of art critics, and to the significance of historical styles and cultural epochs.

A typical problem for investigation is the nature of visual perception in the experience of a picture. This involves the modes in which sensations of color, line, and motion are organized and interpreted, leading to associations and imaginary experiences of space, touch, and movement; the ways in which different types of pictures stimulate different perceptive responses, and different individuals vary in their perception of the same picture. In relation to these, one may study the responses of different sorts which go along with perception, such as memory, feeling-tone, rudimentary movement, volitional attitudes, and the application of conscious standards of value. In relation to such a process as perception of space, one may go on to compare and contrast examples of different arts, such as painting and architecture..

The materials for making a start are available in any college which possesses departments of art, psychology, and sociology or individual teachers with broad interests. It offers an open field for original work, and a means of heightening the interest of students in both subjects, through facing squarely the problem of the meaning of art in human activity.

✦ XVIII ✦

AESTHETICS AND PHILOSOPHY IN
AMERICAN COLLEGES*

Like all other sciences, aesthetics was hatched in the parent nest of
philosophy. It has hesitated long on the edge of the nest, before flying out to set up one of its own. Its elder brother, psychology
(formerly known as "mental philosophy") went through the same
pangs of separation a few decades ago. Psychology has grown
mightily since, and has brought back many a choice morsel of knowledge to its elderly parents. Aesthetics as a formal, academic subject
still feels most at home under the sheltering wing of philosophy.

Since the eighteenth century, it has held a somewhat uncertain
place as a member of the philosophical family. Its position is not unlike that of a late and unexpected arrival, a rather unsought and
accidental infant, come to bless the old age of a couple whose other
children have long since grown up. The infant's awkward attempts
to walk and do things for itself are entertaining but a little embarrassing among its well-poised older brothers. It often talks too much,
and uses big words which it does not understand. When the family
counts noses, in planning a picnic or assigning tasks to be done, its
existence is sometimes forgotten.

Aesthetics is sometimes listed among the recognized branches of
philosophy, sometimes not. The student can read a long list of recent
histories of philosophy and surveys of contemporary problems without discovering that aesthetics exists, or that any great philosophers
have been concerned about art. "Introductions to philosophy" are
worth noticing these days as the nearest approach to comprehensive
philosophical systems. Our philosophers have apparently given up
writing new systems of their own, but they do occasionally produce
these brief epitomes for the young. Friedrich Paulsen's *Introduction
to Philosophy*, still used since William James endorsed it in 1895,
does not mention aesthetics among the branches of philosophy—

* Published in its original form in *The Journal of Aesthetics and Art
Criticism*, IV.3 (March, 1946), pp. 180-187.

logic, ethics, epistemology, and metaphysics. Neither art nor aesthetics is mentioned in its Index. Other textbooks containing no aesthetics (or less than one tenth of one percent) are Bertrand Russell's *The Problems of Philosophy* and R. B. Perry's *Present Philosophical Tendencies*. Several older introductions to philosophy had chapters on aesthetics, or aesthetic value, or "the beautiful"—for example, those by G. T. Ladd (1890) and W. T. Marvin (1912). R. W. Sellars includes aesthetics ("a reflection upon the nature of beauty whether in art or in nature") along with ethics in axiology (theory of values) as one of the main divisions of philosophy. G. T. W. Patrick's *Introduction to Philosophy* has an unusually long chapter on "Aesthetic Values," with sections on objects of beauty, the science of aesthetics, art periods in history, the art impulse, the fine arts, art and morals, art and social morale, the play motive, the imagination, theories of the beautiful, empathy, the psychology of aesthetic experience, music, and beauty as ideal value.

Philosophy in American Education, by a commission of the American Philosophical Association (1945), omits aesthetics from its list of "the basic courses in philosophy" (history of philosophy, ethics, logic, and metaphysics). But it does emphasize art as one of the "specific extraphilosophical subject matters" which should be analyzed by philosophy. "Philosophy," it says, "can fit into such programs of mutual aid between related humanities in three principal ways: (a) through the analytical disciplines of aesthetics and philosophical linguistics; (b) by contributions to the history of ideas; (c) in its interpretation and criticism of the moral and speculative ideals expressed in literature and the arts."

Histories of philosophy in English often pay little attention to aesthetics or the philosophy of art, passing quickly over important works on the subject by leading philosophers. In Bertrand Russell's *History of Western Philosophy,* "aesthetics" receives three brief index references; "art" none. Hegel's monumental *Aesthetik* (translated as *The Philosophy of Fine Art,* in four volumes) is not mentioned in the account of that philosopher; neither are the works of Santayana and Dewey on aesthetics.

What recognition is paid to aesthetics by philosophy departments in our leading universities? This would make an interesting survey, but perhaps it would be fairer to wait until normal conditions return. A casual glance through the catalogues indicates a good deal of difference in this respect. The Harvard Graduate School of Arts and Sciences, in its *Official Register,* lists aesthetics among the topics in systematic philosophy on which a candidate for the Ph.D. may work. The list comprises eleven subdivisions of the field, and is thus notably longer than most traditional lists of the "branches" of philosophy. It includes metaphysics, epistemology, philosophy of science, logic, philosophy of mathematics, ethics, philosophy of history, aesthetics, social philosophy, and political philosophy.

Persistent disagreement on the status of aesthetics in philosophy has not prevented numerous American philosophers from writing books about it. William Knight's *Philosophy of the Beautiful* has a chapter on "The Philosophy of America," which reviews a surprising list of aestheticians from 1815 on—now mostly forgotten, alas!—down to Gayley and a youthful John Dewey in 1887. Since then, substantial writings on aesthetics have appeared under the names of professors in the philosophy departments of Harvard, Columbia, Princeton, Brown, Pennsylvania, Michigan, Ohio, California, Duke, Johns Hopkins, Bryn Mawr, Northwestern, the New School for Social Research, and others. One wonders why the subject of aesthetics itself is still so often treated as an orphan stepchild in American philosophy departments. If someone happens to be around who wants to teach it, well and good; if not, the lack is apparently not considered very serious. Few philosophy departments are inclined to develop aesthetics into a diversified program of detailed courses. One or two half-year courses of a highly abstract nature, on beauty and aesthetic value, are usually considered ample. Few departments assign more than one instructor to the field.

For this slow development, many reasons can be given, including a lack of demand on the part of students. But would there not be more demand if aesthetics were differently taught? One stumbling-block has been the traditionally narrow conception of aesthetics as restricted to the abstract study of beauty and aesthetic value. Some contemporary philosophers restrict it to the linguistic and logical analysis of value judgments. When this is all aesthetics deals with, it can never attract many students to pursue it very far.

Some philosophers in this country and in Germany have gone to great pains to exclude from aesthetics a number of subjects which, everyone concedes, are closely related to it. Unfortunately, these hair-splitting distinctions are still being made, to the continued bewilderment of students and the public. Thus Helmut Kuhn, writing on "Philosophy of Art" in the *Encyclopedia of the Arts* begins, "In order to determine the purpose of a philosophy of art, we must distinguish it from aesthetics . . . Aesthetics, the philosophical analysis of beauty, may be distinguished from the study, philosophical or otherwise, of art as a form of human productivity." On the other hand, as Brand Blanshard remarks, "We must learn to think straight about what art is trying to do, which is the business of aesthetics." [1] Others seem to take the narrow concept of aesthetics as an excuse for neglecting the subject matter of the arts. "It is up to the particular arts to teach this subject matter," they imply. "Let the fine arts, music, and literature departments cover it. Let the psychologists cover the psychology of art." Of course, the psychologists usually don't have time for it either, and of course no one of the particular art departments can undertake to cover the whole field of art in a comprehensive way. It is in many ways a philosophical task, as Dr. Kuhn implies in calling it "philosophy of art."

If the philosophy departments will do the job under that name and define "philosophy of art" broadly enough, well and good. Most American writers now treat "aesthetics" and "philosophy of art" as coextensive. If people can agree to call the field "philosophy of art," or "science of art," or "art theory," or *allgemeine Kunstwissenschaft*, one name will do as well as another. It would not be hard to coin a better name than "aesthetics," if one could start from scratch. But "aesthetics" has achieved more general use than any other term, and it is commonly defined so as to include these closely related fields. So why confuse the issue by needless distinctions and a needless multiplicity of labels? The important thing is to get the job done somehow: to start, in a concerted and vigorous way, systematic investigation of the arts and related types of human experience; to develop instruction in American colleges for the sake of all interested students, and to provide adequate facilities for advanced research.

This is not to say that the distinctions quoted above are false or entirely useless. It is important to distinguish between factual and evaluative studies; between observing works of art and defining general aesthetic categories, etc. These are different tasks, emphases, and approaches within the subject of aesthetics, which should be

[1] "Education as Philosophy," *Swarthmore College Bulletin*, XLII:4 (7th month, 1945).

distinguished as well as interrelated. But it is harmful to erect them at the start into restrictive boundaries for the whole subject: to fence off a little realm of abstract value theory and obstruct free traffic between it and its neighbors. A precise definition of the limits of aesthetics is not urgently needed at the present stage. If made at all, it should be made in terms of more and less. When art criticism becomes sufficiently general and fundamental, covering a wide range of art and scrutinizing value standards, it becomes aesthetics. When art history becomes sufficiently general and fundamental, revealing major culture epochs, styles, trends, and causal relations, it merges with aesthetics. When psychology discloses main recurrent factors in personality and social behavior which affect the creation and use of art, it merges with aesthetics. When semantics deals constructively with aesthetic terms and meanings, it merges with aesthetics.

There is no distinct subject of aesthetics in the nature of things. There is a set of diverse phenomena, called "aesthetic" and "artistic," which can as yet be only roughly marked off. There is a varied group of intellectual approaches to them, for the purpose of raising and answering as well as possible a number of different problems, which seem important to different generations. Aesthetics as a subject will thrive best by freely admitting many scientific, critical, artistic, historical, and educational approaches to its counsels; by admitting many different types of data and hypotheses, whether or not they conform to some pre-established definition of what aesthetics ought to include. In educational administration, as in organizing college departments, some marking off of fields is necessary for practical purposes. But it should never be too exact or obstructive to new approaches which may seek to cut across the old boundaries.

At the present time aesthetics, or the group of subjects loosely designated by that name, is growing too large to be adequately taught within the limits of the ordinary philosophy department, however well-disposed some individual philosophers may be. The philosophical nest is elastic enough to accommodate a sizable fledgling. But there are limits to the growth of any one branch of philosophy, especially when a small department is expected to cover the whole traditional field.

One disadvantage of the term "philosophy of art" is that it seems to tie the subject down to its prescientific status as a branch or a mere application of philosophy. The term "philosophy of mind" was similarly inadequate for scientific psychology. *Kunstwissenschaft* implies science, rather than philosophy, of art. Moreover, "philosophy of art" seems to leave out some important aesthetic phenomena which occur outside the realm of art.

Meanwhile, other college departments are extending in the direction of aesthetics, especially when the philosophers are indisposed to do so. In almost every college, someone on the faculty is interested in problems of general art theory. He may be in the art department, or the English department, or the psychology department, or the history department, or elsewhere. In American colleges, the demarcation of subjects is so flexible that one can expand a course on "art appreciation" or "literary criticism" indefinitely, unless some colleague protests, by bringing in for "background" and "comparison" a variety of materials which should nominally be taught by someone else. For this reason it is hard to discover, from a casual survey of catalogues, just how much aesthetics is being taught in American colleges. Many a course on the history of music or the contemporary novel includes more general aesthetics than its teacher could easily defend on strict theoretical grounds. This is a practical and very American way to let a subject grow, with freedom for different approaches, and for growth along the line of least resistance, in the hands of anyone who seems able and inclined to foster it. Sometimes the next stage is to group several of the arts together for better integration, with or without the help of philosophy.

Some of the most substantial contributions to aesthetics in this country, as in Europe, have been made by persons concerned primarily with the visual arts: for example, Lewis Mumford, Coomaraswamy at the Boston Museum of Fine Arts, Helen Gardner at the Chicago Art Institute, A. P. McMahon at New York University, and A. Torossian at California. Some have been made by literary critics such as R. G. Moulton, I. A. Richards, F. C. Prescott, and Louise Dudley; some by psychologists such as Münsterberg, Langfeld, Witmer, Seashore, Schoen, Ogden, Meier, Farnsworth, Pratt, and Arnheim; some by ethnologists such as Franz Boas at Columbia. In these ways and others, aesthetics is being approached "from below," as Fechner advised, but with solid factual materials from the arts and various sciences.

In approaching aesthetics from any single artistic or scientific point of view, there is an obvious limitation. A certain subdivision of the field, a particular type of phenomenon, is likely to be emphasized to a degree inconsistent with a balanced, comprehensive view. At the present stage some breadth and balance can be secured through supplementing philosophical aesthetics with selected courses in the arts. It is a question how much integration can be achieved through combining a list of specialized courses in different arts, even with the aid of philosophy.

As the subject grows, it will eventually be found advisable to set up distinct departments of aesthetics. Such departments will be separate from philosophy to the extent that psychology has become separate. Let us hope that they will continue to deal with their materials in a philosophic way, through searching criticism of assumptions and methods, along with breadth of synthesis. They will use many of the old philosophical concepts and hypotheses, along with new ones of their own. They will not ignore the old problems of beauty and value, but will approach them with more equipment for intelligent evaluation, in the shape of new knowledge about the arts and their relation to human nature. (Some of this new aesthetic insight may supply American philosophy itself with a much-needed tonic; a fresh approach to its own, nonaesthetic problems. But that is another question.)

It is pleasant at this stage to dream of a fully developed, independent department of aesthetics in a major university, properly staffed and equipped with materials and modern apparatus for studying and experimenting with all the arts; close to museums, libraries, concert halls, and theaters; distinct from specialized departments of philosophy, psychology, literature, music, and visual arts, but co-operating actively with them. An opportunity exists for some university to be the first to build one.

~@I XIX I@~

A COLLEGE PROGRAM IN AESTHETICS
AND THE ARTS*

What kind of education is best suited to prepare a student for postgraduate and professional work in aesthetics, as a writer, teacher, and independent thinker? What training is necessary for original research and creative scholarship in aesthetics?

1. Aesthetics cannot be adequately studied as a single, isolated course or in relation to other courses in philosophy only. It cannot be adequately taught as a highly specialized, abstract subject concerned only with general theories of beauty, value, aesthetic experience, and the like. These studies have their place, but should be based on more specific, concrete studies of various arts and other contributory subjects. Aesthetic theory can best be studied after, and along with, systematic observation and analysis of works of art.

2. Students should be aided in securing a diversified, balanced program of courses on different arts and approaches to art. Those interested in intensive specialization from a technical or historical point of view should be allowed to do so; but those interested in aesthetics should be allowed a more extensive selection. Students should not be forced to specialize on a single art, but should be helped to acquire, as undergraduates, a basic knowledge and appreciation of all the principal arts, including music, literature, the visual arts, and the theater arts. They should not be forced, in advanced courses, to specialize on minute historical periods and problems. They should be helped to combine various approaches to the arts, such as the historical, theoretical, and practical; the philosophical, psychological, and sociological; the appreciative, educational, and critical. They should be helped to gain some experience of the practicing artist's attitude toward his materials and problems, without having to take a long, intensive, professional course on any one medium, technique, or instrument.

* Published in its original form in *The Journal of Aesthetics and Art Criticism,* IV.2 (December, 1945), pp. 115-118.

3. Diversified, extensive study of the arts is not necessarily superficial, "a mere smattering," as specialists often charge. It is possible to specialize on the discovery, testing, and formulation of principles having wide application. Aesthetics is the subject in which this is undertaken with respect to the phenomena of art and related modes of experience. Without a definite course or courses in aesthetic theory, diversified courses on particular arts are in danger of appearing to the student as unrelated. Aesthetics is needed to help integrate them by explicit, systematic comparison and generalization. However, the whole task of presenting a coherent picture of the arts in human experience should not be left to the aesthetics teacher. Courses on particular fields need not be narrowly isolated and self-contained, but should frequently suggest wider relationships. Elementary courses on particular arts, like those on particular sciences, should not all be taught mainly for the benefit of students who are going to specialize in those particular fields. Some of them should try to present, quickly and simply, the essential meaning and importance of each field to the layman, and to the world in general.

4. To prepare a student for effective graduate work in aesthetics, it should be made easy for him to secure undergraduate instruction in the following subjects. "Making easy" involves a recognized, established combination of courses leading toward the bachelor's degree with a major in aesthetics and the arts. It is too much to expect the immature student to pick the right ones for himself, among a bewildering variety of courses in remote departments. Faculty advisers should be prepared to help him do so.

5. *Subjects other than art:*

   a. Logic and introduction to philosophy; history of philosophy; contemporary philosophy. Scientific methods, including elementary statistics. Advanced statistics if desired.

   b. General psychology; psychology of the individual personality and its development; social psychology; abnormal psychology and psychoanalysis. Psychology of art (aesthetic psychology). Educational psychology if desired. Cultural psychology in relation to anthropology.

   c. Survey of social sciences, including anthropology, economics, sociology, political science. History of ideas in these fields.

   d. Cultural history; history of world civilization, with attention to the history of religion, technology, science, and social institutions.

e. Physical geography; topography, climate, raw materials (in brief).

f. Foreign languages: at least French and German; Italian, Latin, and Greek are also valuable.

g. For aesthetics, advanced mathematics and physical science are least necessary among the sciences, and need be studied only from the layman's point of view. Principles of biology, including evolution, are more relevant.

6. *Subjects in the general field of art,* in the broad aesthetic meaning of that term:

a. *Literature:* English composition; history of English and American literature (including the contemporary). Comparative literature; world literature in translation, including primitive and oriental as well as occidental, to be studied historically in relation to cultural history, and also theoretically, through analysis of literary forms, types, and styles. Some reading in foreign languages. Literary criticism; aims and values of different types of literature, including prose and verse, epic, novel, and drama. Opportunity to do some creative writing, and to become acquainted with important living writers.

b. *Visual arts:* "Art appreciation" or introductory survey of the visual arts as to their media, techniques, social functions, aims, and types of value sought, contemporary tendencies and leaders, controversial issues in criticism. Analysis of form, design, and style in various arts. History of the visual arts, including oriental and primitive, and including architecture, city planning, painting, sculpture, landscape design, interior design, furniture, pottery, textiles, and other useful arts, photography, and the visual phases of theater art, dancing, and motion pictures. Opportunity to see good, original examples of these arts. Opportunity to meet living artists, to see them at work, and to experiment with practice of one or more of these arts, to "get the feel of the medium." Travel to American and foreign museums and other art centers.

c. *Music:* "Appreciation of music" or introductory survey of principal types of musical form; instruments in the orchestra; choral music, oratorio; opera; modern styles and trends; issues in criticism. Analysis of form and style. History of music, including medieval, renaissance, oriental, modern, and primitive. Opportunity to hear good music, and play, sing, and compose if desired.

7. *Undergraduate courses on aesthetics* should include an introductory survey, partly theoretical and partly an historical sketch of aesthetics and art criticism. Main past and present theories of the nature of art, beauty, aesthetic experience, and aesthetic value. Transition from the speculative philosophy of art to the empirical, scientific approach. Branches of contemporary aesthetics: current problems and tendencies.

Is this a large order? Certainly, but there is value in stating an ideal clearly, even if its attainment seems remote. In four short years of college, it would of course be impossible to acquire a thorough grasp of all these subjects. But a first step could be taken along many lines, which would help the student to go ahead for himself after graduation. No past or present aesthetician has had the benefit of such a program in college. We have had to seek it out laboriously in later years, with little guidance.

Much more of it can be given in college than is given anywhere at present, by eliminating nonessentials and improving teaching methods. Extreme acceleration is harmful, but we have learned during the war that many kinds of instruction can be speeded up advantageously. Short units are often preferable to the old-time full-year or half-year course. New devices such as motion pictures and television will be useful at certain points in the program, especially as substitutes for distant travel. All subjects can be outlined more selectively, with less dawdling and fumbling by teachers and students alike. More of the subjects mentioned above can be taught in secondary school than at present. There is no reason why a first course in art history, logic, psychology, or cultural history should be postponed until college, for the more intelligent students.

THE EDUCATIONAL FUNCTIONS OF AN
ART MUSEUM*

How much educational work, and of what kinds, should an art museum undertake? What relative emphasis should be placed upon such work, and how should it be related to the museum's other functions? In the last few years the museum has come to take its place as an active teaching agency along with schools, colleges, and art academies, yet the general question of its proper relation to them has never been adequately thought out.

There is no tradition to provide an answer, for the work in its present form is a new and unprecedented development. It has come about, not as a result of much conscious, long-distance planning, or from any theory that the museum ought to do certain things, but step by step, in response to particular demands of the public. This itself is some indication that the services rendered meet genuine needs; and the lack of plan has on the whole been fortunate, for set preconceptions have a way of cramping progress.

Lacking any collective policy, museums have come to differ widely in the extent to which they have undertaken educational work. Some have developed it into large proportions; some have left it in a rudimentary stage or omitted it entirely. Wherever the development does occur, it tends to begin with certain typical services, and then to ramify along divergent paths. The first step may be gallery guidance; this leads to the advance announcement of gallery talks on particular exhibits. Clubs and groups of friends request talks, then series of talks, then systematic courses on some particular art or historical period. New exhibitions bring throngs to the museum and call for repeated explanatory talks. More formal lectures on art, by visiting authorities, are presented in the museum auditorium; these lead to an annual series, which someone must plan and manage.

Meanwhile, teachers are bringing children to observe examples of

* Published in *The Bulletin of The Cleveland Museum of Art*, XX.9 (November, 1933), pp. 141-146.

some art or past civilization about which they have been studying. As more come, their visits must be scheduled in advance; and this itself can become a task of considerable magnitude. Many teachers feel the need of assistance in explaining museum exhibits and ask that museum instructors be assigned to meet their classes. Some alert teachers call for courses on the use of museum materials and on art history and appreciation in general. Children come to sketch in the museum; a special class is started for members' children; an empty room is used as a studio for painting and modeling; talented children from the schools are admitted, then other young and eager applicants, until some hundreds may be coming each Saturday. Qualified special teachers are engaged as part-time assistants. Marionette shows, motion pictures, and illustrated talks are given by and for the children. Classes in music and folk dancing may be added as special privileges of membership. Parents and other adults may wish to use their hands in amateur drawing or in craftwork; advanced students may call for professional technical instruction.

Outside demands may call forth an extension of services to still wider circles in the community. Speakers on art at club meetings, school assemblies, parent-teachers associations are called for; a local radio station may wish a series of fifteen-minute art talks; a local newspaper may print each week the picture which is to be discussed over the radio; television is a promising, new means of mass education in art. The schools clamor for visual materials to be brought to the classroom. Lantern slides, photographs, color prints, small plaster casts are acquired and lent, then small works of foreign handicraft, and ancient artifacts not quite important enough for the main galleries, yet significant for historical study. Works of local artists are presented to the museum, to be circulated among schools and libraries. Distributing, arranging, and caring for these exhibits, and scheduling them in advance, come to demand the whole time of one or more persons. Permanent branch museums in distant parts of the city are discussed.

Thus, under favorable conditions, museum educational work can develop in a few years into a surprisingly elaborate mechanism. On the whole, the cultural value of these functions is so obvious that there has been little disposition to question them. Yet occasional misgivings have been expressed, especially by foreign visitors with quite different conceptions of what a museum should be.

For example, it has been said, "Why do any teaching in a museum at all? Let the works of art speak for themselves. Don't interfere with people's enjoyment of art by asking them to listen to any lectures." But no one urges the mature visitor who would rather look and enjoy by himself to be educated against his will. As a matter of fact, large numbers of people find that art does not always speak for itself, fully and distinctly. Especially with the recent tendency of museums to acquire examples of exotic, primitive, and modernistic art, there has developed a persistent demand for some clue to their understanding and appraisal. Advanced students, moreover, wish to penetrate as deeply as possible into the technique, the aesthetic form, the cultural background of what they see, and not merely to enjoy it in a casual and superficial way. It is in answer to such legitimate demands that museum teaching develops. School children's visits are in a sense involuntary, like all the rest of their studies. But anyone who watches their behavior and expression during museum visits will realize that most of them are having a very good time, and want to know more about the strange and fascinating things they see there. Of course much depends on what is said. Dull facts and sentimental praise can kill their interest and are worse than no talk at all; but the capable instructor can heighten their enjoyment by pointing out interesting details and qualities, and by giving only the right amount and kind of information as a background.

Does museum work make the artist a mere imitator of the past? Will children, in particular, be more creative if kept away from the museum? There again, the answer depends on the kind of instruction. Museum objects can be used, not in excess and for imitation, but for occasional suggestion and stimulus to free imaginative construction. The artist can gain an understanding of how past ages and artists expressed themselves in appropriate forms, and thus of the fundamental meanings of art; but he does not need to copy those symbols literally in expressing modern life or his own personality.

Are American museums developing educational work at the expense of scholarship? This charge, which has been made abroad, is meant to imply that advanced research and writing on the part of curators, in art history and archaeology, have been neglected in favor of popular mass education in simple art appreciation. It may well be that in all subjects this country has tended to overemphasize mass education at the expense of advanced scholarship. Certainly popular lectures and children's classes have been much to the fore in museum educational work, and doubtless undue satisfaction is often felt at large audiences for their own sake. Advanced research is usually regarded as a function, not of the museum educational department, but of the curators in charge of the collections; small advanced courses are regarded as the task of university graduate schools. There seems to be no inherent reason, however, why such lines should be drawn, or why any of these functions should interfere or compete with the rest. It may be necessary in some places to protect museum curators against too persistent demands for popular lectures, and to insure them time for study. It may be necessary to urge museum trustees and supporters not to judge the success of educational work too exclusively in terms of statistics on the number of persons taught, and to approve the spending of time and money on advanced work that reaches a very small public. If these cautions are observed, the development of museum educational work should go hand in hand, and not in competition, with scholarship. In Cleveland, no sharp lines are drawn between museum departments, or between museum and university. Curators from various departments give occasional public talks, but not enough to interfere with their other work. Certain courses, given by the educational staff and attended by museum members, are open for credit to university students; these and other advanced courses are maintained by the museum in spite of their small attendance. Researches and scholarly writing are encouraged in the case of staff members who wish to undertake them.

It has also been suggested that an undue emphasis on education may tend to lower the quality of works of art acquired, in that funds will be diverted from purchases to education; and also in that mediocre objects will be purchased to fill in historical series and thus provide materials for teaching. As to the first, it may seem that every dollar spent for education is one less available for purchases; but the appearance is misleading. Money comes to museums for educational purposes through gifts and grants, fees and paid memberships, which would otherwise not come at all; indeed, gifts of art works and money for purchases are not infrequently stimulated by the knowledge that a large public will learn to appreciate them. On the other point, it is the duty of the museum administration to resist any pressure toward lowering of standards. To build up an extensive collection at the cost of quality would be no real service to education. For study, inexpensive casts and color prints can now be secured in great variety and much-improved quality.

Lastly, it may be asked whether the museum is not stepping out of its proper field into that of the school or college when it becomes an educational institution. Should it not emulate the public library, and be content to provide material for outside teachers to use? Is not its function to collect, exhibit, and preserve works of art, and should it not leave teaching to the schools? Certainly, there can be no doubt that the former is and should be its primary function. But conditions may justify its carrying on education as a secondary function, just as the school or college often buys and exhibits illustrative materials, or even starts a small museum of its own. Rigid specialization is not always the best way for an institution to be socially useful.

For each museum, the extent and character of the educational work it should carry on will be determined by the whole educational structure of its community. If other institutions are at hand, willing and able to carry on a particular branch of art education as well as the museum could, there may be no reason for the museum itself to attempt it. For example, in Cleveland the Art Museum makes no attempt to conduct a school for the training of professional artists, although several museums elsewhere do so. This is due to no objection in principle, but simply to the fact that such an academy already exists nearby. In certain other cities, the proximity of a well-developed institute for popular lectures and courses on art releases the museum from this duty. The nature of art instruction in the local schools and colleges must also be considered, with the aim of avoiding unnecessary duplication. At the same time, there may be worse things than apparent duplication of services within a fairly large community. Competition instead of monopoly is sometimes wholesome; and two ways of teaching the same subject may lead to very different results.

As a center of art instruction, the museum has certain definite advantages over all outside institutions. First and foremost is the fact that art can there be taught in fairly close contact with the indispensable materials for teaching it properly. Teaching it without original works of art, out of textbooks, or even with lantern slides and photographs, is a poor substitute. Assuredly, free imagination and the study of nature are other essential ingredients; but the works of art should also be close at hand, even in creative work, for consultation when needed. Another advantage is the power to co-ordinate work for all age levels.

But should the museum employ its own teachers and conduct its own classes, or merely open its doors to teachers and classes from outside? Either or both may be the wise course, according to local conditions. At Cleveland the situation is flexible and diversified. Outside teachers and classes come freely, and in large numbers. Some teachers, paid by the public school system, are permanently assigned to museum service, where they meet and teach classes, and whence they take art materials for demonstration in the schools. Some teachers, employed by the museum, have their salaries paid in part through appropriations by outside schools, colleges and clubs, for special instruction given. Some are paid entirely out of the museum's operating fund, for instruction to members, their children, and the general public. Such flexibility of arrangement permits great freedom of adjustment to varied and changing local needs. A nucleus of permanent educational personnel, employed and supervised by the museum administration, is, however, essential for the sake of directing and co-ordinating all the manifold activities, including teaching, scheduling, arranging study materials, and advising the outside teacher how to use the museum to best advantage.

The future may bring still further development of the museum as an active teaching agency, or a tendency for other institutions to take over more actively the work of teaching in museums, or such close co-operation between the museum and other agencies that all present lines of demarcation will be obscured. Meanwhile, the museum is actually doing valuable pioneer work along lines which would formerly have been considered out of its field. In many communities, this would have remained undone if the museum had not been at hand, ready and adaptable to the taking on of new functions.

◈ XXI ◈

AIMS AND METHODS IN
ART MUSEUM EDUCATION*

1. The museum as an educational institution

The main purpose of educational work in an art museum is to help make the museum function as actively and beneficially as possible in the cultural life of the community. This means that the museum is not to be a mere treasure house of works of art which remain inert within its walls and cases, seen only by the privileged few; it is to be an active agency for the use and enjoyment of the whole public. It is to welcome and attract the public by important exhibits, well lighted and displayed, and by explanations which add to their meaning and interest. Instead of waiting idly for the public to discover what is there, it is to reach out into the community, inviting and facilitating visits by young and old—especially by the young, who are especially sensitive to what it offers, and who may never come unless someone leads the way. Again, to meet a need beyond its walls, it will send out examples and reproductions of its own and other treasures to be seen in distant parts of the community, with capable teachers to explain their importance.

The essence of this modern conception of an art museum was well set forth in 1939 by Frederick E. Keppel, in his report as President of the Carnegie Corporation. "The shift in emphasis," he said, "from the custodial function of the American museum to its opportunities for educational and other services is now nearly everywhere an accomplished fact." This new emphasis has been more strongly developed in the United States than in any other country.

By private gift and bequest, by foundation grant, and in some cities by government support, American art museums have become the recipients of a vast amount of wealth. Their trustees and staffs feel an obligation to justify this confidence on the part of the public through active community service.

* Published in its original form in the booklet, *Educational Work at The Cleveland Museum of Art,* Cleveland, Ohio, 1952, pp. 7-34.

The art museum as an institution is the custodian of a large and valuable part of the cultural heritage of the American people and of the world. It is charged with selecting, preserving, and exhibiting works of past and contemporary visual arts, which have been chosen as worthy examples of the creative ability of different periods and peoples including our own. The educational department of an art museum has the task of helping to present and interpret this heritage to the people of its own community and others. It is a dynamic agency in the cultural and recreational life of the city.

It can also make a contribution to the creative efforts of artists and craftsmen. By placing at their disposal examples of different styles of art in every medium and technique, it provides a basis for new, original developments. It inspires them with great examples, conveys to them the accumulated, tested skills of past generations of artists, and suggests new possible experiments. It provides a place for them to show and sell their newest products, the best of which may be purchased by the museum for permanent display.

To the layman, the museum is a place for leisure activities which are not only pleasant at the time but permanently valuable. In learning to perceive a great variety of complex forms and subtle qualities of line, shape, and color, he acquires visual powers which carry over into daily life. They intensify his awareness and enjoyment, not only of art itself, but of nature and the life around him. Through developing keener powers of observation, and more discrimination of artistic values, he tends to become more interested in improving the appearance of things around him. Whether professional or amateur, everyone has opportunities for some kind of artistic expression. This may be in beautifying one's clothing and personal appearance, one's home and garden, one's office and factory, or one's neighborhood and community.

The museum's educational department tries to foster and assist these latent artistic interests in boys and girls, men and women of all ages. Through special exhibits and courses, it acquaints the visitor with contemporary trends and possibilities in city planning, interior design, and furnishing. Art in the modern sense is not limited to pictures and statues, but includes every aspect of life in so far as it can affect us aesthetically.

A study of the visual arts contributes greatly to the general education of the student. They are one of our principal means of understanding the civilizations of the past and the cultural trends of our own day. It is well known that art expresses its age as well as the personality of the individual artist. But it is not an easy task to interpret the different attitudes, beliefs, and interests which are thus expressed—those, for example, which distinguish the Greek or Chinese culture from our own.

In saying that the department of education tries to make the museum function as actively as possible we refer primarily, of course, to the works of art in its main galleries. We refer also to its supplementary resources, which are of several kinds. They include other works of art, both originals and reproductions, in the lending or circulating collection. They include the museum library with its books and periodicals on art, its color prints, photographs, and clippings from periodicals which provide information and materials for research and study. They usually include collections of lantern slides and sometimes of films and phonograph records. Among the supplementary resources should also be listed the auditorium with its equipment, including a stage, lantern slide and film projectors, phonographs, sound amplifiers, and spotlights which can be used for dance or other programs. In addition, there are classrooms, studios, and a small supply of materials and equipment for studio work in arts and crafts. Among its most valuable resources must be listed the knowledge and expert judgment of the museum staff; of its various curators, librarians, and others. Most of these have little or no time for direct teaching, but their knowledge and judgment can be communicated first to the museum teachers and through them to the public. Supplementing this permanent staff are visiting lecturers who come to speak in the auditorium and incidentally to advise the staff in their own fields.

2. Its variety of services

Upon all these resources are focused a diversified set of community needs and interests. To meet them, the museum radiates a diversified range of services to various sections of the public. These services never equal the potential demands of the community, for they are always limited by the size and equipment of the staff, by its classroom space and its funds for publication and transportation.

The community thus served is highly diversified as to the kinds of individual and group which it contains. There is need to adapt methods and emphases in various ways. This leads to a diversification in personnel as well as in activities.

For example, the community contains many different age levels. Within the school system, the department of education must meet the needs of students from the lowest grades of elementary school through graduate school of the university. In addition, it must meet the needs of the adult public which is no longer in school, but is still eager to continue its informal education. The community is diversified according to educational levels, both as to general education and as to special training in the arts. The educational program must be adapted to the needs and abilities of the general public, and also to those of the specialized student and advanced connoisseur. Finally, the community is diversified according to special interest and need. Some of the students who come for classes or other guidance are students of art who intend to become professional artists or craftsmen. These are subdivided into various arts, some being interested in painting, others in ceramics, others in textiles, and so on. Most of the classes from schools and colleges are not primarily interested in art as a career or subject of major interest; they are pursuing a liberal education, and they wish to study the visual arts as illustrative material for understanding some period of history. Some of them are primarily interested in social studies, such as anthropology or sociology; some are interested in languages, such as French or Latin; some are interested in the theater; some wish to write stories or essays in a course on English literature. All these types of person can find source material within the art museum for better understanding of their subjects, and perhaps for original work along each line. The more alert teachers in the schools are aware of this; they call upon the museum's educational staff for materials and guidance in many ways, and for adapting the study of works of art in the galleries to these various approaches.

This variety of interests and services requires some diversification in personnel. To some extent, one has to have different teachers for different age levels. Some are more fitted to talk to young children; others to adults or high school students. In addition, one needs teachers specially qualified in various arts and periods of history. The range of world art contained in a great museum is so vast that it is impossible for any one teacher to know all of it thoroughly. The educational department encourages its teachers to specialize to some extent—some on oriental or medieval art, some on textiles or paint-ing; some on contemporary art. At the same time, each teacher in the department may be called upon for a general tour of the museum, and for an elementary interpretation of works in all the galleries. Every member of the staff must therefore familiarize himself in a general, basic way with the whole field of art as represented in the museum.

There is considerable diversification in regard to methods of teach-ing and psychological approach. A mode of presentation which would be adequate for a college student of art history would be quite un-suitable for a class of young children or for a group of casual museum visitors. In case of the youngest visitors, the teacher has to be careful not to strain their span of attention by too long or prosaic a talk, or by staying too long before one object. She must preserve something of the play spirit if possible, and select aspects of the works of art which would interest the youngest children. She must bring out the story interest of pictures and armor. She must not use big words or abstract ideas which would be incomprehensible. The same teacher may talk much more abstractly, technically, and at length to a group of advanced university students. She may present a systematic course on the history of some period of art, on techniques, or aesthetic the-ory. She must find out the animating interest and purpose of each group—for example, one group will be interested in collecting prints or porcelain, oriental or European; another group will be interested in garden art, and in its relation to the whole pattern of oriental culture.

A potential field of activity for the museum and its staff is the relation to industries of the community. In some cities, the art mu-seum is called upon for help in design problems; also for help in providing recreational and cultural opportunities for personnel, espe-cially for those who are newcomers to the city. Systematic relations along these lines with industries provide a possible line of future service.

Some features of museum work in Cleveland are much admired and envied in other cities. First is the arrangement whereby the Cleveland Public Schools provide three teachers for full-time employ-ment in the art museum or in the schools to promote the use of museum materials. The museum educational department does not try to duplicate the work of school art teachers, but to aid and supplement it. It tries to avoid doing things which are and can be better done in the schools. In the short time which children have for a visit to the museum, either on Saturday morning or during the week, one cannot undertake a long, systematic course or a complex project requiring many days for completion. What, then, can one do here which the schools cannot do so well and for which the museum is specially fitted?

3. Distinctive tasks and problems for the museum educator

First of all, of course, is to show and explain its works of art, which the schools do not hope to duplicate. During the weekday visits of the school classes, museum teachers are urged to spend every possible moment in helping the children to look at works of art. This means that teachers are not to spend precious moments of the museum hour delivering long lectures which could be given equally well in the classroom; lectures in which the student's attention is fixed upon the teacher's face and not upon the works of art in the gallery. The primary function of the museum teacher or guide is to *point out;* to call the visitor's attention—either verbally or by actual gesture—to selected works of art which are most relevant to the interests and abilities of the student, and to a few selected features or qualities in these works of art which the student might not otherwise notice. Many museum visitors, especially young children who have never been in the galleries before, are confused and bewildered by the new surroundings and the tremendous number and variety of things which clamor for their attention. In the old way of museum teaching, long files of bewildered children were led quickly through one huge gallery after another, listening only vaguely to a continuous flow of erudite facts from the teacher. They would come out with only a confused memory of what they had seen, and perhaps with a lasting distaste for art and museums. The newer approach is to be selective, not to fatigue or confuse the student—especially the child—with too many unrelated stimuli, and to try above all to help him have a pleasant, satisfying, profitable experience of art, even though of limited scope, which will tempt him to come back for others later.

We are not so much concerned with persuading him to like everything equally well. By showing him how many great styles of art the human race has produced, each with its own distinctive values, we hope to enlarge his range of enjoyment. But taste and preference are largely personal and individual matters, depending on the whole background and character of the individual. A liking for unfamiliar kinds of art is not to be formed all at once; it often requires long study, and for every individual there are some kinds of art which he will not and cannot ever like as much as he likes others. The primary aim, then, in museum gallery teaching, is to help the visitor to *see;* to perceive works of art visually; to develop powers of perceiving the details and subtle qualities in a complex form and how they are organized into a unified work of art. The aim is also to give, in the course of a gallery talk, the indispensable minimum of historical information about the period, the artist, the subject, the use and function of the object, where it was made, and other facts which help in understanding the meaning of the work of art today. But the more of this supplementary information which can be conveyed outside the museum the better, if the time available in it is short. Hence teachers in schools and colleges are encouraged to give preliminary lessons before the visit, so that as much of the time as possible may be spent in undistracted observing. Much attention is paid, in museum classes, to learning to recognize the distinctive styles of various nationalities, periods, and artists.

In the Saturday morning classes also, where studio work in painting, drawing, and modeling is done, the attempt is made to think out what an art museum can do which cannot be done as well in the school, the home, or elsewhere. The answer is not to emphasize "free expression" or creative work based on completely free imagination and experiment. That approach has its merits, although it is sometimes overdone. It is especially valuable for young children, but has to be supplemented for older students by some study of techniques and of the history of the art concerned. In any case, this is not a method for which a museum is peculiarly suited. On the contrary, it can perhaps be practiced better away from a museum than in one, where works of art are everywhere attracting the student's attention. The museum's peculiar opportunity lies in utilizing the works of art—both originals and reproductions—which are at hand within its walls. It lies in helping students to absorb and grow into this phase of their cultural heritage, and to use it constructively.

Academic art teachers used to require too much exact copying of works of art. There is still much value in copying masterpieces, and the most original artists of all periods have done some copying, just as music students learn to play Bach and Beethoven. There has been an undue prejudice against it on the part of extreme "progressives" in education. However, overemphasis on copying may make the student imitative and passive. The problem is to help him study past works of art and use them in a creative, original way. The Saturday classes for children try to achieve a happy medium and a balance between the "free expression" and the old-fashioned "academic" methods. Children are aided and encouraged to spend a part of their time in visiting the galleries, in looking at art, and in making mental notes or actual sketches of what they see there. On returning to their studios, or while in the gallery itself, they are then encouraged to use what they have seen as material and inspiration for an original composition. They are helped to transform what they have seen in some particular way which will involve independent thinking and imagining on their part. The aim is to develop visual, mental and constructive abilities which will be of value later on, in any walk of life.

Another problem in museum education arises from the fact that the same student in the community will come back year after year to see the same works of art, in addition to some new ones. The same child may attend museum Saturday classes for many consecutive seasons. How can his interest be maintained, so that he will want to come back for further study, and so that he will keep on learning to understand and appreciate the same masterpieces more deeply, on more mature levels? This problem is attacked, with varying degrees of success, in both the studio classes and the gallery talks. The teacher is not obliged to say to every class and every student everything which could possibly be said about a particular work of art. About any great painting or statue, a learned professor could talk for hours, pointing out more and more details of its formal organization, more and more of its traits of style, telling more facts about its historical background, its religious, political, and sociological significance. This would not only be unnecessary in the case of young children, but injurious to their natural growth in understanding and appreciation. The museum teacher must have a large amount of this material in his own mind as background, then select whatever seems most relevant for a particular lesson, in relation to the students addressed, the time available, and the purpose of the visit.

In the children's Saturday classes, it is much more common for the same child to come back year after year. Therefore more continuity in instruction can be undertaken. In these classes, an effort is made to grade the instruction in relation to age level. Here a child can be given, not only a growing appreciation of art, but growing ability to handle materials and techniques. Psychological studies of the interests and abilities of children on different age levels have helped us to adapt the method and content of the work in each grade to the children there, so that the same child may come back repeatedly to learn something new about art and the production of art.

Experience has shown that it is not wise to attempt too much within the short period of time—two hours or less—available for actual studio work on a Saturday morning. Ambitious projects requiring many hours of systematic work, such as the working out of a stage play with scenery, costume, and backgrounds, in addition to text and acting, are better suited to schools where much more time is available. They have had to be regretfully put aside in the museum classes, so that children will not be confused and disappointed by beginning projects which they have no time to finish carefully and satisfactorily. It is not a good thing to form habits of hasty, careless work, of dropping too many things unfinished and going on to new ones.

One of the most widely appreciated educational services of the museum is that of circulating exhibits—otherwise called the "lending collection." There has been a great demand for "bringing the museum to the school." This is partly due to the difficulty experienced in all school systems in detaching classes for visits to the museum, especially when the school is at considerable distance from the museum and when transportation is difficult. Some school systems have their own buses and can easily arrange for trips; others have none or so few that hardly any classes can make a trip during the year. In any case, the growing demand for illustrative material from art and other audio-visual sources is far greater than can be met by visits to the museum. Teachers want exhibits and illustrative materials which they can use and talk about in their own classrooms, or at least somewhere in the school. In some schools graduating classes, alumni, and parent-teacher associations have formed the praiseworthy custom of presenting framed pictures and other works of art to the schools. These do a great deal of good in brightening up dark corridors and giving something attractive for the eye to rest upon. But again, they fall far short of meeting the needs of schools for examples of art.

This desire is part of a larger need for examples of fine art to be seen in one's own neighborhood. It is felt more strongly by cultural leaders in the districts more remote from the museum. A similar need has been answered in some cities by the establishment of branch museums; but these have not always justified the trouble and expense involved. Small circulating exhibits have been placed in many branch libraries and other local institutions which can easily assume responsibility for them. If transportation (public and private) improves, adults from all parts of the community will find it easier to visit the main museum. It is the children and the schools that are most in need of having something brought to them. Although our circulating exhibit service operates for adults as well as children, limitations of staff and materials have caused it to be focused largely on the schools.

In some cities, the school system has its own lending agency for audio-visual materials. Its materials deal with many subjects besides art, such as biology and social studies. The schools now own a good many lantern slides, films, and filmstrips on art as well.

A serious obstacle to the success of circulating exhibits is the lack of adequate exhibition space and equipment, such as locked glass cases in the schools and other institutions themselves. All too often a building is completely designed by architects and school officials with no thought for the possible need of exhibition facilities. Consequently, when teachers and museum staff try to arrange for exhibits, they find no suitable accommodations in the building. The ideal place for exhibits in the schools is usually in some part of a large entrance hall near the front entrance, or in a large corridor, or perhaps in a library or a lunchroom. Each of these has advantages and disadvantages. If the corridor is narrow, the crowd of students going through between classes makes it impossible to stand and look at wall displays. Often the entrance hall is too small for large cases or exhibits. Sometimes only a small glass case is provided, and that is poorly lighted, poorly constructed for vision, and perhaps already filled with athletic trophies and other objects which cannot be moved to make way for an art exhibit. It is highly desirable that architects and school officials should plan for a small gallery or other exhibit area in each new school. If possible they should consult with museum officials as well as art teachers on the prospective arrangements. In some cases, after the building is made, it has been found possible to clear an area for art exhibits.

There is no doubt that this phase of museum work has a tremendous future and valuable social possibilities. It is not to be regarded as a substitute for visits to the museum itself, but as a supplement to them. In many cases it is a means of arousing an art interest in children, so that they will later on come to the museum of their own accord. Of course, it will never be possible to lend fragile objects of great value to the schools themselves for constant, daily usage. The functions of the museum galleries and of the circulating exhibit division remain entirely distinct though overlapping. But the possible scope of circulating exhibit service to schools is growing rapidly, partly because of improved methods for reproducing works of art, as in color prints and plaster casts.

The educational department is not the only part of the museum which lends material to outside institutions. The library also carries on an active service in lending lantern slides and color prints. For the large color prints, the practice is to require the borrowing institution to possess a picture frame which can be opened on the back so as to allow different pictures to be inserted. Pictures of this sort, borrowed from the museum library, are often combined with exhibits of solid objects supplied by the educational department.

A division of educational circulating exhibits provides a good way of using many original works of art for which there is otherwise no place in the museum. With limited space at his disposal, the director of an art museum must set high standards of quality for anything that he buys or accepts as part of the first series material. He is constantly forced to decline gifts of works of art, which people would like to give to the museum for the public to enjoy. He may consider the piece a little below first series quality, or may already possess many examples of this particular type of art and not have room for another. If the donor will give the object for educational use, it may do a great deal of good.

The museum should not, of course, accept for such use any work of definitely low quality. It is all too easy to convey low standards of artistic appreciation through exhibiting mediocre objects under the auspices of the museum. However, an object can be of second quality in a sense that it is less rare and precious, less costly on the art market, than something else; at the same time it can be aesthetically worthy and significant for classroom study. This is especially true in the case of reproductions of great works of art; it is also true of much original peasant and folk art. These may be of secondary value in the sense that they are not unique, but are rather continuations of a long tradition within their homeland. Nevertheless, they often show fine workmanship and perpetuate excellent designs. It is quite proper to secure objects of this sort for an educational collection and to bring them to the attention of students.

It would be well for students to handle and get the feel of a textile or a piece of sculpture. Too often they have to look at works of art only in glass cases, or under the eye of some guard, or in photographs. If they can handle a piece of pottery, woodcarving, or silk velvet, they can get a much more intimate idea of what it is and how it is made. This is especially valuable for the blind. Unfortunately, it is seldom possible under present conditions.

What specific educational activities should be undertaken by an art museum, and how far these should be developed, are not questions which can be answered once and for all by some blanket formula. The right solution will depend on many contributing factors, such as (a) the resources of the museum; (b) the interests and civic ideals of its trustees and staff; (c) the educational needs of the community, both conscious and undeveloped; (d) what other near-by institutions are doing to meet these needs, or can and wish to do to meet them properly. These factors are different in every city.

Art museums and their educational work are still so new in this country that precedents are lacking for a definite policy on their proper scope and functions. In any case, the American approach to the problem is based, not so much on precedent, as on practical results. We are still in the pioneer stage of trying to find by experiment what the museum can most effectively do as an educational and cultural agency, and what it can best leave to others.

In a dynamic, growing society like the United States today, no alert institution is satisfied to go on performing a narrow round of traditional duties in a stereotyped, unimaginative way. If its leaders see an important job to be done which no one else is doing, a job which is in their field and for which they are fitted, they feel an impulse to take it on. If they lack sufficient means or staff, they sometimes apply for these and receive them from foundations or individuals; at least after showing by first results that more support is justified. Sometimes the means come first, through the initiative of the donor.

An institution can go too far in thus extending and diversifying its work. It can do so many things that it does nothing very well, and neglects its basic responsibilities. In a city where the spirit of co-operation is active, each institution can go too far in co-operating with others. It can multiply joint boards and committees, and its staff can spend so much time on these as to neglect its work at home. A city institution can be drawn into too much national and international activity, trying to solve the world's problems, and thinning out its work at home to the vanishing point.

4. The museum as a center for many arts

The arts have suffered from too much specialization in the past; too much separation into exclusive compartments in education and in life. In earlier times they were practiced and enjoyed more closely together. There are still great values in bringing them together at times. An art museum, with its spacious building and equipment, is well suited to becoming a community center for all or many arts.

Traditionally, a museum of "fine arts" was limited to the static visual arts of painting and sculpture, with here and there a vase or textile. The Cleveland Museum of Art was, early in its history, presented with a pipe organ, and a music department was established. This department has undertaken year after year programs of fine concerts—most of them free to the public—of a sort which were seldom given elsewhere in the city. The hall is adaptable for concerts of an unusual sort, before a small, discriminating audience; for example, those emphasizing early, unfamiliar music or contemporary musical experiments.

In recent years, the museum educational department has been presented with phonographs, records, and sound-film equipment for its auditorium, with the result that it has been able to include music in its programs for children and adults. In the children's studio classes, it is found that phonograph records often stimulate and inspire creative work in drawing and painting. So do stories and poems, especially for younger children.

By presenting to a class of students the various arts of a people or period, one can convey a more balanced and thorough idea of its culture. Classes often compare the music, literature, folklore, painting, and sculpture of a country such as India or China, which is well represented in the museum's gallery. A dance program in native costume may further develop the comparison. This will be open to the public in the auditorium. On another night a color film with sound, made by travelers in India or China, will show religious festivals and dances against a background of temple architecture and sculpture. Thus students learn how a great oriental civilization expressed itself in music and the dance, in song and legend, as well as in the static visual arts.

Again, while branching out to some extent into these collateral fields, one must keep in mind that this is primarily a museum of visual arts, and that these should hold the main focus of attention. To keep its work in proper balance, and directed upon the museum collections, the educational staff devotes many hours of work each week to staff meetings and discussions of which the public does not learn directly. Week after week, the teachers meet to hear talks on each gallery, by specialists in each field, so that they may be properly briefed on the important qualities to emphasize in their talks to students and the public. They also discuss teaching methods and compare results.

5. *Contemporary arts and problems of evaluation*

Many special exhibits, and some of the purchases of the museum for its permanent collection, include works by contemporary artists whose merits are much disputed. They are likely to baffle and displease some if not many of the public. What is the policy of the educational staff in these matters? First of all, the staff does not feel itself under obligation to convince the public that all works shown in the museum are beautiful, great, or equally important. It does not feel that it has to "sell" all these experimental types of art to the public, or persuade visitors to like them. On the other hand, it does feel an obligation to help the open-minded student or other visitor to understand, if possible, what the artist is trying to do, how this differs from the aims of other artists, and how it fits into the current trend and situation in the world of art. Teachers can explain and interpret controversial art, if they wish, without evaluating it as good or bad, beautiful or ugly. If, on the other hand, they feel strongly about some work of art or artist, favorably or unfavorably, they are free to express their own opinions as such. Frank criticism of a living, local artist is of course rather hard when he or his wife may be looking over one's shoulder. There is no attempt to regiment the individual teachers or to lay down an official line as to what they must approve and disapprove. A teacher can, if she wishes, suggest possible standards for evaluation and point out what values are claimed for a certain work of art by its admirers; then leave it to the audience to decide for itself. Which course is taken will depend to some extent on the nature of the group at the time. Some students are more interested in understanding trends and techniques of art than they are in hearing whether the teacher likes it or not; others want to get a judgment of value as soon as possible.

A wise policy in regard to controversial art is to consider the museum as somewhat like a public forum for political discussion. The museum is not under obligation to endorse everything shown in its galleries, or everything which is said by visiting lecturers. On the other hand, it feels an obligation to acquaint the public with new types of art which are receiving attention elsewhere and which are regarded as important by leading critics, whether we like them ourselves or not. In this way, it can keep the public up to date on trends and experiments, provide the materials for a judgment of value, and help both children and adults to develop their own standards, so as to make their taste in art informed and discriminating without necessarily being the same as that of their neighbors.

As to objects which are purchased by the museum for its permanent collection, the situation is somewhat but not entirely different. Purchase of an object, or even its acceptance as a gift, does imply a belief on the part of museum curators that the object is somewhat important; if not beautiful by every standard, it is at least significant and worth looking at as a work of art. Again, it is up to the museum instructor to find out from the curator concerned why this work of art is considered important, and why it is worth spending money on; why it is worth some effort on the part of the public to understand and appreciate it. The teacher can pass this opinion along to the public, with details to support it. At the same time, the teacher is free to express a divergent opinion if he wishes to.

One of the most interesting aspects of art, especially of contemporary art and of unfamiliar past and primitive styles of art, is the controversy it arouses. If art were completely cut and dried, with no unsettled problems or differences of opinion, it would be much less stimulating. Within limits, controversy is the life of art, and is stimulating alike to keen criticism, interested study, and active creative effort. The museum educational staff does not try to rule out or discourage controversy by pretending to know all the answers; to know exactly what one ought to like and dislike. It undertakes rather to persuade people not to form too hasty, premature, snap judgments about art, but to look carefully, to let the work of art have time to speak for itself and say what it wants to say. The teacher will encourage careful reflection and consideration of the pros and cons in any serious controversy, and then will encourage the student to make up his own mind.

In this regard the museum teacher's job is somewhat different in presenting controversial modern art from what it is in presenting more accepted, familiar traditions. In regard to Renaissance painting and Greek sculpture, there is more agreement among critics and artists as to what is great and why. Here the teacher has a somewhat simpler and more definite task: to convey the reasoned judgment of the art world as to what values may be sought and obtained in the study of each style and period of art. Even here, the world of art is never static. Opinions change, even about the classics; forgotten artists and little-known periods of art are revived and praised while some of the great reputations sink in critical esteem. Standards of value change as people seek new qualities to admire or disparage in the works of old masters. The present trend is toward emphasizing form and design in the evaluation of art, rather than the subject matter represented and its story interest or historical associations. Thus it is always necessary for the museum teacher to keep up with the times by reading books and articles on history, criticism, and educational method, and to pass on the results of his continuing study to the community.

6. Quantity and quality

To what extent should the emphasis be laid on large statistics and quantity of teaching, especially on the popular level? To what extent on high quality and a more advanced level of scholarship? A good solution is to do some of both—to preserve a reasonable balance between the popular and the advanced, between elementary and adult education, and to do all as well as possible. In the early days, most of the museum's educational work was for children and for adults without special training in art.

In the last few years, without neglecting these basic parts of the work, museums have tried to do a little more on the level of advanced scholarship, research, and publication. This increases the sum of human knowledge and appreciation. It aids and guides teachters, critics, school officials, and other cultural leaders.

Some of the free public lectures each year are given to small audiences on scholarly or technical subjects; others fill every seat in the auditorium with talks and entertainments of popular appeal. The annual statistics of attendance could easily be multiplied by giving only popular talks and entertainments; still more so, by emphasizing mass media such as radio and television, which count their hearers by the hundred thousands. But we should then be neglecting something which is at least as important: the education of cultural leaders in a democracy.

Americans have been charged with evaluating everything, including education, too largely in terms of number, size, and quantity. Certainly an art museum is a suitable place to prove that this is not always true. In the presence of enduring masterpieces, carefully wrought with an eye to the highest possible quality, there is a need for study and teaching on an equally high level. A technical lecture or seminar conducted by an outstanding authority, though attended by only a handful of advanced students, may be far more important in the long run than an event which draws large crowds.

It was mentioned above that the educational staff must be somewhat diversified, with different teachers especially fitted for work with children, advanced students, and the general adult public. But the permanent staff is not, and does not have to be, diversified as much as the work itself. It consists essentially in a small nucleus of full-time personnel, capable of handling much of the work themselves and of inviting qualified specialists to help on special occasions in providing a varied and flexible program.

This program contains a central core of basic educational services which are more or less the same from year to year, since they aim to present the same great works of art to successive generations of children and to the ever-changing adult population. In addition, there are courses and events which differ each year. Through these, the museum's clientele of members and friends can find something new to hold their interest in auditoriums and classrooms, as they do in the galleries. The fundamentals of art and education are not neglected, but the community is kept in touch, so far as it desires to be, with new developments in art and the understanding of its values.

ᔥᗰᎥ XXII Ꭵᗰᔥ

ART MUSEUM WORK WITH CHILDREN*

Several basic factors determine the amount of pleasure and profit which children will receive from an art collection. What kinds of art does it include, and how suitable are these to children's interests at different age levels? How are these objects exhibited, explained, and used in instruction? What other activities are available in the museum besides the opportunity of gallery observation? These factors will be touched upon briefly in the paragraphs which follow.

In the first place, *what kinds of art does the museum possess?* It goes without saying that children's tastes have been almost wholly ignored in the art museum of the past. It has been assumed that all good art is adult art, and that if children cannot appreciate adult art, they should stay away from the museum. In fact, the old-fashioned museum director was frank to say that he would be much more comfortable if children would stay out of the galleries entirely. A child to him was an unmitigated nuisance, whose presence in a museum could only mean dirt and disorder, noise, grubby fingerprints, and pencil marks. Experience is proving that these dangers can be almost eliminated through giving children a proper sense of responsibility, and a liking for the museum as a place where one comes to have a good time.

Having admitted the children to the museum, we are now beginning to wonder what there is for them to see there. It is still a debatable question to what extent there is or should be such a thing as "children's art." Should they not be shown the same art that adults are shown, with whatever expurgations our conventions demand, and then helped to appreciate as much of it as they can? Is not so-called children's art usually just bad art, consisting of sentimental and tritely pretty magazine illustrations? Certainly with proper methods of instruction, and sometimes, best of all, with no instruction,

* Published in its original form in the *Western Arts Association Bulletin*, XX.4 (September 1, 1936), pp. 89-97.

children can enjoy and appreciate great adult art—not for its more profound and difficult aspects, but for its more simple and easily understandable ones. At first they may enjoy only the bright colors, or a pretty child or animal somewhere in the picture; but with each successive year they may learn to see more deeply into the same picture, grasping ever more fully its complexities of design and cultural significance.

Nevertheless, certain kinds of art are much more easily and completely enjoyed by children than other kinds. They present simple story situations, familiar objects, types of person, animal and fairy-tale creature which the child can understand, and they do so in art forms which are simple, direct, and vivacious. There is also art which touches directly on the interests of upper age levels in childhood and adolescence, such as machinery, exciting adventure, and romance. Such "art for children" may or may not have been expressly so created. It may have been created for adults of an earlier and simpler time. Yet we must not make the mistake of thinking that all primitive art is suitable for children; much of it is far too complex and remote from the mind of the modern child. Certainly art for children does not have to be inferior, or restricted to the sugary diet of children's magazine illustrations. It can be chosen from the whole range of good art, past and present, on a basis not of lowered aesthetic standards but of simplicity in form and congeniality to the interests of youth. It can be chosen not merely from the standpoint of what children like and prefer at first sight, but of what they can learn to like through effort, and of what will help to develop their powers of appreciation. The problem of making a specific selection for children of different ages and temperaments is one that bristles with difficulties—psychological, moral, and educational. Its solution lies a considerable distance in the future, although numerous educators are beginning to grapple with it. In the meantime, there is perhaps no better way to study the question than to present many different kinds of art to children of different ages, under circumstances as favorable as possible, and see what happens. Let us see how much of the adult art in the main museum galleries they can grasp and enjoy, and let us have, somewhere else, a gallery or two entirely for their benefit. Perhaps it is inadvisable to have a distinct "children's museum" in a building apart from the other, for this may seem to imply that the main museum is not at all for them. But at least we can have separate children's rooms in the main building, where specially planned exhibits are shown.

Whatever kinds we exhibit, we shall have to pay more consideration in future to the problem of *how they can best be exhibited* from the children's standpoint. Here again we have barely made a start. Museum directors and curators in the past have usually had very little of the showman in their makeup. Their attention has been so fixed on the primary tasks of acquiring art works and studying their history that little time has been left for the technique of museum exhibition. Even from the adult standpoint, museum galleries have too often been dark, crowded, and jumbled in arrangement, hence quickly confusing and fatiguing. We are now emerging into a new stage of museum technique, where the art of exhibiting is studied as carefully as it has been for years by department store display experts, whose sales depend on showing objects to their best advantage.

The problem is a many-sided one, involving first of all a sympathetic consideration for the psychology and comfort of museum visitors. It involves proper lighting, to bring out the true color of pictures and textiles, the planes and hollows of sculpture, and the individual quality of every small object. Some things require a spotlight, others a diffused illumination. Cases should not be crowded, even though we have to forego the temptation to display all our treasures at once. Objects should be arranged significantly so as to bring out distinctive shapes and colors, to fit in harmoniously with their neighbors, and perhaps to reveal a historical sequence or principle of art.

If we are just beginning to do these things for the adult visitor, how much farther we have to go before meeting the needs of the youthful one! If he is to see within a case, it must be of the proper height, and this is sometimes hard to arrange without discommoding the adult observer. If crowding, bad arrangement and lighting confuse and tire an adult, how much more quickly will they do so for a child. Children like to handle things, to turn them over and look at them from all sides; and if this cannot be done with precious rarities, then other things should be provided, less precious, but endowed with some aesthetic quality.

Above all, children are depressed and repelled by the atmosphere of chill formality which pervades most museums. So far as possible, children should be able to see, handle, and use art objects under comfortable, informal, and happy conditions. This is very difficult in the main galleries. The situation points again to the desirability of having special rooms for children and inexpensive objects which they can experience at close range, in addition to the main galleries where they must be on best behavior.

We come now to the question of *how museum objects should be presented to children by their guides and teachers*. Here again there is an old way and a new. The old way, and the easiest for a mentally lazy teacher, was a quick general tour of the whole building, in which a docile class was rapidly paraded through a tiring and bewildering series of galleries. Along with this went the heavy informational lecture, replete with names and dates, with abstract principles and dogmatic evaluations. There was little value and much danger in such teaching. It ran the risk of destroying forever the child's delight in art. As a natural reaction, it has sometimes been argued that children should have no formal guidance in a museum whatever, and should merely be turned loose to see whatever they can. Certainly we must agree that every child should be free to wander by himself at times, and to come as often as he wants outside of school hours. But he will miss a great deal in a large museum if he has no help whatever in finding things that might be of special interest, or in paying special attention to important features. He should not be made to see too much in one visit. One or two rooms may well be enough for intensive study on a single trip, and the rest of the time may best be left to free rambling. Straight-ahead informational lecturing should be reduced to a minimum.

In order that a brief museum visit should be devoted as completely as possible to actual selective looking, that visit should in the first place be prepared for and motivated by previous class discussion. Thus interest may be aroused and necessary facts acquired. Sometimes it is worth while to study photographs of the objects in advance, although this runs the risk of giving a misleading first impression. During the visit, considerable planning is required to conduct a tour in a selective and significant way. Comparative studies are very important in a museum, and the objects to be compared may be in widely scattered rooms. To lead a class efficiently from place to place, and help it discern important qualities and relationships amid the profusion of surrounding objects, requires skillful management. The third stage in integrating a museum visit with school work is a follow-up, or discussion on some day a little later, of what was seen at the museum and what was most interesting there. This should lead continuously into new studies, which memories of the visual experience will help to vitalize.

Some classes come to get illustrations for work in social studies, some for specialized studies in art, some for designs to be applied in industrial arts, and so on. For each of these needs, an approach and accessory teaching devices must be differently worked out, and the approach must be varied according to differences in age level.

Contact with works of art should not be limited to passive looking and intellectual discussion, especially for younger children. It should be closely connected with active doing. A little can be done in this direction by letting children make notes and sketches during a visit, and still more by sending them to the museum after school hours to search out independently the materials for some school project. But this is only a start. If the child is to assimilate and apply his visual experiences in any thorough way, both museum and school must actively direct many different kinds of constructive activity in which museum objects are utilized as data, themes, and starting-points.

THE ART MUSEUM AND
THE SECONDARY SCHOOL*

Secondary schools and art museums alike have in the past generation grown rapidly and independently, without much contact or awareness of each other's existence. Each is still changing rapidly, and has its own pressing problems to handle, without bothering to adapt itself to the viewpoint of the other. Only in a few leading centers is the call for mutual adaptation beginning to assert itself. In fact, the number of important art museums in the country is still infinitesimal as compared with the number of high schools. But in those few places, a vast new realm of rich experience for youth is being explored. The new type of museum is eager to be of service to the whole community, and especially to students. When it sees that co-operation with one great branch of the educational system is especially hard—that students and teachers of the high school level seem comparatively hard to work with—it wonders why, and what can be done about it. Leaders in secondary education are also becoming aware that the art museum contains something which ought to be of interest and value to the high school student, and they are asking how this new resource can best be utilized. Superficial obstacles, like the lack of college entrance credit for secondary art, are being removed through conference and experiment in selected high schools. The need for more art is recognized wherever a progressive high school curriculum is undertaken. The time is ripe for a clear understanding of the place of the art museum in these new educational developments.

Since my own position is that of a mediator between an art museum and the neighboring schools, I am forced to look at the situation from both viewpoints. It is brought home to me persistently that each institution possesses serious shortcomings from the stand-

* Published in its original form in *Progressive Education,* XIV.7 (November, 1937), pp. 522–534.

point of the other, which stand in the way of real co-operation. I will try to give a frank summary of the case from each standpoint, with a few suggestions for improvement.

1. Shortcomings of the art museum from the secondary school standpoint

By the "secondary school standpoint," I mean not only the attitude of teachers and of the school as an institution, but—which is far more important—the attitude of the boy or girl of high school age. Why are such students not more eager to come to the museum after school hours, and on Saturdays and Sundays? Why do they not insist more urgently (for their voice is now making itself felt in the running of things) upon trips to the museum as a part of the regular school program?

Let us go right to the heart of the difficulty. There is little in the usual sort of art museum which can make a strong, direct appeal to the student of high school age. It simply does not possess the kinds of art which might attract adolescents. This is not at all to be wondered at if we consider the types of person who have in the past selected the art in our public galleries. Curators and directors have been, for the most part, serious historians and scholars in the field of art. Their interests have been highly specialized and antiquarian, running to solemn classic and medieval products of the far away and long ago. Their donors and trustees have expressed in their purchases the interests of the wealthy, leisured traveler and connoisseur; the collector of antiques and of rarities hallowed by aristocratic approval. Such tastes have, naturally, little in common with those of the ordinary American high school student. Only in the case of students at certain wealthy private preparatory schools, chiefly in New England, has it been possible to arouse an interest in such art through approaching them as future collectors and museum trustees. Otherwise, most of the art in museums is about as remote as could be imagined from the interests of youth.

The adolescent is not likely to be much impressed by the reasons museum people give for their purchases. As a rule they run somewhat as follows: "This painting marked a definite forward step in fifteenth-century art; it shows the influence of a certain early artist, and the characteristics of a certain school; it is genuine, rare, costly, sought after by collectors, and written about by scholars. *Ergo:* it is interesting, valuable, and important to us today." Moreover, there are museum officials who would add: "If the public and the high schools don't appreciate it, so much the worse for them. Let the schools teach their students to appreciate good art—or at least teach the very few who will ever be capable of good taste. Certainly we shall not lower ourselves to gratify the vulgar interests of the rest."

Such an attitude on the part of art museums may fairly be charged with two kinds of snobbery: the one based on an erudite, precious aestheticism; the other on the endowed private wealth of trustees and their employees, some of whom gratify their own tastes with little consideration of the general public. At the same time, I believe that it also contains a genuine awareness of certain profound and subtle values which are worth preserving and fighting for. These are values for which the public of tomorrow may be deeply grateful, as it looks back upon the welter of shoddy commercialism, local politics, and cheap sensationalism by which the present museum is surrounded. In short, the art museum has the values and defects of the social order in which we live. One can easily go too far in charging the museum with indifference to social and educational values. More than a few directors and trustees of museums and foundations are now quite aware of these public duties and eager to perform them. Their staffs are being manned with persons younger in both age and spirit than were those of yesterday, and determined to infuse new life into every corner of their institutions.

Nevertheless, the fact remains that to interest high school students in museum art is about as difficult as to lead a horse to drink some rare and exotic beverage: one can lead them into the museum, but the aesthetic experience is not at all sure to follow. What kind of art would they like? That remains to be seen, for we have never yet built up an art collection psychologically adapted to the artistic needs of adolescents. If we may judge from the rather inarticulate remarks of young people themselves, they might prefer something a bit more modern and American, something more connected with their other interests; something more lively, vigorous, and exciting in its expression and subject matter. Too many museum treasures appear to them as dreary fossils—once alive, perhaps, but now dead and cold, like butterflies on pins. Younger children may passively accept, but the more spirited adolescent will simply stay away, and spend his time where the fun is going on. Perhaps painting, sculpture, and all the static visual arts are too tame for modern American youth; and perhaps this is why we are developing, by preference, the motion picture, the marionette, all manner of mobile theater arts, and the streamlined forms of automobile and airplane. But there are many static visual arts in which adolescents can become interested, provided the right examples are chosen. Unfortunately, few of these are to be seen in the art museum. They include, for girls, costume and textiles in both present and historic styles, the small home and garden in their interior and exterior design, their furnishing and decoration. Boys like contemporary architecture, especially in its constructional aspects, and its functional relations to all manner of present-day uses. They like machine design in industry and are sensitive to appearance in automobiles, sports, and sport equipment. Boys and girls in this age level like works of art which combine realism and romanticism; which tell a story of modern, flesh-and-blood people having exciting adventures and experiences, as in war and love, exploration, intrigue, crime detection, athletics, and social gaiety. They like cartoons and caricatures, vivid posters, and magazine illustrations, portraits of actresses and athletes. Most of them care little for radical trends in art, of the Post-impressionist type, which deal in technical studio problems of abstraction and distortion. They prefer something at once more true to life and more dynamic in form and subject matter. But they can sympathize from a human standpoint with the problem of the modern artist, with his revolt against the dreary museum classics and his desire to create as he pleases. So for personal, if not aesthetic reasons, contemporary art could be made interesting to them. Increasing numbers of high school students, in these days of social unrest, take a serious interest in the art and literature of social controversy, whether of realism, satire, or propaganda.

If we turn from contemporary art of the recent past and seek to find in the art museum materials to illustrate the history of nineteenth-century America, we shall again be disappointed. There is likely to be a good deal of eighteenth and early nineteenth-century portraiture, colonial silver, glass, and furniture, all strongly indebted to European models. But how far do these objects go toward illustrating in visible form the rise of American civilization—the simple craftsmanship of the pioneer, the spread of industrialism with its crude machine products, the visible accessories of life in the small town and mushroom city which constitute our immediate cultural background? Many a high school teacher comes to the museum, sincerely hunting for something that he can connect either with the studies or the extra-curricular interests of his students, and finds little or nothing.

Let me emphasize again that I am not proposing to throw out the old masters, or let the purchase of museum art be guided by high school taste and high school studies. But as long as the museum confines itself to the kinds of art it has been choosing during the past generation, the gulf between it and the high school will continue almost impassable. In fact, the gulf is becoming even wider, now that high schools are turning away from the classics, and from ancient history, to a realistic study of the recent and contemporary world.

One possible concession is for the museum to show occasional, temporary loan exhibits of kinds and qualities of art to which it would not give permanent houseroom. Such, for example, are the exhibits of machine art and of contemporary architecture and housing, circulated by the Museum of Modern Art of New York. When these exhibits came to Cleveland, they were thronged by high school boys and their teachers. Many of these had never come to the museum before, and would have scorned to come for anything labeled "fine arts." If there are such occasional examples, on which the interests of high school people and the aesthetic conscience of museum directors can agree, so much the better for the possibility of their working together. But such unconventional exhibits in an art museum are so few and far between as to be negligible in viewing the general situation. And when they come, they are so brief that no systematic integration between them and the school program can be made.

A second possibility is for the museum to develop its own supplementary collection of exhibits for educational work. These can either be shown in certain designated galleries, apart from the "first series" material, or circulated in the schools themselves. Or, as a third possibility, school systems and individual schools can themselves build up circulating collections of visual material, including art and handcrafts. School authorities would have more hope of success in working along one of these substitute lines than in asking the museum to install a different kind of art in its principal galleries.

Our concept of a museum, in other words, should not be restricted to the white marble building itself and the rarities permanently enshrined in its glass cases. Rather we should broaden the concept, or find a new one, such as "audio-visual education agency," to cover the means of providing those illustrative materials which the high school of tomorrow is sure to demand, but which the conventional art museum will be very slow to provide.

Let us return for a moment to the main museum galleries, and to their disadvantages from the high school student's viewpoint. Entirely apart from the kind of objects which he sees there, he is likely to be somewhat repelled by the conditions under which they are shown. The modern director will insist that his building is no longer a "mausoleum" like museums of the past, and that it has become a friendly, bright, informal place. But in spite of some progress in that direction, there is still an inescapable air of suppression, hush, and austere formality in most museums. It quickly "gets on the nerves" of high school students, and makes them glad to escape into the open air, where they can laugh and chatter, handle things and run about. Even their own school building is a much freer place, as one may learn from the roar of animated conversation in its corridors between classes. There is something chilling in the marble walls, the glass cases, the uniformed guards quick to reprove a loud word or an exploring finger. Moreover, the adolescent is living in a state of rebellion from the authority of parents and the older generation. The more independent children are likely to sense in the museum an air of awed reverence for the past and for solemn religious art, which inhibits and depresses. They would like to giggle and make fun of old "sacred cows," as a defense reaction. This would not indicate that they were failing entirely to appreciate these arts. As I have observed children, those who are first to scoff and ridicule an unfamiliar kind of art may be the most sensitive, while the docile student who accepts everything may have little personality of his own. The basic fact that I am pointing out is that a spirit of superficial irreverence for the past, of mockery and high spirits, plus a love of arguing and disputing, of disagreeing with the teacher, are all essential and valuable elements in the adolescent stage of personality development. They are qualities which cannot thrive or feel comfortable in the usual museum atmosphere. A great deal of rather abstract and esoteric art might appeal rather surprisingly to youth if it could be seen under more relaxed conditions, with greater freedom to live, move, and talk naturally in its presence, and to try one's hand at making something of the sort.

The situation is not helped by the way in which the ordinary museum teacher leads a class through the galleries. He is likely to be at once superior and perfunctory, delivering a "canned" monologue which combines dry, historical erudition with dogmatic praise. The old-fashioned guide at least amused his audience with anecdotes of art and artists, which made the trip entertaining if not instructive. The new type, college-trained in course after course of art history, is more seriously informational, but it is a question whether he brings his audience much nearer to a genuine experience of works of art. His repetition of book-learned facts about obscure names, dates, attributions, influences, and iconographic symbolism not only fails to interest the high school student, but adds one more distracting and oppressive association to the works of art themselves.

In the face of these difficulties, what is the most promising line of advance? As to the museum building and its forbidding atmosphere, it is too much to expect that complete informality can be established. The safety of the exhibits, the rights of adult visitors and of serious students to a modicum of order and quiet in the museum, must all be preserved. But let us hope that museum designers of the future will make a small gesture of welcome to the adolescent as well—perhaps in the form of supplementary galleries, discussion rooms, reading rooms, and studios, where he can be within easy reach of precious objects and yet have a world of his own as well; where he can look, handle, argue, laugh, and work out his own imaginings, among his own friends, either with or without the presence of older teachers.

The interests of the secondary school have been pretty much ignored in museum work up to the present time. The educational staffs of art museums have confined themselves mainly to two types of work: to guidance for adult visitors, and to classes in "creative art" for young children. Let the high school demand attention, and the museum will be encouraged to extend itself in that direction also. Museum teachers who undertake to explain ancient art to modern adolescents must face the psychological problem of how to vitalize it for that age level—for example, through showing the romance of archaeological discovery, and significant comparisons between older cultures and our own.

2. *Shortcomings of the secondary school from the museum standpoint*

It is now time to look at the other side of the shield. Is the present secondary school prepared to take advantage of whatever artistic resources the museum has to offer? After conceding his own faults, the museum worker still finds it a little mystifying that he has to work so hard to urge high school teachers to bring their classes to the galleries; that high school authorities, while boasting of the liberal education their students enjoy, are yet so content to leave them housed up month after month within institutional walls, where there is little upon which to feast one's eyes. Can this be called a liberal education, he wonders, when it fails to make use of the cultural resources at its very door?

The bill of particulars against the school runs somewhat as follows: In most high schools as they are now organized, outside trips, and indeed any variations in the program, are extremely difficult. Their elaborately departmentalized schedule makes them rigid and unwieldy. Where the elementary school teacher can easily decide to take her pupils out of the building for a half day, with little effect on the rest of the school, the high school teacher is caught in an intricate program of scheduled classes for every hour of the day. He teaches a certain subject to one group after another. The student's day is rigidly mapped out into classes here, there, and elsewhere through the building, each under a different teacher. To take a given group of students outside the building for more than fifty minutes requires a rare determination on the part of teacher and principal, and a stupendous amount of conferring and adjusting. Unless and until the secondary school can run upon a more flexible schedule than it does at present, museum visits will continue to be more trouble than they are worth to the average high school teacher. Few schools have enough buses available for outside trips.

These factors have much obstructed high school visits to museums. They have given rise to a city-wide plea: "Bring the museum to the schools." The result has been a vast growth of extension activities on the part of the museum, including circulating exhibits of the types mentioned above, and the constant sending out of museum instructors with sets of lantern slides for illustrated talks in the schools.

Nevertheless, the museum staff is loath to give up entirely its hope of luring high school students within its own walls. The most rigid schedule can be modified where the will to do so exists on the part of teachers, principals, and superintendents. Nothing demonstrates more clearly the difference between alert, energetic, and forward-looking teachers, and those content to plod along in an easy routine, than the amount of use which they make of this and other special neighborhood resources.

Where schools are highly departmentalized upon the traditional subject basis—mathematics, history, English, and the rest—the chief responsibility for art museum contacts is naturally left to the art department. If any part of the faculty has an interest in fostering this relation, it would, one might think, be that of the art department. Yet this has proved a slender reed to lean upon. In many schools, especially boys' private preparatory schools, art is either entirely unrepresented on the faculty or weakly represented by a young, uninfluential instructor. In public high schools which emphasize vocational training, the art department is dominated by an interest in modern commercial and industrial processes, and sees no great practical value in the art museum. Teachers of "fine arts" in the liberal curriculum, whom one might expect to be the most active of all in their demands upon the museum, are often surprisingly backward and indifferent.

The chief explanation of this inertia lies in teacher training. The course of study for high school art teachers, in most cities, includes only a negligible amount of art history, appreciation, or criticism. They secure their degrees and certificates without the need of acquiring more than the scantiest acquaintance with great works of art, old or modern. We are increasing little by little the requirements in art history, but the total is still negligible. Prospective art teachers in the public high schools have been given a stock of rules and technical tricks for the production of stereotyped art forms, through textbooks, diagrams, and "practical" school art magazines. Once learned, these studio formulas can be imparted year after year, without ever leading to the wish for a direct experience with works of art. In the museum, a teacher so trained is likely to be helpless; in the presence of an object which does not conform to the textbook rules, she simply does not know how to respond or what to say. Specific courses in art history and appreciation are still rare in high schools, and are taught mainly from illustrated textbooks and lantern slides.

Occasionally, one finds an art teacher of consciously progressive and modernistic views. The results are not necessarily better, as far as her ability to use the museum is concerned. For among this group of self-styled progressives in every school system, we find a thousand and one new varieties of fad and formula. Some cling to the dream of completely "free expression," against all the evidence of its failure on the higher age level. These, of course, have no need of a museum, for their main concern is to protect the child from all art influences which might corrupt his originality. Others, converted to modern art, merely impose upon their classes a Post-impressionist style instead of an older one, making their students into little Matisses or Kandinskys instead of the Bouguereaus and Kenyon Coxes whom their grandmothers copied. Some of them follow the latest plausible formula for turning out artists in a quick and easy way—the "Dow method," the "Denman Ross method," the "Hofmann method," the "Best-Maugard method," or some other of the sort. Like political and economic panaceas, these methods promise much, and often produce in a short time superficially pleasing, clever results; their barrenness appears only in later years.

All these devices are pretended substitutes for museum observation in the training of artists. Their present popularity in American schools is in part a healthy but extreme reaction against the old idea of museum work as mere copying. In part, it has been due to necessity, for there have been so few art museums, so few opportunities to see even good reproductions of art, that art teachers have simply been forced to get along without them. But that day of frontier isolation is past. The flood of old-world cultural traditions is upon us, and there can be in the next generation no escaping from the art teacher's fundamental task of helping students to understand and assimilate it, to select from it what they need, and reject the rest, developing their eyes and imagination in the process, and producing a new American art—not out of thin air, but upon the rich and diverse foundations of the past.

Whatever the subject, an energetic, intelligent high school teacher can find some way of enriching it through drawing upon the museum for illustrative materials. The exceptional teacher of industrial arts will not only bring his students to observe and sketch in the museum, but will call upon its staff for photographs of new styles in industrial, commercial, and decorative arts. The alert dramatics teacher will come or send his students to find materials for stage design and costume. The alert teacher of English, Latin, French, or German will suggest a trip to the museum for a look at the art products of these peoples, so that concrete visual images may fill out the verbal concepts learned from books. Music teachers are working with comparative arts, and looking for examples of visual design to compare with musical design, or for works of Russian or Spanish art to compare with the folk music of these peoples. Teachers of history and social studies, most of all, come for visual illustrations of past cultures, such as the Egyptian, Greek, and Renaissance.

The present trend is toward an extreme emphasis on social and economic problems. Valuable as it is under present conditions, the impetus of this movement has led to excessive neglect of other valuable approaches, among them the artistic. It has involved an extreme devotion to factual realism, justifiable in its place, but wrong when it leads to a prejudice against all works of imagination and fantasy. It has involved a devotion to the practical, the workable, the useful, which again is wise in a moderate degree, as a protest against the old aristocratic ideal of a gentleman's education. But again it is leading to a wholly unwarranted neglect of worth-while studies which have no obvious practical utility. It involves a concentration upon present-day society, upon the here and now, which is right as contrasted with the antiquarianism of the classical curriculum. But it is bringing up a generation of students much too ignorant of the past to understand even present civilization in any of its deeper aspects, and blind to the wealth of classical, biblical, and other meanings which enriched the old education.

Art is far from being omitted in the new secondary schools. On the contrary, as I have said, there is great use of projects involving some artistic technique. But the constant cry for "creative originality" in these projects keeps the student out of the museum, and tends to delude him with the false belief that he can easily perform great feats of genius by inspired self-expression, with no need of learning from the past.

A liberal education on the secondary level should include far more cultural history, all along the educational process, than it does at present. It should include, not only the recent past in Europe and America, but a more than hasty glance at Egypt, Babylonia, Greece, Rome, and medieval Europe. Still more, to avoid its present provincialism, it should include attention to the great cultures of China and Japan, India, and the Islamic peoples. For all these, the basic necessary materials lie ready at hand in our leading art museums, but they are ignored by many high school teachers. It is not enough for the history teacher to "cover" the history of these peoples in a swift, schematic way, with attention almost wholly on political, social, and economic events, and with no sympathetic experience of the arts of these peoples.

How much of the history of civilization can and should be taught on the high school level? That itself is a problem which has never been faced. It must be experimentally decided, through actual teaching by persons familiar not only with the subject itself, but with the interests and abilities of children at various ages. Only through presenting these materials, as the museum does, to classes of all different age levels, can we arrive at an understanding of what elements within it are suited to the elementary grades, what to the secondary, and what to the college level.

~✿◗ XXIV ◖✿~

ART MUSEUM WORK AND TRAINING*

Those who hope to enter the rapidly growing field of museum work should realize, at an early stage in their training, the wide range of different types of occupation which it involves. The modern museum is a small world in itself, in which there is a high degree of specialization of labor. A type of training which may be excellent for one kind of museum work may fail to prepare for others.

Two important divisions of museum work are the *curatorial* and the *educational.* The department of buildings and grounds may employ secretaries, but most of its personnel consists of men who act as guards, engineers, porters, and the like. The museum library usually employs persons specially trained in library science and also requires attendants for its collections of lantern slides and photographs. The offices of the registrar and cashier or treasurer may also give employment to secretaries, filing clerks, and recorders of accessions. Preparation for clerical or secretarial work in any of these departments should proceed along the same lines as for similar work in any other institution; with the addition that a knowledge of art and artists will help qualify one to handle more responsible tasks.

Since the primary functions of an art museum are to collect, preserve, and exhibit works of art, it is natural that a large and important part of the personnel should be concerned with *curatorial* duties. The staff of a large museum is commonly divided into several departments, such as paintings, decorative arts, textiles, prints, Egyptian art, classical art, Far Eastern art, and Near Eastern art. Each of these usually has at its head a curator, who may be assisted by an associate curator and several clerical assistants. Study for such a position should include the general history of art, foreign languages, and some special field of art within which the assistant hopes to work. It is well to include also some training in secretarial work, typing, stenography, and filing. Frequently a knowledge of art, even though advanced and expert, is insufficient to make the young college graduate acceptable

* Published in *Women's Work and Education,* V.4 (February, 1934).

as a curatorial assistant. On the other hand, one who has achieved a reputation as an art expert may step at once into a responsible position without the need of such secretarial training.

For the person, man or woman, who aspires to become a curator or head of a department of an art museum, there is no doubt that the primary training should be in the field of art history. He or she should have a good general knowledge of art history, and be a genuine connoisseur of one particular field. His or her interest in this field may or may not involve a desire to do scholarly research and writing; some museums encourage this and others do not. But the aspirant should certainly become an expert judge of the authenticity of works of art, so as not to lead the museum into purchasing faked or wrongly attributed objects. This requires a special approach to art history, different from that required by the historian or critic. Since the curator will be called upon to purchase or recommend purchases, not only a developed sense of art values but a practical acquaintance with art markets, current prices, reliable dealers and experts will be highly important. How much of this can be learned in a school, and how much must be acquired through actual museum experience, is at present problematical. As curatorial work becomes more widely recognized as a profession, courses of training for it will no doubt come to stress more and more these specific requirements. Whatever the aspirant can learn informally along these lines, through personal acquaintance, travel, attendance at sales, and the reading of art magazines and news items, will be a distinct advantage.

Another task of the curator is to oversee the care, preservation, cleaning, repairing, and mounting of objects, the relining, framing, revarnishing and perhaps retouching of pictures. Technical experts will do the actual handwork, but the direction and responsibility belong to the curator.

Still another task, whose importance is increasingly emphasized, is that of exhibiting works of art to the best advantage within the museum. Large exhibits must be tastefully and significantly arranged; cases of the right sizes and shapes installed; the position and lighting of every object be such as to bring out its important features and permit easy observation without fatigue. Like many of the others, this branch of the curator's work is one for which intensive training is desirable, but so far not offered in many institutions. The most advantageous place to prepare for a curatorship is in the art department of some large university which possesses an art museum of its own, or co-operates with some near-by museum, so that the scholarly and technical aspects of the work can be studied in close relationship.

The *educational* branch of museum work is more recent in its origin and still less definitely organized as to requirements and training. Few of the present workers in the field were specially trained with that career in view. Most of them have been trained as teachers of art to children, in some art academy or school of education. Employed as museum instructors, their success depends on general mentality and background, and on the ability to adapt themselves to new and unfamiliar problems for whose solution no precedents exist. Here again the most advantageous way to prepare is to study art at some school or college which is near a large museum; and, while finishing one's advanced studies, to gain practical experience by assisting in the museum for whatever financial compensation is offered, or for none at all. There is much to learn in the museum which cannot be taught outside: for example, the procedure of scheduling and conducting gallery visits, of preparing supplementary material for study, of conferring with school teachers on the relation of museum visits to the regular work. If actual work in drawing, painting, or modeling is done within the museum, there are additional problems in the way of distributing and collecting them, and seeing that floors, cases, and exhibits are not damaged.

As museum educational work develops and as competition for the desirable posts becomes keener, the preference will go to those having a broad and thorough training in art and pedagogical method. Not only the history of art should be included and some skill in the handling of an artistic technique, but also a study of aesthetic principles, general and educational psychology, and the philosophy of education—all this with the aim of understanding, not only the meaning of art to the adult, but how it can be made significant and attractive to the child. Working in close contact with outside school teachers, the museum instructor should become acquainted with the whole school curriculum, so as to provide appropriate illustrative material wherever desired. Already the field is tending to subdivide, however, into work with different age levels such as elementary, junior high, senior high school and college; into vocational work for prospective artists and craftsmen, and cultural work for liberal arts students and the general public.

In all its branches, museum work is still in so plastic and rapidly changing a state that no exact course of training, or means of entering employment, can be outlined. Standards of pay, hours, and vacations are likewise variable from museum to museum. On the whole, museums are pleasant and rewarding places in which to work, and the opportunities for pioneer achievement are endless.

THE ART MUSEUM
AND CREATIVE ORIGINALITY*

In this second half of the twentieth century, there are few educators who question the value of the art museum, and of related studies in art history and appreciation, for a liberal education and "cultural background." But there is still a lingering indifference or hostility toward it on the part of many artists and art students. Some are still afraid of being made by it into mere imitators of the past. Some teachers of art, especially in secondary schools, rationalize this attitude in the current Deweyan terminology, by urging that the student's art expression should "grow out of his direct experience," and that "traditional forms should not be imposed upon him."

As commonly interpreted, this goes much farther toward free expression than Dewey himself ever went. It completely ignores his repeated emphasis on the value of looking at visual art as one kind of direct experience, and as material for original thinking. Learning, growing, and creating in the arts are achieved, not through avoiding aesthetic stimuli, but by welcoming them as one phase in active experience; then by reorganizing such experience in memory, imagination, and reflection. The fear of outside influence is a sign of timidity and insecurity. Many artists have not learned how to use tradition selectively and hence assume that it must be followed blindly or ignored. The contents of an art museum are not going to spring upon the aspiring artist, tie him down, and force him to copy them. They are suggestions which he is free to use or not, as he wishes. They are ladders by which he can mount upon the shoulders of the past, taking the work of older artists as a starting-point.

The writer of this article had the pleasure of talking recently in France with both Picasso and Matisse, surely two of the most original artists of our time. In reply to his questions about the best methods of education for a young painter, both stressed the value of some (not too much) academic discipline as a starting-point for the stu-

* Published in the *College Art Journal,* X.3 (Spring, 1951), pp. 257-260.

dent, and of observing art all his life, in museums and elsewhere. Their rooms are strewn with illustrated books on past styles, with here and there an original example of some unusual type of art, other than their own. They know their museums intimately, and have used them for decades as a source of inspiration. Both have achieved what seem to the public highly original styles, partly through selecting elements from past styles (especially unfamiliar ones such as Negro sculpture, Coptic textiles, and Persian miniatures) and partly through fusing these images with other observations and memories from life, in the crucible of an active, powerful imagination. The result is not merely eclectic or imitative, but a creative use of tradition. "There is no danger for the original-minded student," said Picasso, "in doing a conventional, academic task, such as starting to copy an old master. If he is original, he will probably not be able to copy it exactly; he will make something new of it whether he tries to or not."

On the other hand, if it were possible for an art student to avoid seeing, hearing, or reading about past works, and any influence from teachers' demonstrations and directions, what kind of art could we expect him to produce out of his "direct experience" with the outside world? How far would his "creative impulses" take him in translating the life about him and his feelings toward it into pictorial or sculptural form? Not much beyond an infantile stage, and not nearly as far as that of the later Ice Age cave painters, who already had a long artistic tradition behind them. How far could a student of musical composition go without hearing good music of his time? No amount of individual "creative impulse," of "inspiration," or "direct experience" outside the realm of art can suffice to produce a mature, original contribution to the world's art today. The would-be artist must look at life and nature through the eyes of many other artists, through studying their works. He must alternate this with his own observations of nature and his own attempts to control his medium, over long periods of time, before he can develop in himself a real artistic personality, with something to say that has not been said before. Past art shows him how to select from the profusion of images that is constantly pouring in upon him, and how to translate and order them in terms of some particular medium, technique, and stylistic approach. With this as a starting-point, if he has the native ability, he can begin working out some new contribution to art.

The romantic theory that creativeness comes entirely from within, or by communing with nature, had its value in freeing art from the rigid academic rules of the eighteenth century. But it is carried to absurd extremes by the contemporary student who fails to study past art with an open mind, by the teacher who fails to show it to him as an aid to creative experiment, and by the artist who pretends that he has never been influenced by any other artist; that he has thought up all his ideas completely by himself, or by studying nature. Whether he knows it or not, he has always learned to see nature through the eyes of older artists, and could never have imagined as he has without their help. A teacher who fails to help his students see or hear the best available examples of the art they are trying to learn is depriving them of an essential prerequisite for success. He is merely throwing them back upon the thin artistic diet of magazine covers and grocery calendars for nourishment.

At least four major factors go into the making of a really creative artist. One is innate endowment, physical and mental, including the will to create in spite of obstacles, and in spite of all temptations to easy, pleasant living. A second is general education, not necessarily advanced or scholarly, but enough to make him a part of some cultural group, with a share of its inherited stock of basic skills, customs, beliefs, and attitudes. These need not be the dominant ones of the day; he may be part of an oppressed or rebellious minority group. But the atmosphere about him should be encouraging to art expression. Third is a chance to observe and be inspired by some of the art products of his own culture, and perhaps of other cultures; to see or hear how his people have expressed themselves artistically; to feel himself in emotional sympathy with some of these expressions and eager to add his own voice to theirs, while others, perhaps, irritate him into angry counter-statement. Fourth is technical instruction by some skilled practitioner of his chosen medium. American students and teachers still rely too heavily upon this fourth factor, and not enough upon the third.

Museums are, of course, not the only way in which a potential artist can acquire the art traditions of his group. If that group is a primitive or rustic one, he may find them only in the folk arts around him. In medieval Europe and India, cathedrals and temples were centers of the arts. In the larger American cities today, the student can see exhibits of current art in small galleries, and reproductions of some good art in magazines and Sunday newspapers. Many museums are still too much restricted to the long-dead past, and show little or no contemporary art, especially of experimental, avant-garde movements. But on the whole they are trying, with increasing success, to provide the public with a fair cross section of the best in visual art of all major cultures and periods including the present one.

Uncritical veneration of past art and a pedantic spirit of anti-quarian scholarship are not favorable to present creativeness. There has been too much of both in art museums, as well as much timidity in exhibiting present radical experiments. It is understandable that a conservative institution should hesitate to give its full, immediate blessing to all such wild-eyed modernism. The wise solution is to use certain galleries as neutral forums for presenting and discussing con-troversial experiments. One can show them without endorsing them as great or beautiful, so as to help the public study and make up its mind about them.

By exhibiting and helping to sell the artist's recent work, the mu-seum aids creativeness in the most practical of ways. Its educational work, in courses and gallery talks for persons of all ages, is devoted less to rhapsodic praise than in former years, and more to helping people recognize the distinctive features, values, and limitations of each example—especially of the difficult, unfamiliar ones, exotic and contemporary.

Students come to the museum to look, listen, sketch, and take notes; seldom now to make complete, exact copies. They consult ex-hibits and reference files there as an author uses a library: for mate-rial to be freely worked over elsewhere. No doubt the art museum can be of more use to American artists, students, and art teachers in the future, by trying more actively to meet their needs. But up to the present they have not begun to make full use of the resources it now puts at their disposal.

INDEX

Abilities in art, 58; development of, 36
Absolutism, 10
Academic methods, 29, 61, 108, 240, 274, 344
Acting, 101
Action-drawing, 259
Activities, art, 18
Adjustment, social, 26
Administration, 28
Adolescence, 8, 248f; adolescent tastes, 271, 362
Adult art, 68
Advertising art, 148
Aesthetic ability, 112; age, 64, 72, 209; attitude, 4, 118; development, 8, individual, 60, social, 68; education, 3, aims of, 15, methods, 18, subject matter, 22; experience, 3, 115, 122; perception, 123; response, 55, 120, 122
Aesthetics, 14, 33, 50, 174, 176, 316, 321f, 323; training for work in, 328f
Affective attitudes, 121
Age levels, 63, 72, 165, 171, 201, 196, 271, 341, 345
American artistic development, 295; history, 364; Philosophical Association, 322; scene in art, 276
Americanization, 160, 163
Anarchism, 142
Angier, R. P., 180
Anthologies, 23
Anthropology, 318
Apperception, 120
Appreciation, 5, 22, 36, 112, 194, 302, 313, 318; creative, 117; techniques of, 308
Arabian Nights, 157
Architecture, 9, 273
Aristocracy and art, 288, 294
Arnheim, R., 326

Art, 40, 288f, 297; ability, 71; activities, 66; for adults, 357; for children, 356
Art education, aims of, 35, 304, 306; basic problems of, 25; fundamentals in, 107; in U.S.A., 295, 299
Art history, 255, 302f, 313, 315
Art museums, educational work in, 332f, 338f, 356f, 361f; museum work and training, 373
Art principles, 44, 46, 274
Art teacher, inducements to, 34; requirements, 31; training of, 369, 375
Artist, education of, 299, 377; psychology of, 101
Artistic ability, 99; attitude, 4, 118; experience, 3
Arts curriculum, 289
Association, 127
Audiovisual materials, 310, 347

Baade, W., 188
Bach, J. S., 83; family, 58
Bacon, F., 147
Barnhart, E. N., 209n, 213
Beauty, 11, 121
Beethoven, L. van, 91
Behaviorism, 54
Benedict, R., 159
Best-Maugard, A., 278
Binet tests, 209
Biographies, artists', 256
Blanshard, B., 324
Boas, B., 245
Boas, F., 326
Böcklin, A., 238
Boston Museum of Fine Arts, 243
Burns, R., 147

Careers in art, 16, 299
Caricature, 259
Carpentry, 9

DATE DUE

MAY 15 1971			
DE 20'72			
GAYLORD			PRINTED IN U.S.A.